CORVETTE
SERVICE • REPAIR HANDBOOK
ALL MODELS • 1963-1976

By

ERIC JORGENSEN

JEFF ROBINSON
Editor and Publisher

Published by

CLYMER PUBLICATIONS

World's largest publisher of books devoted exclusively to automobiles and motorcycles.

222 NORTH VIRGIL AVENUE, LOS ANGELES, CALIFORNIA 90004

ISBN: 0-89287-082-6

CONTENTS

CHAPTER ELEVEN

CHAPTER TWELVE

CHAPTER THIRTEEN

CHAPTER FOURTEEN

CHAPTER ONE

GENERAL INFORMATION

Since the Corvette's inception in the mid 1950's, the design has had 2 different chassis and 4 different body styles. Prior to 1963, Corvette was a simple 2-seater roadster. Since then, Chevrolet has added all independent suspension, 4-wheel disc brakes, and a variety of V8 engines and transmissions. With these changes, Corvette has become a sophisticated automobile to be taken seriously as a true sports car.

MANUAL ORGANIZATION

This book provides service information and procedures for all 1963-1976 Corvettes.

This chapter provides general information and specifications for the Corvette. **Figure 1** shows the location of all identification tags. **Tables 1 and 2** provide general dimensions and specifications.

Chapter Two explains all periodic lubrication and routine maintenance required to keep your car in top running condition.

Chapter Three includes recommended tune-up procedures, eliminating the need to constantly consult chapters covering the various subassemblies.

Chapter Four provides methods and suggestions for finding and fixing troubles fast.

Table 2   CURB WEIGHT (with base V-8)

	Convertible	Coupe
1963-1968	3,145 lbs.	3,135 lbs.
1969-1971	3,220 lbs.	3,210 lbs.
1972-1973	3,320 lbs.	3,292 lbs.
1974	3,429 lbs.	3,422 lbs.
1975	3,539 lbs.	3,525 lbs.
1976	n.a.	3,525 lbs.

Troubleshooting procedures discuss typical symptoms and logical methods to pinpoint the trouble. They also cover some test equipment useful for both preventive maintenance and troubleshooting.

Subsequent chapters describe specific systems such as the engine, transmission, and electrical system. Each provides complete disassembly, repair, and assembly procedures in easy-to-follow, step-by-step form. If a repair is impractical for the home mechanic, it is so indicated. Such repairs are usually more economically and quickly done by a dealer or other competent repair shop. Specifications concerning a particular system are provided in the applicable chapter.

Some of the procedures in this manual specify special tools. In all cases, the tools are illustrated

① ENGINE AND CHASSIS IDENTIFICATION

Vehicle Identification number located on windshield pillar.

Vehicle serial number and body style, body number trim and paint combination located on instrument panel brace under glove box.

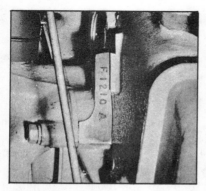

Engine unit number located on pad at front, right hand side of cylinder block.

Rear axle serial number located bottom surface of carrier at cover mounting flange.

Conventional transmission unit number located on rear face of case in the upper right corner.

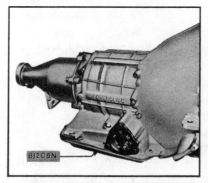

Powerglide source data code stamped on bottom of oil pan.

Table 1   BASIC DIMENSIONS

	1963-1967	1968-1973	1974	1975	1976
Length	175.1 in.	182.5 in.	185.5 in.	185.2 in.	185.2 in.
Width	69.6 in.	69.2 in.	69.0 in.	69.0 in.	69.0 in.
Height					
Convertible	49.8 in.	47.9 in.	47.8 in.	47.8 in.	n.a.
Coupe	49.6 in.	47.8 in.	47.7 in.	47.7 in.	48.0 in.
Wheelbase	98.0 in.	98.0 in.	98.0 in.	98.0 in.	98.0 in.
Track					
Front	56.8 in.	58.7 in.	58.7 in.	58.7 in.	58.7 in.
Rear	57.6 in.	59.4 in.	59.5 in.	59.5 in.	59.5 in.

either in actual use or alone. A well-equipped mechanic may find he can substitute other similar tools he has on hand or can fabricate his own.

IDENTIFICATION NUMBERS

Several identification numbers are important when ordering spare parts or identifying the automobile for registration purposes. Refer to Figure 1.

The vehicle serial number on the 1963-1967 models is under the glove box. On 1968 and later models, the vehicle number is on the top of the instrument panel at the left front edge or on the inside left windshield pillar. The engine serial number is stamped on a pad on the front right-hand side of the cylinder block. Use these numbers when ordering parts.

PARTS REPLACEMENT

Corvette has made frequent changes during the period covered by this book; some minor, some relatively major. When you order parts from a dealer or other parts distributor, always order by year, engine and chassis numbers. Write the numbers down and carry them in your wallet. Compare new parts to old before purchasing them. If they are not alike, have the parts clerk explain the reason for the difference.

SERVICE HINTS

Observing the following practices will save time, effort, and frustration, as well as prevent possible injury.

Throughout this manual keep in mind 2 conventions. "Front" refers to the front of the car. The front of any component such as the engine or transmission is that end which faces toward the front of the car. The left and right side of the car refer to a person sitting in the car facing forward. For example, the steering wheel is on the left side. These rules are simple, but even experienced mechanics occasionally become disoriented.

When working under a car, do not trust a hydraulic or mechanical jack alone to hold the car up. Always use jackstands.

Disconnect the battery ground cable before working near electrical connections and before disconnecting wires. But, *never* run the engine with the battery disconnected; the alternator could be seriously damaged.

Tag all similar internal parts for location and mark all mating parts for position. Record number and thickness of any shims as they are removed. Small parts such as bolts can be identified by placing them in plastic sandwich bags and sealing and labeling bags with masking tape.

Protect finished surfaces from physical damage or corrosion. Keep gasoline and brake fluid off painted surfaces.

Frozen or very tight bolts and screws can often be loosened by soaking with penetrating oil, then sharply strike the bolt head a few times with a hammer and punch (or screwdriver for screws). Avoid heat, unless absolutely necessary, since it may melt, warp, or remove the temper from many parts.

Avoid flames or sparks when working near a charging battery or flammable liquids such as brake fluid or gasoline.

No parts, except those assembled with a press fit, require unusual force during assembly. If a part is hard to remove or install, find out why before proceeding.

Cover all openings after removing parts to keep dirt, small tools, etc., from falling in.

When assembling 2 parts, start all fasteners, then tighten evenly.

Read each procedure in its entirety while looking at the actual parts *before* beginning. Many procedures are complicated and errors can be disastrous. When you thoroughly understand what is to be done, follow the procedure step-by-step.

CHAPTER TWO

LUBRICATION AND MAINTENANCE

To ensure good performance, dependability, and safety, regular preventive maintenance is necessary. This chapter outlines periodic lubrication and maintenance for a car driven by the average owner. A car driven more than average may require more frequent attention; but even without use, rust, dirt, and corrosion cause unnecessary damage. Whether performed by the owner or a Corvette dealer, regular routine attention helps avoid expensive repairs.

The recommended schedule in this chapter includes routine checks which are easily performed at each fuel stop; periodic checks to be performed at each oil change; and periodic maintenance to prevent future trouble. **Table 1** summarizes, in an easy-to-use form, all periodic maintenance required.

ROUTINE CHECKS

The following simple checks should be performed at each fuel stop.

1. Check engine oil. Oil should be checked with the engine warm and the car on level ground. Level should be between 2 marks on the dipstick; never below and never above. Top up if necessary.

2. Check battery electrolyte level. It should be even with the top of the vertical separators. Top up with distilled water.

3. Check tire pressures when tires are cold. See **Table 2**.

4. Check windshield washer fluid level.

Table 2   TIRE PRESSURE

Year	Type	Pressure (psi)
1963-1972	Bias	24
1973-1976	Radial	20

PERIODIC CHECKS

These are performed less frequently than the routine checks. Recommended intervals are discussed below and summarized in Table 1. Many require that the automobile be on a hoist or jackstands.

WARNING
Do not use the tire jack when working under the car. Use only jackstands made specifically for this purpose.

Compression Check

Every **6,000** miles (**7,500** for 1975-1976), check cylinder compression. Record the results and compare them at the next **6,000** (**7,500**) mile check. A running record will show trends in general deterioration so that corrective action can be taken before complete failure.

Table 1   LUBRICATION AND MAINTENANCE SUMMARY

Interval	Item	Check Fluid Level	Replace	Lube	Inspect and/or Clean	Check and/or Adjust
Fuel stop	Engine oil	X				
	Battery electrolyte	X				
	Tire pressure					X
	Windshield washer	X				
6,000 miles (7,500 miles on 1975-1976 models)	Compression					X
	Engine compartment				X	
	Emission control					X
	Manual transmission	X				
	Automatic transmission	X				
	Rear axle	X				
	Clutch free play					X
	Exhaust system				X	
	Power steering	X				
	Drive belts					X
	Manifold heat valve				X	
	Brake fluid	X				
	Tires and wheels				X	
	Engine oil/oil filter		X			
	Front suspension			X		
	Spark plugs				X	X
	Breaker points (if used)				X	X
	Valve clearance					X
	Carburetor					X
12,000 miles (15,000 miles on 1975-1976 models)	Automatic transmission fluid (1965-1970)		X			
	PCV valve (through 1970)		X			
	Air cleaner (1963-1965)				X	
	Fuel filter		X			
	Fuel evaporative filter (1970-1971)		X			
	Spark plugs ①		X			X
	Breaker points (if used)		X			X
24,000 miles (30,000 miles on 1975-1976 models)	Distributor lubrication		X			
	Automatic transmission fluid (1971-1976)		X			
	Turbo-hydramatic strainer		X			
	PCV valve (1971-1974) ②		X			
	Air cleaner (1966-1976)		X			
	Fuel evaporative filter (1972-1976)		X			
30,000 mile	Manual steering gear	X				
	Wheel bearings			X	X	X
	Universal joints			X	X	
36,000 miles	Clutch cross-shaft			X		

① Every 22,500 miles on 1975-1976 models.
② Every 15,000 miles on 1975-1976 models.

Both a dry compression test and a wet compression test may be necessary to isolate cylinder or valve problems. To check compression:

1. Warm the engine to normal operating temperature. Ensure that the choke valve and throttle valve are completely open.

2. Remove the spark plugs.

3. Connect the compression tester to one cylinder, following the manufacturer's instructions. See **Figure 1**.

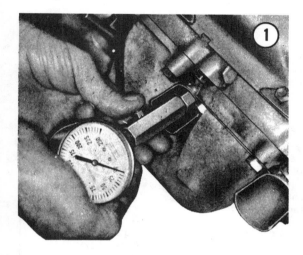

4. Have an assistant crank the engine over until there is no further rise in pressure. Usually this requires at least 4 compression strokes.

5. Remove the tester and record the reading.

6. Repeat Steps 3-5 for each cylinder. When interpreting the results, actual readings are not as important as the difference between readings. All readings should be about 150-160 lb., with a variation of no more than 20 lb. between the highest and lowest cylinders. Greater differences indicate worn or broken rings, sticky or leaky valves, or a combination of all.

7. If one or more cylinders reads low or uneven, inject about a tablespoon of engine oil through the spark plug port. Repeat Steps 3-5. If compression comes up some but still doesn't reach normal, the rings are probably worn. If compression does not improve at all, valves are sticking or seating poorly. If 2 adjacent cylinders indicate low compression and compression does not come up in either, the head gasket may be leaking between them.

Engine Compartment

Every **6,000** miles (**7,500** for 1975-1976), check the entire engine compartment for leaking or deteriorated oil and fuel lines. Check electrical wiring for breaks in insulation caused by deterioration or chafing. Check for loose or missing nuts, bolts, and screws.

Exhaust Emission Control Check

After every tune-up (Chapter Three), check carbon monoxide (CO) content of exhaust gas. Use a good quality exhaust gas analyzer and follow the manufacturer's instructions.

Radiator Coolant Level

Every **6,000** miles (**7,500** for 1975-1976), check the radiator coolant level. Do this only when the engine is cool.

Coolant level should be maintained 3 in. below the bottom of the filler neck when the system is cold. When a surge radiator supply tank is used, coolant level should be maintained at the half-full level in the supply tank.

> NOTE: *Correct fluid level is very important. The sealing ability of the radiator cap is affected when the coolant level is too high.*

Manual Transmission

Every **6,000** miles (**7,500** for 1975-1976), check oil level in transmission. With the transmission at operating temperature, remove the filler plug. The oil level should just reach the bottom of the filler plug hole. If the lubricant level is checked with the unit cold, the level should be ½ in. below the filler plug hole. If quantity is low, top up with gear oil recommended in **Table 3**.

Automatic Transmission

Every **6,000** miles (**7,500** for 1975-1976), check fluid level on dipstick with engine idling, selector lever in neutral position, parking brake set, and transmission at operating temperature. Pull out the dipstick, wipe it with a clean cloth, and reinsert it. Pull the dipstick out again and check that the level is between the 2 marks. If necessary, add fluid, but do not overfill. If level

Table 3   RECOMMENDED LUBRICANTS, COOLANT, AND FUEL CAPACITY

	Temperature Range	Recommended Type	Capacity
Engine oil	Above 90°F. 32°F. - 90°F. 0 - 32°F. Below 0°F.	SAE 30, 10W-30 SAE 20, 20W or 10W-30 SAE 10, 10W-30 SAE 5, 5W-20	4 qts. (327, 350) ① 5 qts. (396, 427, 454) ①

Manual transmission
   3-speed
 	
   4-speed
	
	All temperatures
	
	All temperatures
		
		SAE 90 multipurpose
		   transmission oil
		SAE 90 multipurpose
		   transmission oil
			
			2 pints
			
			2.5 pints

Automatic transmission
   Powerglide
   Turbo-hydramatic
	
	All temperatures
	All temperatures
		
		Dexron
		Dexron
			
			1½ qts. (sump only)
			7½ qts. (sump only)

Rear axle
   w/o Positraction
 	
   w/Positraction
	
	All temperatures
	
	All temperatures
		
		SAE 80 multipurpose gear lube ②
		SAE 90 multipurpose gear lube ② 3.7 pints
		SAE 90 (MIL-L-2205B) ③	

Fuel
 	
   1963-1970
   1971-1974
   1975-1976
	
	All temperatures
	All temperatures
	All temperatures
		Premium
		91 octant regular
		   (unleaded or low lead)
		Unleaded only
			
			20 gals. (std.)

Coolant	All temperatures ④	Ethylene glycol base	17 qts. (1963-1964) 19 qts. (327) 18 qts. (350) ⑤ 23 qts. (427) 24 qts. (454) ⑤

① Add 1 quart with filter change.
② Without limited slip differential.
③ With limited slip differential. Must be marked
   "For limited slip differentials."

④ Mix with water to provide at least 0°F.
   protection, lower if necessary.
⑤ Add 1 quart with air conditioning.

is above the top mark, fluid must be drained to restore proper level, or seals may be damaged.

Rear Axle

Every **6,000** miles (**7,500** for 1975-1976), remove filler plug and check oil level. The oil level should just reach the bottom of the filler plug hole. If necessary, top up with lubricant specified in Table 3.

Clutch

Every **6,000** miles (**7,500** for 1975-1976), check clutch pedal free play on manual shift cars. Depress pedal by hand. Free play should

be ¾-1 in. on 1963-1964 models, 1¼-1¾ in. on 1965-1973 models, and 1-1½ in. for 1974-1976 models. Refer to Chapter Eleven for adjustments.

Exhaust System

Every **6,000** miles (**7,500** for 1975-1976), examine the exhaust pipes, mufflers, and hangers for rust, holes, and other damage. Replace any worn parts.

Manual Steering Gear

Every **30,000** miles, check oil level. To do this, remove the forward and outboard steering gear cover screws. Inject steering gear lubricant into the forward hole until lubricant begins to come out of the other hole. See **Figure 2**. Reinstall the screws. This procedure is not necessary on 1971 and later models.

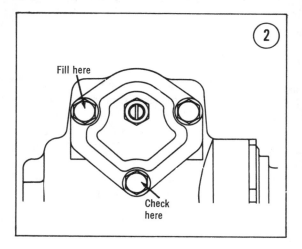

Power Steering Pump

Check fluid level in pump reservoir every **6,000** miles (**7,500** for 1975-1976) or 6 months. Oil should be at operating temperature and wheels in straightahead position. Top up as necessary with Type A automatic transmission fluid (marked AQ-ATF-A).

Drive Belts

Every **6,000** miles (**7,500** for 1975-1976), inspect drive belts for wear, fraying, cracking, and improper tension. A belt should be retightened only when it deflects more than ½ in. with moderate thumb pressure applied midway between pulleys.

Manifold Heat Control Valve

Check valve for freedom of operation every **6,000** miles (**7,500** for 1975-1976). See **Figure 3**. If valve shaft is sticking, free it with GM manifold heat control solvent or equivalent.

Brakes

Every **6,000** miles (**7,500** for 1975-1976), check fluid level in master cylinder. Maintain level ¼ in. below lowest edge of each filler opening. See **Figure 4**. Use brake fluid clearly

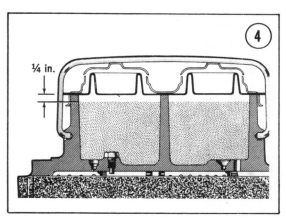

marked SAE 7OR3, SAE J1703 (which supercedes 7OR3), DOT 3, or DOT 4 only.

Air Conditioner

Check the sight glass under the hood every **6,000** miles (**7,500** miles on 1975-1976). After the system has been in operation for several minutes, sight glass should be clear, but during mild weather may show traces of bubbles. Foam or dirt indicates a leak which should be repaired immediately. Every week during winter months, run the system for 10-15 minutes to ensure proper lubrication of the seals and moving parts.

Windshield Wiper Blades

Long exposure to weather and road film hardens the rubber wiper blades and destroys their effectiveness. When blades smear or otherwise fail to clean the windshield, they should be replaced.

Tire and Wheel Inspection

Every **6,000** miles (**7,500** on 1975-1976), check the condition of all tires, including the spare. Check local traffic regulations concerning minimum tread depth. Most recommend replacing tires when tread depth is less than 1/32 in. Corvette original equipment tires have wear indicators which become visible when tread depth reaches 1/16 in. See **Figure 5**. Check lug nuts for tightness.

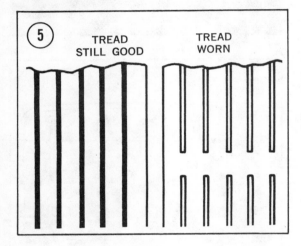

PERIODIC MAINTENANCE

Engine Oil Change

The oil change interval varies depending on the type of driving you do. For normal driving, including some city traffic, change oil every **6,000** miles (**7,500** on 1975-1976) or 6 months. If driving is primarily short distance with considerable stop-and-go city traffic, or if conditions are particularly dusty, change oil more often. Possibly even twice as often. Change oil at least twice a year if the car is driven only a few hundred miles a month.

Any oil used must be rated "FOR SERVICE MS" or with one of the newer designations "FOR API SERVICE SE." Non-detergent oils are not recommended. See Table 3 for recommended oil grades. To drain oil:

1. Warm engine to operating temperature.

2. Remove drain plug from oil pan.

3. Let oil drain for at least 10 minutes.

4. Install oil drain plug.

5. Change oil filter. See procedure below.

6. Remove oil filler cap. Refill with oil grade and quantity recommended in Table 3.

7. Check level on dipstick.

Engine Oil Filter

Replace the oil filter every **6,000** miles (**7,500** on 1975-1976). This should be done after oil is drained and before new oil is poured in.

To remove the filter, unscrew it by hand or use a filter wrench. Wipe the gasket area of the base with a clean, lint-free cloth. Coat the neoprene gasket on the new filter with clean oil. Screw the filter in by hand until the gasket just touches the base, then tighten ½ turn by hand. Do not use a filter wrench.

After adding engine oil, start the engine and check for leaks. Also check the oil level and adjust if necessary.

Distributor

On 1974 and earlier models equipped with conventional ignition systems, turn the distributor cam lubricator end for end every **12,000** miles. See **Figure 6**. Replace the cam lubricator every **24,000** miles.

> CAUTION
> *Never oil the cam lubricator.*

Automatic Transmission

Automatic transmission fluid in the transmission sump must be changed every **12,000** miles on 1965-1970 transmissions, every **24,000** miles on 1971-1974 transmissions, and every **30,000** miles on 1975-1976 transmissions.

To drain automatic transmission fluid, remove all oil pan bolts and the pan itself. Clean oil pan in cleaning solvent. Install oil pan and tighten bolts to 7 ft.-lb.

Refill Powerglide transmissions with approximately 2 quarts of automatic transmission fluid. Refill Turbo-Hydramatics with 7½ pints of automatic transmission fluid. See Table 3 for recommended type. Check oil level as described

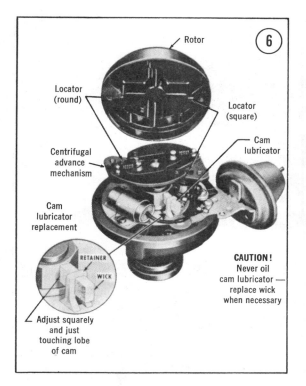

Rotor ⑥

Locator (round)

Locator (square)

Centrifugal advance mechanism

Cam lubricator

Cam lubricator replacement

RETAINER

WICK

Adjust squarely and just touching lobe of cam

CAUTION! Never oil cam lubricator — replace wick when necessary

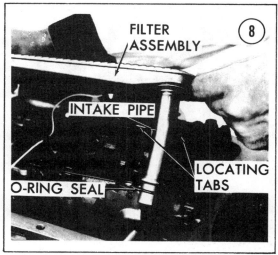

FILTER ASSEMBLY ⑧

INTAKE PIPE

O-RING SEAL

LOCATING TABS

under *Periodic Checks, Automatic Transmissions*. Top up if necessary.

Every **24,000** miles (**30,000** on 1975-1976) on Turbo-Hydramatics, replace the strainer. This is accessible when the oil sump is removed. Remove filter retaining bolt. See **Figure 7**. Then remove filter and intake pipe assembly from case. See **Figure 8**. Installation is the reverse of this procedure.

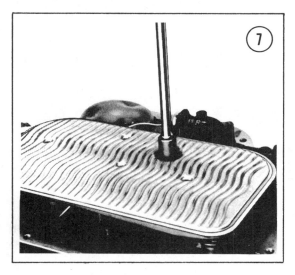

⑦

Front Suspension and Steering Linkage

Every **6,000** miles (**7,500** on 1975-1976) or 4 months, lubricate the upper and lower ball-joints in each wheel. On cars with manual steering, lubricate tie rod end in the relay rod; a total of 5 fittings. See **Figure 9**. On power steering models, lubricate each tie rod end, power steering valve adapter, and the power cylinder; a total of 6 fittings. See **Figure 10**. Use a water resistant EP chassis grease.

PCV System

Replace the PCV valve every **12,000** miles on 1970 and earlier models, every **24,000** miles on 1971-1974 models, and every **15,000** miles on 1975-1976 models.

Air Cleaner

On 1963-1965 models, remove polyurethane element and clean it every **12,000** miles. To do this, remove support screen from element and wash element in kerosene. Squeeze out excess solvent. See **Figure 11**.

CAUTION
Do not use a hot degreaser or any solvent containing acetone or similar chemicals.

Dip element in light engine oil and gently squeeze excess oil out. Install the screen support and replace the element in the air cleaner housing.

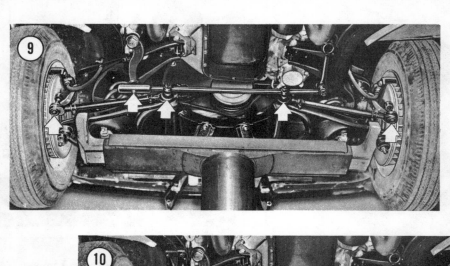

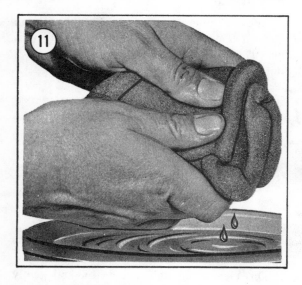

On 1975-1976 models, replace the filter every **30,000** miles.

Fuel Filter

On 1966-1974 models, rotate the filter 180° in the housing every **12,000** miles. See **Figure 12**. Every **24,000** miles, replace the entire element.

On 1963-1965 models with a Carter AFB carburetor or fuel injection system, replace the inline fuel filter every **12,000** miles. See **Fig-**

ure 13. Be sure the flow arrow on the fuel filter is pointed in the direction of the fuel flow.

On 1963-1965 models, with a Carter WCFB and all 1966 and later models, replace the fuel filter in the carburetor every **12,000** miles (**15,000** on 1975-1976). See **Figures 14 and 15**. The bronze filter in Holley carburetors must be installed with the small section of the cone facing out.

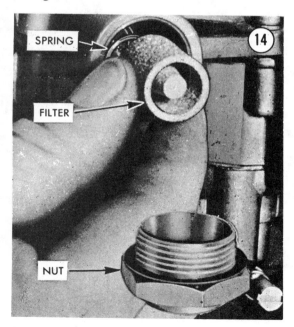

Fuel Evaporation Control System Filter

The filter is on the bottom of the fuel evaporation control canister, located on the left side of

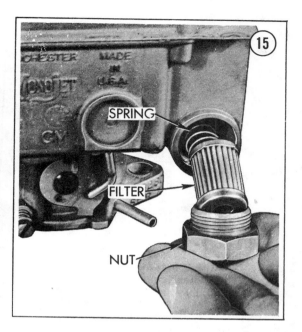

the engine compartment. This should be changed every **12,000** miles on 1970-1971 models, every **24,000** miles on 1972-1974 models, and every **30,000** miles on 1975-1976 models.

To replace the filter, raise the vehicle on a hoist. Mark position of hoses on canister and disconnect them from the canister. Loosen the clamp securing the canister and remove it. Remove bottom of canister and pull the filter out. Install the canister by reversing this procedure. See **Figure 16**.

Cooling System

The cooling system should be drained, flushed with clean water, and refilled with anti-freeze at least every 2 years. See Chapter Nine for procedures.

Wheel Bearings

Clean, pack, and adjust the front wheel bearings every **30,000** miles. See Chapter Twelve for cleaning and packing procedures. See Chapter Thirteen for adjustment procedure.

Universal Joints

Every **30,000** miles, clean and pack universal joints on propeller shaft and rear axles. See Chapter Fourteen for both procedures.

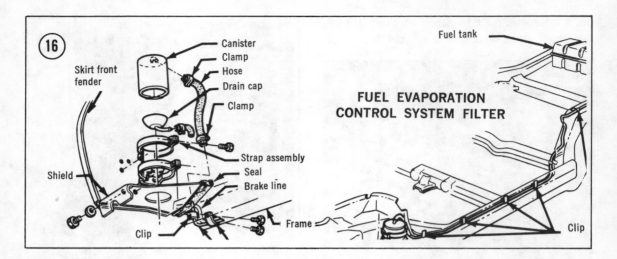

FUEL EVAPORATION
CONTROL SYSTEM FILTER

Clutch Cross-shaft

On 1963-1964 models, lubricate the clutch cross-shaft every **6,000** miles. See **Figure 17**. On 1965 and later models, remove the plug on clutch cross-shaft and install Zerk fitting. Lubricate cross-shaft at **36,000** miles and every 36,000 miles thereafter.

Body

Once a year, apply light engine oil to hood latch mechanism and hinges, rear compartment lid release and hinges, side hinge pins, and gas filler cap hinge. Lubricate the lock cylinders with powdered graphite. Lubricate the door lock rotor and striker plate with a stainless stick lubricant such as Door-Ease. Lightly coat the

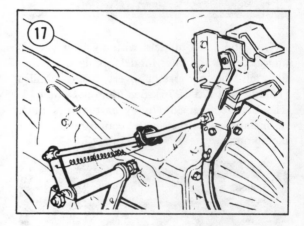

weatherstripping and rubber bumpers with special rubber lubricant or glycerine.

CHAPTER THREE

ENGINE TUNE-UP

In order to maintain your Corvette in proper running condition, the engine must receive periodic tune-ups. Procedures outlined here are performed every 6,000 miles on 1974 and earlier models. However, every 12,000 miles, spark plugs and breaker point should be replaced, not merely cleaned. Since different systems in an engine interact to affect overall performance, tune-up must be performed in the following order.

1. Valve clearance (lash) adjustment (solid lifters only)
2. Ignition adjustment and timing
3. Carburetor adjustment

On 1975-1976 models, which are equipped with the Chevrolet High Energy Ignition System, the tune-up consists of spark plug replacement and timing and carburetor adjustments, and is required every 22,500 miles.

VALVE CLEARANCE (LASH)

Solid Lifters

This is a series of simple mechanical adjustments performed while the engine is hot.

1. Warm the engine to normal operating temperature.
2. Remove rocker arm covers.

CAUTION
Do not pry rocker arm cover loose. Instead, tap end of rocker arm cover rearward with palm of hand or rubber mallet. This will loosen the gasket without distorting the rocker arm cover.

3. With engine running at idle, insert a feeler gauge between rocker arm and valve stem. See **Figure 1**. Valve clearance is shown in **Table 1**.

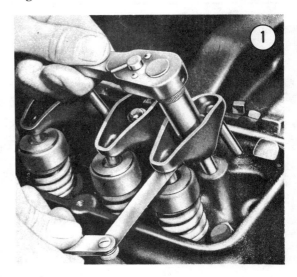

4. With a socket wrench on the rocker arm stud nut, adjust nut until proper clearance is established.

Table 1   VALVE CLEARANCES (Solid Lifters)

1963-1964		
340 HP	0.008″	0.018″
360 HP	0.008″	0.018″
1965		
365 HP	0.030″	0.030″
375 HP	0.030″	0.030″
1966		
425 HP	0.020″	0.024″
1967		
425 HP	0.022″	0.024″
435 HP	0.024″	0.028″
1968		
430 HP	0.022″	0.024″
435 HP	0.024″	0.028″
1969		
370 HP	0.030″	0.030″
430 HP	0.022″	0.024″
435 HP	0.024″	0.028″
1970		
370 HP	0.030″	0.030″
465 HP	0.024″	0.028″
1971		
330 HP	0.024″	0.030″
425 HP	0.024″	0.028″
1972		
255 HP	0.024″	0.030″

5. Stop the engine. Clean the gasket surfaces on cylinder heads and rocker arm covers with degreaser, then install rocker arm covers using new gaskets.

Hydraulic Lifters (1963-1971)

NOTE: *Hydraulic valve lifters seldom require adjustment. The following procedures should be used for adjustment after engine overhaul or valve mechanism installation.*

1. Warm engine to normal operating temperature.

2. Remove rocker arm covers and gaskets.

CAUTION
Do not pry rocker arm cover loose. Instead, tap end of rocker arm cover rearward with palm of hand or rubber

mallet. This will loosen the gasket without distorting the rocker arm cover.

3. With engine running at idle, back off rocker arm nut with socket wrench until the valve rocker arm starts to clatter.

4. Turn rocker arm nut down slowly until the clatter just stops. This is the "0" lash position.

5. Turn nut down an additional ¼ turn and pause 10 seconds until engine runs smoothly. Turn nut down 3 additional ¼ turns, pausing 10 seconds each time, until nut has been turned down one full turn from the "0" lash position.

CAUTION
This one-turn preload adjustment must be done slowly to allow the filter to adjust itself. Otherwise, the inlet valve and the piston may collide, resulting in serious internal damage.

6. Repeat Steps 3-5 for the rest of the valves.

7. Install rocker arm cover using new gasket.

Hydraulic Lifters (1972-1976)

1. Warm engine to normal operating temperature, and shut it off.

2. Remove rocker arm covers and gaskets.

CAUTION
Do not pry rocker arm cover loose. Instead, tap end of rocker arm cover rearward with palm of hand or rubber mallet. This will loosen the gasket without distorting the rocker arm cover.

3. Rotate the engine crankshaft until piston No. 1 is at TDC on its compression stroke. This is evident when the mark on the harmonic balancer lines up with the center or "0" mark on the timing tab (**Figure 2**), and neither valve for cylinder No. 1 is moving. If the valves move as the mark comes up to the "0" mark on the timing tab, cylinder No. 6 is in firing position and the crankshaft should be rotated one more revolution to reach the No. 1 position.

4. Back off the adjusting nut on both valves for cylinder No. 1 until there is play in the pushrod. See **Figure 3**. Tighten the nuts just enough to remove all pushrod clearance. Tighten the nuts

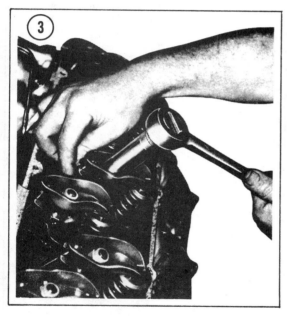

an additional turn to place the hydraulic lifter plunger in the center of its travel.

5. With the engine still in the No. 1 firing position, adjust the exhaust valves for cylinders No. 3, No. 4, and No. 8, and the intake valves for No. 2, No. 5, and No. 7 in the same manner as cylinder No. 1 intake and exhaust valves were adjusted in Step 4.

6. Crank the engine one revolution until the timing tab "0" mark and harmonic balancer mark are again in alignment. With the engine in this position, adjust the exhaust valves for cylinders No. 2, No. 5, No. 6, and No. 7 and the

intake valves for cylinders No. 3, No. 4, No. 6, and No. 8.

7. Install the rocker arm covers with new gaskets.

IGNITION SYSTEM (1963-1974)

Once valve clearance is properly adjusted, work on the ignition system.

Spark Plugs

Blow out any foreign material from around spark plugs with compressed air. Disconnect the spark plug wires and remove the plugs. Keep the plugs in order so they may be matched to the cylinder they came from.

Examine spark plugs and compare their appearance to **Figure 4**. Electrode appearance is a good indication of performance in each cylinder and permits early recognition of trouble. Clean the plugs and inspect the insulator and body of each plug for signs of cracks and chips; replace if necessary. Regap the plugs and reinstall them using new gaskets.

Distributor Cap and Rotor

Remove distributor cap and wipe off any dirt or corrosion. Examine inside of the cap for wear and signs of carbon tracks (arcing). Install a new cap if carbon tracks are evident. Remove the rotor and check for excessive wear or burning around the metal contact surfaces. Replace the rotor if defective, or any time breaker points are replaced.

Breaker Points

Check breaker points for signs of pitting, discoloration, and misalignment. If this is a 12,000 mile tune-up, replace the points and condenser.

Every 12,000 miles, replace breaker points. Disconnect the primary lead to the distributor and remove the points. Note carefully how they are connected and install new points in exactly the same way. Replace the condenser also. Check that the contacts on the points are properly aligned as shown in **Figure 5**. If not, carefully bend the fixed contact to align the contacts.

SPARK PLUG CONDITION

NORMAL

- Identified by light tan or gray deposits on the firing tip.
- Can be cleaned.

GAP BRIDGED

- Identified by deposit buildup closing gap between electrodes.
- Caused by oil or carbon fouling. If deposits are not excessive, the plug can be cleaned.

OIL FOULED

- Identified by wet black deposits on the insulator shell bore electrodes.
- Caused by excessive oil entering combustion chamber through worn rings and pistons, excessive clearance between valve guides and stems, or worn or loose bearings. Can be cleaned. If engine is not repaired, use a hotter plug.

CARBON FOULED

- Identified by black, dry fluffy carbon deposits on insulator tips, exposed shell surfaces and electrodes.
- Caused by too cold a plug, weak ignition, dirty air cleaner, defective fuel pump, too rich a fuel mixture, improperly operating heat riser, or excessive idling. Can be cleaned.

LEAD FOULED

- Identified by dark gray, black, yellow, or tan deposits or a fused glazed coating on the insulator tip.
- Caused by highly leaded gasoline. Can be cleaned.

WORN

- Identified by severely eroded or worn electrodes.
- Caused by normal wear. Should be replaced.

FUSED SPOT DEPOSIT

- Identified by melted or spotty deposits resembling bubbles or blisters.
- Caused by sudden acceleration. Can be cleaned.

OVERHEATING

- Identified by a white or light gray insulator with small black or gray brown spots and with bluish-burnt appearance of electrodes.
- Caused by engine overheating, wrong type of fuel, loose spark plugs, too hot a plug, low fuel pump pressure, or incorrect ignition timing. Replace the plug.

PREIGNITION

- Identified by melted electrodes and possibly blistered insulator. Metallic deposits on insulator indicate engine damage.
- Caused by wrong type of fuel, incorrect ignition timing or advance, too hot a plug, burned valves, or engine overheating. Replace the plug.

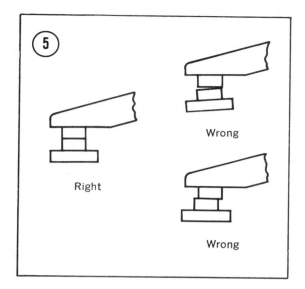

5

Right

Wrong

Wrong

Carefully rotate the distributor body or the crankshaft pulley until the high cam lobe opens the points to the maximum gap. Loosen the screw holding the points, insert a feeler gauge in the gap, and adjust to 0.019 in. Tighten the retaining screw.

More accurate point gap measurement is possible by measuring dwell angle which should be $30° \pm 2°$. Connect the dwell meter, following the manufacturer's instructions. To adjust the dwell, run engine at idle and turn the adjusting screw with an Allen wrench (**Figure 6**) until the specified dwell is obtained.

On engines without exhaust emission controls, dwell can be set fairly close without a dwell meter. With the engine running at idle, turn the adjusting screw clockwise until the engine starts to misfire, then turn the screw ½ turn in the opposite direction.

Ignition Timing

After adjusting the breaker gap, set the ignition timing. Always use a stroboscopic timing light to adjust timing.

1. Turn the engine, without starting it, until the timing mark on the harmonic balancer is visible. Rub the mark with white chalk to make it even more noticeable when lit by the strobe light.

2. Disconnect the distributor spark advance hose at the distributor, and plug the hose.

3. Start the engine and run at idle speed. See **Table 2** at the end of the chapter.

4. Aim the timing light at the timing tab.

5. Loosen the distributor clamp and rotate the distributor body as required to line up the mark on the harmonic balancer with the appropriate mark on the timing tab. See **Figure 7**. Refer to Table 2 to determine the appropriate mark for your engine.

> NOTE: *The markings on the timing tab are in 2° increments. See Figure 7. The "0" mark is* TDC. *The greatest number of markings occur on the* BTDC *side of the timing tab.*

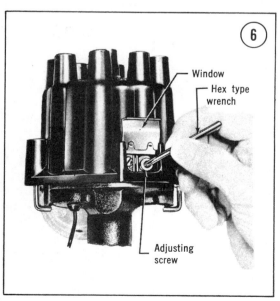

6

Window

Hex type wrench

Adjusting screw

7

6. Tighten the distributor clamp and recheck the timing.

7. Stop the engine and disconnect the timing light. Reconnect the spark advance hose.

HIGH ENERGY IGNITION SYSTEM
(1975-1976)

All 1975-1976 Corvette engines are equipped with the Chevrolet High Energy Ignition (HEI) system (**Figure 8**). The HEI is a pulse-triggered, transistor controlled, inductive discharge system. Conventional breaker points are not used. Principal system elements are the ignition coil, electronic module, pickup assembly, and the centrifugal and vacuum advance mechanisms. All of these elements are contained in the distributor.

Ignition Coil

The HEI coil operates in basically the same way as a conventional coil, but is smaller in size and generates higher secondary voltage when the primary circuit is broken. The coil is built into the cap of the distributor.

Electronic Module

Circuits within the electronic module perform 5 functions. These are spark triggering, switching, current limiting, dwell control, and distributor pickup.

Pickup Assembly

The pickup assembly consists of a rotating timer core with external teeth (turned by the distributor shaft), a stationary pole piece with internal teeth, and a pickup coil and magnet located between the pole piece and a bottom plate.

Centrifugal and Vacuum Advance

The centrifugal and vacuum advance mechanisms are basically identical to units used in breaker point ignition systems.

Operation

As the distributor shaft turns the timer core teeth out of alignment with the pole piece teeth,

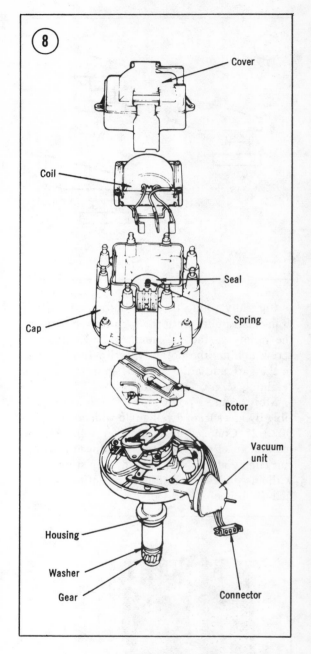

a voltage is created in the magnetic field of the pickup coil. The pickup coil sends this voltage to the electronic module, which determines from the rotational speed of the distributor shaft when to start building current in the ignition coil primary windings. When the timer core teeth are again aligned with the pole piece teeth, the magnetic field is changed, creating a different voltage. This signal is sent to the electronic module by the pickup coil and causes the module to shut off the ignition coil primary circuit. This collapses the coil magnetic field and induces a high secondary voltage to fire one spark plug.

The electronic module limits the 12-volt current to the ignition coil to 5-6 amperes. The module also triggers the opening and closing of the coil primary circuit with zero energy loss. In a conventional breaker point ignition system some energy can be lost due to point arcing and/or capacitor charging time lag. (Although a capacitor is present in the HEI system, it is used only as a radio noise suppressor.) The efficiency of the triggering system allows up to approximately 35,000 volts to be delivered through the secondary wiring system to the spark plugs.

The module circuit controlling dwell angle causes the angle to increase as engine speed increases.

Tune-up

Routine maintenance is not required for the HEI system itself. If parts or components fail, they are not repairable and must be replaced. However, engine timing should be checked and the distributor components visually checked for cracks, wear, dust, moisture, burns, etc., every 18 months or 22,500 miles, whichever comes first. At the same time, the secondary wiring (spark plug wires) should be inspected, checked out with an ohmmeter, and replaced if necessary.

> NOTE: *The HEI system has larger (8mm) diameter, silicon-insulated spark plug wires. While these gray-colored wires are more heat resistant and less vulnerable to deterioration than conventional wires, they should not be mistreated. When removing wires from spark plugs, grasp only on the boots. Twist boot a half turn in either direction to break seal, then pull to remove.*

Spark plugs also should be replaced after every 22,500 miles.

The procedure for ignition timing is identical to that given above for conventional ignition systems, except that timing light connections should be made in parallel using an adapter at the No. 1 spark plug wire terminal on the distributor. The distributor cap also has a special terminal marked "Tach". Connect one lead of the tachometer to this terminal and the other lead to ground.

> NOTE: *Some tachometers must connect from the "Tach" terminal to the battery positive terminal. Check the manufacturer's instructions before making connections.*

CARBURETTED FUEL SYSTEM

Carburetor adjustments should not be attempted until valve clearances and the ignition system have been adjusted.

Idle Speed and Mixture Adjustment (1963-1967 Without AIR)

The following procedures apply to 1963-67 models without the Air Injection Reactor system (AIR).

1. Connect a tachometer to the engine.

2. Connect a vacuum gauge in the distributor spark advance line with a T-fitting.

3. Set handbrake and start engine. Place transmission in NEUTRAL and let the engine warm thoroughly.

4. When the engine is thoroughly warmed up, be sure that the choke is fully open and the carburetor is on "slow idle."

5. Adjust idle speed screw (**Figure 9**) to idle speed given in Table 2.

> NOTE: *Manual transmission should be in NEUTRAL, automatic transmission should be in DRIVE.*

6. Adjust each idle mixture screw alternately to give peak steady vacuum at given idle speed. These screws interact considerably, so each will have to be adjusted several times.

7. Hold choke valve closed and ensure that fast idle cam index mark lines up with fast idle adjustment screw. See **Figure 10**. If necessary, bend fast idle rod at the lower angle to adjust.

8. Start engine and connect tachometer. With fast idle screw on index of cam, adjust fast idle screw to obtain approximately 1,750 rpm with a warm engine.

⑨

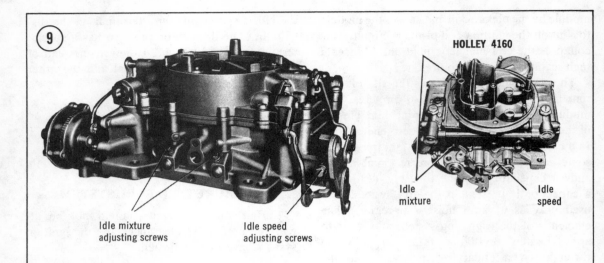

HOLLEY 4160

Idle
mixture

Idle
speed

Idle mixture
adjusting screws

Idle speed
adjusting screws

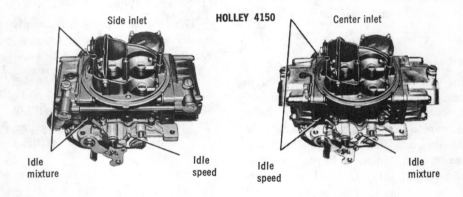

Side inlet   HOLLEY 4150   Center inlet

Idle
mixture

Idle
speed

Idle
speed

Idle
mixture

HOLLEY 2300
(SECONDARY)

HOLLEY 2300C
(PRIMARY)

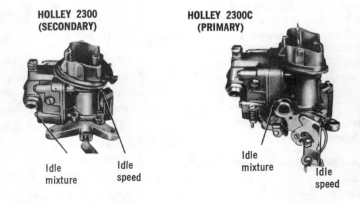

Idle
mixture

Idle
speed

Idle
mixture

Idle
speed

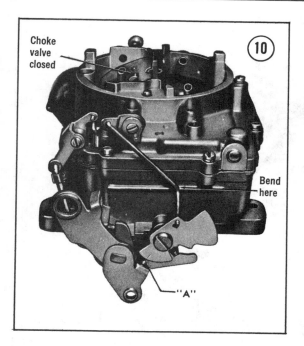

Choke valve closed

⑩

Bend here

"A"

Idle Speed and Mixture Adjustment
(1967-1969 with AIR)

The following procedures apply to 1967-1969 models with the Air Injection Reactor system (AIR).

1. Connect a tachometer to the engine.

2. Connect a vacuum gauge in the distributor spark advance with a T-fitting.

3. Set handbrake. Start engine. Place transmission in NEUTRAL and let the engine warm thoroughly.

> NOTE: *Consult tune-up decal on your engine to determine whether the air conditioner should be on or off.*

4. When the engine is thoroughly warmed up, be sure that the choke is fully open and the carburetor is on "slow idle."

5. Adjust idle speed screw (Figure 9) to idle speed given in Table 2.

> NOTE: *Manual transmission should be in* NEUTRAL, *automatic transmission should be in* DRIVE.

6. Adjust each idle mixture screw alternately to give peak steady vacuum at given idle speed. These screws interact considerably, so each will have to be adjusted several times.

7. Turn one idle mixture screw in until the rpm drops 20-30 rpm. Back the screw out ¼ turn from this point.

8. Repeat Step 7 for the other screw, if so equipped.

9. Repeat the entire procedure as often as necessary to ensure the adjustments are correct.

Idle Speed and Mixture Adjustment
(1970-1971 with Holley Carburetor)

1. Connect a tachometer to the engine. Remove the gas cap.

2. Connect a vacuum gauge in the distributor spark advance line with a T-fitting.

3. Set handbrake. Start engine. Place transmission in NEUTRAL and let the engine warm thoroughly.

> NOTE: *Consult tune-up decal on your engine to determine whether the air conditioner should be on or off.*

4. When the engine is thoroughly warmed up, be sure that the choke is fully open and the carburetor is on "slow idle."

5. Adjust idle speed screw (**Figure 11**) to idle speed given in Table 2.

> NOTE: *Manual transmission should be in* NEUTRAL; *automatic transmission should be in* DRIVE. *Be sure handbrake is firmly set. Wheel blocks add to safety.*

6. Adjust each idle mixture screw alternately to give peak steady vacuum at given idle speed. These screws interact considerably, so each will have to be adjusted several times.

7. Turn one idle mixture screw in until the rpm drops 20-30 rpm. Back the screw out ¼ turn from this point.

8. Repeat Step 7 for other screw, if equipped.

9. Repeat the entire procedure as often as necessary to ensure the adjustments are correct.

Idle Speed Adjustment
(1970-1973 With Rochester Carburetor)

All carburetors are equipped with idle mixture limiter caps. Do not remove the mixture

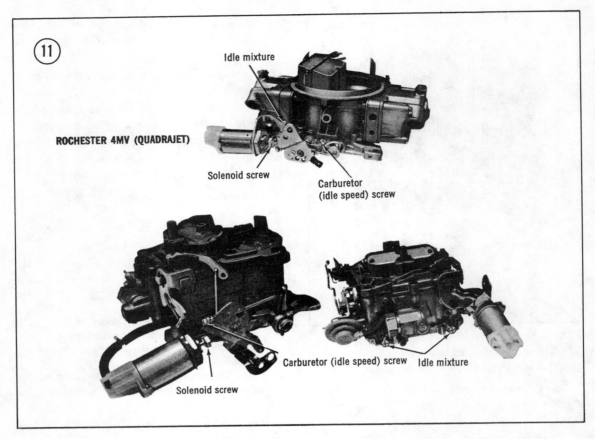

⑪

Idle mixture

ROCHESTER 4MV (QUADRAJET)

Solenoid screw

Carburetor
(idle speed) screw

Carburetor (idle speed) screw   Idle mixture

Solenoid screw

screw caps. Do not adjust the mixture of these carburetors.

1. Disconnect distributor spark advance line at distributor and plug the line.

2. Remove the fuel tank gas cap.

3. Connect a tachometer to the engine.

4. With air conditioning off, adjust idle stop solenoid screw (Figure 11 and **Figure 12**) to idle speed listed in Table 2.

5. Place fast idle cam follower on second step of fast idle cam. With air conditioning off, adjust fast idle to 1,350 rpm with manual transmission in NEUTRAL, or 1,500 rpm with automatic transmission in PARK.

6. Reconnect distributor spark advance line and install fuel tank gas cap.

Idle Speed Adjustment
(1972-1973 With Holley Carburetor)

All carburetors are equipped with idle mixture limiter caps. Do not remove the mixture

screw caps and do not adjust the mixture of these carburetors.

1. Disconnect distributor spark advance line at distributor. Plug the line.

2. Remove the fuel tank gas cap.

3. Connect a tachometer to the engine.

4. With air conditioning off, adjust idle stop solenoid screw (**Figure 13**) to idle speed listed in Table 2.

5. Reconnect distributor spark advance line and install fuel tank gas cap.

Idle Speed Adjustment
(1974-1976 Rochester Carburetor)

Engine should be at normal operating temperature, air cleaner on, choke open, air conditioner off, and automatic transmission in DRIVE or manual transmission in NEUTRAL. Set parking brake and block rear wheels.

NOTE: *Consult the tune-up decal on your engine for the correct idle speeds*

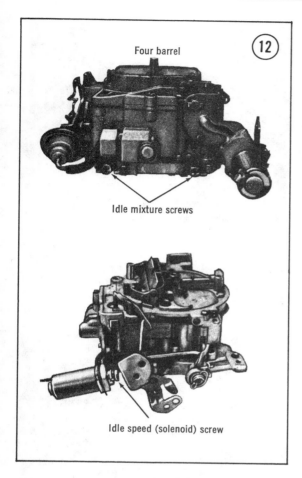

Four barrel ⑫

Idle mixture screws

Idle speed (solenoid) screw

1. On 1974 models, remove gas tank cap. On 1975-1976 models, disconnect fuel tank hose from vapor canister.

2. Disconnect (at distributor) and plug vacuum advance hose.

3. Verify that engine timing is correctly set. Reconnect vacuum advance hose, and attach tachometer, using manufacturer's instructions.

4. Disconnect idle stop solenoid electrical connector. Turn low idle stop screw to obtain low idle speed specified on tune-up decal.

5. Reconnect idle stop solenoid connector and crack throttle slightly to extend solenoid plunger.

6. Set curb idle speed to specified rpm by screwing solenoid plunger in or out, as required.

7. Kill engine and remove tachometer.

NOTE: *Idle mixture is preset at the factory and the idle mixture screws are capped with plastic limiter caps. These caps should not be removed or damaged unless the engine and/or carburetor have been overhauled.*

FUEL INJECTION

The engine must be at normal operating temperature before attempting these procedures.

Idle Speed and Mixture Adjustment

1. Preset the idle mixture screw 1½ turns out from fully closed position. See **Figure 14**.

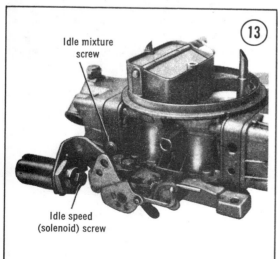

Idle mixture screw ⑬

Idle speed (solenoid) screw

and other specifications. If the decal specifications differ from those given in Table 2, use those shown on the decal.

⑭

2. With the engine running, adjust idle speed screw (**Figure 15**) to approximately 800 rpm.

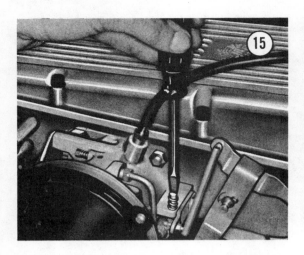

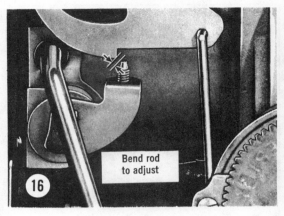

3. Adjust idle mixture screw (Figure 14) for maximum idle speed.

4. Readjust idle speed if necessary to 800-850 rpm.

Fast Idle Speed Adjustment

1. With the cold enrichment valve fully open, check that there is about 0.040 in. between fast idle cam and adjusting screw. See **Figure 16**. Bend the rod if necessary to obtain clearance.

2. With engine off, crank the throttle valve and manually position the cold enrichment valve to its fully closed position. Release the throttle linkage. The fast idle cam should remain positioned as for cold engine operation.

3. Without disturbing the throttle valve or the cold enrichment valve, restart the engine and adjust the fast idle screw to obtain 2,200 rpm on 1963-1964 models, and 2,600 rpm on 1965 models. See **Figure 17**.

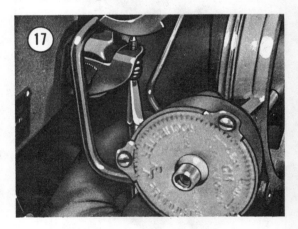

Table 2 TUNE-UP SPECIFICATIONS

Year	1963				1964				1965					
Engine displacement	327	327	327	327	327	327	327	327	327	327	327	327	327	396
Horsepower	250	300	340	360	250	300	365	375	250	300	350	365	375	425
Spark plug type														
Standard	AC-44	AC-44	AC-44	AC-44	AC-44	AC-44	AC-44	AC-44	AC-44	AC-44	AC-44	AC-44	AC-44	43N
Colder	AC-43	AC-43	AC-43	AC-43	AC-43	AC-43	AC-43	AC-43	AC-43	AC-43	AC-43	AC-43	AC-43	AC-C42N
Hotter	—	—	—	—	—	—	—	—	AC-45	AC-45	AC-45	AC-45	AC-45	—
Spark plug gap	0.035"	0.035"	0.035"	0.035"	0.035"	0.035"	0.035"	0.035"	0.035"	0.035"	0.035"	0.035"	0.035"	0.035"
Breaker point														
Gap	0.019"	0.019"	0.019"	0.019"	0.019"	0.019"	0.019"	0.019"	0.019"	0.019"	0.019"	0.019"	0.019"	0.019"
Dwell	28-32°	28-32°	28-32°	28-32°	28-32°	28-32°	28-32°	28-32°	28-32°	28-32°	28-32°	28-32°	28-32°	31-34°
Ignition timing														
Manual														
Without AIR[2]	4° BTDC	8° BTDC	10° BTDC	10° BTDC	4° BTDC	8° BTDC	10° BTDC	10° BTDC	4° BTDC	8° BTDC	8° BTDC	12° BTDC	12° BTDC	10° BTDC
With AIR[2]	—	—	—	—	—	—	—	—	4° BTDC	8° BTDC	—	—	—	—
Automatic														
Without AIR[2]	4° BTDC	8° BTDC	—	—	4° BTDC	8° BTDC	—	—	4° BTDC	8° BTDC	—	—	—	—
With AIR[2]	—	—	—	—	—	—	—	—	4° BTDC	8° BTDC	—	—	—	—
Engine idle speed														
Manual														
Without AIR[2], rpm	475	475	750	850	475	475	800	850	450-500	450-500	650-750	750-850	850 (min.)	800
With AIR[2], rpm	—	—	—	—	—	—	—	—	—	—	—	—	—	—
Automatic														
Without AIR[2], rpm	450	450	—	—	450	450	—	—	450-500	450-500	—	—	—	—
With AIR[2], rpm	—	—	—	—	—	—	—	—	450-500	450-500	—	—	—	—

1. Vacuum advance line disconnected and plugged.
2. Air injection reaction system.
3. Air conditioner off, hot idle compensator closed.
4. Adjust at 800 rpm.

Table 2   TUNE-UP SPECIFICATIONS (continued)

	1966				1967					1968					
Year	327	327	427	427	327	327	427	427	427	327	327	427	427	427	427
Engine displacement	327	327	427	427	327	327	427	427	427	327	327	427	427	427	427
Horsepower	300	350	390	425	300	350	390	400	435	300	350	390	400	430	435
Spark plug type															
Standard	AC-44	AC-44	AC-43N	AC-43N	AC-44	AC-44	AC-43N	AC-43N	AC-43N	AC-44	AC-44	AC-43N	AC-43	AC-43XL	AC-43N
Colder	AC-43	AC-43	AC-C42N	AC-C42N	AC-43	AC-43	AC-C42N	AC-C42N	AC-C42N	AC-43	AC-43	AC-C42N	AC-C42N	AC-42XL	AC-C42N
Hotter	—	—	—	—	—	—	—	—	—	—	—	—	—	—	—
Spark plug gap	0.035"	0.035"	0.035"	0.035"	0.035"	0.035"	0.035"	0.035"	0.035"	0.035"	0.035"	0.035"	0.035"	0.035"	0.035"
Breaker point															
Gap	0.019"	0.019"	0.019"	0.019"	0.019"	0.019"	0.019"	0.019"	0.019"	0.019"	0.019"	0.019"	0.019"	0.019"	0.019"
Dwell	28-32°	28-32°	28-32°	28-32°	28-32°	28-32°	28-32°	28-32°	28-32°	28-32°	28-32°	28-32°	28-32°	28-32°	28-32°
Ignition timing															
Manual															
Without AIR[2]	6° BTDC	10° BTDC	4° BTDC	8° BTDC	6° BTDC	10° BTDC	4° BTDC	4° BTDC	5° BTDC	4° BTDC	4° BTDC	4° BTDC	4° BTDC	12° BTDC[4]	4° BTDC
With AIR[2]	6° BTDC	10° BTDC	4° BTDC	—	6° BTDC	10° BTDC	4° BTDC	4° BTDC	5° BTDC	4° BTDC	4° BTDC	4° BTDC	4° BTDC	12° BTDC[4]	4° BTDC
Automatic															
Without AIR[2]	—	—	—	—	6° BTDC	—	4° BTDC	4° BTDC	—	4° BTDC	4° BTDC	4° BTDC	4° BTDC	—	—
With AIR[2]	4° ATDC	—	4° BTDC	—	4° ATDC	—	4° BTDC	4° BTDC	—	4° BTDC	4° BTDC	4° BTDC	4° BTDC	—	—
Engine idle speed															
Manual															
Without AIR[2], rpm	450-500	650-750	500-600	750-850	500	700	550	550	750	700	750	700	750	1000	750
With AIR[2], rpm	700[3]	—	600	—	700[3]	700	700	750	750	750	750	700	750	1000	750
Automatic															
Without AIR[2], rpm	450-500	—	500-600	—	500	—	550	550	—	600	—	600	600	—	—
With AIR[2], rpm	600[3]	—	550	—	600[3]	—	550	600	—	600	—	600	600	—	—

1. Vacuum advance line disconnected and plugged.
2. Air injection reaction system.
3. Air conditioner off, hot idle compensator closed.
4. Adjust at 800 rpm.

Table 2   TUNE-UP SPECIFICATIONS   (continued)

	1969							1970				
Year												
Engine displacement	350	350	350	427	427	427	427	350	350	350	454	454
Horsepower	300	350	370	390	400	430	435	300	350	370	390	465
Spark plug type												
Standard	AC-R44	AC-R44	AC-R43	AC-R43N	AC-R43N	AC-R43XL	AC-R43N	AC-R44	AC-R44	AC-R4	AC-R42TS	AC-R42TS
Colder	AC-R43	AC-R43	AC-R42-1C	AC-RC42N	AC-RC42N	AC-R42XL	AC-RC42N	AC-R43	AC-R43	AC-R42-1C	—	—
Hotter	—	—	—	—	—	—	—	—	—	—	—	—
Spark plug gap	0.035"	0.035"	0.035"	0.035"	0.035"	0.035"	0.035"	0.035"	0.035"	0.035"	0.035"	0.035"
Breaker point												
Gap	0.019"	0.019"	0.019"	0.019"	0.019"	0.019"	0.019"	0.019"	0.019"	0.019"	0.019"	0.019"
Dwell	28-32°	28-32°	28-32°	28-32°	28-32°	28-32°	28-32°	28-32°	28-32°	28-32°	28-32°	28-32°
Ignition timing												
Manual												
Without AIR[2]	4° BTDC	4° BTDC	4° BTDC	4° BTDC	4° BTDC	12° BTDC[4]	4° BTDC	4° BTDC	4° BTDC	4° BTDC	8° BTDC	8° BTDC
With AIR[2]	4° BTDC	4° BTDC	4° BTDC	4° BTDC	4° BTDC	—	4° BTDC	4° BTDC	4° BTDC	4° BTDC	8° BTDC	8° BTDC
Automatic												
Without AIR[2]	4° BTDC	—	—	4° BTDC	4° BTDC	—	4° BTDC	4° BTDC	—	4° BTDC	12° BTDC	12° BTDC
With AIR[2]	4° BTDC	—	—	4° BTDC	4° BTDC	—	4° BTDC	4° BTDC	—	4° BTDC	12° BTDC	12° BTDC
Engine idle speed												
Manual												
Without AIR[2], rpm	700	750	750	800[3]	800[3]	1000	750	700	750	750	600	600
With AIR[2], rpm	700	750	750	800[3]	800[3]	1000	750	700	750	750	600	600
Automatic												
Without AIR[2], rpm	600	—	—	600[3]	600[3]	—	750	600	—	750	700	700
With AIR[2], rpm	600	—	—	600[3]	600[3]	—	750	600	—	750	700	700

1. Vacuum advance line disconnected and plugged.
2. Air injection reaction system.
3. Air conditioner off, hot idle compensator closed.
4. Adjust at 800 rpm.

Table 2   TUNE-UP SPECIFICATIONS   (continued)

	1971				1972			1973		
Year	1971				1972			1973		
Engine displacement	350	350	454	454	350	350	454	350	350	454
Horsepower	270	330	365	425	200	255	270	190	250	275
Spark plug type										
Standard	AC-R44TS	AC-R44TS	AC-R42TS	AC-R42TS	AC-R44T	AC-R44T	AC-R44T	AC-R44T	AC-R44T	AC-R44T
Colder	AC-R43TS	AC-R43TS	—	—	AC-R43T	AC-R43T	AC-R43T	AC-R43T	AC-R43T	AC-R43T
Hotter	—	—	—	—	—	—	—	—	—	—
Spark plug gap	0.035"	0.035"	0.035"	0.035"	0.035"	0.035"	0.035"	0.035"	0.035"	0.035"
Breaker point										
Gap	0.019"	0.019"	0.019"	0.019"	0.019"	0.019"	0.019"	0.019"	0.019"	0.019"
Dwell	29-31°	29-31°	29-31°	29-31°	29-31°	29-31°	29-31°	29-31°	29-31°	29-31°
Ignition timing										
Manual										
Without AIR[2]	8° BTDC	8° BTDC	8° BTDC	8° BTDC	8° BTDC	4° BTDC	8° BTDC	12° BTDC	8° BTDC	10° BTDC
With AIR[2]	8° BTDC	8° BTDC	8° BTDC	8° BTDC	8° BTDC	4° BTDC	8° BTDC	12° BTDC	8° BTDC	10° BTDC
Automatic										
Without AIR[2]	12° BTDC	12° BTDC	8° BTDC	12° BTDC	8° BTDC	8° BTDC	8° BTDC	12° BTDC	8° BTDC	10° BTDC
With AIR[2]	12° BTDC	12° BTDC	8° BTDC	12° BTDC	8° BTDC	8° BTDC	8° BTDC	12° BTDC	8° BTDC	10° BTDC
Engine idle speed										
Manual										
Without AIR[2], rpm	600	700	600	700	800	900	750	900	900	900
With AIR[2], rpm	600	700	600	700	800	900	750	900	900	900
Automatic										
Without AIR[2], rpm	550	700	600	700	600	700	600	600	700	600
With AIR[2], rpm	550	700	600	700	600	700	600	600	700	600

1. Vacuum advance line disconnected and plugged.
2. Air injection reaction system.
3. Air conditioner off, hot idle compensator closed.
4. Adjust at 800 rpm.

Table 2   TUNE-UP SPECIFICATIONS (continued)

Year	1974			1975		1976	
Engine displacement	350		454	350		350	
Horsepower	195	250	270	165	205	180	210
Spark plug type							
Standard	AC-R44T	AC-R44T	AC-R44T	AC-R44TX	AC-R44TX	AC-R45TS	AC-R45TS
Colder	AC-R43T	AC-R43T	AC-R43T	—	—	—	—
Spark plug gap	0.035"	0.035"	0.035"	0.060"	0.065"	0.045"	0.045"
Breaker points							
Gap	0.019"	0.019"	0.019"	Not used	Not used	Not used	Not used
Dwell	29-31°	29-31°	29-31°	—	—	—	—
Ignition timing							
Manual	8° BTDC ①	8° BTDC	10° BTDC	6° BTDC	6° BTDC	8° BTDC ②	12° BTDC
Automatic	8° BTDC	8° BTDC	10° BTDC	6° BTDC	6° BTDC	8° BTDC ②	12° BTDC
Engine idle speed							
Manual	900	900	800	800	800	1,000	1,000
Automatic	600	700	600	600	600	700	700

① 4° BTDC for vehicles sold new in California.

② 6° BTDC for vehicles sold new in California.

CHAPTER FOUR

TROUBLESHOOTING

Troubleshooting the Corvette can be a relatively simple matter if it is done logically. The first step in any troubleshooting procedure must be defining the symptoms as closely as possible. Subsequent steps involve testing and analyzing areas which could cause the symptoms. A haphazard approach may eventually find the trouble, but in terms of wasted time and unnecessary parts replacement, it can be very costly.

The troubleshooting procedures in this chapter analyze typical symptoms and show logical methods of isolation. These are not the only methods. There may be several approaches to a problem, but all methods must have one thing in common—a logical, systematic approach.

TROUBLESHOOTING INSTRUMENTS

The following equipment is necessary to properly troubleshoot any engine:

a. Voltmeter, ammeter, and ohmmeter
b. Hydrometer
c. Compression tester
d. Vacuum gauge
e. Fuel pressure gauge
f. Dwell meter
g. Tachometer
h. Strobe timing light
i. Exhaust gas analyzer

Items a-f are basic for any car. Items g-i are necessary for exhaust emission control compliance. The following is a brief description of each instrument. Consult a basic repair manual for more detailed information.

Voltmeter, Ammeter, and Ohmmeter

For testing the ignition system and electrical system, a good voltmeter is required. For automotive use, an instrument covering 0-20 volts is satisfactory. One which also has a 0-2 volt scale is necessary for testing relays, points, or individual contacts where voltage drops are much smaller. Accuracy should be $\pm\frac{1}{2}$ volt.

An ohmmeter measures electrical resistance. This instrument is useful for checking continuity (open and short circuits) and for testing fuses and lights.

The ammeter measures electrical current. Ammeters for automotive use should cover 0-50 amperes and 0-250 amperes. These are useful for checking battery charging and starting current. The starter and alternator procedures in this manual use the ammeter to check for defective windings.

Several inexpensive VOM's (volt-ohmmeters) combine all 3 instruments into one which fits easily in any tool box. The ammeter ranges are usually too small for automotive work, though.

Hydrometer

The hydrometer gives a useful indication of battery condition and charge by measuring the specific gravity of the electrolyte in each cell. Complete details on use and interpretation of readings are given in Chapter Ten.

Compression Tester

The compression tester measures the compression pressure built up in each cylinder. The results, when properly interpreted, can indicate general cylinder and valve condition. Chapter Two explains the use of this instrument on the Corvette.

Vacuum Gauge

The vacuum gauge is one of the easiest instruments to use, but one of the most difficult for the inexperienced mechanic to interpret. The results, when interpreted with other findings, can provide valuable clues to possible trouble.

Connect the vacuum gauge with a T-connection in the hose from the carburetor to the vacuum advance on the distributor. Start engine; let it warm up thoroughly. Vacuum reading should be about 20 in. at idle.

NOTE: *Subtract one in. from reading for every 1,000 feet of altitude.*

Figure 1 shows numerous typical readings with interpretations. Results are not conclusive without comparing to other tests, such as compression.

Fuel Pressure Gauge

This instrument is vital for evaluating fuel pump performance. Fuel system troubleshooting procedures in this chapter use a fuel pressure gauge. Usually a vacuum gauge and fuel pressure gauge are combined.

Dwell Meter

A dwell meter measures the distance in degrees of cam rotation that the breaker points remain closed while the engine is running. Since this angle is determined by the breaker point gap, the dwell angle is an accurate indication of point gap.

Many tachometers intended for tuning and testing incorporate a dwell meter as well. Follow the manufacturer's instructions to measure dwell on the Corvette.

Tachometer

A tachometer is necessary for tuning Corvettes with exhaust emission control. Ignition timing and carburetor adjustments must be performed at the specified idle speed. The best instrument for this purpose is one with a range of 0-2,500 rpm. Extended range (0-6,000 or 8,000) instruments lack accuracy at lower speeds. The instrument should be capable of detecting changes of 25 rpm.

Strobe Timing Light

This instrument is necessary for Corvettes with exhaust emission control and is recommended for all Corvettes. It permits very accurate ignition timing. By flashing a light at the precise instant cylinder No. 1 fires, the position of the crankshaft pulley (harmonic balancer) at that instant can be seen. The mark on the pulley is lined up with the appropriate mark on the timing tab while the engine is running.

Suitable lights range from inexpensive neon bulb types ($2-6) to powerful xenon strobe lights ($20-60). Neon timing lights are difficult to see and must be used in dimly lit areas. Xenon strobe timing lights can be used outside in bright sunlight. Both types work on the Corvette; use according to the manufacturer's instructions.

Exhaust Analyzer

Of all instruments described here, this is the least likely to be owned by a home mechanic. The instrument samples the exhaust gases from the tailpipe and measures the thermal conductivity of the exhaust gases. Since different gases conduct heat at varying rates, thermal conductivity of the exhaust is a good indication of gases present.

This instrument is vital for accurately checking the effectiveness of exhaust emission control adjustments. These instruments are relatively expensive to buy, but several large rent-all dealers have them available for a modest fee.

①

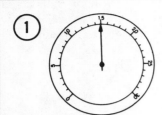

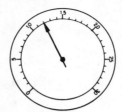

1. NORMAL READING .
Reads 15 in. at idle.

**2. LATE IGNITION
TIMING**
About 2 inches too
low at idle.

**3. LATE VALVE
TIMING**
About 4 to 8 inches
low at idle.

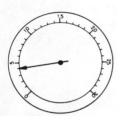

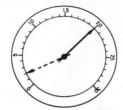

4. INTAKE LEAK
Low steady reading.

5. NORMAL READING
Drops to 2, then rises
to 25 when accelera-
tor is rapidly de-
pressed and released.

**6. WORN RINGS,
DILUTED OIL**
Drops to 0, then rises
to 18 when accelera-
tor is rapidly de-
pressed and released.

**7. STICKING
VALVE(S)**
Normally steady.
Intermittently flicks
downward about 4 in.

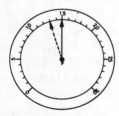

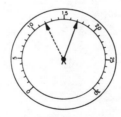

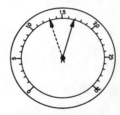

8. LEAKY VALVE
Regular drop about 2
inches.

**9. BURNED OR
WARPED VALVE**
Regular, evenly
spaced down-scale
flick about 4 in.

**10. WORN VALVE
GUIDES**
Oscillates about 4 in.

**11. WEAK VALVE
SPRINGS**
Violent oscillation
(about 10 in.) as rpm
increases. Often
steady at idle.

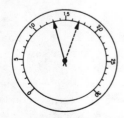

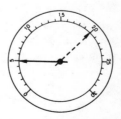

**12. IMPROPER IDLE
MIXTURE**
Floats slowly between
13-17 in.

**13. SMALL SPARK
GAP or DEFECTIVE
POINTS**
Slight float between
14-16 in.

**14. HEAD GASKET
LEAK**
Gauge floats between
5-19 in.

**15. RESTRICTED
EXHAUST SYSTEM**
Normal when first
started. Drops to 0 as
rpm increases. May
eventually rise to
about 16.

STARTER

Starter system troubles are relatively easy to isolate. The following are common symptoms and cures.

1. *Engine cranks very slowly or not at all*—Turn on the headlights; if the lights are very dim, most likely the battery or the connecting wires are at fault. Check the battery using the procedures described in Chapter Ten. Check the wiring for breaks, shorts, and dirty connections. If the battery and connecting wires check good, turn the headlights on and try to crank the engine. If the lights dim drastically, the starter is probably shorted to ground. Remove the starter and test it by using procedures described in Chapter Ten.

If the lights remain bright or dim slightly when trying to crank the engine, the trouble may be in the starter, solenoid, or wiring. To isolate the problem, short the 2 large solenoid terminals together (not to ground); if the starter cranks normally, check the solenoid and wiring up to the ignition switch. If the starter still fails to crank properly, remove the starter and test it.

2. *Starter turns, but does not engage with the engine*—The trouble is usually a defective pinion or solenoid shifting fork. It may also be that the teeth on the pinion, flywheel ring gear, or both, are worn down too far to engage properly.

3. *Starter engages, but will not disengage when ignition switch is released* — This is usually caused by a sticking solenoid, but occasionally the pinion can jam on the flywheel. With manual transmissions, the pinion can be temporarily freed by rocking the car in high gear. Naturally, this is not possible with automatics; the starter must be removed.

4. *Loud grinding noises when starter runs*—May mean the teeth on the pinion and/or flywheel are not meshing properly or it may mean the overrunning clutch is broken. In the first case, remove the starter and examine the gear teeth. In the latter, remove the starter and replace the pinion drive assembly.

CHARGING SYSTEM

Troubleshooting an alternator system is somewhat different from troubleshooting a generator. For example, never short any terminals to ground on the alternator or the voltage regulator. The following symptoms are typical of alternator charging system troubles.

1. *The ammeter indicates constant discharge*—Before suspecting the alternator, check the fan belt tension as described in Chapter Two. Check the condition of the battery with a hydrometer. See Chapter Ten. Check and clean all electrical connections in the charging system. If the trouble still persists, check the alternator and voltage regulator as described later in this section.

2. *Battery requires frequent additions of water, or lamps require frequent replacement*—The alternator system is probably overcharging the battery. Have the voltage regulator checked, or replace it.

3. *Noisy alternator*—Check for loose alternator mounting. Check for faulty alternator bearings. Replace the bearings using procedures provided later in this section.

ENGINE

These procedures assume the starter cranks the engine over normally. If not, refer to *Starter* section in this chapter.

1. *Engine won't start*—Could be caused by the ignition system or the fuel system. First determine if high voltage to spark plugs occurs. To do this, disconnect one of the spark plug wires. Hold the exposed wire terminal about ¼ to ½ in. from ground (any metal in engine compartment) with an insulated screwdriver.

Crank engine over. If sparks do not jump to ground or are very weak, trouble may be in the ignition system. See *Ignition System*, later in this chapter, to further isolate the trouble. If sparks occur properly, trouble may be in fuel system. See *Carburetted Fuel System* or *Fuel Injection System*.

2. *Engine misses steadily*—Remove one spark plug wire at a time and ground the wire. If engine miss increases, that cylinder was working properly. Reconnect the wire and check the others. When a wire is disconnected and engine miss remains the same, that cylinder is not firing. Check spark as described in Step 1. If no spark occurs for one cylinder only, check distributor cap, wire, and spark plug. If spark occurs prop-

erly, check compression and intake manifold vacuum to isolate the trouble.

3. *Engine misses erratically at all speeds*—Intermittent trouble like this can be difficult to find. The trouble could be in the ignition system, exhaust system (exhaust restriction), or fuel system. Carefully follow troubleshooting procedures for these systems to isolate the trouble.

4. *Engine misses at idle only*—Trouble could exist anywhere in ignition system. Follow *Ignition System* procedure carefully. Trouble could also exist in the carburetor idle circuit. Check idle mixture adjustment and check for restrictions in the idle circuit.

5. *Engine misses at high speed only*—Troubles could exist in fuel system or ignition system. Check accelerator pump operation, fuel pump delivery, fuel lines, etc., as described under *Carburetted Fuel System* or *Fuel Injection System*. Also check spark plugs and wires. See *Ignition System*.

6. *Low performance at all speeds, poor acceleration*—Trouble usually exists in ignition or fuel systems. Check each with the appropriate troubleshooting procedure.

7. *Excessive fuel consumption*—This can be caused by a wide variety of seemingly unrelated factors. Check for clutch slippage, brake drag, defective wheel bearings, and poor front end alignment. Check ignition system and fuel system as described later.

8. *Oil pressure gauge reads low*—This may mean low, or complete loss of the oil pressure. *Stop the engine immediately*; coast to stop with clutch disengaged or the transmission in neutral. This may simply be caused by a low oil level or an overheating engine. Check the oil level and fan belt tension (see Chapter Two). Check for shorted oil pressure sender with an ohmmeter or other continuity tester. Listen for unusual noises indicating bad bearings, etc. Do not restart the engine until you know why oil pressure read low.

IGNITION SYSTEM

The procedures assume the battery is in good enough condition to crank the engine at a normal rate.

1. *No spark to one plug*—The only possible causes are a defective distributor cap or spark plug wire. Examine the distributor cap for moisture, dirt, carbon tracking caused by flashover, cracks, etc.

2. *No spark to any plugs*—This could be caused by trouble in the primary or secondary circuits. First remove the coil wire from the center post of the distributor. Hold the wire end about ¼ in. from ground with an insulated screwdriver. Crank the engine. If sparks are produced, the trouble is in the rotor or distributor cap. Remove the cap and check for burns, moisture, dirt, carbon tracking, cracks, etc. Check the rotor for excessive burning, pitting, or cracks. Replace both if necessary.

If the coil does not produce any spark, check the secondary wire for opens. If the wire is good, turn the engine over so the breaker points are open. Examine them for excessive gap, burning, pitting, or looseness. Replace and adjust them if necessary. With the points open, check voltage from minus terminal on the coil to ground with a voltmeter or test lamp. If voltage is present, the coil is probably bad. Have it checked or substitute a coil known to be good.

If voltage is not present, check wire connections to coil and distributor. Temporarily disconnect the wire from minus terminal on the coil to the distributor and measure from minus terminal to ground. If voltage is present, the distributor is shorted; examine breaker points and connecting wires carefully. If voltage is still not present, measure plus terminal of the coil. Voltage on plus terminal, but not on minus terminal, indicates a defective coil. No voltage on plus terminal indicates an open wire between minus terminal and the battery.

3. *Weak spark*—If the spark is so small that it cannot jump from the wire ¼ to ½ in. to ground, check the battery condition as described in Chapter Ten. Other causes are bad breaker points, condenser, incorrect breaker point gap, or dirty or burned rotor or distributor. Also check for worn distributor cam lobes.

4. *Missing*—This is usually caused by fouled or damaged plugs, plugs of the wrong heat range, or incorrect plug gap. Clean and regap the spark plugs. This trouble can also be caused by weak spark (see Symptom 3) or incorrect ignition timing.

Spark Polarity

Less voltage is required to cause electron flow from a relatively hot electrode to a cooler one. Since the center electrode is hottest, this electrode should be negative. Electron flow is then from the center electrode to the outer electrode. From 20 to 40% more voltage is required to cause electron flow from the outside electrode to the hotter center electrode. This occurs when the spark voltage is positive.

The coil must be connected so that the double wire (from the battery) goes to the minus terminal and the single wire (from the distributor) goes to the plus terminal. This ensures that the spark will be negative.

CARBURETTED FUEL SYSTEM

Fuel system troubles must be isolated at the carburetor, fuel pump, or fuel lines. These procedures assume the ignition system has been checked and properly adjusted.

1. *Engine will not start*—First, determine that fuel is delivered to carburetor. Remove the air cleaner, look into the carburetor throat and depress the accelerator several times. There should be a stream of fuel from the accelerator pump discharge tube each time the accelerator is depressed. If not, check fuel pump delivery (described later), float valve, and float adjustment (Chapter Six). If engine still will not start, check automatic choke parts for sticking or damage. If necessary, rebuild or replace the carburetor. See Chapter Six.

2. *Engine runs at fast idle*—Usually this is caused by defective automatic choke. Correct this trouble as soon as possible; the resulting overrich mixture washes oil from cylinder walls, dilutes oil, and leads to expensive wear and damage.

3. *Rough idle or engine miss with frequent stalling*—Check idle mixture and idle speed adjustments. See Chapter Three.

4. *Engine "diesels" when ignition is turned off*—Check idle mixture (probably too rich) and idle speed adjustments. See Chapter Three.

5. *Stumbling when accelerating from idle*—Check accelerator pump diaphragm (Chapter Six) and idle speed adjustment (Chapter Three).

6. *Engine misses at high speed or lacks power*—This indicates possible fuel starvation. Check fuel pump pressure and capacity. Clean main jet and float needle valve.

7. *Black exhaust smoke*—Black exhaust smoke means a badly overrich mixture. Check idle mixture and idle speed adjustment. Check for excessive fuel pump pressure, leaky float, or worn needle valve.

8. *Excessive fuel consumption*—Another indication of an overrich mixture. Check that automatic choke operates. Check idle mixture and idle speed. Check for excessive fuel pump pressure, leaky float, or worn float needle valve. Also check that jets are proper size. Compare with specifications in Chapter Six.

Fuel Pump Testing

1. Disconnect the fuel line at the carburetor.

2. Disconnect the primary ignition wire from the coil to the distributor so that the engine can be cranked without starting.

3. Place a container at the end of the fuel line to catch the fuel, and crank the engine a few revolutions. If little or no gasoline flows from the open end of the fuel line, then the line is clogged or the pump is defective.

4. If a good volume of fuel flows from the pump, connect a fuel pump pressure gauge to the disconnect end of the fuel line.

5. Reconnect the primary ignition lead.

6. Run the engine at approximately 950-1,000 rpm and note reading on pressure gauge; (there is enough fuel in the carburetor bowl to do this.)

7. Pressure should be: 327 cu. in. engine, 5-6½ lb.; 350 cu. in. engine, 7-8½ lb.; 396 cu. in. engine, 5½-7½ lb.; and 427 and 454 cu. in. engines, 5-8½ lb. If pressure is too low or too high, or varies significantly at different speeds, the pump should be rebuilt or replaced. See Chapter Six.

FUEL INJECTION SYSTEM

Before suspecting the fuel injection system, check for air or vacuum leaks, faulty ignition system, or low engine compression.

1. *Engine fails to start*—Check fuel tank supply and engine fuel pump output. Check for broken

fuel meter pump drive cable. Check for leaking or ruptured main control diaphragm, defective cranking signal valve, or broken main control diaphragm linkage.

2. *Difficulty starting*—Check fast idle cam setting. See Chapters Three and Seven. Check for defective cranking signal valve or enrichment solenoid. Check for vacuum leaks at main control diaphragm or signal line.

3. *Engine will not idle; high speed operation OK* —Ensure that idle speed is set correctly. See Chapters Three and Seven. Check for dirty air meter passages, vacuum or air leaks, or defective main diaphragm. Check for plugged nozzle vent tubes and nozzles. Check for defective nozzle-to-insulator gaskets. Check for defective cranking signal valve or signal boost valve. Check for plugged main control diaphragm vent tube, sticking spill plunger, or excessive air meter throttle valve-to-bore clearance.

4. *Rough idle; high speed operation OK*— Check for defective cranking signal valve, or cold enrichment housing operation. Check nozzle vent tube, nozzles, and main diaphragm vent tube for clogging. Check engine valve lash settings. See Chapter Three.

5. *Erratic engine idle speeds*—If engine fails to return to same idle speed, check for sticking throttle valve shaft and air meter bushings or linkage binding. Also, check for sticking spill plunger or choke valve.

6. *Poor acceleration; idle and wide-open throttle operation OK*—Check for defective fuel meter pump drive cable or pump drive shaft. Check for dirty signal tube, cold enrichment housing valve. Check for interference between enrichment housing and diaphragm. Check for incorrect power stop settings or sticking spill plunger.

7. *Hesitation or "flat" spot*—Check for defective main control diaphragm or vacuum leaks, faulty spill plunger operation, or incorrect economy stop setting. See Chapter Seven.

8. *Surging at steady engine speed*—Check for plugged nozzles or nozzle vent tubes. Check for incorrect economy stop setting. Check for faulty integral siphon breaker operation, or plugged main control diaphragm vent tube.

9. *Excessive fuel consumption*—Check for defective cranking signal valve or sticking cold enrichment valve. Check for open electric choke coil, fuel leaks, or faulty integral siphon breaker operation. Ensure that spark plugs are the correct heat range.

10. *Engine misses during wide-open throttle operation*—Check fuel meter pump drive cable and drive shaft for out-of-square condition. Check engine fuel pump for low output. Check for dirty air cleaner or air filter. Check for defective spark plugs.

EXHAUST EMISSION CONTROL

The following symptoms assume you have adjusted the ignition and carburetor as described in Chapter Three and you have checked the results on an accurate exhaust gas analyzer.

1. *CO content too low*—Ensure that idle speed is not too low. Check idle mixture adjustment (too lean). Check carburetor jets and channels. Clean and/or replace as necessary. Check engine condition with a compression and vacuum test.

2. *CO content too high*—Check idle mixture adjustment (too rich). Check for sticking air cleaner, warm air flap, and sticking or defective automatic choke. Check carburetor jets and channels. Check and/or replace as necessary. Check engine condition with a compression and vacuum test.

3. *Hydrocarbon level too high*—Make sure throttle valve closes completely. Check spark plug condition and gap. Check breaker points. Check ignition timing (too early). Check intake manifold for leaks. Check valve clearance (too small). Check condition of valves with compression test.

CLUTCH

All clutch troubles except adjustments require transmission removal for isolation and repair.

1. *Slippage*—This condition is most noticeable when accelerating in a high gear at relatively low speed. To check slippage, park the car on a level surface with the handbrake set. Shift to second gear and release the clutch as if driving off. If

the clutch is good, the engine will slow and stall. If the clutch slips, continued engine speed will give it away.

CAUTION

This is a severe test. Perform this test only when slippage is suspected, not periodically.

Slippage results from insufficient clutch pedal free play, oil or grease on the clutch disc, worn pressure plate, or weak springs. Also check for binding in the clutch linkage which may prevent full engagement.

2. *Drag or failure to release*—This trouble usually causes difficult shifting and gear clash, especially when downshifting. The cause may be excessive clutch pedal free play, warped or bent pressure plate or clutch disc, broken or loose linings, or burrs on the main shaft splines.

3. *Chatter or grabbing*—Worn or misaligned pressure plate binding clutch linkage.

4. *Other noises*—Noise usually indicates a dry or defective release (throw-out) or pilot bearing. Check the bearings and replace if necessary. Also check all parts for misalignment and uneven wear.

MANUAL TRANSMISSION

Transmission troubles are evidenced by one or more of the following symptoms:
   a. Difficulty shifting gears
   b. Gear clash when downshifting
   c. Slipping out of gear
   d. Excessive noise in neutral
   e. Excessive noise in gear
   f. Oil leaks

Transmission troubles are sometimes difficult to distinguish from clutch troubles. Eliminate the clutch as a source of trouble before suspecting the transmission.

AUTOMATIC TRANSMISSION

Most automatic transmission repairs require considerable specialized knowledge and tools. It is impractical for the home mechanic to invest

in tools which cost more than a properly rebuilt transmission.

The following symptoms and tests will help you find and verify transmission troubles. You may perform adjustments as described in Chapter Eleven; all other troubles require dismantling the transmission and must be handled by your dealer or a competent, well-equipped shop.

Powerglide Transmission

To diagnose Powerglide trouble:

1. *No drive in any gear*—Low fluid level check. Defective fluid pump; check pressure as described later. Broken gears.

2. *No drive in* REVERSE—Incorrect manual valve lever adjustment. Defective reverse clutch.

3. *Engine races excessively during upshifts*—Improper fluid level. Improper band adjustment. Burnt or worn high clutch friction linings. Improper fluid pressure. Check as described later.

4. *Transmission will not upshift*—Low band not releasing. This could be caused by improperly adjusted manual valve lever, stuck low drive valve, defective governor, stuck or improperly adjusted throttle valve, or defective rear pump.

5. *Harsh upshifts*—Improper low band adjustment. Defective vacuum modulator or modulator line. Defective hydraulic modulator.

6. *Harsh downshifts when throttle is closed*—Improper low band adjustment. High engine idle speed. Defective downshift timing valve. High mainline pressure.

7. *Transmission will not downshift*—Sticking low drive shift valve. High governor pressure. Low throttle valve pressure.

8. *Incorrect shift points*—(**Table 1**) Carburetor to transmission linkage incorrectly adjusted. Defective governor. Rear pump priming valve stuck.

9. *Poor acceleration; engine output good*—Normally caused by defective torque converter. Could also be low fluid level, slipping bands or clutches.

10. *Transmission fluid discolored or smells burnt*—Burnt band or clutch friction lining.

Table 1   POWERGLIDE SHIFT POINTS

Year and Engine	Throttle Position					
	Closed		Detent Touch		Full Detent	
	Upshift	Downshift	Upshift	Downshift	Upshift	Downshift
1963-1964 327 engine 3.36 : 1 axle	12-15	11-14	50-62	15-18	61-68	58-65
1965 327 engine 3.36 : 1 axle	14-18	13-17	50-62	17-24	62-70	59-67
1966 327 engine 3.08 axle	14.0-17.3	12.8-16.3	50.4-61.0	14.8-26.2	61.3-68.5	57.4-65.0
1967 327 engine (Hi Perf.) 3.36 axle 7.75-15 tire	13.8-17.0	12.6-16.0	49.3-59.7	15.5-25.5	60.3-67.4	56.4-63.9
427 engine (L36) 3.36 : 1 axle 7.75-15 tire	13.8-17.0	12.6-16.0	55.7-66.9	15.5-28.5	68.1-75.6	63.7-71.6

11. *Unusual scraping, grinding, or screeching noises*—Defective converter or planetary gear.

12. *Excessive fluid consumption*—If accompanied by smoky exhaust, vacuum unit is probably leaking and engine is drawing fluid out. Otherwise, check for oil leaks around transmission case and extension, transmission oil pan gasket, and converter cover pan.

13. *Oil forced out of filler tube*—Oil level too high. Water in oil. Leak in pump suction circuits.

14. *Vehicle "creeps" excessively at idle; transmission in* DRIVE—Idle speed too high.

15. *Car "creeps" in* NEUTRAL—Incorrect manual valve lever adjustment. High clutch or low band not releasing.

16. *Unable to push-start (1963-1966 only)*—Rear pump drive gear not engaged with drive pin on output shaft. Drive pin sheared off. Rear pump priming valve not sealing.

Basic Pressure Checks (Powerglide)

Several basic pressure checks are used to diagnose Powerglide troubles. All checks should be made only after thoroughly warming up the transmission.

1. Warm engine by idling at 750 rpm for 2 minutes in the DRIVE range. Be sure to set the parking brake tight. As an alternative, run the car approximately 5 miles, with frequent starts and stops. Return engine to proper idle after warm up.

2. Connect pressure gauge at the low servo apply test point. See **Figure 2**. Route connecting hose so car can be driven with gauge visible.

3. Ensure that a wide open throttle upshift occurs at the pressure indicated in **Table 2**.

Table 2   **POWERGLIDE MAINLINE PRESSURES***

Vacuum	Low Servo Apply (Mainline) Pressure	
	1963-1964	1965-1967
16″ Hg	60-70	63-72
10″ Hg	89-99	90-99

*Parking brake applied, transmission in DRIVE.

4. Apply parking brake and move the shift selector to DRIVE. Compare idle pressure to values in Table 2.

5. Connect a tachometer. Apply the parking brake and move the shift selector to LOW. Adjust engine speed to 1,000 rpm. Compare mainline pressure to Table 2.

6. With the vehicle coasting in the DRIVE range, at 20-25 mph and engine vacuum at approximately 20 in. of mercury, mainline pressure should be 48-54 psi.

Turbo Hydramatic

To diagnose Turbo Hydramatic trouble:

1. Does not drive in DRIVE range—Could be caused by low fluid level, incorrectly adjusted manual linkage, low fluid pressure, malfunctioning forward clutch, or defective roller clutch.

2. Fluid pressure is high or low (see fluid pressure checks below)

   a. If line pressure is high, check for disconnected or leaking vacuum, or leak in other vacuum operated accessories. This symptom also can be caused by the modulator (stuck, damaged, or presence of water), a fault in the detent system (defective detent switch, shorted wiring, defective solenoid, restricted feed orifice, or damaged valve bore plug), or by a defective oil pump.

   b. If line pressure is low, check for low fluid level, or a restricted or blocked filter or screen. Low pressure also can be caused by a defective oil pump, internal circuit leaks, defective regulator valves, and leaky or damaged case assemblies.

3. If transmission shifts from first to second at full throttle only, the cause could be a sticking (or misadjusted linkage) detent valve, faulty or leaking vacuum line or fittings, a defective control valve assembly, or a porous or leaking case assembly. Suspect a sticking detent switch if symptom occurs only in wet or cold weather.

4. If transmission refuses to shift from first to second, check for a binding detent (downshift) cable. This also may be caused by a sticking or damaged governor assembly, damaged control valves or gaskets, or faulty intermediate clutch case defects may also cause the problem.

5. If shifting occurs between first and second, but the transmission will not shift from second to DRIVE, suspect a defective control valve, detent switch or solenoid, or a damaged or malfunctioning direct clutch.

6. If the transmission skips first and starts in second, suspect a defective intermediate clutch.

7. If drive occurs while the transmission is in NEUTRAL, check the manual linkage for correct adjustment. This symptom also can be caused by damaged internal linkage, defective fluid pump, or a damaged forward clutch.

8. If no motion or slippage occurs in REVERSE, check for low fluid level, misadjusted manual linkages, or low fluid pressure. This can also be caused by defective control valve, defective or sticking servos, and malfunctioning clutches.

9. If slipping occurs in all ranges, or when starting, check for low fluid level, low fluid pressure, or leaking case assembly. This can also be caused by defective direct or forward clutch.

10. If slipping occurs during the first-second shift, check for low fluid level, low fluid pressure, or leaking case. Possible causes also include defective control valves, mispositioned or damaged pump-to-case gasket, or damaged intermediate clutch.

11. If slipping occurs during the second-third shift, again check for low fluid level and/or pressure, or a leaking case. This can also be caused by a defective direct clutch.

12. If rough shifting occurs in the first-second shift, check for high fluid pressure. Other possible causes include defective control valve, damaged intermediate clutch, and damaged case.

13. If roughness occurs in the second-third shift, check for high fluid pressure. This can also be caused by defective servo accumulators, or damaged direct clutch.

14. If engine braking does not occur in L1 or L2, check for low fluid pressure. This also can be caused by defective control valves, clutches, and servos.

15. If downshift does not occur at part throttle, check for high or low fluid pressure. This can also be caused by defective detent valve and linkage, or damaged control valve.

16. If no detent downshift (wide open throttle) occurs, check for improperly adjusted or disconnected detent downshift cable or retainer, or malfunctioning valve body or solenoid.

17. If low or high shift points occur, check for high or low fluid pressure and for vacuum leaks and/or faulty vacuum connections. This symptom also can be caused by a faulty governor, a stuck detent valve and/or linkage, a sticking control valve assembly, or a leaking case assembly.

18. If the transmission will not hold in PARK, check the adjustment of the manual linkage.

This also can be caused by defective internal linkage.

19. If the transmission seems to sound noisy, verify that the noise is not coming from the water pump, alternator, power steering, air conditioner compressor, or other belt-driven accessories. This can be done by removing the belt to each accessory and operating the engine momentarily. If this procedure isolates the noise to the transmission, check for low fluid level or for external transmission or cooler lines grounded against underbody of vehicle, or loose or broken engine mounts. Also check for water in fluid. If these checks fail to uncover the problem, the transmission should be taken to a competent mechanic.

Basic Pressure Check
(Turbo Hydramatic)

1. Warm engine by idling at approximately 750 rpm for 2 minutes in DRIVE range with parking brake set and wheels blocked. As an alternative, drive the car for about 5 miles, making frequent starts and stops.

2. Connect oil pressure gauge to line pressure tap (**Figure 3**). Route connecting hose so gauge is visible from driver's position in car.

3. Disconnect vacuum modulator tube and firmly apply parking brake. Operate the engine at 1,200 rpm (connect tachometer if required) and check pressures obtained in the various transmission ranges against those given in **Table 3** (350) or **Table 4** (375-400).

4. Reconnect the vacuum modulator tube and connect a vacuum gauge to the intake manifold.

5. Operate engine at a speed required to maintain an absolute manifold pressure of 16 in. Hg (operate engine at 600-800 rpm for Turbo Hydramatic 375-400). Compare the pressures obtained in the various transmission ranges with those given in **Table 5** (Turbo Hydramatic 350) or **Table 6** (Turbo Hydramatic 375-400).

BRAKES

1. *Brake pedal goes to floor*—There are numerous causes for this including excessively worn linings, air in the hydraulic system, leaky brake lines, leaky wheel cylinders, and leaky or worn

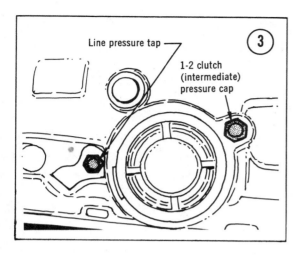

Line pressure tap — ③

1-2 clutch (intermediate) pressure cap

Table 4
TURBO HYDRAMATIC 375-400 OIL PRESSURES*

Approximate Altitude of Check (Ft. above sea level)	Drive Neutral Park	L1 or L2	Reverse
0	150	150	244
2,000	150	150	233
4,000	145	150	222
6,000	138	150	212
8,000	132	150	203
10,000	126	150	194
12,000	121	150	186
14,000	116	150	178

*Zero output speed, vacuum modulator tube disconnected, engine speed 1,200 rpm.

master cylinder. Check for leaks and thin brake linings. Bleed and adjust the brakes. If this does not cure the trouble, rebuild wheel cylinders and/or master cylinder.

2. *Spongy pedal*—Normally caused by air in the system; bleed and adjust the brakes.

3. *Brakes pull*—Check brake adjustment. Also check for contaminated brake linings (from leaks), leaky wheel cylinders, loose calipers, frozen or seized pistons, and restricted brake lines or hoses. In addition, check front end alignment and suspension damage such as a broken front or rear torsion bar. Tires also affect brak-

Table 3   TURBO HYDRAMATIC 350 FLUID PRESSURE CHECK

Check taken at 1,200 rpm						
	1968			**1969-1970**		
Altitude (in feet above sea level)	Drive, Neutral, Park	L1 or L2	Reverse	Drive, Neutral, Park	L1 or L2	Reverse
0	150	150	244	149	149	255
2,000	150	150	233	149	149	241
4,000	145	150	222	149	149	228
6,000	138	150	212	142	144	215
8,000	132	150	203	134	138	203
	1971-1972			**1973-1976**		
Altitude (in feet above sea level)	Drive, Neutral, Park	L1 or L2	Reverse	Drive, Neutral, Park	L1 or L2	Reverse
0	162	162	254	178	174	270
2,000	157	158	240	169	167	256
4,000	147	151	226	160	160	242
6,000	135	142	213	151	154	230
8,000	126	135	202	144	148	218

Table 5   TURBO HYDRAMATIC 350 TRANSMISSION FLUID PRESSURE CHECK

Check taken at 16 in. Hg absolute manifold pressure											
		1969-1970				1971-1972				1973-1976	
Altitude (In Feet Above Sea Level)	Relative Engine Vacuum (In. Hg)	Drive, Neutral, Park	L1 or L2	Reverse	Drive, Neutral, Park	L1 or L2	Reverse	Drive, Neutral, Park	L1 or L2	Reverse
0	13.92	86	103	131	86	106	129	60	87	92
2,000	11.83	89	105	136	88	108	134	69	93	104
4,000	9.86	92	107	140	90	110	138	77	99	117
6,000	7.96	95	109	144	92	112	142	85	105	129
8,000	6.23	97	117	148	95	114	146	91	110	139

Table 6   TURBO HYDRAMATIC 375-400 TRANSMISSION FLUID PRESSURE CHECK

Check taken at 600-800 rpm with vacuum tube connected; applies at all altitudes for all engines		
Drive, Neutral, Park	L1 or L2	Reverse
60	150	107

ing; check tire pressure and condition. Replace or repair defective parts.

4. *Brake squeal or chatter*—Check brake lining thickness and brake drum roundness. Ensure that the shoes have chamfered ends and are not loose. Clean away all dirt on shoes and drums.

5. *Dragging brakes*—Check brake adjustment, including handbrake. Check for broken or weak shoe return springs, swollen rubber parts due to improper brake fluid or contamination, and obstructed master cylinder bypass port. Clean or replace defective parts.

6. *Hard pedal*—Check brake linings for contamination. Also check for restricted brake lines and hoses.

7. *High speed fade*—Check for distorted or out-of-round drums and contaminated brake linings. Make sure that recommended brake fluid is used. Drain entire system and refill if in doubt.

8. *Pulsating pedal*—Check for distorted or out-of-round brake drum. Check for excessive brake disc runout.

STEERING AND SUSPENSION

Trouble in the system is evident when:

a. Steering is hard

b. Car pulls to one side

c. Car wanders or front wheels wobble

d. Steering has excessive play

e. Tire wear is abnormal

Unusual steering, pulling, or wandering is usually caused by bent or otherwise misaligned suspension parts. This is difficult to check without proper alignment equipment. See Chapter Thirteen for repairs which you can perform and those that must be left to a dealer or front end specialist.

If the trouble seems to be excessive play, check wheel bearing adjustment first. This is the most frequent cause. Next check steering free play as described in Chapter Thirteen. Then check ball-joint play. Finally, check tie rod end ball-joints by shaking each tie rod. Also check pitman arm nut for tightness.

Tire wear may be caused by suspension troubles, but may have many other causes. See *Tire Wear Analysis* below.

TIRE WEAR ANALYSIS

Abnormal tire wear should always be analyzed to determine the cause and correct it. The most common causes are:

a. Incorrect tire pressure

b. Improper driving

c. Overloading

d. Bad road surfaces

e. Incorrect wheel alignment

Figure 4 identifies wear patterns and indicates the most probable causes.

WHEEL BALANCING

All 4 wheels and tires must be in balance along 2 axes. To be in static balance, **Figure 5**, weight must be evenly distributed around the axis of rotation. (A) shows a statically unbalanced wheel; (B) shows the result—wheel tramp or hopping; (C) shows proper static balance.

To be in dynamic balance, **Figure 6**, the centerline of the weight must coincide with the centerline of the wheel. (A) shows a dynamically unbalanced wheel; (B) shows the result—wheel wobble or shimmy; (C) shows proper dynamic balance.

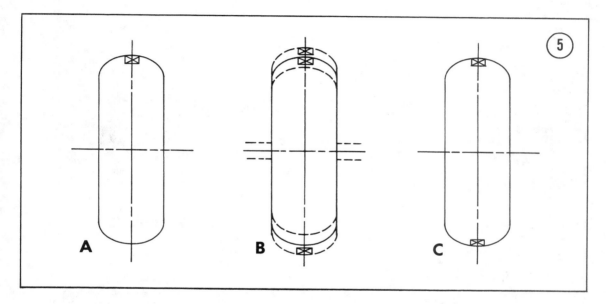

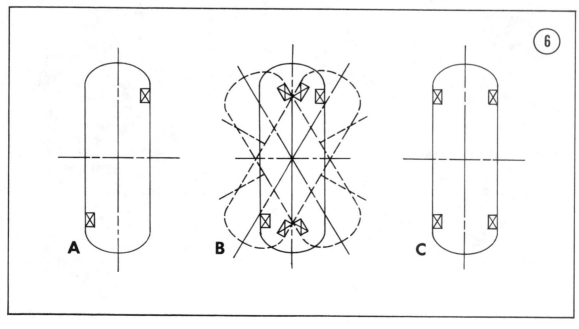

④

Underinflation—Worn more on sides than in center.

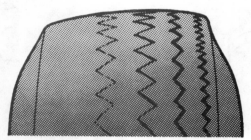

Wheel Alignment—Worn more on one side than the other. Edges of tread feathered.

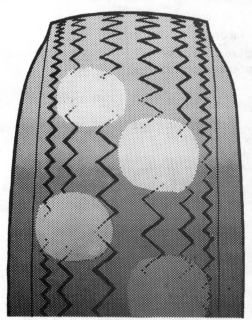

Wheel Balance — Scalloped edges indicate wheel wobble or tramp due to wheel unbalance.

Road Abrasion—Rough wear on entire tire or in patches.

Overinflation—Worn more in center than on sides.

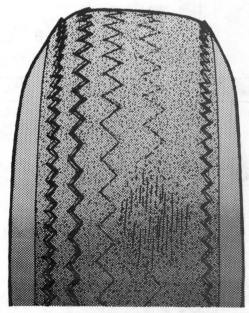

Combination—Most tires exhibit a combination of the above. This tire was overinflated (center worn) and the toe-in was incorrect (feathering). The driver cornered hard at high speed (feathering, rounded shoulders) and braked rapidly (worn spots). The scaly roughness indicates a rough road surface.

CHAPTER FIVE

ENGINE

All Corvettes use conventional overhead valve V8 engines. **Figure 1** is typical. A single camshaft operates the valves through solid or hydraulic valve lifters, pushrods, and rocker arms. The camshaft also drives the distributor, fuel pump, and oil pump. Four replaceable bearings support the crankshaft. Belts, driven by the crankshaft, operate the cooling fan, alternator, air injection reactor pump, and power steering pump (if so equipped).

Chevrolet divides its Corvette engine designs into "small" V8's (327, 350), and "large" V8's (396, 427, 454). In addition, the 454 engine is called a Mark IV V8. Fortunately, all these engines are remarkably close in appearance; and service procedures differ very little.

This chapter includes repair procedures for all Corvette engines used from 1963-1976. Specifications (**Table 1**) and tightening torques (**Table 2**) are found at the end of the chapter. **Table 3** lists the different engines and the years in which they were available.

ENGINE REMOVAL

The engine is removed separately without the transmission on all Corvettes.

1. Drain cooling system and crankcase.

2. Remove hood. See Chapter Fifteen.

3. Remove air cleaner and cover carburetor with a clean cloth.

4. Remove distributor shielding.

5. Remove fan shroud and radiator.

6. Disconnect:

   a. Battery cables at battery
   b. Starter solenoid wires
   c. Alternator wiring
   d. Engine-to-body ground straps
   e. Oil pressure indicator at engine
   f. Water temperature sender wire at sender
   g. Primary lead at coil
   h. Tachometer cable at distributor
   i. Fuel tank line at fuel pump
   j. Accelerator rod at pedal bellcrank
   k. Throttle valve rod (lower) at throttle valve bellcrank
   l. Heater hose at engine connections
   m. Power brake hose at carburetor

7. Remove fan and fan pulley as described in Chapter Nine.

8. Remove the power steering pump bolts and swing the pump into radiator opening. As an alternative, disconnect pump lines and plug open ends.

9. Remove rocker arm covers.

10. Remove distributor cap and pull it forward.

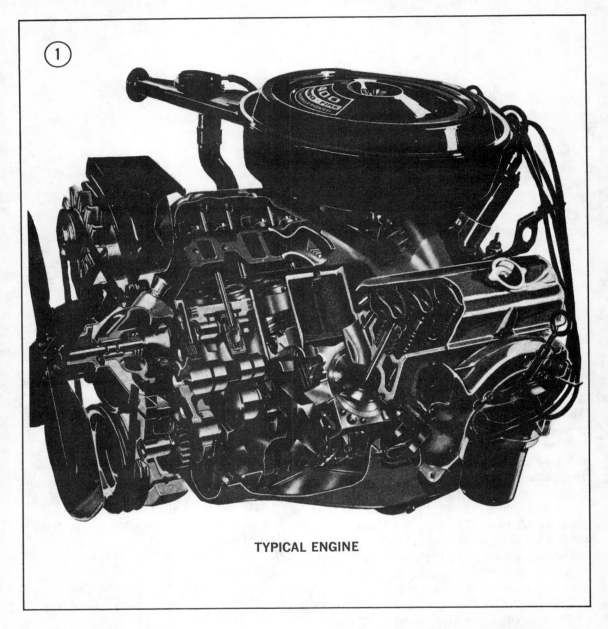

TYPICAL ENGINE

11. Raise vehicle on jackstands.

12. Disconnect exhaust pipes at exhaust manifold flanges. See **Figure 2**.

13. Remove oil filter.

14. Block clutch pedal up. Remove clutch cross-shaft (frame bracket end first). See Chapter Eleven.

15. Remove starter. See Chapter Ten.

16. Remove flywheel cover plate (manual) or converter underpan (automatic).

17. Remove engine front mount through-bolts. See **Figure 3**.

18. Position floor jack under transmission. Raise it just enough to take the weight of the transmission.

19. Remove all but the top 2 bell housing-to-engine bolts.

20. Connect engine hoist to engine. Take strain of engine on hoist, then remove 2 top bell housing bolts.

Table 3 ENGINE APPLICATION

Year	327	350	396	427	454
1963	X				
1964	X				
1965	X		X		
1966	X			X	
1967	X			X	
1968	X			X	
1969		X		X	
1970		X			X
1971		X			X
1972		X			X
1973		X			X
1974		X			X
1975		X			
1976		X			

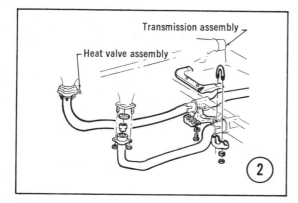

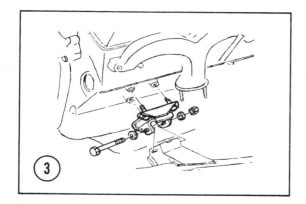

21. On automatics, remove flywheel-to-converter bolts. Install bracket over bell housing to hold converter in place. See **Figure 4**.

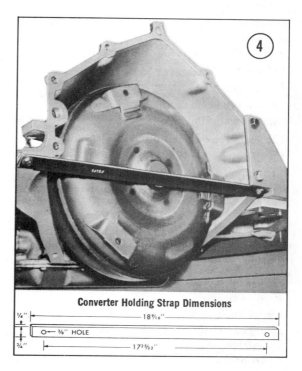

Converter Holding Strap Dimensions

22. Alternately raise engine and move it forward as needed to remove engine from vehicle.

ENGINE INSTALLATION

1. Clean transmission case and engine flange thoroughly.

2. On automatics, remove temporary restraining bracket installed during Step 21, *Engine Removal*.

3. On manual shift cars, make sure that clutch plate is properly centered (Chapter Eleven). Inspect clutch release bearing and release plate for wear and cracks. Replace them if necessary. if necessary.

4. On manual shift cars, apply molybdenum disulphide powder or a very light coat of heavy duty grease to the main drive shaft spline. Use a clean cloth or a brush.

5. Put the transmission in gear to steady the main drive shaft.

6. Connect engine hoist to engine.

7. Tilt and lower engine into vehicle.

8. Work engine hoist and floor jack under transmission together as needed to line up transmission main shaft into clutch plate on manuals, or

converter into the pilot area of flywheel on automatics.

9. Install bell housing-to-engine bolts. Tighten to 25-35 ft.-lb.

10. Remove jack from under transmission.

11. Lower engine into place with hoist. Connect engine mount through bolts.

12. Remove engine hoist.

13. Reverse Steps 1-16, *Engine Removal*.

14. Perform tune-up as described in Chapter Three. Check for oil and water leaks.

ENGINE DISASSEMBLY

The following sequences are designed so that the engine need not be disassembled any further than necessary. Unless otherwise indicated, procedures for major assemblies in these sequences are included in this chapter. The procedures are arranged in the approximate order in which they are performed.

To perform a step, turn to the procedure for the major assembly indicated, e.g., cylinder head, and perform the removal and inspection procedures. Move to the next step, perform removal and inspection procedures etc., until the engine is disassembled. To reassemble, reverse the disassembly sequence and perform the installation procedure for each major assembly involved.

Valve Service

This procedure does not require engine removal.

1. Remove cylinder heads.

2. Remove and inspect pushrods and rocker arms.

3. Remove and inspect valves, guides, and seats.

4. Assembly is the reverse of these steps.

Valve and Ring Service

This procedure does not require engine removal unless cylinder bores need boring and/or honing. However, the job is often easier with the engine removed.

1. Perform *Valve Service* Steps 1-3.

2. Remove oil pan.

3. Remove piston/connecting rod assemblies.

4. Remove piston rings and check piston clearance.

5. Install new rings.

6. Install piston/rod assemblies.

7. Check connecting rod bearing condition and clearance.

8. Install oil pan.

9. Perform Step 4, *Valve Service*.

General Overhaul Sequence

1. Remove alternator.

2. Remove carburetor(s) or fuel injection unit.

3. Remove distributor and coil.

4. Remove water pump and thermostat. See Chapter Nine.

5. Remove intake and exhaust manifolds.

6. Remove rocker arms, pushrods, and valve lifters.

> NOTE: *Keep valve parts in a rack so they may be returned to their original location during assembly.*

7. Remove cylinder heads.

8. Remove crankcase ventilation from block.

9. Remove oil pan.

10. Remove harmonic balancer.

11. Remove timing gear cover and crankshaft oil slinger.

12. Remove timing chain and both gears.

13. Remove camshaft.

14. Remove oil pump.

15. Remove piston/connecting rod assemblies.

16. Remove piston rings.

17. Remove crankshaft.

18. Remove clutch assembly. See Chapter Eleven.

19. Remove flywheel.

20. Assembly is the reverse of these steps.

ENGINE MOUNTS
Front Mount Replacement

1. Raise car on jackstands.

2. Remove through bolt from mount(s). See Figure 3.

3. Raise engine with jack to clear mount from frame.

CAUTION
Do not jack directly under oil pan. Use wood supports wherever possible to distribute load.

4. Remove 3 bolts securing mount to engine and remove mount.

5. Installation is the reverse of these steps.

Rear Mount Replacement

1. Raise car on jackstands.

2. Remove 2 mount-to-support and 2 mount-to-transmission bolts. See **Figure 5**.

3. Raise transmission clear of mount with a jack. Remove mount.

4. Installation is the reverse of these steps.

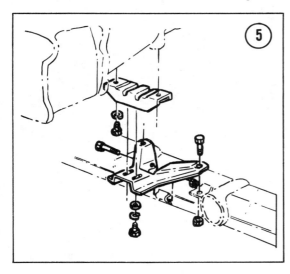

CYLINDER HEAD
Removal

1. Disconnect battery cables.

2. Remove intake manifold as described in Chapters Six and Seven.

3. Disconnect spark plug wires and remove spark plug shields.

4. Remove nuts securing exhaust manifold(s). Pull manifold(s) free of head(s).

5. On fuel injected engines, remove air cleaner assembly if removing left cylinder head.

6. On 1963-1964 engines, remove alternator if removing right cylinder head.

7. Remove rocker arm covers.

8. Back off rocker arm nuts until rocker arms can be pivoted clear of pushrods, then remove pushrods. See **Figure 6**. Keep pushrods in a holder so that they may be reinstalled in exactly the same way. See **Figure 7**.

9. Drain cooling system including block.

10. Remove cylinder head bolts as shown in **Figure 8**.

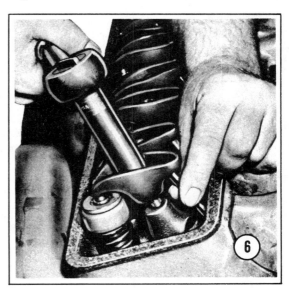

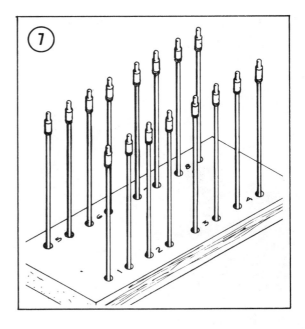

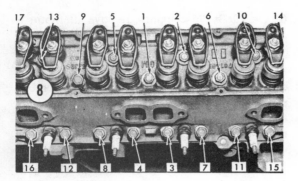

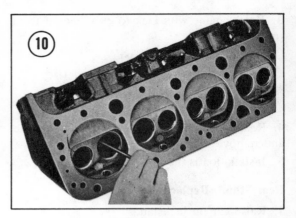

11. Lift cylinder head off. Remove and discard gasket. Place head on 2 blocks of wood to prevent damage to sealing surface.

Inspection

1. Without removing valves, remove all carbon deposits from combustion chambers with a wire brush. A blunt screwdriver or chisel may be used if care is taken not to damage head or valves.

2. Remove valves as described later.

3. Clean carbon from valve parts. See **Figure 9**.

4. Clean carbon and varnish valve guides with a stiff spiral wire brush. See **Figure 10**.

5. Check cylinder heads for cracks in the exhaust ports, combustion chambers, and external surfaces.

6. Check all studs for tightness. Studs on 327 and 350 engines are a press-fit into the head. If loose, have a machinist ream the hole to accept either a 0.0003 or 0.013 in. oversize stud. See **Figure 11**.

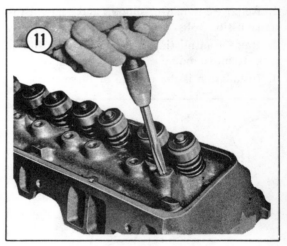

Installation

1. Thoroughly clean cylinder head bolt holes in head and all cylinder head bolts.

2. Make sure that cylinder head seating surface and mating surface on block are thoroughly clean.

3. On engines using a steel gasket, apply a thin uniform coat of cylinder head gasket sealer to both sides of the gasket and place over the dowel pins on the block with the bead up. Do *not* use sealer on composition steel/asbestos gaskets.

4. Guide the cylinder head into place over the dowel pins.

5. Coat cylinder head bolts with thread sealing compound (GM Perfect Seal or equivalent). Install all bolts finger-tight.

> NOTE: *On some engines, bolts at No. 14 and No. 17 are shorter than the others. See Figure 8.*

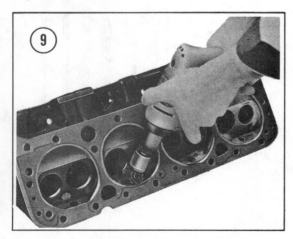

6. Tighten all cylinder head bolts a little at a time in the sequence shown in Figure 8 until the torque specified in Table 1 (at the end of the chapter) is reached.

7. Install lifters (if removed), pushrods, and rocker arms (if removed) in their original positions.

8. Adjust valve lash. See Chapter Three.

9. Install intake and exhaust manifolds as described in Chapters Six and Seven.

10. Install spark plugs (if removed) and reconnect spark plug wires.

11. On 1963-1964 engines, reinstall alternator and adjust drive belt tension. See Chapter Two.

12. Refill cooling system as described in Chapter Nine.

13. Install rocker arm covers.

14. Reconnect battery cables.

15. Perform entire engine tune-up as described in Chapter Three.

VALVE LIFTERS

Two different lifters may be found in 1965 and later engines. The complete lifter assemblies are interchangeable, but parts from one type cannot be interchanged with another. **Figure 12** shows both types.

Removal/Installation

1. Remove rocker arm covers.

2. Remove intake manifold. See Chapters Six and Seven.

3. Back off rocker arm nuts until arms can be pivoted away from pushrods. See Figure 6. Remove pushrods. Store them so that they may be returned to the same location. See Figure 7.

4. Remove hydraulic valve lifters. Store them so that they may be returned to the same locations. See Figure 7.

5. Installation is the reverse of these steps. Coat bottoms of lifters with Molykote or equivalent. Adjust valve lash as described in Chapter Three.

Disassembly/Assembly (Hydraulic Lifters)

Refer to Figure 12 for the following procedure.

1. Hold plunger down with a pushrod.

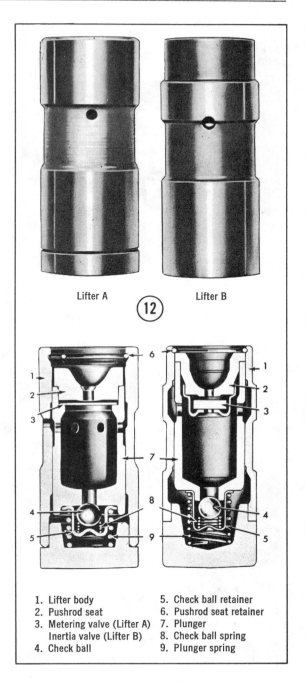

Lifter A   (12)   Lifter B

1. Lifter body
2. Pushrod seat
3. Metering valve (Lifter A) Inertia valve (Lifter B)
4. Check ball
5. Check ball retainer
6. Pushrod seat retainer
7. Plunger
8. Check ball spring
9. Plunger spring

2. Pry seat retainer out with a small screwdriver or awl.

3. Remove pushrod seat, metering valve (lifter "A"), plunger, and spring from lifter body.

CAUTION
Do not remove inertia valve from pushrod seat on lifter "B".

4. Pull check valve ball retainer from bottom of plunger. See **Figure 13**. Remove ball and spring.

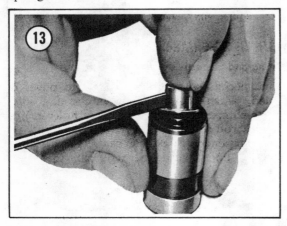

5. Clean all parts thoroughly in solvent. Inspect all parts carefully. If any are damaged, the entire lifter must be replaced.

6. Place check valve ball on small hole in plunger.

7. Insert check valve spring in ball retainer and place retainer over ball so spring rests on ball. Carefully squeeze retainer and press into position in plunger. See **Figure 14**.

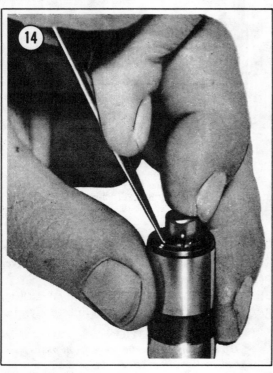

8. Place plunger spring over ball retainer and slide lifter body over spring and plunger.

9. Install pushrod seat and metering valve in open end of plunger. Push plunger into body and install retainer.

10. Compress plunger to open oil holes. Fill plunger with SAE 10 oil. Work plunger up and down and refill.

Cleaning and Inspection (Mechanical Lifter)

Mechanical lifters should never be disassembled.

1. Clean lifters thoroughly in solvent and blow them dry.

2. Blow out oil holes in lifter body and pushrod seat with compressed air.

3. Check pushrod seat and retainer. If seat is loose, replace entire lifter.

4. Check lifter body for scuffing or wear. Check cylinder block if sides of the lifter are worn. Check camshaft lobes if bottom of lifter is worn. Check pushrod if seat is worn.

ROCKER ARMS

Removal/Installation

1. Remove nut in center of rocker arm. See **Figure 15**.

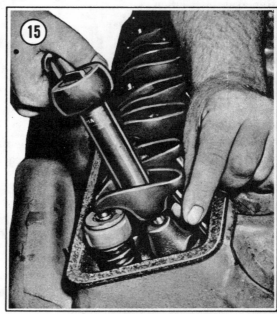

2. Remove rocker arm ball and rocker arm.

3. Installation is the reverse of these steps.

4. Adjust valve lash as described in Chapter Three.

VALVES AND VALVE SEATS

Valve Removal

1. Remove, clean and inspect cylinder head as described earlier.

2. Remove rocker arms as described earlier.

3. Lay cylinder head on its side.

4. With a valve spring compressor, compress valve spring and remove valve locks. See **Figure 16**.

5. Release tool and remove spring retainer, valve shield, spring, and valve guide seal.

6. Remove valve from head.

7. Repeat for each valve.

> NOTE: *Keep valves in a rack indicating location so that they may be reassembled in the same location.*

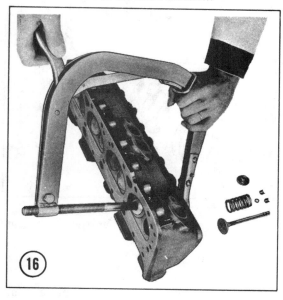

Valve Inspection

1. Clean valves with a wire brush and solvent. Discard burned, warped, or cracked valves.

2. Remove all carbon and varnish from valve guides with a stiff spiral wire brush.

3. Insert each valve in its guide. Hold valve just slightly off its seat and rock it sideways. If it

rocks more than slightly, the guide and/or valve stem is worn and should be checked more accurately as described in the procedure below, *Measuring Valve Stem*.

4. Measure valve spring heights. All should be equal, with no bends or other distortion. Replace defective springs.

5. Test valve springs under load. Springs should compress to 1-45/64 in. at 74.5 lb. See **Figure 17**. Replace springs which are not within 10 lb. of above load.

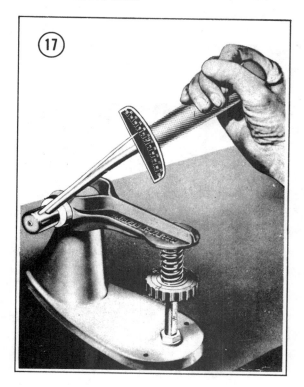

Measuring Valve Stem Clearance

There are 2 ways to measure valve stem clearance. Either way is satisfactory and depends on tools you have on hand.

First Method:

1. Perform Steps 1-3, *Valve Inspection*.

2. Measure valve stems with a micrometer at top, center, and bottom.

3. Measure valve guide diameter with a telescope hole gauge at its center.

4. Subtract highest reading in Step 2 from guide diameter measured in Step 3 to obtain stem-to-

guide clearance. Clearance for intake valves should be 0.001-0.003 in.; for exhaust valves, 0.002-0.004 in.

Second Method:

1. Perform Steps 1-3, *Valve Inspection*.

2. Clamp a dial indicator to the cylinder head as shown in **Figure 18**. The indicator stem must contact the side of the valve stem just above the valve guide.

3. Drop the valve head about 1/16 in. off the valve seat.

4. Move the stem of the valve from side to side against the dial indicator with light pressure. Compare clearance obtained with Table 1 (end of chapter).

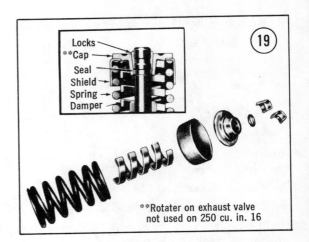

Locks — ****Cap** — **Seal** — **Shield** — **Spring** → **Damper** →

**Rotater on exhaust valve not used on 250 cu. in. 16

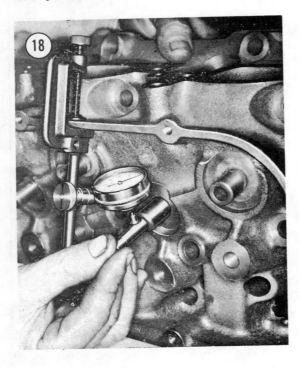

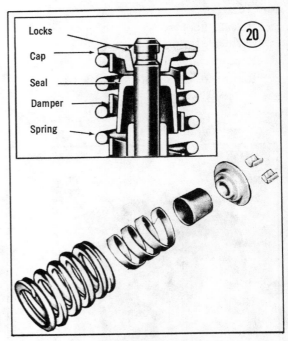

Locks — **Cap** — **Seal** — **Damper** — **Spring** →

Valve Installation

Refer to **Figure 19** (327, 350) **or** 20 (396, 427, 454) for following procedure.

1. Make certain that cylinder head, valve guides, valve seats, and valves are clean.

2. Insert valve in head.

3. On 396, 427 and 454 engines, lubricate valve stem oil seals and install over valve guides.

4. Fit valve spring and damper over valve stem, with the close pitched end against head.

5. Install valve shield (327 and 350) and retainer over spring.

6. Compress spring with valve spring compressor. See Figure 16.

7. On 327 and 350 engines, install oil seal in lower valve stem groove. Make sure it is flat and not twisted in groove.

8. Install valve locks and release tool.

NOTE: *Locks can be greased to hold them in place while releasing tool.*

9. Assemble remaining valves in the same manner.

10. Measure installed height of all valve springs from top of spring seat (or shims, if any) in the head to the top of the valve spring shield. See **Figures 21 and 22**. If height is greater than specified in Table 1 (end of chapter), install a 1/16 in. shim in the spring seat.

CAUTION
Installed height must never be less than specified or coil bind may occur.

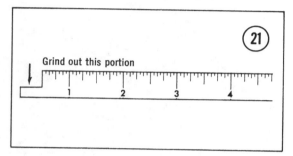

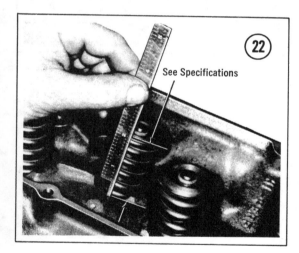

See Specifications

Valve Guide Reconditioning

When valve guides are worn so that there is excessive stem-to-guide clearance or valve tipping, they must be reamed to the next oversize. Valves are available with stems 0.003 in., 0.015 in., and 0.030 in. oversize.

Valve Seat Reconditioning

Proper valve seating is very important if the engine is to deliver the original power and performance. Valve seats and valve faces must be in good condition to provide perfect sealing and proper heat transfer from valve to cylinder head.

Several types of equipment are available for reseating valves. This job is best left to your dealer or local machine shop. They have the special equipment and knowledge required for this exacting job.

Valve seat widths should be within specifications shown in Table 4 and concentric within 0.002 in. See **Figure 23**. To provide an interference fit, valves faces are ground at 45° angle and valve seats at 46° angle. See **Figure 24**.

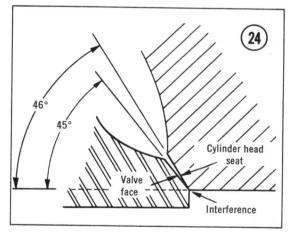

46°
45°
Cylinder head seat
Valve face
Interference

OIL PAN

Removal

1. Disconnect battery cables at battery.

2. Raise front of car on jackstands.

3. Drain engine oil. Remove the oil dipstick and the tube.

4. Remove underpan for starter and flywheel.

5. Disconnect steering linkage idler at frame (Chapter Thirteen) and lower linkage.

6. Remove oil pan bolts and remove pan. Discard old gasket.

> NOTE: *On 396, 427 and 454 engines, there are 3 ¼ in. x 20 bolts attaching oil pan to crankcase front cover.*

Installation

1. Clean sealing surfaces on oil pan and block thoroughly.

2. Install side gaskets on pan rails of block using gasket sealer to hold them in place.

3. Install rear oil pan seal in groove in rear main bearing cap with ends butting side gaskets.

4. Install front oil pan seal in groove in crankcase front cover with ends butting side gaskets.

5. Install oil pan with bolts. Torque to 80 in.-lb.

> NOTE: *On 396, 427 and 454 engines, start 3 bolts into crankcase front cover before tightening other bolts.*

OIL PUMP

Removal

1. Remove oil pan as described earlier.

2. Remove oil baffle on high performance engines.

3. Remove bolt securing pump to rear main bearing cap. See **Figure 25**. Remove pump and extension shaft.

Disassembly

Refer to **Figure 26** (327, 350) **or 27** (396, 427 and 454) for the following procedure.

1. Remove extension shaft from pump.

2. Remove screws securing pump cover and lift cover off.

3. Remove idler and drive gears.

4. If intake pipe and/or screen require replacement, hold cover in a vise with copper or wood-covered jaws and pull intake pipe out.

Inspection

1. Clean all pump parts thoroughly in solvent and blow dry.

2. Check the pump body for cracks and excessive wear.

3. Check gears for excessive wear or damage.

4. Check drive gear for excessive clearance in pump body.

5. Check inside surface of cover for excessive wear.

6. Check oil pickup screen for damage to screen bypass valve or body.

Assembly

1. Clean all parts in solvent just prior to final assembly.

2. Lubricate all internal parts and surfaces with assembly lubricant.

3. Install drive gear in pump body.

4. Install idler gear with smooth side towards pump cover.

5. If intake pipe and screen have been removed, hold pipe in a vise with soft jaws and carefully tap cover on with a plastic hammer.

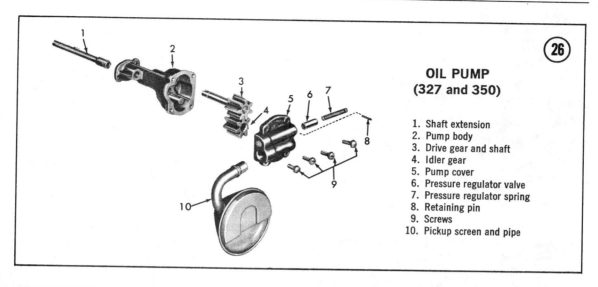

OIL PUMP (327 and 350)

1. Shaft extension
2. Pump body
3. Drive gear and shaft
4. Idler gear
5. Pump cover
6. Pressure regulator valve
7. Pressure regulator spring
8. Retaining pin
9. Screws
10. Pickup screen and pipe

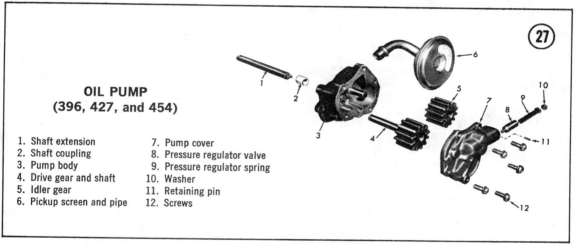

OIL PUMP (396, 427, and 454)

1. Shaft extension
2. Shaft coupling
3. Pump body
4. Drive gear and shaft
5. Idler gear
6. Pickup screen and pipe
7. Pump cover
8. Pressure regulator valve
9. Pressure regulator spring
10. Washer
11. Retaining pin
12. Screws

CAUTION
Do not collapse suction tube. Also, do not subject tube to shearing or twisting forces, as air leaks may occur.

6. Install cover and tighten screws to 6-9 ft.-lb. Make certain that the drive shaft turns freely.

7. Fit extension shaft over drive gear shaft.

Installation

1. Install pump on rear main bearing cap. Turn extension shaft if necessary to align slot in shaft with drive tang on distributor shaft.

2. Install the pump retaining bolt and tighten to 45-50 ft.-lb.

3. Install oil pan as described earlier.

REAR MAIN BEARING OIL SEAL

Replacement

The rear main bearing oil seal can be replaced without removing the crankshaft.

1. Remove oil pan.

2. Remove rear main bearing cap.

3. Remove oil seal half from cap with a small screwdriver. See **Figure 28**.

CAUTION
Do not nick cap with screwdriver.

4. Tap one end of the upper half with a brass pin punch (**Figure 29**) until the other end protrudes enough to grab it with pliers.

7. Install the bearing cap and torque bolts to 60-70 ft.-lb.

8. Install oil pan.

9. Refill with engine oil, run engine and check for leaks.

CRANKSHAFT

The engine must be removed to replace crankshaft. However, main bearings may be replaced with or without the engine installed.

Bearing and Journal Inspection

Generally, the lower bearing halves wear more rapidly than the upper halves. If the lower halves are good, it is safe to assume the uppers are good also. If lower halves require replacement, replace corresponding upper halves at the same time.

1. Remove rear main bearing cap and wipe oil from journal and bearing cap.

2. Check bearing insert and journal for evidence of wear, abrasion, or scoring.

3. Remove both halves of the rear oil seal as described earlier.

4. Place a piece of Plastigage on the journal, parallel to the crankshaft. See **Figure 31**.

5. Install new lower seal half in bearing cap in direction shown in **Figure 30**. Lubricate lip with assembly lubricant or engine oil.

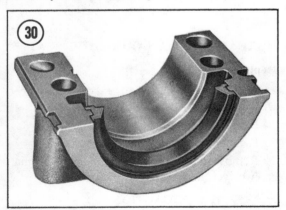

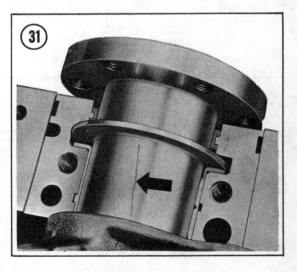

5. Install bearing cap and tighten the retaining bolts evenly to 60-70 ft.-lb.

CAUTION
Do not rotate the crankshaft while Plastigage is in place.

6. Lubricate lip of upper seal half and insert end in groove. Gradually push the seal with a hammer handle until it rolls into place above the crankshaft.

6. Remove the bearing cap.

7. Measure the width of flattened Plastigage according to manufacturer's instructions. See **Figure 32**. Measure at both ends of the Plastigage strip. A difference of 0.001 in. or more indicates a tapered journal. Confirm with a micrometer. If bearing clearance is not over 0.004 in. or less than 0.001 in., the bearing insert is good. Otherwise, replace bearing insert.

8. Repeat Steps 1-7 for each of the other bearings.

9. Install new rear oil seal as described previously.

10. Install the bearing cap and tighten the bolts to 60-70 ft.-lb.

11. Force crankshaft as far forward as possible. Insert feeler gauge between rear main bearing and crankshaft as shown in **Figure 33**. End play should be 0.002-0.006 in. with a new rear main bearing. If greater than 0.009 in., replace rear bearing.

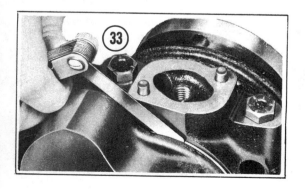

Main Bearing Replacement

Main bearings may be replaced with engine installed or not. Replace bearings in sets.

With Engine Installed:

1. Remove oil pan.

2. Remove rear bearing cap and remove bearing insert from cap.

3. Remove rear oil seal.

4. Insert long cotter pin into crankshaft journal oil hole. Rotate crankshaft to roll the bearing out.

5. Clean crankshaft journal. Insert unnotched side of bearing into notched side of block. Using same techniques as for removal, roll new bearing insert into place.

> NOTE: *Only the upper bearing insert has an oil hole.*

6. Install new bearing insert in cap.

7. Install cap with strip of Plastigage and measure clearance as described in Steps 4-7, *Bearing and Journal Inspection.*

8. If bearing clearance is satisfactory, lubricate journal and bearing halves with assembly lubricant.

9. Install new rear oil seal as described earlier.

10. Install the bearing caps and tighten the bolts to 10-12 ft.-lb.

11. Repeat Steps 2-10 (except Step 9) for other main bearings.

12. Tap crankshaft rearward with a lead hammer to locate bearing caps and bearings.

13. Tighten main bearing cap bolts to 60-70 ft.-lb.

14. Force crankshaft as far forward as possible. Insert feeler gauge between rear main bearing and crankshaft as shown in Figure 33. End play should be 0.002-0.006 in. with a new rear main bearing.

15. Reinstall oil pan and refill with engine oil.

With Engine Removed:

If the engine is removed, simply follow the *Crankshaft Removal and Installation* procedures below.

Crankshaft Removal

1. Remove oil pan and oil pump. On high performance engines, remove oil baffle.

2. Mark all main bearing caps and connecting rod caps so that they can be reinstalled in exactly the same location.

3. Remove connecting rod bearing caps. Push piston/rod assemblies towards the heads.

4. Remove main bearing caps.

5. Carefully lift crankshaft out of cylinder block.

6. Remove rear oil seal as described previously.

7. Remove main bearing inserts from cylinder block and main bearing caps. If they are reusable, mark their location on the back of the insert with a pencil.

8. Remove connecting rod bearing inserts from rods and rod caps. If they are reuseable, mark their location on the back of the insert with pencil.

Crankshaft Inspection

1. Check connecting rod side clearance and bearing clearance as described under *Connecting Rod Bearing and Crankpin Inspection.*

2. Clean crankshaft thoroughly with solvent. Clean oil holes with rifle type brushes; flush thoroughly and blow dry with air. Lightly oil all journal surfaces immediately to prevent rust.

3. Carefully inspect each journal for scratches, ridges, scoring, nicks, etc. Very small nicks and scratches may be removed with crocus cloth. More serious damage must be removed by grinding, a job for a machine shop.

4. If the surface finish on all journals is satisfactory, take the crankshaft to your dealer or local machine shop. They can check for out-of-roundness, taper, and wear on the journals. They can also check crankshaft alignment and inspect for cracks.

Crankshaft Installation

1. Make certain that cylinder block bearing saddles, bearing caps, bearing inserts and crankshaft journals are perfectly clean. A small piece of grit behind a bearing insert could deform the bearing and lead to very early failure.

2. Install new upper main bearing inserts in cylinder block. Upper halves have an oil hole, the lower halves do not. Make sure that the bearing tang fits in the cut-out in the block.

CAUTION
Do not file bearings or bearing saddles to get a "better" fit. The ends of the bearings normally protrude slightly. This "bearing crush" causes the bearing to be forced tightly against the saddle and cap when the caps are tightened down. See **Figure 34**, *which is exaggerated for clarity.*

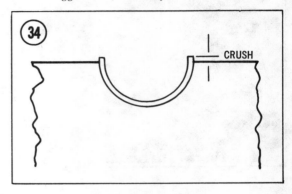

3. Install new lower bearing inserts in main bearing caps. Make certain that the bearing tang fits in the cut-out in the cap and observe the CAUTION, above.

4. Install new bearing inserts in connecting rods and rod caps.

5. Carefully lower crankshaft into place. Be careful not to damage bearing or journal surfaces.

6. Check clearance of each main bearing. See Steps 4-7, *Bearing and Journal Inspection.*

7. If bearing clearance is satisfactory, lubricate journal and bearing halves with assembly lubricant.

8. Install new rear oil seal as described earlier.

9. Install bearing caps and tighten to 10-12 ft.-lb.

10. Tap crankshaft rearward with a lead hammer to locate bearing caps and bearings.

11. Tighten main bearing cap bolts to 60-70 ft.-lb.

12. Force crankshaft as far forward as possible. Insert feeler gauge between rear main bearing

and crankshaft as shown in Figure 33. End play should be 0.002-0.006 in. with a new rear main bearing.

13. Install rods on crankshaft as described under *Pistons and Connecting Rods.*

HARMONIC BALANCER (TORSIONAL DAMPER)

Removal

1. Remove hood as described in Chapter Fifteen.

2. On 327 and 350 engines, remove radiator and shroud as described in Chapter Nine. This step is not necessary on 396, 427 and 454 engines unless other operations, such as timing gear or camshaft service, are required.

3. On 427 and 454 engines, remove through bolts from front engine mounts and jack engine high enough so that harmonic balancer clears frame crossmember.

4. Remove fan and fan pulley. See Chapter Nine.

5. Remove bolts securing crankshaft pulley and remove pulley. See **Figure 35**.

6. On 340 and 360 hp 327 engines, remove balancer retaining bolt and washer from end of crankshaft.

7. Remove harmonic balancer with a suitable puller. Chevrolet dealers use tool J-6978 shown in **Figure 36**.

Installation

1. Lubricate front cover seal with engine oil.

2. Position balancer on crankshaft. Align crankshaft key with balancer keyway.

3a. On all except 340-360 hp 327 engines, drive balancer on crankshaft (use tool J-5590 or equivalent) until it bottoms on crankshaft gear. See **Figure 37**.

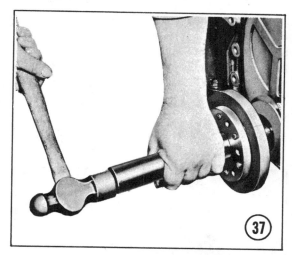

3b. On 340-360 hp 327 engines, pull balancer on with a large bolt to fit in end of crankshaft and suitable spacers. See **Figure 38**.

4. Install crankshaft pulley on balancer.

5. Install fan, fan pulley, and fan belt.

6. Install radiator and fan shroud. Refill with coolant and check for leaks.

TIMING GEAR COVER

Removal/Installation

1. Remove harmonic balancer as described earlier.

2. Remove oil pan.

3. Remove heater hose from water pump.

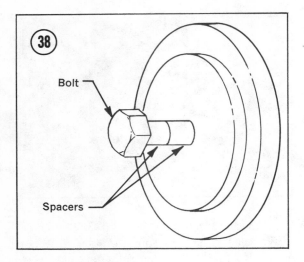

4. Remove water pump. See Chapter Nine.

5. Remove bolts securing timing gear cover and remove cover.

6. Clean away oil and all traces of old gasket from block and cover.

7. Make certain oil slinger is in place against crankshaft timing sprocket.

8. Lubricate oil seal with light grease.

9. On 396, 427 and 454 engines, install centering tool J-22102 in oil seal. See **Figure 39**.

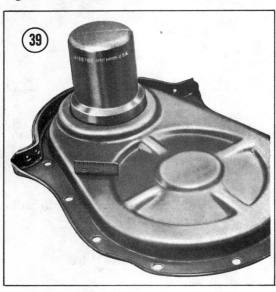

10. Install cover and new gasket over cylinder block dowel pins.

11. Install cover bolts and tighten to 6-8 ft.-lbs.

12. Install water pump and heater hose. See Chapter Nine.

13. Install harmonic balancer as described earlier.

TIMING GEAR COVER OIL SEAL

The oil seal may be replaced with the timing gear cover installed or not. Both procedures follow.

Timing Gear Cover, Installed

1. Remove harmonic balancer as described previously.

2. Pry old seal out of cover with a large screwdriver. Do not damage crankshaft or cover.

3. Clean the recess between cover and crankshaft.

4. Install new seal with open end facing inward. One method is to put the seal in place and gently tap it with a hammer, using a small block of wood. Working slowly and evenly around the seal, tap until it is flush with cover. Another method requires a special tool (J-8340 for 327 and 350 engines, J-22102 for 396, 427 and 454 engines) which presses the seal in evenly. See **Figure 40**.

5. Install harmonic balancer.

Timing Gear Cover, Removed

1. Pry old seal out of cover with a large screwdriver. Do not damage cover.

2. Clean cover in solvent. Make certain sealing surface for seal is perfectly clean.

3. Install new seal with open end facing inward. Use tool J-995 (**Figure 41**) on 327 and 350 en-

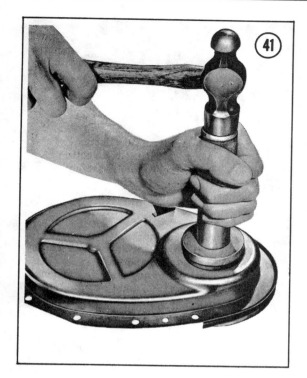

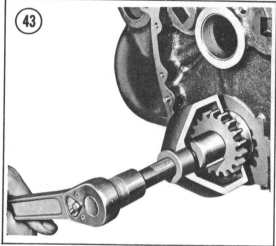

gines, tool J-22102 on 396, 427 and 454 engines or tap in place with a hammer as described in previous procedure, Step 4.

TIMING CHAIN OR SPROCKET

Replacement

1. Remove harmonic balancer and timing gear cover as described in previous procedures.

2. Remove crankshaft oil slinger.

3. Turn crankshaft until "0" marks on camshaft and crankshaft sprockets are aligned. See **Figure 42**.

4. Remove bolts securing camshaft sprockets.

5. Remove camshaft sprocket and timing chain together.

> NOTE: *If sprocket does not come off easily, a light blow with a plastic-faced hammer on the lower edge of the sprocket should dislodge it.*

6. If crankshaft sprocket is to be replaced, remove it using a suitable puller. See **Figure 43**.

7. Install crankshaft sprocket (if removed). Align keyway, fit a length of pipe over crankshaft, and tap sprocket on. See **Figure 44**.

8. Install timing chain on camshaft sprocket. Hold sprocket vertical with chain hanging below. Orient camshaft sprocket so that "0" points straight down.

9. Fit chain under crankshaft sprocket and fit camshaft sprocket on camshaft. Make sure that camshaft dowel aligns with hole in sprocket. Also ensure that "0" on both sprockets align as in Figure 42. If not, remove camshaft sprocket, reposition on chain, and reinstall.

10. Draw sprocket onto camshaft with the 3 mounting bolts. Tighten to 15-20 ft.-lb.

CAUTION
Do not drive camshaft sprocket onto shaft or the expansion plug at rear of engine can be dislodged.

11. Lubricate timing chain with engine oil.

12. Install timing gear cover and harmonic balancer.

CAMSHAFT

Removal/Installation

The camshaft may be removed and installed without removing the engine.

1. Remove intake manifold and timing gear cover.

2. Remove rocker arm covers, pushrods, and valve lifters.

3. Remove fuel pump and allow pump pushrod to fall against the adapter plate so that it clears the cam.

4. Remove front grille as described in Chapter Fifteen.

5. Remove timing chain and camshaft sprocket as described earlier.

6. Install two 5/16 in. - 18 x 4 bolts in camshaft (**Figure 45**) and carefully pull camshaft from engine.

CAUTION
All camshaft journals are the same size. Be very careful that bearings in block are not damaged when pulling camshaft out.

7. Installation is the reverse of these steps. Whenever a new camshaft is installed, coat lobes with Molykote or equivalent.

CAMSHAFT BEARING REPLACEMENT

Bearing replacement requires special tools not easily improvised. The best solution is to take empty cylinder block to a dealer or local machine shop. For a small bench fee he will replace bearings.

CYLINDER BLOCK

Inspection

1. Check cylinder block for cracks in the cylinder walls, water jacket, and main bearing webs.

2. Check cylinder walls for taper, out-of-round, or excessive ridge at the top of ring travel. Use a dial gauge as shown in **Figure 46**. More than 0.002 in. out-of-round requires reboring cylinders.

Reconditioning

Cylinder walls may be reconditioned by boring and/or honing to correct out-of-round or taper.

If only slight wear is evident, usually 0.005 in. or less, the bores may be lightly honed and high

limit standard size pistons fitted to maintain proper piston-to-cylinder clearance. Measure piston clearance as described later.

If wear is excessive, cylinders should be bored and honed for 0.020 in., 0.030 in., or 0.040 in. oversize. Measure piston clearance as described later.

PISTONS AND CONNECTING RODS

Several piston configurations are used in Corvette engines. Refer to **Figure 47**.

Removal

1. Remove oil pan and oil pump.

2. Remove cylinder heads.

3. Rotate crankshaft until piston is at bottom of travel. Place an oil soaked cloth over the piston to collect cuttings, then remove ridge and/or deposits from upper end of cylinder bores with a ridge reamer.

4. Turn crankshaft until piston is at top of its stroke. Remove cloth and cuttings.

5. Repeat Steps 3 and 4 for all other pistons to be removed.

6. Mark connecting rod bearing caps 1, 3, 5, 7 on the left bank, and 2, 4, 6, 8 on the right bank, working from front to rear.

7. Remove rod caps.

8. Push piston/rod assembly out top of cylinder bore. **Figure 48** shows a special tool made for this purpose. If this is not available, tape end of rod to prevent damage to cylinder walls and push out with a piece of hardwood or hammer handle.

Disassembly

1. Remove rings with a ring expander tool.

2. Before removing the piston pin, hold the rod tightly and rock the piston as shown in **Figure 49**. Any rocking movement (do not confuse with sliding motion) indicates wear in the piston pin, rod bushing, pin bore, or more likely, a combination of all three. Mark the piston, pin, and rod for further examination later.

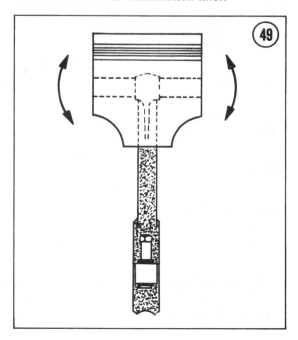

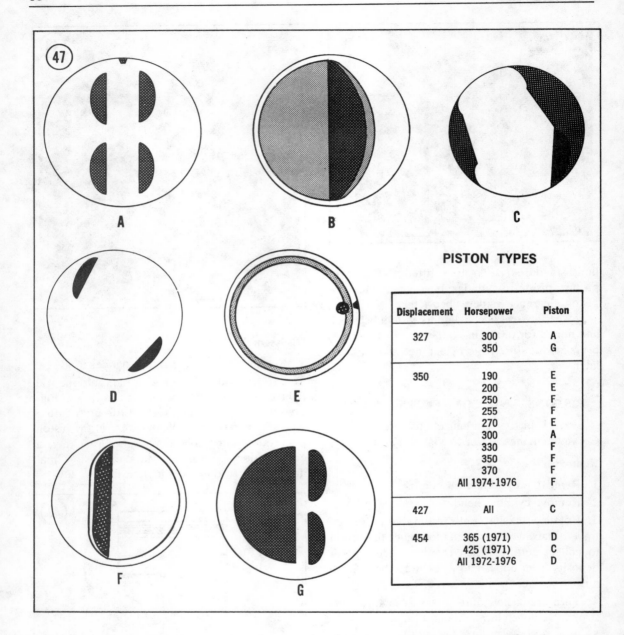

PISTON TYPES

Displacement	Horsepower	Piston
327	300	A
	350	G
350	190	E
	200	E
	250	F
	255	F
	270	E
	300	A
	330	F
	350	F
	370	F
	All 1974-1976	F
427	All	C
454	365 (1971)	D
	425 (1971)	C
	All 1972-1976	D

Inspection

1. Clean pistons thoroughly in solvent. Scrape carbon deposits from the top of the piston and ring grooves. Don't damage the pistons.

CAUTION
Do not wire brush piston skirts.

2. Examine each ring groove for burrs, dented edges, and side wear. Pay particular attention to the top compression ring groove, as it usually wears more than the others.

3. Measure piston-to-cylinder clearance as described below.

4. If damage or wear indicate piston replacement, select a new piston as described under *Piston Clearance* procedure.

5. Measure any parts marked in Step 4, *Piston Removal*, with a micrometer and dial bore gauge to determine which part or parts are worn. Any machinist can do this for you if you do not have micrometers. Replace piston/pin set as a unit if either or both are worn.

Piston Clearance (1963-1964)

This procedure should be performed at normal room temperature (68°F.). Pistons and cylinder walls must be clean and dry.

1. Insert piston upside down in cylinder bore so that the center of the pin bore is flush with the top surface of the block.

2. Make a feeler gauge ½ in. wide by 0.0015 in. (250, 300 hp) or 0.0040 in. (340, 360 hp) thick. Attach it to a spring scale as shown in **Figure 50**.

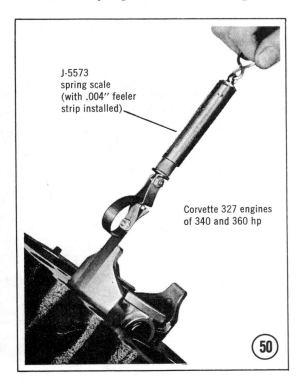

J-5573
spring scale
(with .004″ feeler strip installed)

Corvette 327 engines
of 340 and 360 hp

3. Insert feeler gauge between piston skirt and cylinder wall, 90° from piston pin holes.

4. Pull up on the spring scale. See Figure 50. If the force required to pull the feeler gauge out is 7-17 lb. (250, 300 hp) or 11-18 lb. (340, 360 hp), then the piston clearance is within specifications. If more force is required, clearance is too small. Try another piston or hone the cylinder bore slightly to obtain proper clearance.

If force required is less, clearance is too large. Try another piston or if standard size, try a standard high limit piston. If proper clearance cannot be obtained, rebore cylinder to next oversize piston and repeat procedure.

5. Permanently mark the piston for the cylinder to which it has been matched.

Piston Clearance (1965-1976)

1. Make sure the piston and cylinder walls are clean and dry.

2. Measure cylinder bore with a telescope bore gauge. See **Figure 51**.

3. Measure the outside diameter of the piston at the bottom of the skirt. See **Figure 52**.

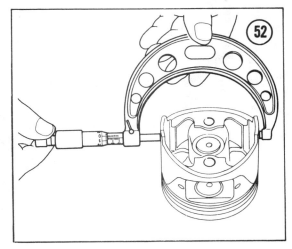

4. The difference between the 2 readings is the piston clearance. Compare this difference with the specifications in **Table 4**. If difference is greater than specification, select another piston from Table 4 or **Table 5**.

Table 4   PISTON SELECTION (1966-1976)

Displacement & hp	Piston-to-Bore Clearance		Pistons Available				
	New	Wear Limit	Std.	Oversize			
				0.001"	0.020"	0.030"	0.060"
327 (300 hp) 350 (300 hp)	0.0005-0.0010"	0.0025"	4.0000" 4.0010"	4.0010" 4.0020"	4.0187" 4.0207"	4.0287" 4.0307"	————
327 (350 hp) 350 (350 & 370 hp)[1]	0.0024-0.0030"	0.0050"	3.9965" 3.9975"	3.9975" 3.9985"	————	4.0264" 4.0284"	————
350 (205, 210, 250, 255, 330 & 370 hp)[2]	0.0036-0.0042"[3]	0.0061"	3.9953" 3.9963"	3.9963" 3.9973"	4.0138" 4.0158"	4.0252" 4.0272"	————
350 (165, 180, 190, 195, 200, 270, 300 hp)	0.0007-0.0013"[3]	0.0027"	3.9998" 4.0008"	4.0008" 4.0018"	4.0183" 4.0203"	4.0283" 4.0303"	————
350 (350 hp)[2]	0.0020-0.0026"	0.0040"	————	————	————	————	————
427 (430 hp)	0.0054-0.0063"	0.0085"	4.2440" 4.2450"	4.2450" 4.2460"	————	4.2700" 4.2720"	4.3000" 4.3020"
427 (390 & 400 hp)	0.0009-0.0015"	0.0025"	4.2488" 4.2498"	4.2498" 4.2508"	4.2678" 4.2698"	4.2778" 4.2798"	————
427 (425 & 435 hp)	0.0037-0.0043"	0.0065"	4.2455" 4.2465"	4.2465" 4.2475"	————	4.2760" 4.2780"	4.3060" 4.3080"
454 (425 & 465 hp)	0.0040-0.0048"	0.0065"	4.2465" 4.2475"	4.2475" 4.2485"	4.2657" 4.2677"	4.2757" 4.2777"	————
454 (235, 275, 270, 365, 390 hp)	0.0024-0.0032"	0.0049"	4.2481" 4.2491"	4.2491" 4.2501"	4.2675" 4.2695"	4.2775" 4.2795"	————

1. 1969 only   2. 1970-1973   3. Increase clearances by 0.0010" for 1975-1976.

Piston Selection, 1965

On all except 1965 engines, select pistons on the basis of the *Piston Clearance* procedures described above. On 1965 engines only, selection is based on procedure below.

1. Measure cylinder bore with a telescope bore gauge.

2. Subtract base bore (specified bore in Table 1) from measured bore.

3. Locate the difference in Table 5, *Piston Selection*. Piston markings are stamped in ink on the piston crown. There are four standard pistons, four 0.020 in. oversize pistons, and four 0.030 in. oversize pistons.

Table 5   PISTON SELECTION (1965)

Base Cylinder Diameter	Piston Marking							
				Example "A"				
3.9995"	Base Dia.	.001	.002	.003	.004	.005	.020" O.S.	.021	.022
	Cylinder Oversize							
250 hp 300 hp	Piston Marking							
				Example "B"				
350 hp 365 hp 375 hp	.030" O.S.	.031	.032	.033	.034	.035		
	Cylinder Oversize							

For example, suppose actual measured bore of a 250 hp engine is 4.0025 in. Base bore for this 327 engine is 3.9995 in.

4.0025 in.	actual bore
−3.9995 in.	base bore
0.0030 in.	difference

According to the *Piston Selection Chart*, a difference of 0.003 in. over base diameter calls for an S7 piston. If this had been a 350-375 hp engine, an S4 piston would be called for with the same 0.003 in. difference.

As another example, suppose the cylinder had been bored to 0.030 in. oversize and that actual measurement reveals a 4.0315 in. bore.

4.0315 in.	actual bore
−3.9995 in.	base bore
0.0320 in.	difference

Piston selection chart indicates an 0.030 in. oversize piston marked 4.

Refer to Figure 47 for illustrations of various pistons used in Corvette engines.

Installation

1. Coat pistons, rings, and cylinder walls with light engine oil.

2. Install each piston in its respective bore. Orient rod as shown in **Figure 53**. Use tool J-6305, if available (Figure 48), to guide rod bearing into place. If not available, work slowly and have an assistant guide it on by hand.

CAUTION
The cast depression in the top of the piston must face toward the front of the engine.

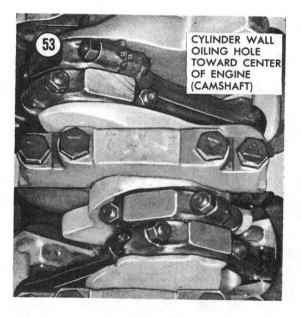

CYLINDER WALL OILING HOLE TOWARD CENTER OF ENGINE (CAMSHAFT)

3. Compress rings with a ring compressor tool and press pistons into bores with a hammer handle. See **Figure 54**.

4. Guide bearing onto journal as described above.

5. Install bearing caps and check bearing clearance as described later.

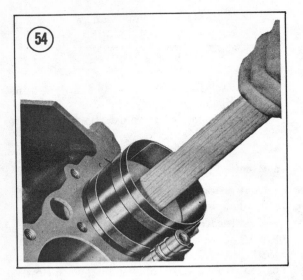

CONNECTING ROD BEARINGS

Bearing and Crankpin Inspection

1. Remove oil pan and oil pump.

2. On high-performance engines, remove oil baffle.

3. Remove connecting rod bearing caps. Push piston/rod assembly toward head.

4. Wipe bearing inserts and crankpins clean. Check bearing inserts and crankpins for evidence of wear, abrasion, or scoring.

5. Place a piece of Plastigage on one crankpin parallel to crankshaft. See **Figure 55**.

6. Install the rod cap and tighten the nuts evenly to 30-35 ft.-lb.

> **CAUTION**
> *Do not rotate crankshaft while Plastigage is in place.*

7. Remove bearing cap.

8. Measure width of flattened Plastigage according to manufacturer's instructions. See **Figure 56**. Measure at both ends of the Plastigage strip. A difference of 0.001 in. or more indicates a tapered crankpin. Confirm with a micrometer. If bearing clearance is not over 0.004 in. or less than 0.001 in., then bearing insert is good. Otherwise, replace bearing insert.

9. Repeat Steps 5-8 for each of the other rods.

10. Lubricate bearings and crankpins and install rod caps. Tighten nuts to 30-35 ft.-lb.

11. Rotate crankshaft to be sure bearings are not too tight.

12. Insert feeler gauge between connecting rods. Clearance should be 0.008-0.014 in. See **Figure 57**.

PISTON RINGS

Replacement

1. Remove old rings with a ring expander tool. See **Figure 58**.

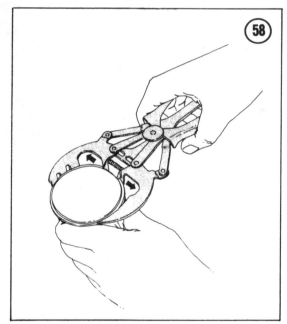

feeler gauge as shown in **Figure 59**. Compare gap with Table 1. If the gap is smaller than specified, hold a small file in a vise, grip the ends of the ring with your fingers and enlarge the gap. See **Figure 60**.

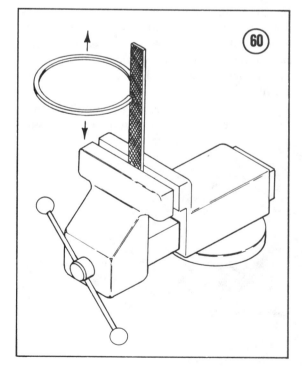

2. Carefully remove all carbon from ring grooves. Inspect grooves carefully for burrs, nicks, and broken or cracked lands. Recondition or replace piston, if necessary.

3. Select rings comparable in size to the piston being used.

4. Check ring gap of each ring. To check ring, insert it in the bottom of the cylinder bore, and square it with the wall by tapping with a piston. The ring should be in about 2 inches. Insert a

5. Roll each ring around its piston groove as shown in **Figure 61** to check for binding. Minor binding may be cleaned up with a fine cut file.

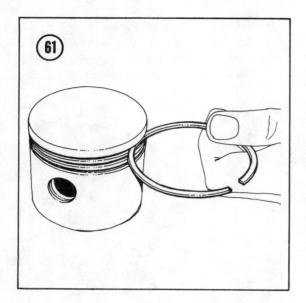

6. Install oil ring spacer in oil ring groove with a ring expander tool. Position gap in line with piston pin hole. Hold spacer ends butted and install steel rail on the top side of spacer. Position gap at least one in. to the left of spacer gap. Install second rail on lower side of spacer. Position gap at least one in. to right of spacer gap.

7. Flex oil ring assembly in its groove to make sure ring is free and does not bind at any point. Minor binding can be cleaned up with a fine cut file.

8. Install 2 compression rings carefully with a ring expander tool. See **Figure 62**. The side marked "G. M." *must* be up.

9. Check side clearance of each ring as shown in **Figure 63**. Compare with specifications for your engine.

10. Distribute ring gaps around piston as shown in **Figure 64**.

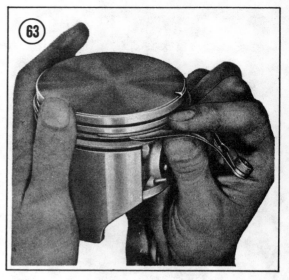

FLYWHEEL

Removal

1. Remove clutch pressure plate and clutch disc. See Chapter Eleven.

2. Remove 6 bolts securing flywheel to crankshaft.

3. Pull flywheel off.

Inspection

1. Check ring gear teeth for wear or damage.

2. Check clutch friction surface of flywheel for cracks and grooves. If necessary, recondition or replace flywheel.

Installation

1. Clean mating surface of flywheel and crankshaft to make certain there are no burrs.

2. Lightly oil threads of flywheel mounting bolts. Fit flywheel on crankshaft flange. Insert mounting bolts and tighten finger-tight.

> NOTE: *On manual transmission models, dowel holes in crankshaft and flywheel must align. On automatics, flange collar must face transmission. See* **Figure 65**.

3. Tighten diagonally opposite bolts evenly and progressively until all are tightened to 60 ft.-lb. on 327 and 350 engines, 65 ft.-lb. on larger engines.

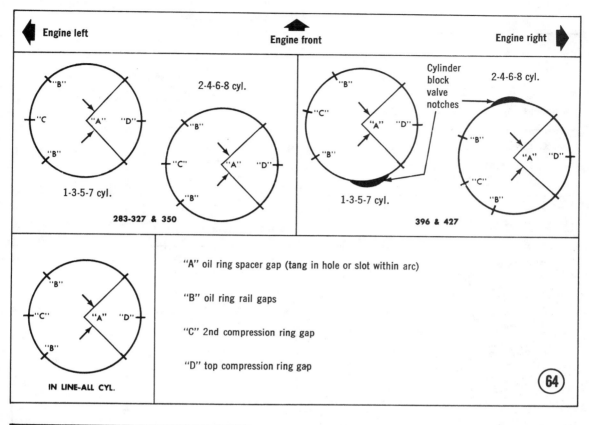

Engine left   Engine front   Engine right

2-4-6-8 cyl.

1-3-5-7 cyl.

283-327 & 350

Cylinder block valve notches

2-4-6-8 cyl.

1-3-5-7 cyl.

396 & 427

"A" oil ring spacer gap (tang in hole or slot within arc)

"B" oil ring rail gaps

"C" 2nd compression ring gap

"D" top compression ring gap

IN LINE-ALL CYL.

(64)

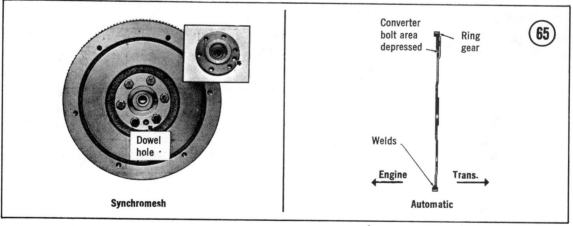

Dowel hole

Synchromesh

(65)

Converter bolt area depressed — Ring gear

Welds

Engine   Trans.

Automatic

Table 1   327 ENGINE SPECIFICATIONS

GENERAL

Type	V8
Displacement	327 cu. in.
Bore	4.0"
Stroke	3.25"

CYLINDER BORE

Diameter	3.9995-4.0025"
Out-of-round, new (wear limit)	0.001" (0.002")

PISTON

Clearance in bore	See Table 3, Chapter Five

PISTON RINGS

No. per cylinder	3
Ring end gap	
Top	0.013-0.023"[1], 0.010-0.020"[2]
2nd	0.013-0.025"[1], 0.013-0.023"[2]
Oil control	0.015-0.055"
Ring side clearance	
Top	0.0012-0.0027"[1], 0.0012-0.0032"[2]
2nd	0.0012-0.0032"[1], 0.0012-0.0027"[2]
Oil control	0.000-0.005"

PISTON PINS

Diameter	0.9270-0.9273"
Clearance	
In piston	0.00015-0.00025"[1], 0.00045-0.00055"[2]
In rod	0.0008-0.0016"

CRANKSHAFT

End play	0.003-0.011"[3,4], 0.002-0.006"[5,7]
Main bearing journal	
Diameter	
No. 1	2.2984-2.2993"[4], 2.2987-2.2997"[3], 2.2978-2.2988"[5,7]
No. 2, 3, 4	2.2983-2.2993"[3,4], 2.2978-2.2988"[5,7]
No. 5	2.2978-2.2988"
Taper	0.0002"
Out-of-round	0.0002"
Main bearing clearance	
No. 1	0.0008-0.0020"[4], 0.0008-0.0034"[3,7]
No. 2, 3, 4	0.0018-0.0020"[4], 0.0008-0.0034"[3,7]
No. 5	0.0010-0.0036", 0.0008-0.0034"[7]
Crankpin	
Diameter	1.999-2.000"
Taper, new (wear limit)	0.0003"
Out-of-round, new (wear limit)	0.0002"

(continued)

Table 1   327 ENGINE SPECIFICATIONS (continued)

CONNECTING RODS	
Side clearance	0.009-0.013", 0.0017-0.0038"[7]
Bearing clearance	0.0007-0.0028"

CAMSHAFT	
Journal diameter	1.8682-1.8692"
Run-out	0.0015"
VALVE SYSTEM	
Lifter type	Hydraulic, solid[6]
Rocker arm ratio	1.50:1
Valve lash	See Table 1, Chapter Three
Intake valve	
Face angle	45°
Seat angle	46°[9]
Seat width	1/32-1/16"
Stem-to-guide clearance	0.0010-0.0027"
Seat run-out	0.002" max.
Exhaust valve	
Face angle	45°
Seat angle	46°[8]
Seat width	1/16-3/32"
Stem-to-guide clearance	0.0010-0.0027", 0.0016-0.0033"[5,7]
Seat run-out	0.002" max.
Valve springs (outer)	
Free length	2.03"[4], 2.08"[3,5,7]
Load @ length (lbs. @ in.)	78-86 @ 1.66[3,5,7]
	170-178 @ 1.26[1,3,5,7], 180-185 @ 1.21[2,3]
Installed height	1 5/32±1/32"[4], 1 21/32±1/32"[3]
Damper free length	1.94", (2.00")

Notes: 1. 250, 300 hp   5. 1965
             2. 350, 365, 375 hp   6. 365, 375, 340, 360 hp
             3. 1966   7. 1963-1964
             4. 1967   8. 45° on aluminum heads

Table 1   350 ENGINE SPECIFICATIONS

GENERAL	
Type	V8
Displacement	350 cu. in.
Bore	4.0 in.
Stroke	3.48 in.
CYLINDER BORE	
Diameter	3.9995-4.0025 in.
Out-of-round, new (wear limit)	0.001 in. (0.002 in.)
PISTON	
Clearance in bore	See Table 3, Chapter 5
PISTON RINGS	
No. per cylinder	3
Ring end gap	
Top	0.010-0.020 in.
2nd	0.013-0.025 in.
Oil control	0.015-0.055 in.
Ring side clearance	
Top	0.0012-0.0032 in.
2nd	0.0012-0.0032 in.
Oil control	0.005 (maximum) in.
PISTON PINS	
Diameter	0.9270-0.9273 in.
Clearance	
In piston	0.00015-0.00025 in. (0.001 in.)
In rod	0.0008-0.0016 in.
CRANKSHAFT	
End play	0.002-0.006 in.
Main bearing journal	
Diameter	
No. 1	2.4484-2.4493 in. ①②③④⑧⑨⑩⑪
	2.7481-2.7490 in. ⑩
	2.4479-2.4488 in. ⑤⑥⑦
No. 2, 3, 4	2.4481-2.4490 in. ①②③④⑩⑪
	2.4484-2.4493 in. ⑧⑨
	2.4479-2.4488 in. ⑤⑥⑦
No. 5	2.4479-2.4488 in. ①②③④⑤⑥⑦⑧⑨⑩⑪
	2.7473-2.7483 in. ⑩
Taper	0.0002 in.
Out-of-round	0.0002 in.
Main bearing clearance	
No. 1	0.0008-0.0020 in. ①②③④⑤⑥⑦⑧⑨⑩⑪⑫
	0.0013-0.0025 in. ⑩⑪⑫⑬, 0.0019-0.0031 in. ⑭
No. 2, 3, 4	0.0011-0.0023 in. ①②③④⑤⑥⑦⑧⑨⑩⑪⑫
	0.0013-0.0025 in. ⑩⑪⑫⑬⑭
No. 5	0.0017-0.0033 in. ①②③④⑤⑥⑦⑧⑨⑩⑪⑫
	0.0023-0.0033 in. ⑩⑪⑫⑬⑭
Crankpin	
Diameter	2.099-2.100 in.
Taper, new (wear limit)	0.0003 in. (0.001 in.)
Out-of-round, new (wear limit)	0.0002 in. (0.001 in.)

(continued)

Table 1   **350 ENGINE SPECIFICATIONS**   (continued)

CONNECTING RODS	
Side clearance	0.008-0.014 in.
Bearing clearance	0.0013-0.0035 in.
CAMSHAFT	
Journal diameter	1.8682-1.8692 in.
Runout	0.0015 in. maximum
VALVE SYSTEM	
Lifter type	Hydraulic①②③⑤⑥⑧⑨⑩⑪, Solid④⑦⑩
Rocker arm ratio	1.50:1
Valve lash	See Table 1, Chapter 3
Intake valve	
Face angle	45°
Seat angle	46°
Seat width	$\frac{1}{32}$-$\frac{1}{16}$ in.
Stem-to-guide clearance	0.0010-0.0027 in.
Seat runout	0.002 in. maximum
Exhaust valve	
Face angle	45°
Seat angle	46°
Seat width	$\frac{1}{16}$-$\frac{3}{32}$ in.
Stem-to-guide clearance	0.0012-0.0029 in.
Seat runout	0.002 in. maximum
Valve springs (outer)	
Free length	2.03 in.
Load @ length (lbs. @ in.)	76-84 @ 1.70
	194-206 @ 1.25
Installed height	$1\frac{5}{8} \pm \frac{1}{32}$ in.①②⑫
	$1\frac{23}{32} \pm \frac{1}{32}$ in.③④⑧⑨⑩⑬⑭
	$1\frac{5}{32} \pm \frac{1}{32}$ in.⑤⑥⑦
Valve springs (inner)	
Free length	——
Load @ length (lbs. @ in.)	——
Installed height	——
Damper free length	1.94 in.

Notes:

① 190 hp	⑥ 350 hp	⑪ All 1974-1976
② 200 hp	⑦ 370 hp	⑫ 1974 185 hp
③ 250 hp	⑧ 270 hp	⑬ 1975-1976 man. trans.
④ 255 hp	⑨ 300 hp (1970)	⑭ 1975-1976 auto. trans.
⑤ 300 hp (1969)	⑩ 330 hp	

Table 1   427 ENGINE SPECIFICATIONS

GENERAL	
Type	V8
Displacement	427 cu. in.
Bore	4.25″
Stroke	3.76″
CYLINDER BORE	
Diameter	4.2495-4.2525″
Out-of-round, new (wear limit)	——
PISTON	
Clearance in bore	See Table 3, Chapter Five
PISTON RINGS	
No. per cylinder	3
Ring end gap	
Top	0.010-0.020″
2nd	0.010-0.020″
Oil control	0.010-0.030″
Ring side clearance	
Top	0.0017-0.0032″, 0.0012-0.0032″[6]
2nd	0.0017-0.0032″, 0.0012-0.0032″[6]
Oil control	0.0005-0.0065″, 0.0012-0.0060″[6]
PISTON PINS	
Diameter	0.9895-0.9898″
Clearance	
In piston	0.00025-0.00035″[1,2], 0.00045-0.00055″[3],
	0.00030-0.00040″[4]
In rod	0.0001-0.0008″[3], 0.0008-0.0016″[1,2,4]
CRANKSHAFT	
End play	0.006-0.010″
Main bearing journal	
Diameter	
No. 1, 2	2.7481-2.7490″, 2.7487-2.7497″[6]
No. 3, 4	2.7481-2.7490″, 2.7482-2.7492″[6]
No. 5	2.7478-2.7488″
Taper	0.0002″
Out-of-round	0.0002″
Main bearing clearance	
No. 1, 2	0.0013-0.0025″, 0.0004-0.0020″[6]
No. 3, 4	0.0013-0.0025″, 0.0009-0.0025″[6]
No. 5	0.0015-0.0031″, 0.0013-0.0029″[6]
Crankpin	
Diameter	2.199-2.200″[1,2,8], 2.1985-2.1995″[3,7]
Taper, new (wear limit)	0.0003″
Out-of-round, new (wear limit)	0.0002″

(continued)

Table 1   427 ENGINE SPECIFICATIONS   (continued)

CONNECTING RODS	
Side clearance	0.015-0.021"[1,2,8], 0.019-0.025"[3,7]
Bearing clearance	0.0009-0.0025"[3,4], 0.0014-0.0030"[3,4], 0.0007-0.0028"[6]
CAMSHAFT	
Journal diameter	1.9482-1.9492"
Run-out	0.0015" max.
VALVE SYSTEM	
Lifter type	Hydraulic[1,2], solid[3,4,5]
Rocker arm ratio	1.70:1
Valve lash	See Table 1, Chapter Three
Intake valve	
Face angle	45°
Seat angle	46°
Seat width	1/32-1/16"
Stem-to-guide clearance	0.0010-0.0025"
Seat run-out	0.002" max.
Exhaust valve	
Face angle	45°
Seat angle	46°
Seat width	1/16-3/32"
Stem-to-guide clearance	0.0012-0.0027"
Seat run-out	0.002" max.
Valve springs (outer)	
Free length (in.)	2.09"[1,2,4,6], 2.21"[3]
Load @ length (lbs. @ in.)	94-106 @ 1.88[1,2,4], 69-81 @ 1.88[3]
	303-327 @ 1.38[1,2,4], 181-205 @ 1.32[3]
Installed height	1 7/8±1/32"
Valve springs (inner)[3]	
Free length	2.12"
Load @ length (lbs. @ in.)	37-45 @ 1.78
	92-110 @ 1.22
Installed height	1 3/4±1/32"
Damper spring free length	1.94-2.00"[1,2,4], 1.95-2.07"[3]

Notes: 1. 390 hp   5. 425 hp (1966)
        2. 400 hp   6. 1966-1967 engines
        3. 430 hp   7. 435 hp (except 1967)
        4. 435 hp, all years   8. 435 hp (1967 only)

Table 1   454 ENGINE SPECIFICATIONS

GENERAL
Type	V8
Displacement	454 cu. in.
Bore	4.25″
Stroke	4.0″

CYLINDER BORE
Diameter	4.2495-4.2525″
Out-of-round, new (wear limit)	0.001″ (0.002″)

PISTON
Clearance in bore	See Table 3, Chapter Five

PISTON RINGS
No. per cylinder	3
Ring end gap	
Top	0.010-0.020″
2nd	0.010-0.020″
Oil control	0.015-0.055″
Ring side clearance	
Top	0.0017-0.0032″
2nd	0.0017-0.0032″
Oil control	0.0005-0.0065″

PISTON PINS
Diameter	0.9895-0.9898″
Clearance	
In piston; new (wear limit)	0.00025-0.00035″
In rod	0.0008-0.0016″

CRANKSHAFT
End play	0.006-0.010″
Main bearing journal	
Diameter	
No. 1	2.7485-2.7494″[1], 2.7481-2.7490″[2]
No. 2, 3, 4	2.7481-2.7490″
No. 5	2.7478-2.7488″
Taper; new (wear limit)	0.0002″
Out-of-round; new (wear limit)	0.0002″
Main bearing clearance	
No. 1	0.0013-0.0025″
No. 2, 3, 4	0.0013-0.0025″
No. 5	0.0024-0.0040″[1], 0.0029-0.0045″[2]
Crankpin	
Diameter	2.199-2.200″[1], 2.1985-2.1995″[2]
Taper, new (wear limit)	0.0003″
Out-of-round, new (wear limit)	0.0002″

(continued)

Table 1   454 ENGINE SPECIFICATIONS (continued)

CONNECTING RODS	
Side clearance	0.015-0.021"[1], 0.019-0.025"[2]
Bearing clearance	0.0009-0.0025"
CAMSHAFT	
Journal diameter	1.9482-1.9492"
Run-out	0.0015" max.
VALVE SYSTEM	
Lifter type	Hydraulic[1], solid[2]
Rocker arm ratio	1.70:1
Valve lash	See Table 1, Chapter Three
Intake valve	
Face angle	45°
Seat angle	46°
Seat width	1/32-1/16"
Stem-to-guide clearance	0.0010-0.0027"
Seat run-out	0.002" max.
Exhaust valve	
Face angle	45°
Seat angle	46°
Seat width	1/16-3/32"
Stem-to-guide clearance	0.0012-0.0027"
Seat run-out	0.002" max.
Valve springs (outer)	
Free length	2.10"[3], 2.12"[4]
Load @ length (lbs. @ in.)	74-86 @ 1.88[3], 69-81 @ 1.88[4]
	288-312 @ 1.38[3], 228-252 @ 1.38[4]
Installed height	1 7/8±1/32"
Valve springs (inner)[4]	
Free length	2.06"
Load @ length (lbs. @ in.)	26-34 @ 1.78
	81-99 @ 1.28
Installed height	1 25/32±1/32"
Damper spring free length[3]	1.86"

Notes: 1. Except 425 & 450 hp   3. 235 & 275 hp
        2. 425 & 450 hp   4. Except 275 hp

Table 2   TIGHTENING TORQUES

	Torque*	
	Small V8	Large V8
Crankcase front cover	80 in.	—
Flywheel housing pans	80 in.	—
Oil filter bypass valve	80 in.	—
Oil pan (to crankcase)	80 in.	—
Oil pan (to front cover)	—	80 in.
Oil pump cover	80 in.	80 in.
Rocker arm cover	55 in.	50 in.
Connecting rod cap	35 ft.	50 ft.
Camshaft sprocket	20 ft.	20 ft.
Oil pan (to crankcase)	65 in.	135 in.
Oil pump	65 ft.	65 ft.
Water pump	30 ft.	30 ft.
Distributor clamp	10 ft.	10 ft.
Flywheel housing	30 ft.	30 ft.
Manifold (exhaust)	20 ft.	20 ft.
Manifold (inlet)	30 ft.	30 ft.
Water outlet	20 ft.	20 ft.
Cylinder head	65 ft.	80ft.
Main bearing cap	80 ft.	—
Rocker arm stud	—	50 ft.
Flywheel	60 ft.	65 ft.
Torsional damper	60 ft.	85 ft.
Main bearing cap (2 bolt)	—	95 ft.
Main bearing cap (4 bolt)	—	115 ft.
Temperature sending unit	20 ft.	20 ft.
Oil filter	25 ft.	25 ft.
Oil pan drain plug	20 ft.	20 ft.
Spark plug	25 ft.	25 ft.

*Note carefully whether torque is in foot-pounds (ft.) or inch-pounds (in.)

CHAPTER SIX

CARBURETTED FUEL SYSTEM

The fuel system consists of a rear mounted fuel tank connected through a line to a mechanical fuel pump which feeds the carburetor(s).

Numerous carburetors are used on Corvettes. These are designed to meet particular requirements of engines and transmissions. Therefore, carburetors that look alike are not always interchangeable. Refer to **Table 1** to determine the proper carburetor for a particular vehicle.

This chapter covers removal, installation, repair and/or replacement of all carburetors, fuel pumps, and fuel tanks used on Corvettes.

CARTER AFB

The Carter AFB (Aluminum Four Barrel) is a 4-barrel downdraft type which provides the advantages of a dual 2-barrel installation in one compact unit. See **Figure 1**. Table 1 lists usage of this carburetor. **Table 2** includes specifications.

Removal/Installation

1. Remove air cleaner, gasket, and stud.

2. Disconnect vacuum, fuel, and choke pipes at carburetor.

3. On automatic models, disconnect transmission control rod from throttle lever.

Table 2   CARTER AFB (1963-1965)

	Primary	Secondary
Float level	7/32″	7/32″
Float drop	3/4″	3/4″
Pump rod	1/2″	——
Idle vent	——	——
Choke setting	1 lean	——
Unloader	1/4″	——
Fast idle (rpm)	1,750	——
Throttle lockout adjustment	0.020″	
Vacuum break adjustment	0.070″	——
Main jet	0.104″	0.0689″
Metering rod sizes	0.060	——
	0.069″	——
Throttle bore	1-9/16″	1-11/16″
Main venturi	1-1/4″	1-9/16″
Pump discharge jet	0.028″	——
Idle speed jet	0.035″	——

4. On models with positive crankcase ventilation (PCV), disconnect ventilation hose at valve on carburetor base.

5. Disconnect accelerator rod and throttle return spring at carburetor.

6. Remove mounting nuts and lift carburetor from manifold.

Table 1   CARBURETOR USAGE

Year	Horsepower	Carburetor	Type
1963-1964	250 hp	Carter WCFB	1 x 4-barrel
	300, 340 hp	Carter AFB	1 x 4-barrel
1965	250 hp	Carter WCFB	1 x 4-barrel
	300 hp	Carter AFB	1 x 4-barrel
	350, 365, 425 hp	Holley 4150	1 x 4-barrel
1966	300, 350, 390 hp	Holley 4160	1 x 4-barrel
	425 hp	Holley 4150	1 x 4-barrel
1967	300, 350, 390 hp	Holley 4160	1 x 4-barrel
	400, 435 hp	Holley 2300/2300c	3 x 2-barrels
1968	300, 350, 390 hp	Rochester 4MV	1 x 4-barrel
	400, 435 hp	Holley 2300/2300c	3 x 2-barrels
	430 hp	Holley 4150	1 x 4-barrel
1969	300, 350 hp	Rochester 4MV	1 x 4-barrel
	370 hp	Holley 4150	1 x 4-barrel
	400, 435 hp	Holley 2300/2300c	3 x 2-barrels
1970	300, 350, 370, 390, 465 hp	Rochester 4MV	1 x 4-barrel
1971	270, 365 hp	Rochester 4MV	1 x 4-barrel
	330, 425 hp	Holley 4150	1 x 4-barrel
1972	200, 270 hp	Rochester 4MV	1 x 4-barrel
	255 hp	Holley 4150	1 x 4-barrel
1973	190, 215, 245 hp	Rochester 4MV	1 x 4-barrel
1974	195, 235, 250 hp	Rochester 4MV	1 x 4-barrel
1975	165, 205 hp	Rochester M4MC	1 x 4-barrel
1976	180, 210 hp	Rochester M4MC	1 x 4-barrel

7. Installation is the reverse of these steps. Make certain that base of carburetor and manifold flange are clean.

Disassembly

Refer to Figure 1, **Figure 2 and Figure 3** for the following procedure.

1. Remove retainer from upper end of pump rod and disconnect pump rod from arm.

2. Remove hairpin clip from upper end of inter-mediate choke rod and disconnect rod.

3. Remove screw from end of choke shaft and remove outer lever and washer. Remove inner lever and fast idle rod from carburetor as an assembly.

4. Remove screws securing cover plates shown in **Figure 4**. Remove cover, piston, metering rod, and spring on each side.

5. Remove fuel inlet fitting, gasket, and strainer.

6. Remove screws securing top cover of carbu-retor (**Figure 5**). Lift cover off as shown in

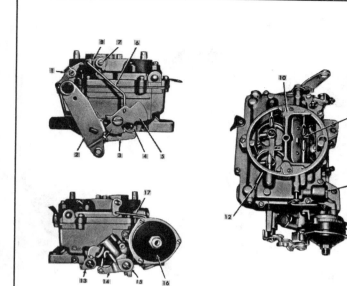

CARTER AFB

1. Pump lever
2. Primary throttle shaft lever
3. Secondary throttle lockout lever
4. Secondary throttle shaft lever
5. Fast idle cam
6. Fast idle rod
7. Choke shaft outer lever
8. Choke shaft kick lever
9. Choke valve
10. Piston cover plate
11. Fuel inlet fitting
12. Choke clean air pickup tube
13. Secondary throttle shaft dog lever
14. Secondary throttle trip lever
15. Primary throttle shaft lever
16. Choke coil and housing cover
17. Intermediate choke rod

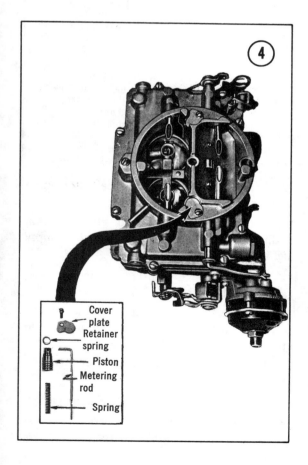

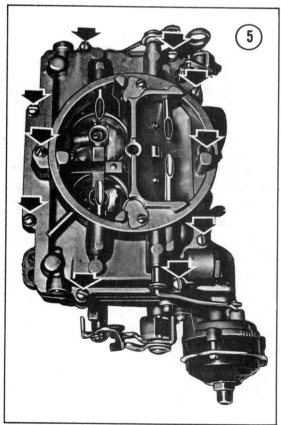

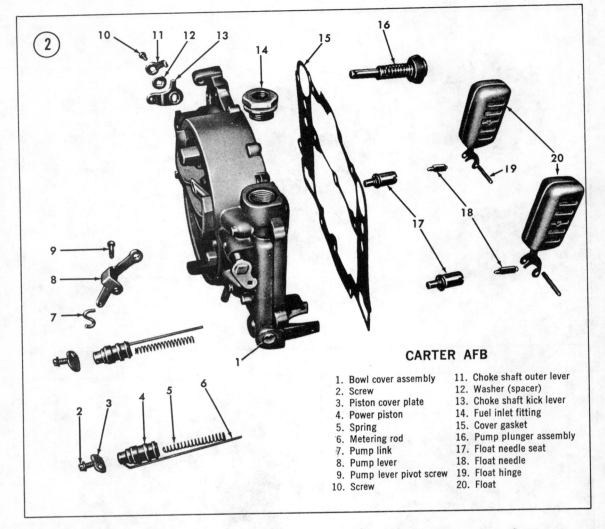

CARTER AFB

1. Bowl cover assembly	11. Choke shaft outer lever
2. Screw	12. Washer (spacer)
3. Piston cover plate	13. Choke shaft kick lever
4. Power piston	14. Fuel inlet fitting
5. Spring	15. Cover gasket
6. Metering rod	16. Pump plunger assembly
7. Pump link	17. Float needle seat
8. Pump lever	18. Float needle
9. Pump lever pivot screw	19. Float hinge
10. Screw	20. Float

Figure 6. Do not damage floats or accelerator pump plunger.

7. Remove float lever pins and floats.

8. Remove float needles, seats, and gaskets.

9. Remove pump lever pivot screw and pump lever. Remove S-1 link and plunger.

10. Remove cover gasket.

> NOTE: *Ordinarily, the choke valve and shaft are not disassembled from cover. If shaft is binding or valve is damaged, perform Step 11. Otherwise, proceed to Step 12.*

11. File choke valve screws (staked ends) level with shaft to prevent damage to threads in shaft. Remove screws and choke valve. Slide shaft from top cover.

12. Remove lower spring of accelerator pump from carburetor body.

13. Check fuel left in bowl for contamination by dirt, gum, or other foreign matter, then empty fuel from bowl.

14. Remove choke housing retainer, cover, gasket, and baffle plate.

15. Remove choke housing mounting screws and housing. Remove O-ring from vacuum opening.

16. Remove choke piston lever screw. Remove piston and 2 levers.

17. Remove pump discharge nozzle and gasket.

18. Remove primary and secondary venturi clusters (**Figure 7**) and idle compensator valve.

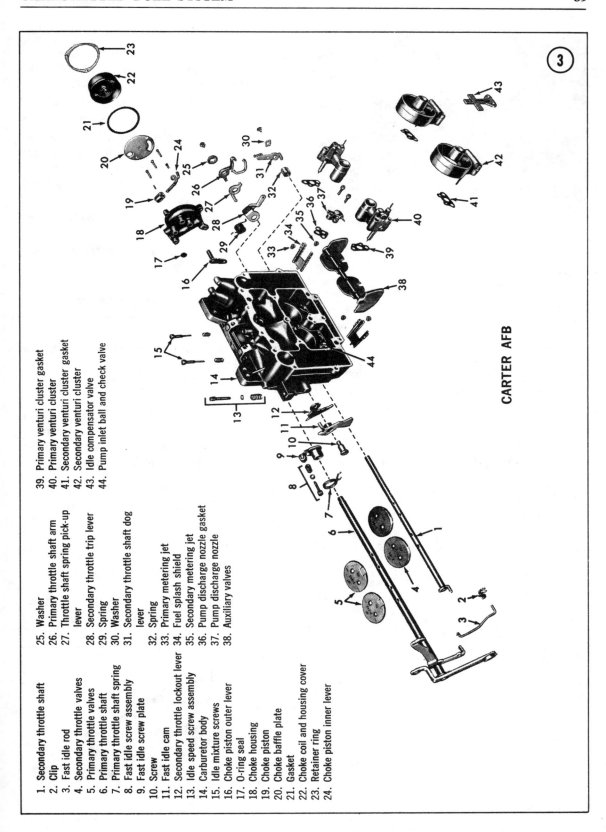

CARTER AFB

1. Secondary throttle shaft
2. Clip
3. Fast idle rod
4. Secondary throttle valves
5. Primary throttle valves
6. Primary throttle shaft
7. Primary throttle shaft spring
8. Fast idle screw assembly
9. Fast idle screw plate
10. Screw
11. Fast idle cam
12. Secondary throttle lockout lever
13. Idle speed screw assembly
14. Carburetor body
15. Idle mixture screws
16. Choke piston outer lever
17. O-ring seal
18. Choke housing
19. Choke piston
20. Choke baffle plate
21. Gasket
22. Choke coil and housing cover
23. Retainer ring
24. Choke piston inner lever
25. Washer
26. Primary throttle shaft arm
27. Throttle shaft spring pick-up lever
28. Secondary throttle trip lever
29. Spring
30. Washer
31. Secondary throttle shaft dog lever
32. Spring
33. Primary metering jet
34. Fuel splash shield
35. Secondary metering jet
36. Pump discharge nozzle gasket
37. Pump discharge nozzle
38. Auxiliary valves
39. Primary venturi cluster gasket
40. Primary venturi cluster
41. Secondary venturi cluster gasket
42. Secondary venturi cluster
43. Idle compensator valve
44. Pump inlet ball and check valve

19. Lift auxiliary throttle valves from body. See **Figure 8**.

20. Remove idle mixture screws and springs.

21. Remove all 4 metering jets. See Figure 7.

22. Remove pump inlet ball and check valve. See Figure 7.

> NOTE: *Further disassembly is not necessary or advisable unless throttle valves or linkages are worn or damaged. If necessary to replace these components, perform following steps.*

23. Remove fast idle screw and cam.

24. Remove the primary to secondary connecting link.

25. Remove primary and secondary throttle dog lever screws and remove levers and springs.

26. File off staked ends of throttle valve screws. Remove screws and throttle valves. Slide shafts out of body.

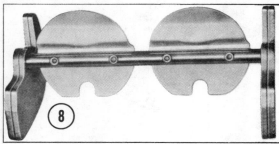

Cleaning and Inspection

The most frequent causes of carburetor trouble are dirt, gum, and water in the carburetor. Carefully clean and inspect all parts before assembling carburetor.

1. Clean all parts except choke housing and accelerator pump plunger in solvent. Special carburetor cleaners available from any auto parts supplier work best.

2. Check bearing surfaces of all operating levers, shafts, and castings for excessive wear.

3. Check floats for dents. Immerse floats in hot water. If bubbles appear, float is leaking, and the float must be *replaced*. Do not attempt to solder the hole. This increases float weight and causes high fuel level.

4. Check pump plunger leather for cracks and creases.

5. Check float needles and seats for burrs and ridges. If present, replace needle and seat; never replace either alone.

6. Check metering rods and jets for bends, burrs, ridges, or other distortion. Replace rod and jet if either is damaged.

7. Inspect edges of throttle valves for nicks or gouges. Replace if necessary.

8. Check all springs for obvious distortion or bends.

9. Make certain all gasket mating surfaces of choke housing, top cover and carburetor body are free of burrs, gouges, deep scratches or other irregularities which could prevent a good seal.

Assembly

Refer to Figures 1, 2, and 3 for the following procedure.

> NOTE: *The first 4 steps apply only if throttle shafts were removed in Steps 23-26 of* Disassembly *procedure.*

1. Install primary and secondary throttle shafts.

2. Install primary throttle shaft dog levers and spring. See **Figure 9**.

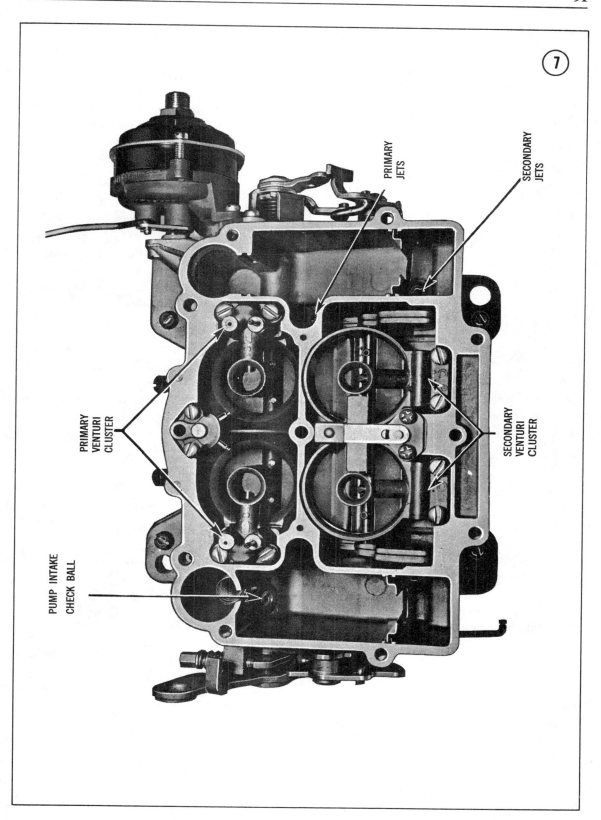

3. Install secondary throttle shaft dog lever and spring. Wind spring one turn. See **Figure 10**.

4. Install throttle valves in shafts with part number identification toward bottom of carburetor. Secure with new screws. Use Loctite to prevent loosening.

5. Install pump inlet ball and check valve. See Figure 7.

6. Install primary and secondary metering jets.

NOTE: *Primary jets have larger orifices than secondary jets.*

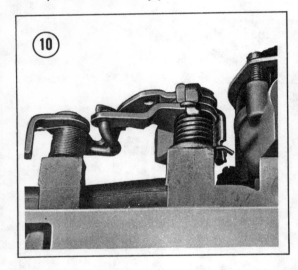

7. Install pump discharge needle, housing, and gasket.

8. Fit auxiliary throttle valve assembly in place with screws down.

9. Install primary and secondary venturi clusters in place. Use new gaskets.

10. Screw idle mixture screws in place. Seat very lightly, then back them out 1½ turns.

11. Install choke piston housing shaft, lever, and rod in piston housing. Place O-ring in housing recess, then install piston housing on main body with 3 screws.

12. Install choke piston, pin link, and lever assembly in housing. Install piston lever on flats of shaft so that inner and outer levers are pointing in the same general direction. Install special washer and screw.

13. Place pump plunger in position in cover and install pump link. Install pin spring in upper end of link.

14. Install float needle seats and gaskets. Install float needles, floats, and lever pins.

NOTE: *Steps 15-17 adjust float level.*

15. Align float parallel with outer edge of cover. See **Figure 11**. Bend end of float, if necessary, while holding float lever with thumb. Make sure that float operates freely.

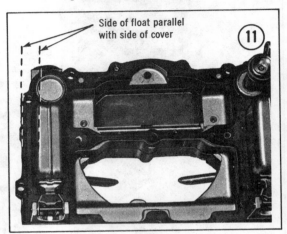

Side of float parallel with side of cover

16. Invert top cover of carburetor with gasket in place. Check clearance between outer end of each float and gasket with float gauge J-9550 or 5/16 in. drill. See **Figure 12**. Bend float lever if necessary, then recheck Step 15.

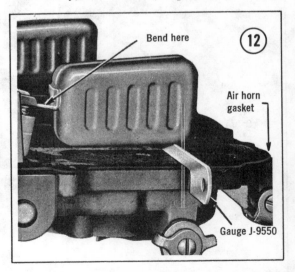

Bend here

Air horn gasket

Gauge J-9550

17. Hold top cover upright. Check float drop by measuring vertical distance shown in **Figure 13**. Bend float arm tang as required to obtain ¾ in. measurement.

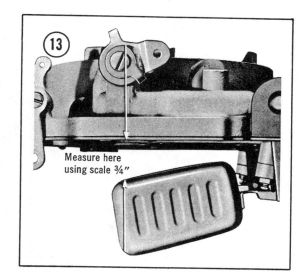

Measure here using scale ¾"

18. Place lower pump spring in pump well.

19. Fit top cover over body. Do not disturb float adjustment. Install cover screws. The 2 longest screws go in middle holes.

20. Install fuel strainer, gasket, and inlet in cover.

21. If removed, install choke shaft in cover. Install choke valves with markings *up*. Do not tighten screws. Align valves carefully to ensure that there is uniform clearance and no binding. Tighten screws; use Loctite to prevent loosening.

22. Install fast idle rod and choke lever by first engaging fast idle cam. Place lever over end of choke shaft so that it points toward accelerator pump. Install special washer on shaft, then install choke shaft outer lever so that tang on outer lever is above tang on inner lever when choke valve is open.

23. Install metering rod springs. Install assembled piston, rod, and rod retainer spring. Carefully push down on each piston and rod until rod enters metering jet; do not bend rod. Install cover plates.

24. Install upper end of pump rod in pump arm.

NOTE: *Steps 25-27 adjust automatic choke.*

25. Open choke valve and insert 0.026 in. wire gauge between bottom of slot in piston and top of slot in choke piston housing. See **Figure 14**. Close choke piston against gauge with rubber band. Check clearance between top of choke

valve and web of top cover (Figure 14) with an 0.070 in. wire gauge. If necessary, bend intermediate choke rod to achieve 0.070 in. clearance. Remove gauges and rubber band.

26. Install choke baffle plate, gasket, and coil housing with retainer ring and screws.

27. Align index on coil cover with center mark on choke housing.

NOTE: *Steps 28-30 adjust accelerator pump.*

28. Push fast idle cam aside and back out throttle stop screw until throttle valves seat in throttle bores.

29. Measure from top cover to top of plunger shaft with scale. See **Figure 15**. Bend pump rod at lower angle if necessary to obtain ½ in. measurement.

30. Turn throttle stop screw in ½ turn (from fully closed throttle).

NOTE: *Steps 31-33 adjust unloader.*

31. Hold throttle wide open.

32. Check clearance between upper edge of choke valve and inner wall of top cover with a ¼ in. drill. See **Figure 16**.

½" MEASUREMENT WITH THROTTLE FULLY CLOSED

THROTTLE STOP SCREW

BEND HERE USING TOOL J-4552

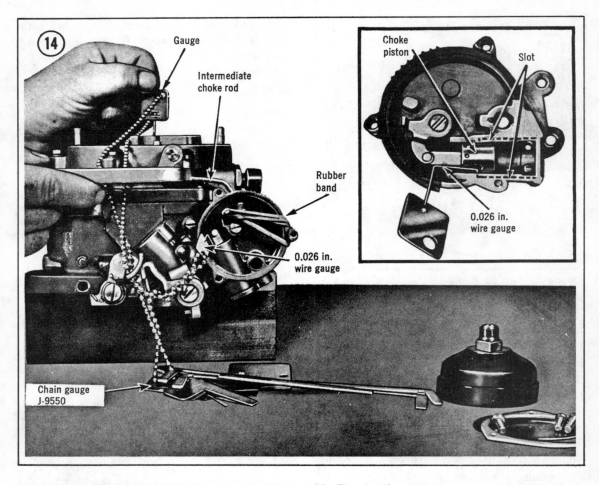

Gauge

Intermediate
choke rod

Rubber
band

0.026 in.
wire gauge

Chain gauge
J-9550

Choke
piston

Slot

0.026 in.
wire gauge

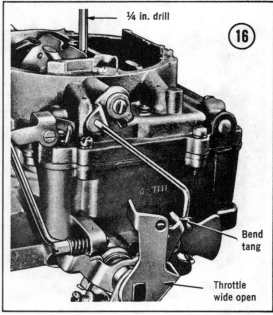

¼ in. drill

16

Bend
tang

Throttle
wide open

33. Bend unloader tang on throttle shaft lever as necessary to obtain proper clearance. See Figure 16.

NOTE: *Steps 34-35 adjust closing shoe.*

34. With primary and secondary throttle valves closed, check clearance between positive closing shoes with 0.020 in. feeler gauge. See **Figure 17**.

35. Bend secondary closing shoe if necessary to obtain proper clearance.

NOTE: *Steps 36-37 adjust secondary throttle opening.*

36. Rotate pickup lever on primary shaft. Ensure that lever contacts points (A) and (B) in **Figure 18** at exactly the same time. Bend lever if necessary to achieve this.

37. Open throttles wide open. Make sure that primary and secondary throttle valves reach

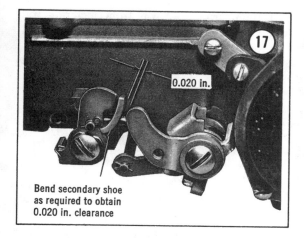

Bend secondary shoe as required to obtain 0.020 in. clearance

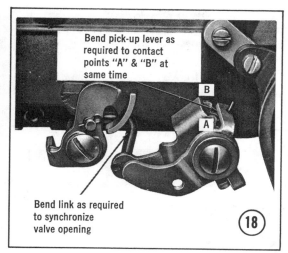

Bend pick-up lever as required to contact points "A" & "B" at same time

Bend link as required to synchronize valve opening

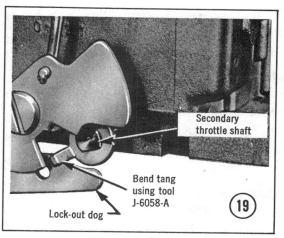

Secondary throttle shaft

Bend tang using tool J-6058-A

Lock-out dog

Table 3   CARTER WCFB (1963-1965)

	Primary	Secondary
Float level	7/32"	1/4"
Float drop	3/4"	3/4"
Pump rod	1/2"	—
Idle vent	3/32"	—
Automatic choke setting	Index	—
Unloader	3/16"	—
Fast idle (rpm)	1,750	—
Throttle lockout adjustment	0.020"	—
Vacuum break adjustment	0.060"	—
Manual transmission	0.060"	—
Automatic transmission	0.035"	—
Main jet	0.086"	0.0635"
Metering rod sizes		—
	0.067"	—
Throttle bore	1-7/16"	1-7/16"
Main venturi	1-1/16"	1-1/4"
Pump discharge jet	0.021"	—
Idle speed jet	0.031"	—

wide open position simultaneously. If necessary, bend connecting link. See Figure 18.

NOTE: *Remaining step adjusts secondary throttle lockout.*

38. Open primary throttle valves slightly. Manually open and close choke valve. Tang on secondary throttle lever should freely engage in notch of lockout dog while barely missing edge of notch. See **Figure 19**. Bend tang if necessary.

CARTER WCFB

The Carter WCFB Climatic Control Carburetor is essentially two 2-barrel carburetors in one assembly. It consists of 4 basic castings; choke housing, bowl cover, carburetor body, and throttle flange. Table 1 lists usage of this carburetor. **Table 3** lists specifications.

Removal/Installation

1. Remove air cleaner, gasket, and stud.

2. Disconnect vacuum, fuel, and choke pipes at carburetor.

3. On automatic models, disconnect transmission control rod from throttle lever.

4. On models with positive crankcase ventilation (PCV), disconnect ventilation hose at valve on carburetor base.

5. Disconnect accelerator rod and throttle return spring at carburetor.

6. Remove mounting nuts and lift carburetor from manifold.

7. Installation is the reverse of these steps. Make certain that base of carburetor and manifold flange are clean.

Disassembly

Refer to **Figures 20-23** for the following procedure.

1. Remove inlet nut and gasket. Lift filter out.

> NOTE: *Tap filter nut lightly with hammer before loosening with wrench.*

2. Remove both ends of choke connector rod and intermediate choke rod.

3. Remove retainer securing throttle rod to pump countershaft lever and disconnect rod.

4. Remove metering rod dust cover and gasket.

5. Remove vent arm screw and vent arm.

6. Loosen, but do not remove, screws securing pump operating arm and metering rod arm to countershaft. Pull countershaft out of bowl cover. See **Figure 24**.

7. Lift metering rod arm from metering rod well. Push connecting link out of pump shaft and remove arm and link. See Figure 24.

8. Rotate each metering rod ½ turn and remove from hanger. Do not lose 2 metering rod discs.

> NOTE: *Further disassembly is not necessary or advisable unless throttle valves or shaft are worn or damaged. If necessary to replace these components, perform Step 9. Otherwise, proceed to Step 10.*

9. Remove 2 choke valve screws and choke valve. Remove shaft.

10. Remove 16 bowl covers screws. See **Figure 25**. Lift bowl cover straight up (**Figure 26**) to prevent damaging floats. Be sure that bowl cover gasket does not stick to bowl and bend floats.

11. Place bowl cover upside down on a clean surface. Remove 2 float hinge pins and lift out primary and secondary floats.

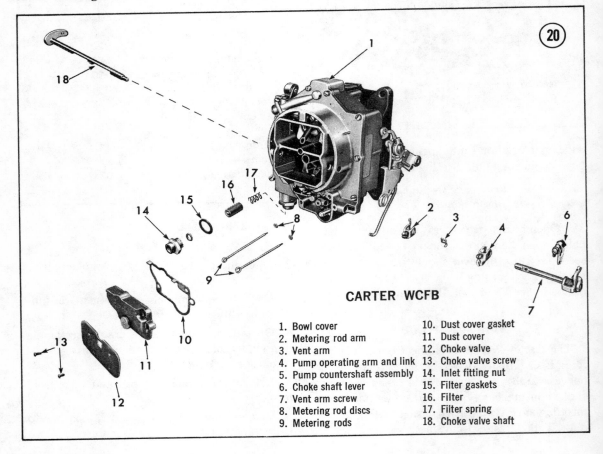

CARTER WCFB

1. Bowl cover
2. Metering rod arm
3. Vent arm
4. Pump operating arm and link
5. Pump countershaft assembly
6. Choke shaft lever
7. Vent arm screw
8. Metering rod discs
9. Metering rods
10. Dust cover gasket
11. Dust cover
12. Choke valve
13. Choke valve screw
14. Inlet fitting nut
15. Filter gaskets
16. Filter
17. Filter spring
18. Choke valve shaft

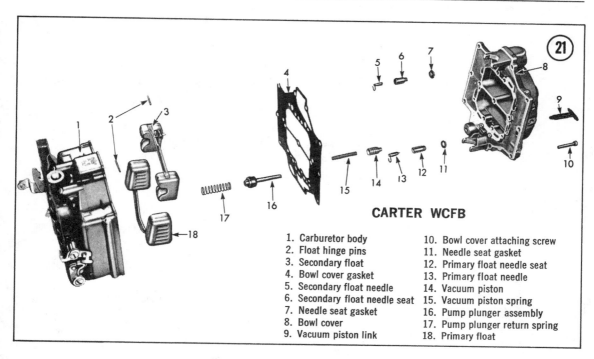

CARTER WCFB

1. Carburetor body
2. Float hinge pins
3. Secondary float
4. Bowl cover gasket
5. Secondary float needle
6. Secondary float needle seat
7. Needle seat gasket
8. Bowl cover
9. Vacuum piston link
10. Bowl cover attaching screw
11. Needle seat gasket
12. Primary float needle seat
13. Primary float needle
14. Vacuum piston
15. Vacuum piston spring
16. Pump plunger assembly
17. Pump plunger return spring
18. Primary float

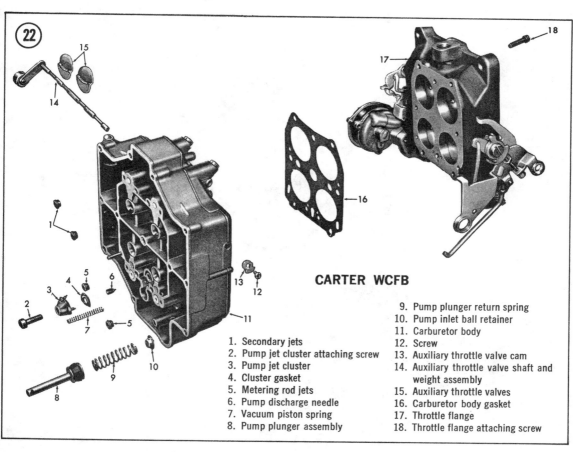

CARTER WCFB

1. Secondary jets
2. Pump jet cluster attaching screw
3. Pump jet cluster
4. Cluster gasket
5. Metering rod jets
6. Pump discharge needle
7. Vacuum piston spring
8. Pump plunger assembly
9. Pump plunger return spring
10. Pump inlet ball retainer
11. Carburetor body
12. Screw
13. Auxiliary throttle valve cam
14. Auxiliary throttle valve shaft and weight assembly
15. Auxiliary throttle valves
16. Carburetor body gasket
17. Throttle flange
18. Throttle flange attaching screw

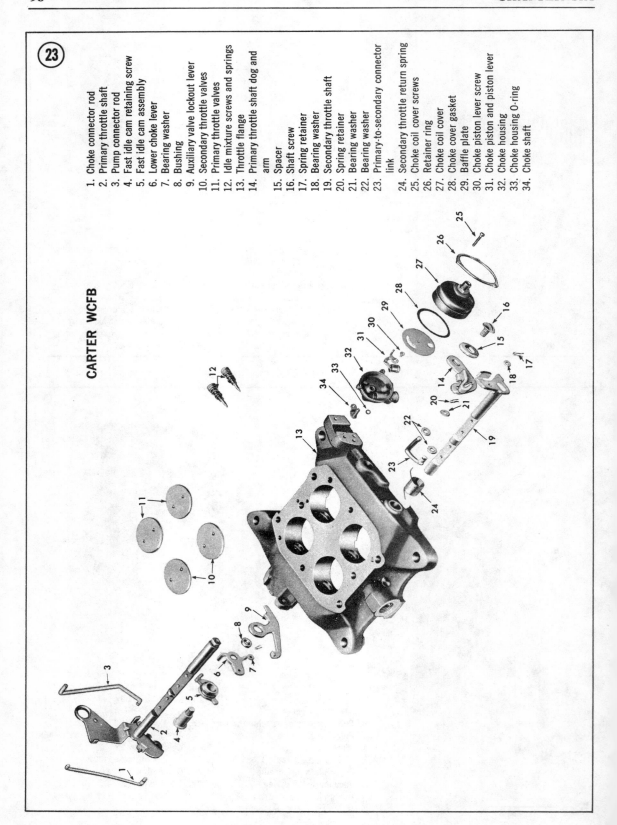

CARTER WCFB

1. Choke connector rod
2. Primary throttle shaft
3. Pump connector rod
4. Fast idle cam retaining screw
5. Fast idle cam assembly
6. Lower choke lever
7. Bearing washer
8. Bushing
9. Auxiliary valve lockout lever
10. Secondary throttle valves
11. Primary throttle valves
12. Idle mixture screws and springs
13. Throttle flange
14. Primary throttle shaft dog and arm
15. Spacer
16. Shaft screw
17. Spring retainer
18. Bearing washer
19. Secondary throttle shaft
20. Spring retainer
21. Bearing washer
22. Bearing washer
23. Primary-to-secondary connector link
24. Secondary throttle return spring
25. Choke coil cover screws
26. Retainer ring
27. Choke coil cover
28. Choke cover gasket
29. Baffle plate
30. Choke piston lever screw
31. Choke piston and piston lever
32. Choke housing
33. Choke housing O-ring
34. Choke shaft

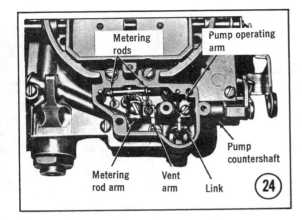

Metering rods — Pump operating arm — Pump countershaft — Metering rod arm — Vent arm — Link

(24)

12. Remove secondary float needle seat and gasket. Keep these 3 parts together to aid reassembly.

13. Remove primary float needle, seat, and gasket. Keep together to aid reassembly.

14. Lift pump plunger out of bowl cover and remove return spring from carburetor body. Place plunger in gasoline or kerosene to prevent leather from drying out.

15. Rotate vacuum piston 90° to disconnect from vacuum piston link. Remove link.

16. Remove vacuum piston spring.

17. Check fuel in bowl for contamination by dirt, water, grime, or other foreign matter. Drain fuel from bowl.

18. Remove pump jet cluster and gasket. See **Figure 27**.

(25)

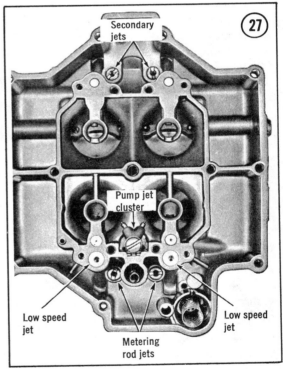

Secondary jets — Pump jet cluster — Low speed jet — Low speed jet — Metering rod jets

(27)

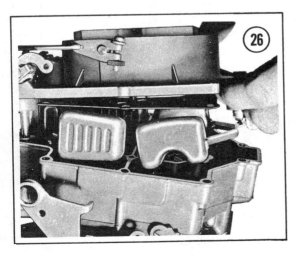

(26)

19. Invert carburetor. Remove small brass pump discharge needle.

20. Pry pump inlet ball retainer sideways with a 5/16 in. 6-point socket. Remove retainer and check ball.

21. Remove 2 primary metering rod jets. See Figure 27.

22. Remove 2 secondary main jets (Figure 27).

> NOTE: *Do not mix primary and secondary jets. They have different size openings.*

23. Remove 6 screws securing throttle flange and separate flange from carburetor body. Remove gasket.

> NOTE: *Further disassembly is not necessary or advisable unless throttle valves or shaft are worn or damaged. If necessary to replace these components, perform Step 24. Otherwise, proceed to Step 25.*

24. File staked ends of screws on auxiliary throttle valves. Remove screws and valves. Pull shaft out.

25. Remove 2 idle mixture screws and springs.

26. Remove throttle lever adjusting screw, washer, and spring.

27. Remove 3 choke cover retainer screws. Remove retainer, cover, gasket, and baffle plate.

28. Remove 3 choke housing screws.

29. Remove O-ring from vacuum opening.

30. Remove choke piston lever screw. Disassemble piston and 2 levers.

> NOTE: *Further disassembly is not necessary or advisable unless throttle valves or linkage are damaged. If necessary to replace these components, perform following steps.*

31. Remove fast idle cam screw, cam assembly, and lockout arm.

32. Remove primary-to-secondary connector rod pin, springs, and washers. Remove rod.

33. Remove primary throttle shaft screw and washer.

34. Remove primary throttle levers.

35. Unhook secondary throttle return spring.

36. File off staked ends of throttle valve screws. Remove screws and valves from bores.

37. Remove primary and secondary throttle shafts.

Cleaning and Inspection

Cleaning and inspection procedures for the Carter WCFB are identical to the Carter AFB procedures.

Assembly

Refer to Figures 20-23 for the following procedure.

> NOTE: *The first 3 steps apply only if throttle shafts were removed in Steps 31-37 of Disassembly procedure.*

1. Install primary and secondary shafts.

2. Install return spring on secondary shaft. Wind spring 1½ turns and hook onto secondary throttle lever as shown in **Figure 28**.

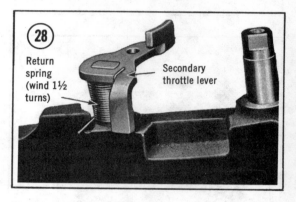

3. Install primary and secondary throttle valves in shafts with part number facing manifold side. Secure with new screws; use Loctite to prevent loosening.

4. Install 2 idle mixture screws with springs finger-tight. Back them out one turn.

5. Install throttle shaft dog spacer and screw on primary throttle shaft. Adjust parts relationships as shown in **Figure 29**.

6. Using a bearing washer on each side of the secondary throttle lever and inner arm, install connector rod (Figure 29). Secure rod with 2 spring retainers.

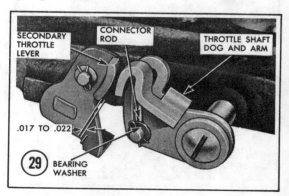

7. Assemble fast idle cam, lower choke lever, and auxiliary lockout lever on retaining screw. See **Figure 30**. Make certain tang of lower choke lever is installed under spring of fast idle cam as illustrated.

8. Position secondary lockout lever(**Figure 31**) against boss of throttle flange. Secure with retaining screw in fast idle cam assembly. Check that levers and cam operate freely.

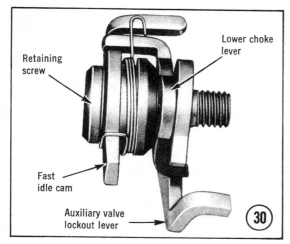

Figure 30

9. Install choke rod in fast idle cam. Secure with spring retainer. See Figure 31.

10. Install throttle lever adjusting screw, spring, and washer. See Figure 31.

11. Install choke piston on lever. Position assembly in choke housing.

12. Install choke shaft and lever assembly in

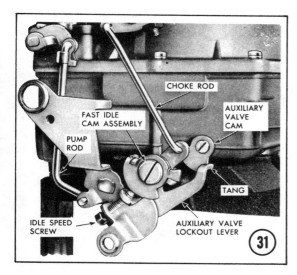

Figure 31

housing and attach to choke piston lever assembly with attaching screw.

13. Mount choke housing on throttle flange. Be certain that O-ring in vacuum passage stays in place.

14. Install baffle plate, cover gasket, cover and retainer.

15. If auxiliary throttle valves were disassembled in Step 9, *Disassembly* procedure, insert auxiliary throttle shaft into bowl and install throttle valves.

16. Install throttle flange on carburetor body with new gasket.

17. Install primary metering rod jets. See Figure 27.

> NOTE: *Primary jets have larger orifice than secondary jets.*

18. Install secondary jets.

19. Install pump inlet ball check and retainer.

20. Install brass pump discharge check needle. Be sure needle point is down.

21. Install pump discharge cluster assembly with new gasket.

22. Install vacuum piston spring in bore.

23. Install lower pump spring in pump cylinder. See Figure 21.

24. Place bowl cover upside down on bench and install primary and secondary needles or seats. Furthermore, if seat or needle requires replacement, replace both as a set.

> NOTE: *Steps 25-28 adjust float level.*

25. Temporarily install primary and secondary floats without bowl cover gasket.

26. Invert bowl cover. Check clearance between primary floats and bowl cover with gauge J-7665 or $1/8$ in. drill. See **Figure 32**. Bend float arms if necessary.

27. Repeat Step 26 on secondary floats with $1/4$ in. drill or gauge. Bend float arms if necessary.

28. Turn bowl cover right side up. Measure from lowest point of floats to the bottom of the bowl cover. This measurement should be 2 in. for primary and secondary floats. See **Figure 33**. Bend float tangs if necessary.

29. Remove floats and install new bowl cover gasket.

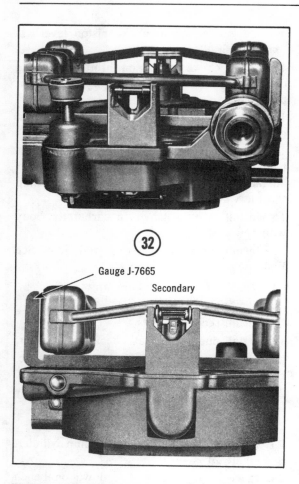

Gauge J-7665　　　　　　　　Secondary

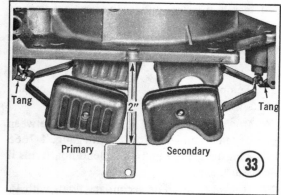

Tang　　　　　　2″　　　　　　Tang

Primary　　　　　Secondary

33. Fit bowl cover on carburetor body. Do not disturb float adjustment. Secure with 16 screws. Tighten all screws evenly starting with inner screws, then working around outer edge of carburetor.

34. Use metering rod to position metering rod discs over holes in bowl cover. Countersunk side of disc goes down. Catch metering rod spring loop with lower end of rod before rod is inserted, then twist "eye" of rod onto vacuum piston link assembly.

35. Place metering rod arm in place.

36. Slide pump countershaft through operating arm and metering rod arm.

> NOTE: *Be certain that metering rod operating arm is positioned in slot in vacuum piston link.*

37. Tighten pump arm screw.

38. Install vent arm with screw.

39. Install throttle connector rod into throttle lever while holding lever in closed position. Secure with spring and retainer.

40. Install throttle connector rod in pump countershaft lever and secure with clip.

> NOTE: *Steps 41-44 are required only if choke shaft and valves were disassembled.*

41. Install choke shaft through bowl cover.

42. Install choke valve on shaft with "C" on valve facing the top of the carburetor. Center valve and install new screws. Use Loctite to keep them from loosening.

43. Make sure that neither valve nor shaft bind in any position.

44. Install choke operating lever on shaft. Tighten screw just enough to permit lever to be moved.

45. Install choke connector rod in choke operating lever and choke lower lever. Secure lower end with pin spring.

46. Install fuel filter, inlet fitting, gaskets, and filter spring in primary side.

> NOTE: *Steps 47-49 adjust accelerator pump.*

47. Back out idle speed screw.

30. Install vacuum piston link and piston. Lip on link must face air horn.

31. Insert pump shaft through bowl cover. Secure with link and pump arm assembly.

32. Reinstall primary and secondary float assemblies. Float tension spring goes on secondary assemblies.

48. Hold gauge J-813-3 (**Figure 34**) on dust cover boss.

49. Visually check relationship between top of flat of pump arm and top of gauge. These surfaces should be parallel. Bend pump rod (Figure 34) if necessary.

> NOTE: *Steps 50-53 adjust the metering rods.*

50. Back out throttle lever adjusting screw to allow throttle valves to seat fully.

51. Loosen screw in metering rod arm. See **Figure 35**.

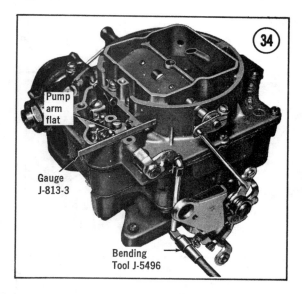

Pump arm flat

Gauge J-813-3

Bending Tool J-5496

34

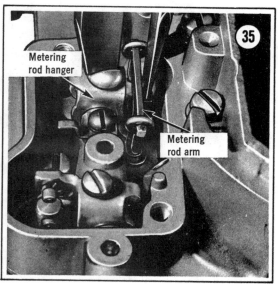

Metering rod hanger

Metering rod arm

35

52. Press metering rod arm down until rods bottom. Rotate metering rod arm upward until arm lightly contacts hanger. Lock arm in this position by tightening screw.

53. Install dust cover over metering rods with new gasket.

> NOTE: *Steps 54-56 adjust fast idle.*

54. Loosen choke lever clamp screw on choke shaft. See **Figure 36**.

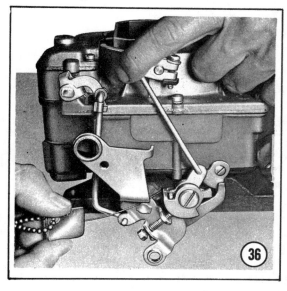

36

55. Insert 0.020 in. wire gauge between lip of fast idle cam and boss of throttle flange. See Figure 36.

56. Hold choke valve tightly closed. Pull choke shaft lever upward to eliminate all slack from linkage. Tighten screw in choke lever clamp.

> NOTE: *Steps 57-58 adjust bowl vapor venting.*

57. Back out throttle lever stop screw to allow throttle valves to seat fully closed.

58. Insert 1/16 in. gauge between lower edge of vapor vent and well in dust cover. See **Figure 37**. Remove dust cover and bend vent arm tang if necessary.

> NOTE: *Steps 59-60 adjust unloader.*

59. Open throttle valves wide open with linkage.

60. Measure distance between inboard edge of choke valve and center wall of bowl cover with

3/16 in. gauge. See **Figure 38**. Bend unloader tang if necessary to achieve 3/16 in. measurement.

NOTE: *Steps 61-64 adjust secondary throttle lever.*

61. Operate throttle linkage to wide open position. Primary valves (visible from bottom) should be wide open. Secondary valves must be within 4-7° of wide open.

62. To adjust primary valves, bend connector rod at upper angle. See **Figure 39**.

63. To adjust secondary valves, hold valves open 5½° with tool J-7665 as shown in **Figure 40**. Bend tang on secondary throttle dog (shoe) if necessary to achieve proper angle.

64. With throttle valves tightly closed, there should be 0.017-0.022 in. clearance between positive closing shoes on primary and secondary throttle levers. Bend shoe on primary lever, if necessary.

NOTE: *Steps 65-66 adjust auxiliary valve lockout.*

65. Close choke valve. Ensure that tang on auxiliary valve lockout lever should engage in auxiliary valve cam. See **Figure 41**.

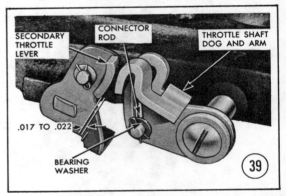

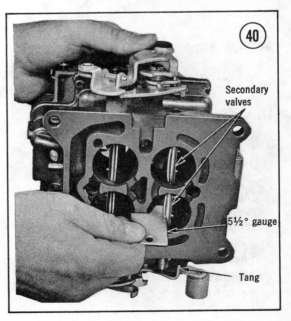

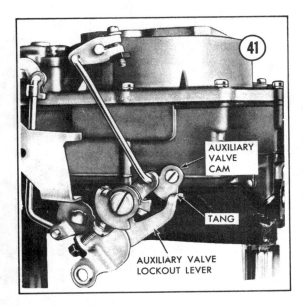

66. Open choke valve fully. Make sure that tang disengages lockout lever from cam so auxiliary valve operates freely.

HOLLEY 4150 AND 4160 CARBURETORS

These 4-barrel, 2-stage carburetors consist of 7 subassemblies: throttle body; main body; primary and secondary fuel bowls; primary and secondary metering bodies, and the secondary throttle operating assembly.

The primary and secondary metering bodies on the Model 4150 are similar. The primary metering body on the Model 4160 is similar to the ones on the 4150, but the secondary metering body is different. The secondary throttle operating assembly on both models is vacuum operated.

Table 1 lists usage of this carburetor. **Table 4** lists specifications.

Disassembly

The carburetor is disassembled into subassemblies; then each subassembly is disassembled separately. See **Figures 42 and 43** for initial disassembly.

1. Loosen fuel inlet fitting, fuel bowl sight plugs, and needle/seat assembly lock screws.

2. Remove 4 primary fuel bowl screws and remove bowl, metering body, splash shield, and gaskets.

3. Remove fuel tube if so equipped.

4. Remove 4 secondary fuel bowl screws. Remove fuel bowl.

5a. On 4150 carburetors, remove metering body and gasket.

5b. On 4160 carburetors, remove 6 secondary metering body screws. Remove metering body assembly and fuel bowl gasket.

6. Disconnect secondary throttle operating rod at throttle lever.

7. Remove secondary throttle operating assembly and gasket from main body.

8. Disconnect vacuum break hose at vacuum break.

9. Remove throttle body screws and separate throttle body from main body.

> NOTE: *Steps 10-14 disassemble the fuel bowls. Refer to* **Figure 44** *for these steps.*

10. Remove float hinge pin retainer. Slide float from bowl.

11. Turn adjusting nut on needle and seat assembly counterclockwise. Remove needle and seat assembly.

12. Remove sight plug and gasket.

13. Remove inlet fitting, fuel filter, spring, and gaskets.

14. On primary bowl only, remove air vent assembly. Remove pump diaphragm screws, cover assembly, diaphragm, and spring.

> NOTE: *Steps 15-17 disassemble metering bodies. Refer to* **Figures 45 and 46** *for these steps.*

15. On 4150 primary and secondary metering bodies and 4160 primary metering body, remove main metering jets with a *wide* blade screwdriver. Remove power valves with a 1 inch 12-point socket.

16. On 4150 primary only, remove vacuum fitting, idle mixture screws, and seals.

17. On 4160 secondary only, remove plate and gasket from metering body.

> NOTE: *Steps 18-19 disassemble secondary throttle operating assembly. See* **Figure 47**.

Table 4   HOLLEY 4150/4160

Year	1966	1966	1966	1967 w/o AIR	1967 w/o AIR	1967 w/AIR	1967 w/AIR	1968	1969	1971	1972
Holley model number	4150	4160	4160	4160	4160	4160	4160	4150	4150	4150	4150
Engine displacement	427	327	427	327	427	327	427	427	350	350, 454	350
Float level Primary	0.350"	0.170"	0.170"	0.170"	0.170"	0.170"	0.170"	0.350"	0.350"	centered	centered
Float level Secondary	0.450"	0.300"	0.300"	0.300"	0.300"	0.300"	0.300"	0.500"	0.500"	centered	centered
Accelerator pump	0.015"	0.015"	0.015"	0.015"	0.015"	0.015"	0.015"	0.015"	0.015"	0.015"	0.015"
Idle vent	0.065"	0.065"	0.065"	0.065"	0.065"	0.065"	0.065"	0.065"	—	—	—
Fast idle Measurement	0.025"	0.035"	0.035"	0.035"	0.035"	0.035"	0.035"	0.025"	0.025"	0.025"	0.025"
Fast idle rpm	2,200	2,200	2,000	2,000	2,200	2,000	2,200	2,200	2,200	2,200	2,350
Vacuum break	0.350"	0.170"	0.180"	0.190"	0.175"	0.175"	0.175"	0.350"	0.300"	0.350"	0.350"
Unloader	0.350"	0.260"	0.260"	0.265"	0.265"	0.265"	0.265"	0.350"	0.350"	0.350"	0.350"
Main metering jet Primary	#70	#65	#65	#65	#65	#63	#67	#69	#68	#70	#68
Main metering jet Secondary	0.076"	0.076"	0.076"	0.076"	0.073"	0.076"	0.073"	#76	#76	#76	#73
Throttle bore Primary	1-11/16"	1-9/16"	1-9/16"	1-9/16"	1-9/16"	1-9/16"	1-9/16"	1-11/16"	1-11/16"	1-11/16"	1-11/16"
Throttle bore Secondary	1-11/16"	1-9/16"	1-9/16"	1-9/16"	1-9/16"	1-9/16"	1-9/16"	1-11/16"	1-11/16"	1-11/16"	1-11/16"

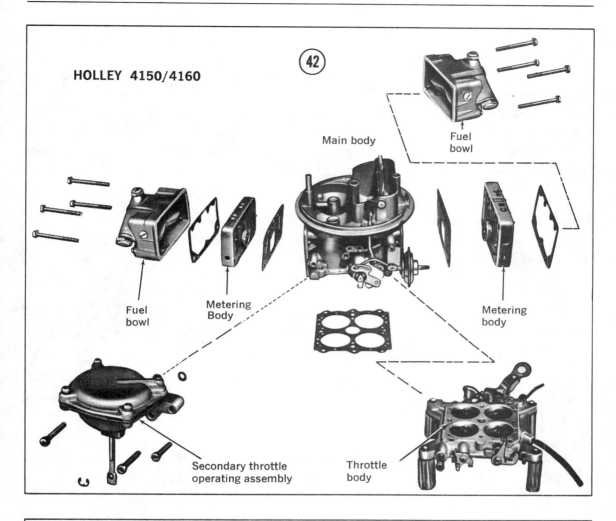

HOLLEY 4150/4160

(42)

Main body

Fuel bowl

Fuel bowl

Metering Body

Metering body

Secondary throttle operating assembly

Throttle body

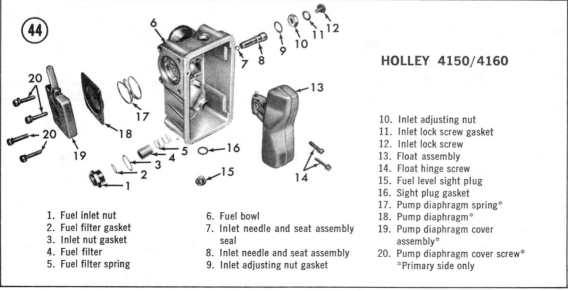

(44)

HOLLEY 4150/4160

1. Fuel inlet nut
2. Fuel filter gasket
3. Inlet nut gasket
4. Fuel filter
5. Fuel filter spring

6. Fuel bowl
7. Inlet needle and seat assembly seal
8. Inlet needle and seat assembly
9. Inlet adjusting nut gasket

10. Inlet adjusting nut
11. Inlet lock screw gasket
12. Inlet lock screw
13. Float assembly
14. Float hinge screw
15. Fuel level sight plug
16. Sight plug gasket
17. Pump diaphragm spring*
18. Pump diaphragm*
19. Pump diaphragm cover assembly*
20. Pump diaphragm cover screw*
   *Primary side only

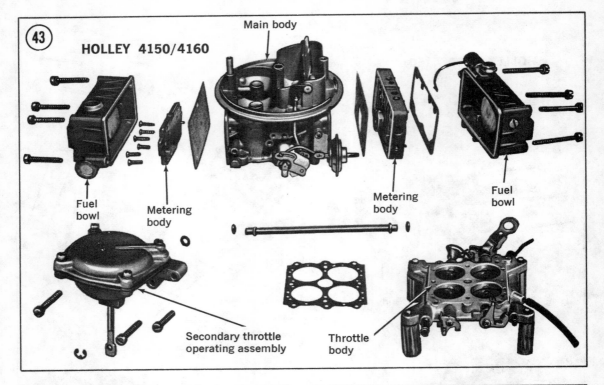

(43) HOLLEY 4150/4160

Main body

Fuel bowl

Metering body

Metering body

Fuel bowl

Secondary throttle operating assembly

Throttle body

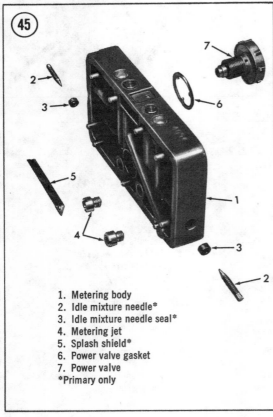

(45)

7

2

3

6

5

1

4

3

2

1. Metering body
2. Idle mixture needle*
3. Idle mixture needle seal*
4. Metering jet
5. Splash shield*
6. Power valve gasket
7. Power valve
*Primary only

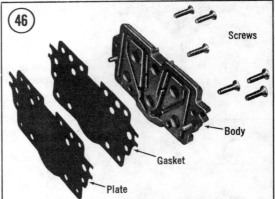

(46)

Screws

Body

Gasket

Plate

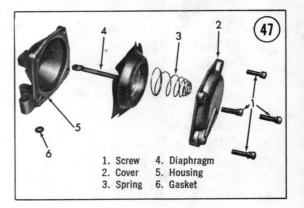

4

3

2

(47)

1

5

6

1. Screw   4. Diaphragm
2. Cover   5. Housing
3. Spring   6. Gasket

18. Remove diaphragm cover.

19. Remove spring and diaphragm.

> NOTE: *Steps 20-22 disassemble main body. See* **Figure 48.**

20. Remove choke vacuum break. Disconnect link at choke lever.

21. Remove choke lever and fast idle cam.

22. Remove pump discharge nozzle and gasket. Invert body to remove pump discharge needle valve.

> NOTE: *Steps 23-31 disassemble throttle body. See* **Figure 49.** *Normally, the throttle body should not be disassembled unless parts are worn or damaged.*

23. Remove pump operating lever assembly. Disassemble the spring, bolt, and nut only if necessary.

24. Remove idle speed screw and spring.

25. Remove diaphragm lever from secondary throttle shaft and fast idle cam lever from primary throttle shaft.

26. Disconnect throttle connecting link from shaft levers.

27. File off staked ends of throttle plate screws. Remove screws and plates.

28. Slide shafts out.

29. Remove secondary throttle stop screw.

30. Remove accelerator pump cam from throttle lever.

31. Remove vacuum break hose from body.

Cleaning and Inspection

The most frequent causes of carburetor trouble are dirt, gum, and water in the carburetor. Carefully clean and inspect all parts before assembling carburetor.

1. Clean all parts except choke housing and accelerator pump plunger in solvent. Special carburetor cleaners available from any auto parts supplier work best.

2. Check bearing surfaces of all operating levers, shafts, and castings for excessive wear.

3. Check floats for dents. Immerse floats in hot water. If bubbles appear, float is leaking and the float must be *replaced*. Do not attempt to solder the hole. This increases float weight and causes high fuel level.

4. Check pump diaphragm for damage.

5. Check float needles and seats for burrs and ridges. If present, replace needle and seat; never replace either alone.

6. Inspect edges of throttle valves for nicks or gouges. Replace if necessary.

7. Check secondary throttle operating diaphragm for free operation and leakage. To do this, push diaphragm arm up and cover vacuum passage with thumb. Diaphragm should stay up. Remove thumb and diaphragm rod should move down readily.

8. After washing in solvent, clear all passages in metering bodies and main body with compressed air.

Assembly

The assembly procedure consists of first assembling each subassembly, making adjustments, then assembling subassemblies together.

> NOTE: *Steps 1-10 assemble throttle body if it was disassembled. Refer to Figure 49.*

1. Install secondary throttle stop screw.

2. Install throttle shafts in body. Roll new plastic bushings on shaft to shape them for easier installation.

3. Install throttle valves on shaft with identification numbers down. Do not tighten screws.

4. Center throttle valves on shaft by holding valves closed. Tighten screws; use Loctite to prevent loosening.

5. Install throttle connecting link to throttle shaft levers.

6. Install fast idle cam lever on primary throttle shaft. Install diaphragm lever on secondary throttle shaft.

7. Install idle speed screw and spring. Turn idle speed screw clockwise until it contacts throttle lever. Turn additional 1½ turns.

8. Install accelerator pump cam on throttle lever.

9. Assemble and install pump operating lever assembly.

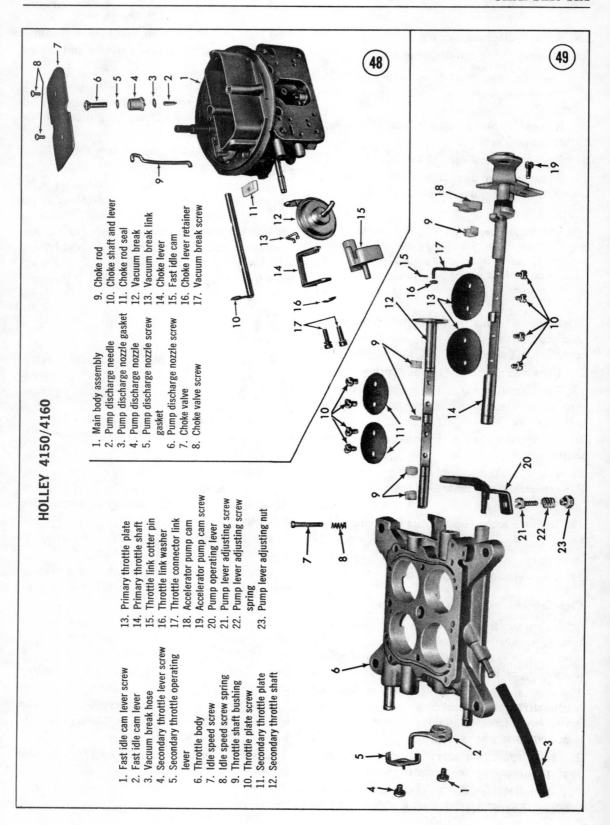

HOLLEY 4150/4160

1. Main body assembly
2. Pump discharge needle
3. Pump discharge nozzle gasket
4. Pump discharge nozzle
5. Pump discharge nozzle screw gasket
6. Pump discharge nozzle screw
7. Choke valve
8. Choke valve screw
9. Choke rod
10. Choke shaft and lever
11. Choke rod seal
12. Vacuum break
13. Vacuum break link
14. Choke lever
15. Fast idle cam
16. Choke lever retainer
17. Vacuum break screw

1. Fast idle cam lever screw
2. Fast idle cam lever
3. Vacuum break hose
4. Secondary throttle lever screw
5. Secondary throttle operating lever
6. Throttle body
7. Idle speed screw
8. Idle speed screw spring
9. Throttle shaft bushing
10. Throttle plate screw
11. Secondary throttle plate
12. Secondary throttle shaft
13. Primary throttle plate
14. Primary throttle shaft
15. Throttle link cotter pin
16. Throttle link washer
17. Throttle connector link
18. Accelerator pump cam
19. Accelerator pump cam screw
20. Pump operating lever
21. Pump lever adjusting screw
22. Pump lever adjusting screw spring
23. Pump lever adjusting nut

10. Install vacuum break hose on fitting.

NOTE: *Steps 11-17 assemble main body. Refer to Figure 48. Steps 13-15 apply only if these parts were disassembled.*

11. Install pump discharge valve.

12. Install pump discharge nozzle. Use new gaskets.

13. Install choke rod and seal.

14. Install choke shaft and connect upper end of choke rod.

15. Install choke valve on shaft. Hold valve closed while tightening screws to keep valve centered. Use Loctite on screws to prevent loosening.

16. Install choke lever and fast idle cam.

17. Connect vacuum break link to choke lever, then install vacuum break.

NOTE: *Steps 18-19 assemble secondary throttle operating assembly. See Figure 47.*

18. Install diaphragm assembly and spring in housing.

19. Install diaphragm cover and tighten securely.

NOTE: *Steps 20-22 assemble metering bodies. Refer to Figures 45 and 46.*

20. On all except 4160 secondary, install power valve with a new gasket. Tighten securely with a one in. 12-point socket. Install main metering jets with a wide blade screwdriver.

21. On 4150 and 4160 primaries only, install idle mixture screws. Turn all the way in *lightly* to seat them, then back off one turn.

22. On 4160 secondary, install metering plate over metering body with a new gasket. Tighten screws securely.

NOTE: *Steps 23-29 assemble fuel bowls and set float adjustment. Steps apply to primary and secondary bowls unless otherwise specified (Figure 44).*

23. Install sight plugs with new gaskets.

24. Install inlet needle and seats with new gaskets. Leave locknuts loose.

25. Install inlet fitting, fuel filter spring, and gaskets.

26. Assemble spring to float, slide float into bowl and install float hinge pin retainer.

27. Install inlet baffle.

28. On primary bowl only, install pump spring and diaphragm. Install air vent valve assembly.

29. Invert each fuel bowl. Turn adjustable needle seat until top of float is 0.170 in. (primary float) or 0.300 in. (secondary float) from top of fuel bowl. See **Figure 50**.

NOTE: *Steps 30-37 are final assembly of individual subassemblies.*

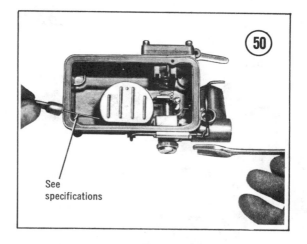

See specifications

30. Invert main body. Install throttle body with new gasket.

31. Install secondary throttle operating assembly on main body with new gasket.

32. Install secondary metering body onto main body with new gasket. Secure 4160 metering body with 6 screws.

33. Install secondary fuel bowl with gaskets under screw heads.

34. Install primary metering body onto main body with new gasket.

35. Lubricate O-rings and install on very ends of fuel tube (if so equipped). O-rings will roll into position when installed. Install fuel tube end into secondary bowl inlet.

36. Install splash shield, new gasket, and primary fuel bowl. Align fuel tube into inlet (if so equipped).

37. Align pump lever under operating lever

duration spring. Install fuel bowl retaining screws with new gaskets under heads.

> NOTE: *Steps 38-39 adjust secondary throttle valve stop.*

38. Back off stop screw (see **Figure 51**) until throttle plates are fully closed.

39. Turn stop screw in until it just touches throttle lever. Turn in additional ½ turn.

> NOTE: *Steps 40-43 adjust air vent. See* **Figure 52.**

40. Back off idle speed screw until throttle valves are fully closed.

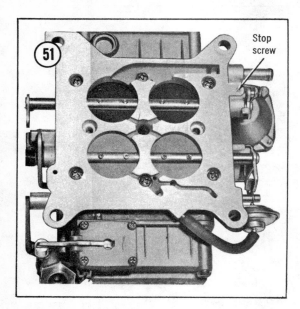

Stop screw

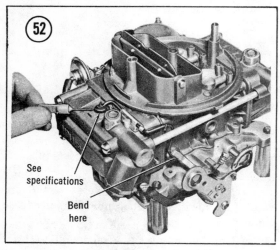

See specifications

Bend here

41. Check clearance between choke valve and seat. Clearance should be 0.065 in.

42. Bend rod shown in Figure 52 to adjust.

43. Turn idle screw in until it just touches throttle lever. Screw in additional 3 turns.

> NOTE: *Steps 44-46 adjust the fast idle cam.*

44. Open throttle slightly. Close fast idle lever against top step of cam.

45. Check clearance between throttle plate and bore as shown in **Figure 53**. The clearance should be 0.025 in. on 4150 carburetors; 0.035 in. on 4160 carburetors.

46. Bend fast idle lever to adjust.

> NOTE: *Steps 47-50 adjust accelerator pump.*

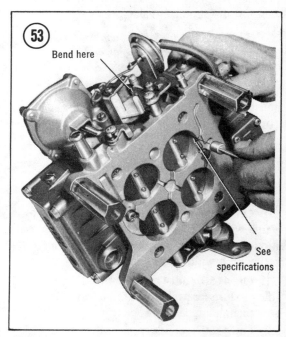

Bend here

See specifications

47. Hold throttle lever wide open with rubber band. See **Figure 54**.

48. Hold pump lever fully down.

49. Measure clearance between spring adjusting nut and arm of pump lever. Clearance should be 0.015 in. See Figure 54.

50. Turn nut or screw as required to adjust.

> NOTE: *Steps 51-54 adjust vacuum break.*

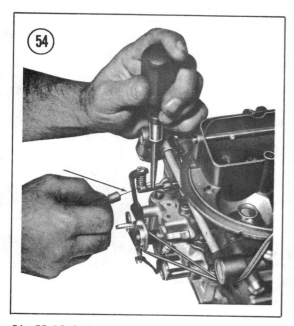

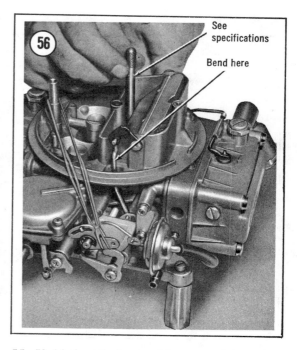

51. Hold choke valve closed with a rubber band.

52. Hold vacuum break in against stop.

53. Measure distance between lower edge of choke valve and main body. See **Figure 55**. Proper distance is shown in specifications.

54. Bend vacuum break link to adjust.

> NOTE: *Steps 55-58 adjust choke un-loader. See* **Figure 56.**

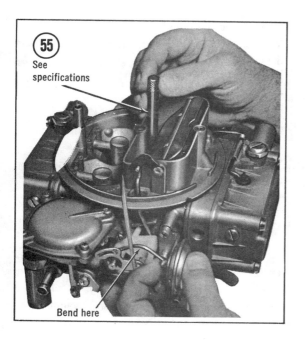

55. Hold throttle lever wide open with rubber band.

56. Hold choke valve toward closed position against unloader tang of throttle shaft.

57. Measure opening between lower edge of choke valve and main body. See specifications for proper measurement.

58. Bend choke rod (Figure 56) to adjust.

HOLLEY 2300 and 2300C

Some Corvettes use 3 Holley 2-barrels mounted on a common manifold. See Table 1. One Holley 2300C primary carburetor is used in the center and 2 Holley 2300 secondary carburetors are mounted fore and aft.

The Holley 2300 secondary carburetors contain all normal regulatory systems, but do not contain choke, power enrichment, or accelerator pump systems found in the 2300C primary carburetor. Primary carburetor throttles are mechanically operated while secondaries are vacuum operated. See **Table 5** for specifications.

Removal/Installation

1. Remove air cleaner, gasket, and stud.

2. Disconnect vacuum, fuel, and choke pipes at carburetor.

Table 5   HOLLEY 2300

	1967 427	1968 427	1969 427
Float level			
Primary	0.350"	0.350"	0.350"
Secondary (400, 435 hp manual)	0.350"	0.350"	0.350"
Secondary (400 hp automatic)	0.350"	0.500"	0.350"
Accelerator pump	——	0.015"	0.015"
Fast idle			
Measurement	0.025"	0.025"	0.025"
rpm	2,200	2,200	2,200
Vacuum break (primary only)	0.250"	0.250"	0.250"
Unloader (primary only)	0.275"	0.275"	0.275"
Main metering jet			
Primary (except 400 hp automatic)	#64	#64	#63
Primary (400 hp automatic)	#62	#62	#61
Secondary	0.076"	0.076"	#76
Throttle bore			
Primary	1½"	1½"	1½"
Secondary	1¾"	1¾"	1¾"

3. On automatic models, disconnect transmission control rod from throttle lever.

4. On models with positive crankcase ventilation (PCV), disconnect ventilation hose at valve on carburetor base.

5. Disconnect accelerator rod and throttle return spring at carburetor.

6. Remove mounting nuts and lift carburetor from manifold.

7. Installation is the reverse of these steps. Make certain that base of carburetor and manifold flange are clean.

Disassembly

The carburetor is disassembled into subassemblies, then each subassembly is further disassembled separately. Refer to **Figures 57 and 58** for initial disassembly.

1. Loosen fuel inlet fitting, fuel bowl sight plugs, and needle/seat lock screw.

2. Remove fuel bowl screws, fuel bowl, metering body (2300C carburetor), splash shield, and gasket.

3. On 2300 carburetors, remove metering block screws; remove metering body and gasket.

4. On 2300C carburetors, disconnect vacuum break hose at vacuum break.

5. On 2300 carburetors, disconnect secondary diaphragm housing assembly at throttle lever. Remove diaphragm housing assembly from carburetor body.

6. Remove throttle body from main body.

NOTE: *Steps 7-12 disassemble fuel bowl. Refer to* **Figures 59 and 60.**

7. Remove fuel inlet baffle.

8. Remove float hinge screws and remove float.

9. Loosen inlet needle and seat lock screw. Turn adjusting nut counterclockwise to remove needle/seat assembly.

10. Remove sight plug and gasket.

11. Remove fuel inlet fitting, fuel filter, spring, and gasket.

12. On 2300C carburetor, remove pump cover, diaphragm, and spring.

NOTE: *Steps 13-15 disassemble metering body. Refer to* **Figures 61 and 62.**

13. On 2300C carburetor, remove main metering jets with a *wide* blade screwdriver. Remove power valve with a one in. 12-point socket.

14. On 2300C carburetor, remove vacuum fitting and idle mixture needles and seals.

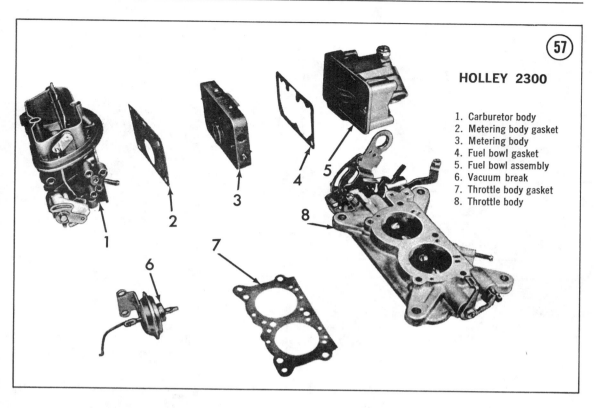

(57)

HOLLEY 2300

1. Carburetor body
2. Metering body gasket
3. Metering body
4. Fuel bowl gasket
5. Fuel bowl assembly
6. Vacuum break
7. Throttle body gasket
8. Throttle body

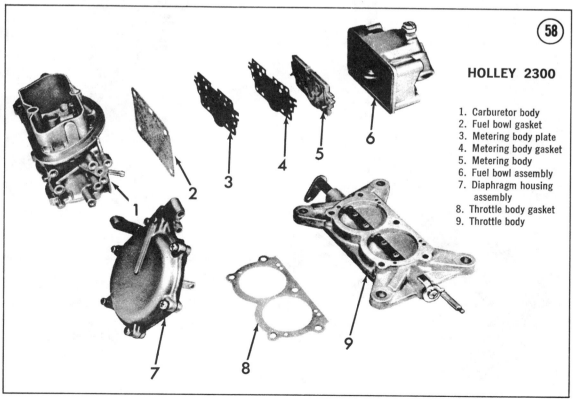

(58)

HOLLEY 2300

1. Carburetor body
2. Fuel bowl gasket
3. Metering body plate
4. Metering body gasket
5. Metering body
6. Fuel bowl assembly
7. Diaphragm housing assembly
8. Throttle body gasket
9. Throttle body

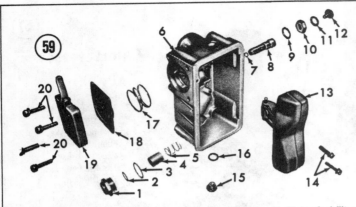

59

7. Inlet needle and seat assembly
   seal
8. Inlet needle and seat assembly
9. Inlet adjusting nut gasket
10. Inlet adjusting nut
11. Inlet lock screw gasket
12. Inlet lock screw
13. Float assembly
14. Float hinge screw
15. Fuel level sight plug
16. Sight plug gasket
17. Pump diaphragm spring
18. Pump diaphragm
19. Pump diaphragm cover
    assembly
20. Pump diaphragm cover screw

1. Fuel inlet nut　　3. Inlet nut gasket　　5. Spring fuel filter
2. Fuel filter gasket　4. Fuel filter　　　　6. Fuel bowl

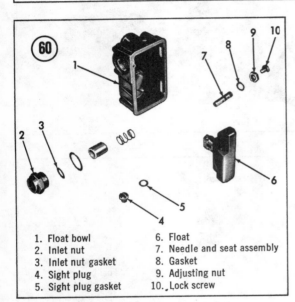

60

1. Float bowl
2. Inlet nut
3. Inlet nut gasket
4. Sight plug
5. Sight plug gasket
6. Float
7. Needle and seat assembly
8. Gasket
9. Adjusting nut
10. Lock screw

61

1. Metering body
2. Idle mixture needle
3. Idle mixture needle seal
4. Metering jet
5. Splash shield
6. Power valve gasket
7. Power valve

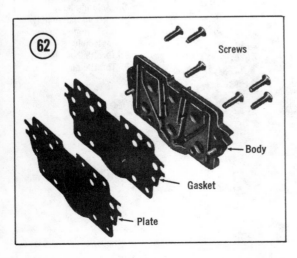

62

Screws

Body

Gasket

Plate

15. On 2300 carburetor, remove plate and gasket from secondary metering body.

NOTE: *Steps 16-17 disassemble secondary throttle operating assembly. See* **Figure 63.**

16. Remove diaphragm cover.

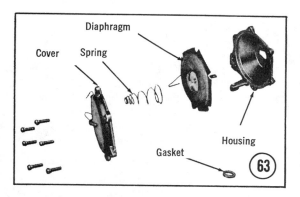

17. Remove spring and diaphragm.

NOTE: *Steps 18-22 disassemble main body of 2300C (primary) carburetor only. Main body of 2300 (secondary) carburetor cannot be disassembled. Refer to* **Figure 64.**

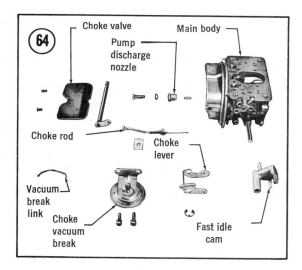

18. Remove vacuum break from body and disconnect link at choke lever.

19. Remove choke lever and fast idle cam.

20. Remove pump discharge nozzle and gasket. Invert body to remove check valve.

NOTE: *Further disassembly is not necessary or advisable unless throttle valve or shaft parts require replacement. If necessary, perform remaining steps. See* **Figure 65.**

21. File off staked ends of throttle valve screws. Remove screws and valves. Slide shaft out of body.

22. On 2300C carburetor, remove accelerator pump cam from throttle lever shaft.

Cleaning and Inspection

The most frequent causes of carburetor trouble are dirt, gum, and water in the carburetor. Carefully clean and inspect all parts before assembling carburetor.

1. Clean all parts except choke housing and accelerator pump plunger in solvent. Special carburetor cleaners available from any auto parts supplier work best.

2. Check bearing surfaces of all operating levers, shafts, and castings for excessive wear.

3. Check floats for dents. Immerse floats in hot water. If bubbles appear, float is leaking and the float must be *replaced*. Do not attempt to solder the hole. This increases float weight and causes high fuel level.

4. Check pump diaphragm for damage.

5. Check float needles and seats for burrs and ridges. If present, replace needle and seat; never replace either alone.

6. Inspect edges of throttle valves for nicks or gouges. Replace if necessary.

7. Check secondary throttle operating diaphragm for free operation and leakage. To do this, push diaphragm arm up and cover vacuum passage with thumb. Diaphragm should stay up. Remove thumb and diaphragm rod should move down readily.

8. After washing in solvent, clear all passages in the metering bodies and main body with compressed air.

Assembly

Assembly procedure involves assembly of components in each subassembly, then final assembly of subassemblies into a complete carburetor.

NOTE: *Steps 1-7 assemble throttle body if disassembled earlier.*

1. On 2300C carburetor, install accelerator cam on throttle lever shaft.

2. Install throttle shaft in throttle body.

3. Install throttle valves with numbers down. Hold valves closed to center them while tighten-

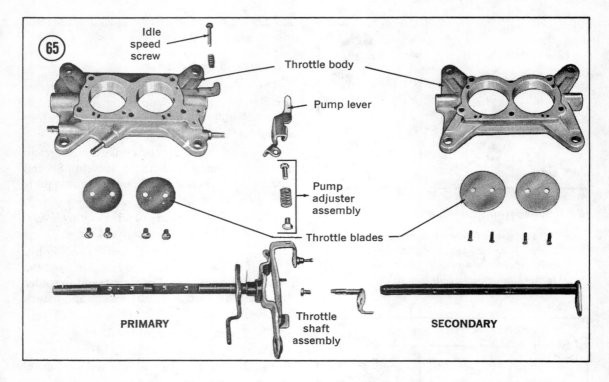

Idle speed screw
Throttle body
Pump lever
Pump adjuster assembly
Throttle blades
PRIMARY
Throttle shaft assembly
SECONDARY

ing screws. Use Loctite to keep screws from loosening.

4. On 2300 carburetor, install throttle diaphragm lever.

5. On 2300C carburetor, install fast idle cam lever.

6. Install idle speed screw and spring on 2300C carburetor.

7. Install accelerator pump actuating lever assembly.

NOTE: *Steps 8-13 assemble 2300C main body.*

8. Install pump discharge valve and nozzle.

9. Install choke rod and seal.

10. Install choke shaft and connect upper end of choke rod.

11. Install choke valve on choke shaft. Hold valve closed while tightening screws. Use Loctite to keep screws from loosening.

12. Install choke lever and fast idle cam.

13. Connect vacuum link to choke lever, then install vacuum break.

NOTE: *Steps 14-15 assemble secondary diaphragm housing assembly.*

14. Install diaphragm and spring in housing.

15. Install diaphragm cover and tighten screws.

NOTE: *Steps 16-17 assemble metering body.*

16. On 2300C carburetor, install vacuum fitting, idle mixture needles, and new needle seals. Turn needles until they rest *lightly* on their seats; back off one turn.

17. On 2300 carburetor, install metering plate on metering body with new gasket.

NOTE: *Steps 18-24 assemble fuel bowl, adjust float, and install vacuum fitting.*

18. Install fuel lever sight plug with new gasket.

19. Install fuel inlet needle and seat with new gasket. Leave lock screw loose.

20. Install fuel inlet fitting, fuel filter, spring, and new gasket.

21. Place fuel float in bowl and install float hinge screws.

22. Install fuel inlet baffle.

23. On 2300C carburetor, install accelerator pump spring, diaphragm, and cover.

24. Invert fuel bowl. Turn adjustable needle

until clearance between top of float and top of fuel bowl is as specified in Table 5 (**Figure 66**). Snug lock screw down, but do not tighten.

NOTE: *Steps 25-29 assemble various subassemblies into complete carburetor.*

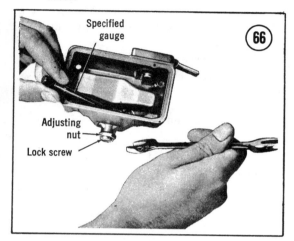

25. Invert main body and install throttle body.

26. On 2300 carburetors, install throttle operating assembly with new gasket. Connect rod to throttle lever.

27. On 2300C carburetor, connect vacuum break hose to vacuum break.

28. On 2300 carburetor, install metering body on main body with new gaskets and 6 screws. Install fuel bowl with new gaskets under screw heads.

29. On 2300C carburetors, assemble fuel bowl, fuel bowl gasket, metering body, and metering body gasket. Hold in alignment with mounting screws. Install assembly on main body. Use new gaskets under screw heads.

NOTE: *Steps 30-32 are preliminary adjustment.*

30. Turn idle screw in until it just touches the throttle lever. Turn in an additional 1½ turns.

31. Open throttle slightly. Close fast idle lever against top step of fast idle cam.

32. Insert 0.025 in. wire gauge where shown in **Figure 67**. Bend fast idle lever as shown to establish proper clearance.

NOTE: *Step 33 adjusts accelerator pump.*

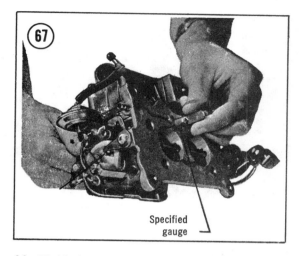

33. Hold throttle lever wide open with rubber band. Hold pump lever down. Measure clearance between spring adjusting nut and arm of pump lever. See **Figure 68**. Clearance should be 0.015 in. Adjust by turning nut or screw as necessary to establish proper clearance.

NOTE: *Steps 34-37 adjust vacuum break on 2300C carburetor.*

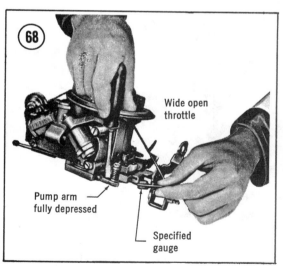

34. Hold choke valve closed with a rubber band.

35. Hold vacuum break in against stop.

36. Measure distance between lower edge of choke valve and main body. See **Figure 69**. Proper distance is shown in specifications.

37. Bend vacuum break link to adjust.

NOTE: *Steps 38-41 adjust choke unloader. See **Figure 70**.*

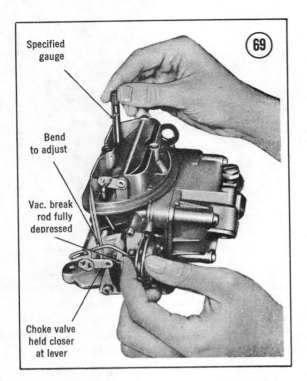

Specified gauge

(69)

Bend to adjust

Vac. break rod fully depressed

Choke valve held closer at lever

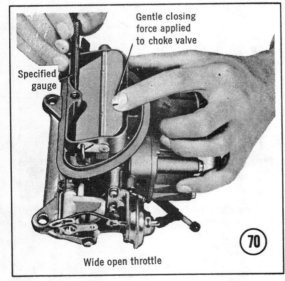

Gentle closing force applied to choke valve

Specified gauge

(70)

Wide open throttle

38. Hold throttle lever wide open with rubber band.

39. Hold choke valve toward closed position against unloader tang of throttle shaft.

40. Measure opening between lower edge of choke valve and main body. See specifications for proper measurement.

41. Bend choke rod to adjust.

ROCHESTER 4MV

This is a 4-barrel, 2-stage carburetor which is easily adapted for small to large engines without design changes. See Table 1 for years used and **Table 6** for specifications.

The fuel bowl is centrally located to avoid fuel slosh. The float needle valve is pressure balanced to permit use of a small single float.

The primary side has small bores and a triple venturi for fine fuel control in the idle and economy ranges. The secondary side has large bores and an air valve for high air capacity.

Removal/Installation

1. Remove air cleaner, gasket, and stud.

2. Disconnect vacuum, fuel, and choke pipes at carburetor.

3. On automatic models, disconnect transmission control rod from throttle lever.

4. On models with positive crankcase ventilation (PCV), disconnect ventilation hose at valve on carburetor base.

5. Disconnect accelerator rod and throttle return spring at carburetor.

6. Remove mounting nuts and lift carburetor from manifold.

7. Reverse procedures to install. Be sure carburetor base and manifold flange are clean.

Disassembly

NOTE: *Steps 1-5 remove and disassemble the air horn. See* **Figure 71.**

1. Remove idle vent valve.

2. Disconnect choke rod from upper choke shaft lever and remove choke rod.

3. Disconnect and remove pump rod from the pump lever.

4. Remove 7 screws around air horn and lift straight up. Leave air horn gasket on bowl. Do not damage or remove 2 small main well air bleed tubes protruding from air horn.

5. Hold air valve wide open. Tilt secondary metering rods, then slide from holes in hanger.

NOTE: *Steps 6-27 disassemble the float bowl and throttle body. Refer to* **Figures 72 and 73.**

Table 6　　ROCHESTER 4MV

Note: All dimensions given in inches.								
Year	**1968**	**1969-70**		**1971**	**1972**		**1973**	**1974**
Engine displacement	327	350	427	350, 454	350	454	350, 454	350	454
Float level	9/32	7/32	3/16	1/4	1/4	1/4	7/32	1/4	3/8
Float drop	—	—	—	—	—	—	—	—	—
Accelerator pump	9/32	5/16	9/32	—	3/8	3/8	13/32	13/32	13/32
Idle vent	3/8	3/8	3/8	—	—	—	—	—	—
Fast idle									
Measurement	2 turns	2 turns	2 turns	—	—	—	—	—	—
rpm	2,400	2,400	2,400	—	—	—	—	—	—
Choke rod	0.100	0.100	0.100	0.100	0.100	0.100	0.430	0.430	0.430
Vacuum break									
Manual transmission	0.245	0.245	0.245	0.275	0.215	0.250	0.250	0.230	0.250
Automatic transmission	0.160	0.180	0.160	0.260	0.215	0.250	0.250	0.230	0.220①
Unloader	0.300	0.450	0.300	—	—	—	0.450	0.450	0.450
Secondary closing	0.020	0.020	0.020	—	—	—	—	—	—
Secondary opening	0.070	0.070	0.070	—	—	—	—	—	—
Secondary lockout	0.010	0.015	0.010	—	—	—	—	—	—
Main metering jet	0.071	0.067	0.071	—	—	—	—	—	—
Throttle bore									
Primary	1 3/8	1 3/8	1 3/8	1 3/8	—	1 3/8	1 3/8	1 3/8	1 3/8
Secondary	2 1/4	2 1/4	2 1/4	2 1/4	—	2 1/4	2 1/4	2 1/4	2 1/4
Air valve dashpot	0.015	0.015	0.015	0.020	0.020	0.020	—	—	—
Secondary metering rod	27/32	—	27/32	—	—	—	—	—	—

① 0.250 on models first sold in California.

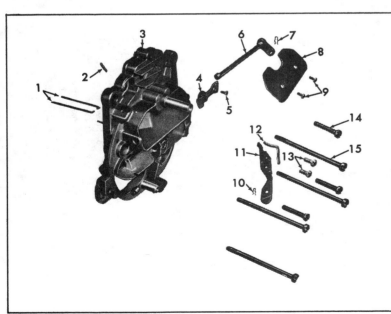

ROCHESTER 4MV

1. Secondary metering rod
2. Pump lever roll pin
3. Air horn assembly
4. Idle vent valve
5. Idle vent valve screw
6. Choke shaft and lever assembly
7. Choke rod clip
8. Choke valve
9. Choke valve screw
10. Pump rod clip
11. Pump actuating lever
12. Idle vent valve lever
13. Air horn screw
14. Air horn screw (short)
　　(counter sunk)
15. Air horn screw (long)

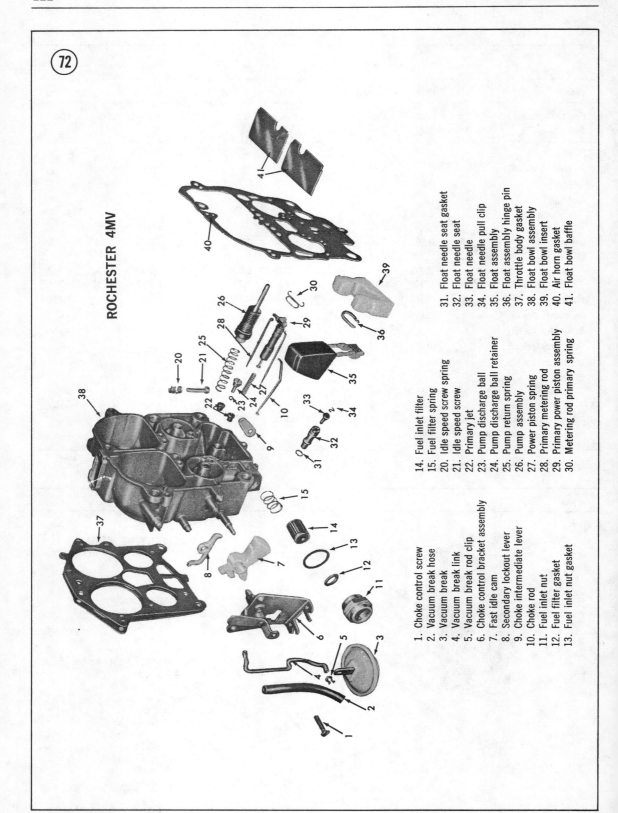

ROCHESTER 4MV

1. Choke control screw
2. Vacuum break hose
3. Vacuum break
4. Vacuum break link
5. Vacuum break rod clip
6. Choke control bracket assembly
7. Fast idle cam
8. Secondary lockout lever
9. Choke intermediate lever
10. Choke rod
11. Fuel inlet nut
12. Fuel filter gasket
13. Fuel inlet nut gasket
14. Fuel inlet filter
15. Fuel filter spring
20. Idle speed screw spring
21. Idle speed screw
22. Primary jet
23. Pump discharge ball
24. Pump discharge ball retainer
25. Pump return spring
26. Pump assembly
27. Power piston spring
28. Primary metering rod
29. Primary power piston assembly
30. Metering rod primary spring
31. Float needle seat gasket
32. Float needle seat
33. Float needle
34. Float needle pull clip
35. Float assembly
36. Float assembly hinge pin
37. Throttle body gasket
38. Float bowl assembly
39. Float bowl insert
40. Air horn gasket
41. Float bowl baffle

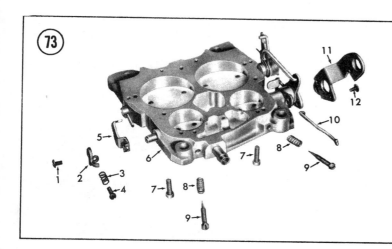

⑦③

ROCHESTER 4MV

1. Cam and fast idle levers screw
2. Fast idle lever
3. Fast idle screw spring
4. Fast idle adjusting screw
5. Cam lever
6. Throttle body assembly
7. Throttle body screw
8. Idle needle spring
9. Idle needle
10. Accelerator pump rod
11. Throttle lever
12. Throttle lever screw

6. Remove pump plunger from pump well.

7. Lift air horn gasket from dowels on secondary side of bowl, then remove gasket from around power piston and primary metering rods.

8. Remove pump return spring.

9. Remove plastic filler over float valve.

10. Remove power piston and primary metering rods. See **Figure 74**.

11. Disconnect tension spring at top of each primary metering rod. Rotate each rod and remove from hanger on power piston.

12. Remove float assembly.

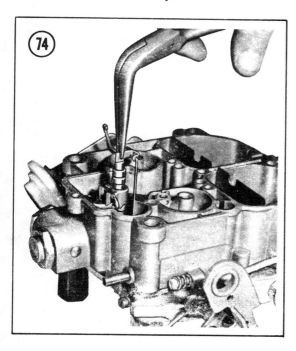

⑦④

13. Remove pull clip and fuel inlet needle.

14. Remove fuel inlet needle seat with *wide* blade screwdriver.

15. Remove primary metering jets.

CAUTION
Do not remove secondary metering discs.

16. Remove pump discharge check ball retainer and check ball.

17. Remove baffle from secondary side of bowl.

18. Remove vacuum hose.

19. Remove choke assembly from bowl.

20. Remove secondary lockout link from bowl.

21. Remove vacuum break rod and vacuum break.

22. Remove fast idle cam.

23. Remove lower choke rod and lever from inside float bowl well.

24. Remove fuel inlet filter nut, gasket, filter, and spring.

25. Remove throttle body from bowl.

26. Remove pump rod from throttle lever.

27. Remove idle mixture screws and springs.

Cleaning and Inspection

The most frequent causes of carburetor trouble are dirt, gum, and water in the carburetor. Carefully clean and inspect all parts before assembling carburetor.

1. Clean all carburetor castings and metal parts in carburetor cleaner.

CAUTION
Do not immerse any rubber parts, plastic parts, diaphragms, or pump plungers in carburetor cleaner. The delrin cam on the air valve shaft, however, will withstand normal cleaning in carburetor cleaner.

2. Check bearing surfaces of all operating levers, shafts, and castings for excessive wear.

3. Check floats for dents. Immerse floats in hot water. If bubbles appear, float is leaking and the float must be *replaced*. Do not attempt to solder the hole. This increases float weight and causes high fuel level.

4. Check pump plunger leather for cracks and creases.

5. Check float needles and seats for burrs and ridges. If present, replace needle and seat; never replace either alone.

6. Check metering rods and jets for bends, burrs, ridges, or other distortion. Replace rod and jet if either is damaged.

7. Inspect edges of throttle valves for nicks or gouges. Replace if necessary.

8. Check all springs for obvious distortion or bends.

9. Make certain all gasket mating surfaces of choke housing, top cover and carburetor body are free of burrs, gouges, deep scratches or other irregularities which could prevent a good seal.

Assembly

NOTE: *Steps 1-24 assemble float bowl and throttle body. See Figures 72 and 73.*

1. Install idle mixture needles and springs. Screw in until they seat *lightly*, then back them out 2 turns.

2. Install pump rod in throttle lever.

3. Install throttle body with new gasket.

4. Install fuel inlet filter spring, filter, new gasket, and nut.

5. Install vacuum break and rod.

6. Install fast idle cam on vacuum break assembly.

7. Connect choke rod to choke rod actuating lever. Hold choke rod with grooved end pointing

inward. Position lever in well of float bowl and install choke assembly so that shaft engages with hole in actuating lever. See **Figure 75**. Install retaining screw. Remove choke rod from lever temporarily.

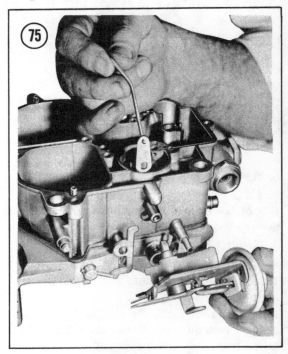

8. Install vacuum hose to bowl and vacuum break.

9. Install baffle in secondary side of bowl with notches toward top.

10. Install pump discharge check ball and retainer in passage next to pump well.

11. Install primary main metering jets.

12. Install fuel inlet needle seat and gasket. Use *wide* blade screwdriver.

13. Install fuel inlet needle. Secure with the pull clip.

14. Install float.

15. Measure from top of float bowl gasket surface (gasket removed) to top of float at toe. See **Figure 76**. Proper measurement is listed in Table 6.

16. Bend float as necessary to adjust.

17. Install power piston spring in well.

18. Install main metering rods to power piston assembly.

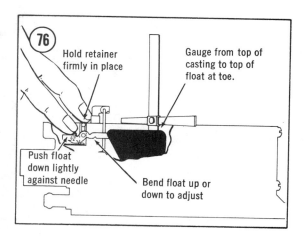

Hold retainer firmly in place

Gauge from top of casting to top of float at toe.

Push float down lightly against needle

Bend float up or down to adjust

26. Place air horn on float bowl carefully. Secure with 7 screws. Tighten screws in sequence shown in **Figure 78**.

27. Install idle vent rod in pump lever.

28. Connect pump rod in pump lever and secure with spring clip.

29. Connect choke rod in lower choke lever. Secure upper end with spring clip.

30. Install idle vent valve.

NOTE: *Steps 31-33 adjust the accelerator pump.*

31. Close throttle valves.

32. Measure from top of choke valve wall (next to vent stack) to top of pump stem. See **Figure 79** for method and Table 6 for specifications.

19. Install power piston assembly in well with main metering rods positioned in jets. Secure with retainer.

20. Install plastic filler over float needle.

21. Install pump return spring in pump well.

22. Install air horn gasket over bowl.

23. Press power piston down firmly to insure correct alignment.

24. Install pump plunger in pump well.

NOTE: *Steps 25-31 assemble air horn.*

25. Install secondary metering rods. Refer to **Figure 77**.

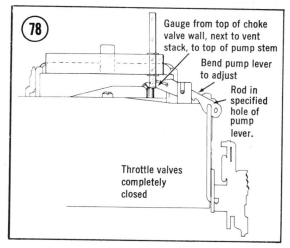

Gauge from top of choke valve wall, next to vent stack, to top of pump stem

Bend pump lever to adjust

Rod in specified hole of pump lever.

Throttle valves completely closed

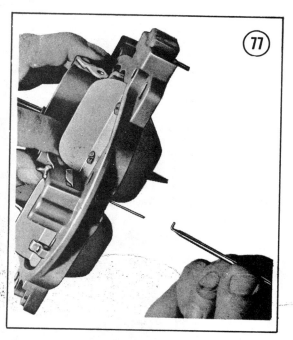

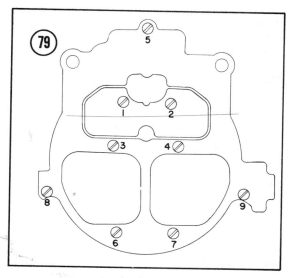

33. Bend pump lever if necessary.

NOTE: *Steps 34-37 adjust idle vent.*
See **Figure 80.**

34. Hold vent valve closed.

35. Open primary throttle until vent valve arm just contacts the bi-metal strip adjacent to the vent valve.

36. Measure distance from top of choke valve wall to top of pump plunger stem. See Figure 80.

37. Bend wire tang on pump lever to adjust if necessary.

NOTE: *Steps 38-40 adjust fast idle.*
See **Figure 81.**

38. Close primary throttle valves completely.

39. With cam follower over the high step of the fast idle cam, turn fast idle screw in or out until it just touches lever. Screw in 3½ turns from this point.

NOTE: *Steps 40-43 adjust choke rod.*
See **Figure 82.**

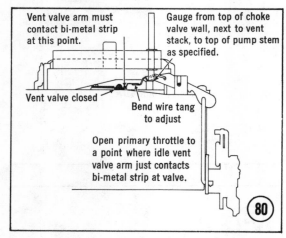

Vent valve arm must contact bi-metal strip at this point.

Gauge from top of choke valve wall, next to vent stack, to top of pump stem as specified.

Vent valve closed

Bend wire tang to adjust

Open primary throttle to a point where idle vent valve arm just contacts bi-metal strip at valve.

80

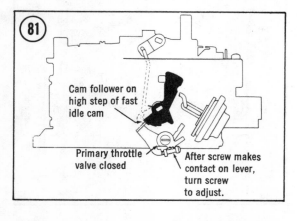

81

Cam follower on high step of fast idle cam

Primary throttle valve closed

After screw makes contact on lever, turn screw to adjust.

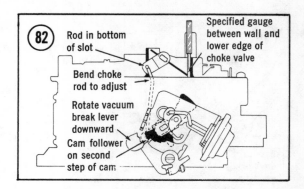

82

Rod in bottom of slot

Specified gauge between wall and lower edge of choke valve

Bend choke rod to adjust

Rotate vacuum break lever downward

Cam follower on second step of cam

40. Place cam follower on second step of fast idle cam.

41. Rotate choke valve toward closed position by pushing down on vacuum break tang.

42. Measure between lower edge of choke valve and wall. See Table 6 for dimensions.

43. Bend choke rod if necessary to adjust.

NOTE: *Steps 44-47 adjust vacuum break. See* **Figure 83.**

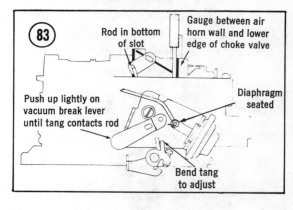

83

Rod in bottom of slot

Gauge between air horn wall and lower edge of choke valve

Push up lightly on vacuum break lever until tang contacts rod

Diaphragm seated

Bend tang to adjust

44. Hold choke valve closed with a rubber band. Cam follower must be on highest step of fast idle cam.

45. Hold vacuum break diaphragm stem against its seat so vacuum link is at end of slot.

46. Measure between lower edge of choke valve and air horn at choke lower end.

NOTE: *Steps 47-51 adjust secondary lockout. See* **Figure 84.**

47. With choke valve wide open, rotate vacuum break lever *counterclockwise* toward closed position.

48. Bend lever to provide minimum 75% contact. See Figure 84, inset 1.

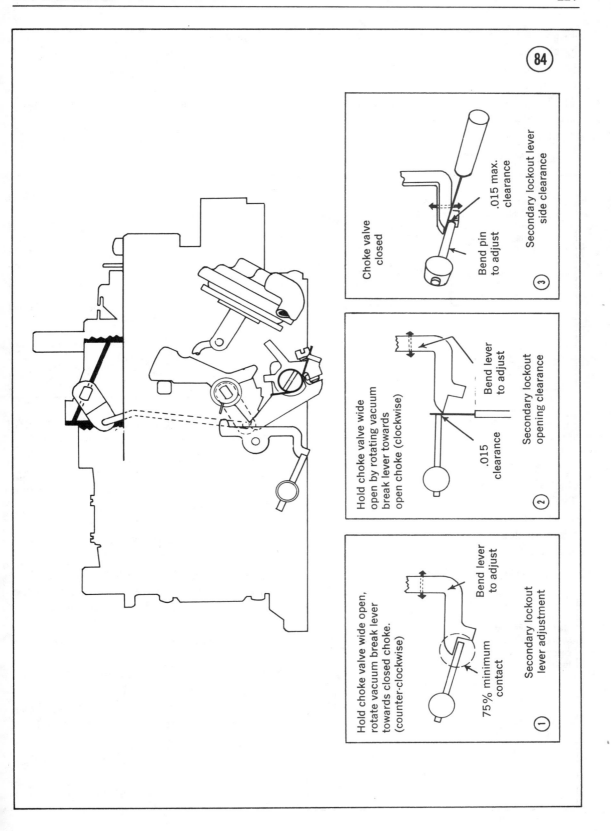

(84)

Choke valve closed

.015 max. clearance

Bend pin to adjust

Secondary lockout lever side clearance

(3)

Hold choke valve wide open by rotating vacuum break lever towards open choke (clockwise)

Bend lever to adjust

.015 clearance

Secondary lockout opening clearance

(2)

Hold choke valve wide open, rotate vacuum break lever towards closed choke. (counter-clockwise)

Bend lever to adjust

75% minimum contact

Secondary lockout lever adjustment

(1)

49. With choke valve wide open, rotate vacuum break lever clockwise toward open position.

50. Bend lever to provide clearance specified in Figure 84, inset 2.

51. With choke valve closed, bend lever to provide clearance specified in Figure 84, inset 3.

NOTE: *Steps 52-54 adjust air valve spring adjustment. See* **Figure 85**.

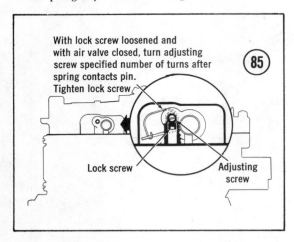

52. Loosen lock screw (Allen screw) and turn spring adjusting screw counterclockwise to relieve all spring tension.

53. With air valve closed, turn adjusting screw clockwise the number of turns specified in Table 6.

54. Hold adjusting screw in this position and tighten lock screw.

NOTE: *Steps 55-57 adjust secondary metering rod. See* **Figure 86**.

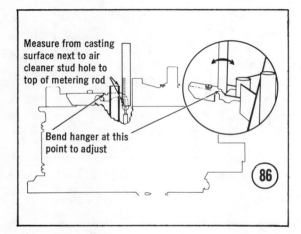

55. Close air valve.

56. Measure from top of casting surface behind air clearance stud hole to top of metering rod.

57. Adjust if necessary by bending secondary metering rod hanger with tool J-22514 or equivalent until rod height is correct. See Table 6.

NOTE: *Steps 58-59 adjust secondary opening. Refer to* **Figure 87**.

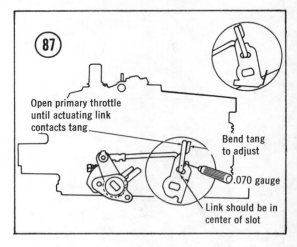

58. Open primary throttle valves until actuating link contacts tang on secondary lever.

59. Ensure that bottom of link is in the center of the secondary lever slot. Also be sure that there is 0.070 in. clearance between link and tang. See Figure 87.

ROCHESTER M4MC

The M4MC model Quadrajet carburetor (**Figure 88**) is used on 1975-1976 model Corvettes. This carburetor was developed from the 4MV series, and has the following additional features.

1. Calibration to meet 1975-1976 performance and emission requirements.

2. Choke coil mounted on carburetor float bowl (instead of exhaust manifold).

3. Dual vacuum break system to improve choke operation during warmup (on 1975 models).

4. Larger fuel filters.

5. Filter block and baffle added to fuel bowl to reduce slosh.

6. "Windowless" needle seat to improve fuel handling.

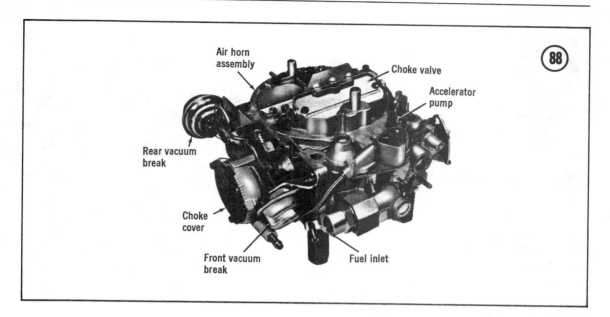

Air horn assembly

Choke valve

Accelerator pump

Rear vacuum break

Choke cover

Front vacuum break

Fuel inlet

7. Adjustable Part Throttle (APT) added to provide better fuel control and fuel/air ratio control.

8. Expander spring added to accelerator pump to improve fuel delivery.

Installation/Removal

This procedure is identical to that given above for the 4MV carburetor.

Disassembly

Idle Stop Solenoid

1. If equipped with idle stop solenoid, remove attaching screws and remove solenoid and bracket from carburetor float bowl.

CAUTION
Do not immerse solenoid in any type of cleaning solvent.

Air Horn Removal

1. Remove lever from end of choke shaft (one screw). Rotate lever to remove choke rod. See **Figure 89**.

2. Hold lower lever (inside float bowl casting) outward with a small screwdriver and rotate choke rod counterclockwise to remove rod.

3. Remove hose from front vacuum break.

4. Remove retaining screw in top of metering rod hanger and remove secondary metering rods.

Lift up on hanger until rods are completely out of air horn. Rotate rods out of holes in end of hanger to remove (**Figure 90**).

5. Use a small drift punch (GM Part No. J-25322 or equivalent) to drive pump lever pivot pin inward far enough so pump lever can be removed (**Figure 91**).

CAUTION
Use care in driving pump lever pivot pin to avoid causing damage to pump lever casting bosses in air horn.

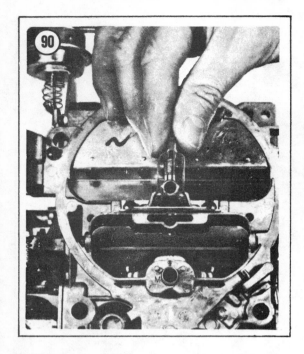

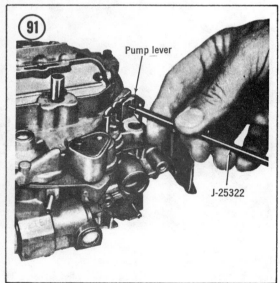

Pump lever

J-25322

6. Remove 9 attaching screws (**Figure 92**) and remove secondary air baffle deflector plate (if so equipped). Remove air horn from float bowl by lifting straight up (**Figure 93**).

CAUTION

Use care to avoid damage to small tubes protruding from air horn. These tubes are permanently pressed into air horn casting and shouldn't be removed.

Air Horn Disassembly

1. Remove front vacuum break bracket (2 screws) and then remove air valve dashpot rod from diaphragm assembly and air valve lever (**Figure 94**).

CAUTION

Do not immerse vacuum break assembly in carburetor solvent.

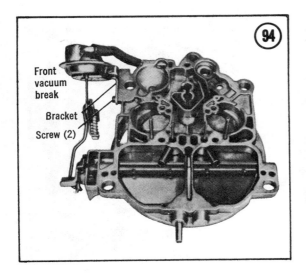

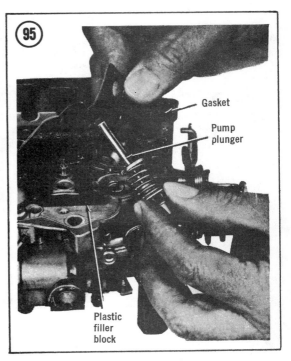

NOTE: *Further disassembly of air horn for cleaning purposes is not required. If part replacement is necessary, use the following steps as appropriate.*

2. Remove choke valve (2 screws) and choke valve shaft. Use a file to remove staking on attaching screws.

CAUTION
Do not remove air valves or air valve shaft.

3. If replacement of air valve closing spring or center plastic eccentric cam is necessary, follow instructions contained in repair kit.

Float Bowl Disassembly

1. Remove air horn gasket, taking care not to distort metering rod springs (**Figure 95**).

2. Remove pump plunger and pump return spring from pump well.

3. Remove power piston and metering rods (press down on piston stem and allow it to snap free). See **Figure 96**.

CAUTION
Do not use pliers to remove power piston. Repeat Step 3 as often as necessary to remove.

4. Disconnect tension spring from top of each metering rod and rotate rods to remove them from power piston (**Figure 97**).

CAUTION
Use care to avoid distortion of tension springs and metering rods. Carefully note position of springs for reassembly.

5. Remove plastic filler block over float valve.

6. Pull up on retaining pin and remove float assembly and float needle. Remove needle seat and gasket (**Figure 98**).

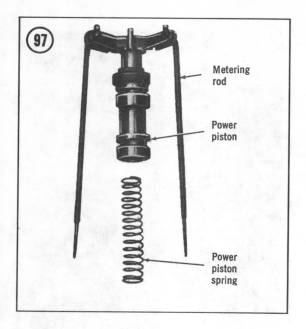

Metering rod

Power piston

Power piston spring

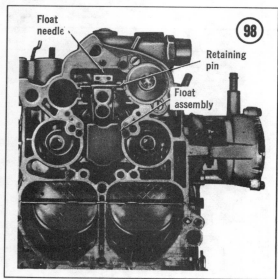

Float needle

Retaining pin

Float assembly

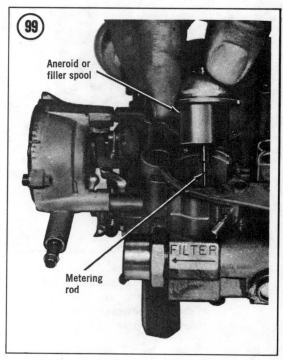

Aneroid or filler spool

Metering rod

8. Remove primary main metering jets (**Figure 100**).

> NOTE: *Do not attempt to remove* APT *metering jet or secondary metering orifice plates, as they are fixed. If these jets are damaged, the float bowl must be replaced.*

7. Remove Adjustable Part Throttle (APT) cover (2 screws) and carefully lift out filler spool or aneroid and metering rod (**Figure 99**).

CAUTION

> *The* APT *metering rod assembly is very fragile and care must be taken to avoid damage. Do not immerse the assembly in carburetor cleaner. No attempt should be made to adjust the metering rod. If replacement is required, see procedure below.*

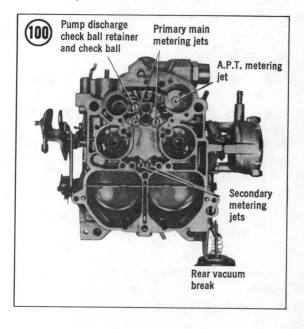

Pump discharge check ball retainer and check ball

Primary main metering jets

A.P.T. metering jet

Secondary metering jets

Rear vacuum break

9. Remove retainer and pump discharge check ball.

10. Remove rear vacuum break control unit and bracket (2 screws) and vacuum hose. Remove vacuum break rod from slot in plunger head by rotating assembly (**Figure 101**).

CAUTION
Do not immerse vacuum break assembly in carburetor solvent.

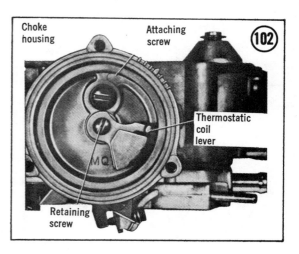

11. Disengage vacuum break rod from hole in intermediate choke lever.

Choke Disassembly

1. Remove choke cover and coil assembly (3 screws) by pulling straight outward. Remove gasket.

> NOTE: *Do not remove baffle plate located under thermostatic coil, as distortion could result.*

2. Remove choke housing from float bowl (one screw). See **Figure 102**.

3. Remove secondary throttle valve lockout lever (**Figure 103**).

4. Invert float bowl and remove lower choke lever from bowl cavity.

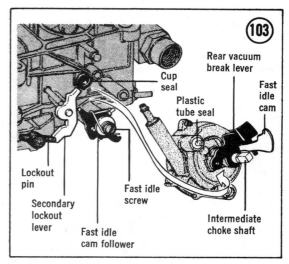

5. Remove plastic seal tube from choke housing (Figure 103).

CAUTION
Do not immerse plastic tube in carburetor solvent.

6. Remove coil lever from intermediate choke shaft (one screw). See Figure 102. Slide intermediate choke shaft outward and remove. Remove fast idle cam from intermediate choke shaft (Figure 103).

CAUTION
Remove cup seal from inside choke housing shaft hole before immersing housing in carburetor solvent. Also, remove cup seal from float bowl. **Do not** *remove plastic insert.*

Float Bowl Disassembly

1. Remove inlet nut, fuel filter, spring, and gasket (**Figure 104**).

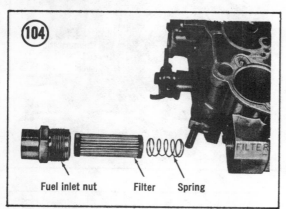

Fuel inlet nut   Filter   Spring

2. If replacement is required, remove secondary air baffle and/or pump well fill slot baffle.

3. Remove throttle body from float bowl (2 screws) and remove gasket (**Figures 105 and 106**).

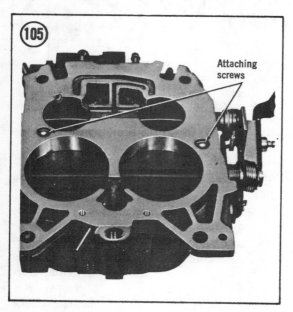

Attaching screws

Throttle Body Disassembly

1. Disengage pump rod from throttle body.

> NOTE: *Further disassembly is not necessary unless the idle mixture screws require replacement or if normal cleaning fails to clean idle passages.*

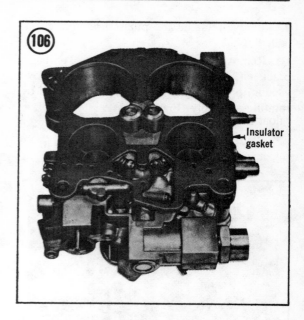

Insulator gasket

2. Destroy plastic limiter cap and **remove idle** mixture screws and springs.

Cleaning and Inspection

1. Thoroughly clean castings and metal parts in carburetor solvent.

> CAUTION
> *Do not immerse idle stop solenoid, throttle stop vacuum unit, rubber parts, plastic parts, pump plunger, filler spool or aneroid, or choke vacuum break in carburetor solvents. However, throttle valve shaft may be immersed.*

2. Blow all passages dry with compressed air.

> CAUTION
> *Do not clean passages or jets with drills or wire.*

3. Examine all needles, seats, lever holes, levers, valves and metering rods for wear, damage and binding. Replace parts as necessary.

Assembly

Throttle Body Assembly

1. If removed, install idle mixture needles and springs until lightly seated. Back out 4 turns.

> NOTE: *Make final idle mixture adjustment on engine, using the procedure given in Chapter Four.*

2. Install pump rod in throttle lever. End of rod should point outward.

Float Bowl Assembly

1. Install new gasket over locating dowels on float bowl.

2. Place throttle body on float bowl, indexing dowels on bowl with depressions in throttle body. Install attaching screws and securely tighten.

3. Install carburetor on holding fixture (GM part J-8328 or equivalent).

4. Install fuel filter element, spring, new gasket, and inlet nut and securely tighten (18 ft.-lb.).

CAUTION

Do not over tighten inlet nut, as nylon gasket could be damaged.

Choke Assembly

1. Install new cup seal in plastic insert in side of float bowl (seal lip facing outward).

2. Place secondary throttle valve lockout lever on float bowl boss with recess in lever hole facing inward.

3. Install new cup seal in choke housing shaft hole with lips of seal facing inside of housing.

4. Place fast idle cam on intermediate choke shaft with cam steps facing down (Figure 103).

5. Install fast idle cam and intermediate choke shaft assembly through seal in choke housing. Install thermostatic coil lever on intermediate choke shaft (inside and outside levers must face toward fuel inlet). Install and securely tighten retaining screw.

6. Install lower choke rod lever in float bowl cavity. Install plastic tube seal in choke housing cavity and install choke housing to bowl, sliding intermediate choke shaft into lower choke lever **(Figure 107)**.

NOTE: *Fast idle cam and intermediate choke shaft lever are in proper relationship when lever tang is below the cam. Do not install choke cover and coil until coil lever is adjusted (see procedure below).*

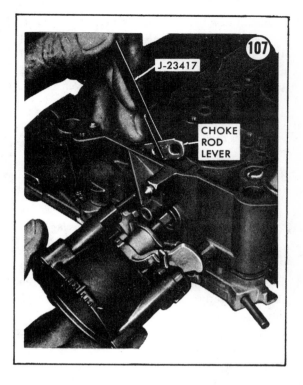

Float Bowl Assembly

1. Install end of vacuum break rod in hole in intermediate choke lever while holding down on fast idle cam (hot idle position).

2. Install other end of vacuum break rod in rear vacuum break plunger head slot. Install vacuum break and bracket assembly to float bowl (2 screws) and securely tighten (Figure 101).

NOTE: *Do not attach hose to vacuum break until it has been adjusted. See procedure below.*

3. Install air baffle (if removed) in secondary side of fuel bowl. Notches must be at top and top edge of baffle must be flush with bowl casting.

4. Install pump well fill slot baffle, if removed.

5. Install check ball and retainer in passage next to pump well and securely tighten retainer.

6. Install primary main metering jets (Figure 100).

7. Using care, install APT metering rod and cover assembly into float bowl. The tab on cover should be aligned with slot in bowl nearest to fuel inlet nut. Securely tighten screws.

8. Install new needle seat assembly and gasket.

9. Install float by sliding float lever under pull clip from front to back. Hold float at toe and install retaining pin from APT metering side. Adjust float level, using procedure given below.

CAUTION
Do not install float needle pull clip into holes in float arm.

APT Metering Rod Replacement

Refer to **Figure 108**.

CAUTION
Do not attempt to adjust APT metering rod unless it is damaged and requires replacement.

1. Carefully note position of adjusting screw slot and lightly scribe a mark on the cover of the metering rod assembly.

2. Remove cover screws and lift out metering rod and cover assembly.

3. Hold assembly upright and turn adjusting screw counterclockwise, carefully counting the number of turns until metering rod bottoms on cover. Record the number of turns for later reference.

4. Remove retainer (E-clip) from threaded end of rod and turn rod clockwise until it disengages from cover.

CAUTION
Rod is spring loaded and care should be exercised during removal.

5. Install spring on replacement rod and thread rod into cover until rod bottoms on cover.

6. Turn adjusting screw clockwise the exact same number of turns counted in Step 3.

NOTE: *When properly adjusted the screw slot may not line up exactly with the scribe mark on the cover.*

7. Install E-clip in rod assembly groove and lock securely in place.

8. Carefully install metering rod and cover assembly in float bowl. Tab should be aligned with slot nearest to fuel inlet nut. Do not bend or damage metering rod tip.

9. Install and securely tighten screws.

Float Level Adjustment

Refer to **Figure 109**.

1. While firmly holding float retainer in place, press float lightly down against needle.

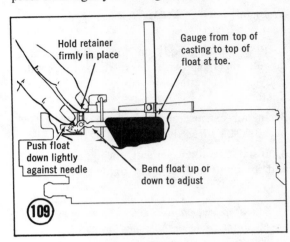

Hold retainer firmly in place

Gauge from top of casting to top of float at toe.

Push float down lightly against needle

Bend float up or down to adjust

109

2. Use adjustable T-scale to measure from top of float bowl casting (air horn gasket removed) to top of float (1/16 in. back from toe).

3. Bend float arm if adjustment is required. See **Table 7** for specifications.

4. Visually check float alignment.

Table 7   ROCHESTER M4MC

	1975	1976
Float level	15/32 in.	13/32 in.
Pump rod	0.275 in.	0.275 in.
Choke coil lever	0.120 in.	0.120 in.
Choke rod	0.300 in.	0.325 in.
Air valve dashpot	0.015 in.	0.015 in.
Front vacuum break	0.180 in.	0.185 in.
Rear vacuum break	0.170 in.	—
Spring windup	7/8 in.	7/8 in.
Unloader	0.325 in.	0.325 in.

Float Bowl Final Assembly

1. Install plastic filler block over float needle. Press down to properly seat filler block.

2. Install power piston in well. If removed, install main metering rods on hanger, making sure tension springs are connected to top of each rod (Figure 96). Make sure metering rods are properly inserted into metering jets and plastic power

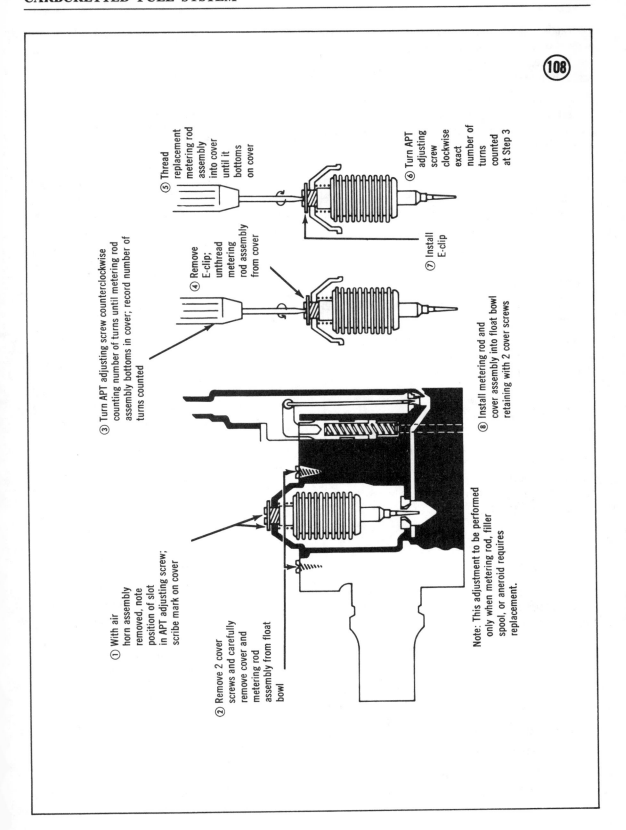

(108)

③ Turn APT adjusting screw counterclockwise counting number of turns until metering rod assembly bottoms in cover; record number of turns counted

⑤ Thread replacement metering rod assembly into cover until it bottoms on cover

⑥ Turn APT adjusting screw clockwise exact number of turns counted at Step 3

④ Remove E-clip; unthread metering rod assembly from cover

⑦ Install E-clip

① With air horn assembly removed, note position of slot in APT adjusting screw; scribe mark on cover

② Remove 2 cover screws and carefully remove cover and metering rod assembly from float bowl

⑧ Install metering rod and cover assembly into float bowl retaining with 2 cover screws

Note: This adjustment to be performed only when metering rod, filler spool, or aneroid requires replacement.

piston is seated in recess in bowl (press down with finger until flush with top of bowl casting, or, if necessary tap lightly with drift punch and small hammer).

3. Install pump return spring in pump well, then install air horn gasket, carefully sliding gasket tab around main metering rods and below power piston hanger. Place gasket over 2 dowel pins on float bowl.

4. Using care, lift a corner of gasket and install pump plunger in pump well. Push plunger to bottom of well against spring tension. Align plunger stem with hole in gasket and press gasket into place.

Air Horn Assembly

1. Install choke shaft and choke valve (2 screws).

2. Check choke valve for free movement and proper alignment. Securely tighten screws and lightly stake in place.

Air Horn-to-Bowl Assembly

1. Carefully lower air horn onto float bowl while holding down on gasket at pump plunger location. Make sure that bleed tubes, accelerating well tubes, pull-over enrichment tubes (if used) and pump plunger stem are properly positioned through gasket holes.

CAUTION
Do not use force. Air horn should be lightly lowered into place.

2. Install attaching screws and evenly and securely tighten, using the pattern shown in Figure 92.

NOTE: *If used, install secondary air baffle under 2 center screws.*

3. Install vacuum break rod in air valve shaft lever and install other end of rod in vacuum break diaphragm plunger. Install front vacuum break and bracket (2 screws) to air horn and securely tighten screws.

NOTE: *Adjust vacuum break, using procedure below, before installing vacuum hose.*

4. Connect pump rod to pump lever. Use a small screwdriver to push pump lever roll pin back through casting until end of pin is flush with casting bosses in air horn.

CAUTION
Take care to avoid damage to pump lever casting bosses.

5. Install secondary metering rods into hanger with upper ends of rods pointing toward each other. Install hanger and rods on air valve cam follower. Install and securely tighten retaining screw. Check air valves for free movement.

6. Connect choke rod to lower choke lever (inside bowl cavity) and to slot in upper choke lever. Retain choke lever to shaft with screw and securely tighten.

NOTE: *At this point, use procedures below to adjust front and rear vacuum break units, fast idle cam (choke rod) and thermostatic choke coil lever.*

7. Install choke coil and cover assembly and gasket. Coil tang must be installed in slot in inside choke coil lever pickup arm. Line up alignment marks on choke cover and body and securely tighten screws.

8. If so equipped install idle stop solenoid and bracket assembly or decel throttle stop vacuum assembly.

Pump Rod Adjustment

Refer to **Figure 110**.

1. With follower off steps of fast idle cam, back out idle speed screw until throttle valves are completely closed.

NOTE: *Make sure secondary actuating rod is not keeping primary throttle valves from closing. If necessary, bend secondary closing tang out of way and readjust later.*

2. Place pump rod in specified hole in lever.

3. Gauge from top of choke valve wall, next to vent stock, to top of pump stem. See Table 7 for specifications.

4. If adjustment is required, support pump lever with screwdriver and bend lever.

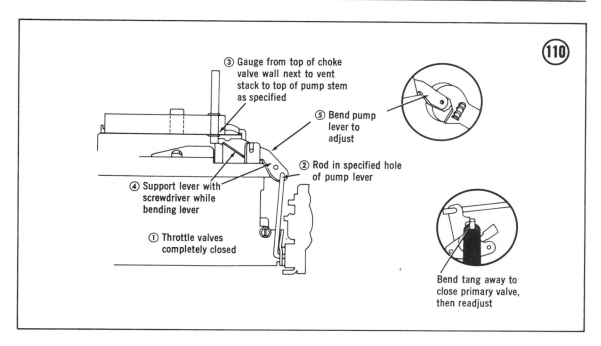

③ Gauge from top of choke valve wall next to vent stack to top of pump stem as specified

⑤ Bend pump lever to adjust

② Rod in specified hole of pump lever

④ Support lever with screwdriver while bending lever

① Throttle valves completely closed

Bend tang away to close primary valve, then readjust

Fast Idle Adjustment

Refer to **Figure 111**.

1. Place cam follower on highest step of fast idle cam.

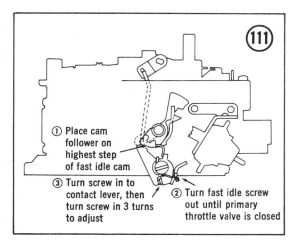

① Place cam follower on highest step of fast idle cam

③ Turn screw in to contact lever, then turn screw in 3 turns to adjust

② Turn fast idle screw out until primary throttle valve is closed

2. Adjust fast idle screw out until primary throttle valves are closed.

3. Turn fast idle screw in to contact lever, then give screw 3 additional turns.

4. Connect tachometer to engine, start engine and check fast idle against specification listed on Vehicle Emission Control Information decal. Readjust as required.

Choke Coil Lever Adjustment

Refer to **Figure 112**.

1. Loosen retaining screws and remove thermostatic cover and coil assembly from choke housing.

2. Move thermostatic coil tang counterclockwise until choke valve is closed.

3. Insert plug gauge (Table 7) in hole in choke housing. Lower edge of choke coil lever should just contact side of gauge.

4. Bend choke rod at point shown in Figure 112 inset to make adjustments.

5. Replace coil assembly and thermostatic cover. Adjust coil, using procedure given below.

Fast Idle Cam (Choke Rod) Adjustment

Refer to **Figure 113**.

1. Turn fast idle screw in until contact is made with fast idle cam follower lever, and then turn screw an additional 3 turns in.

2. Place cam follower lever on Step 2 of fast idle cam, firmly against rise of cam high step.

3. Close choke valve by pushing up on choke coil lever inside choke housing.

4. Insert gauge between upper edge of choke valve and air horn inside wall. See Table 7 for gauge size.

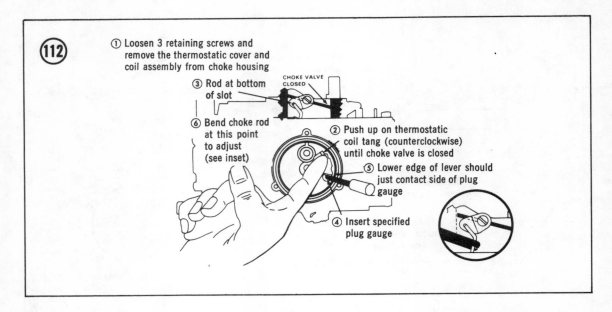

① Loosen 3 retaining screws and remove the thermostatic cover and coil assembly from choke housing

③ Rod at bottom of slot

⑥ Bend choke rod at this point to adjust (see inset)

CHOKE VALVE CLOSED

② Push up on thermostatic coil tang (counterclockwise) until choke valve is closed

⑤ Lower edge of lever should just contact side of plug gauge

④ Insert specified plug gauge

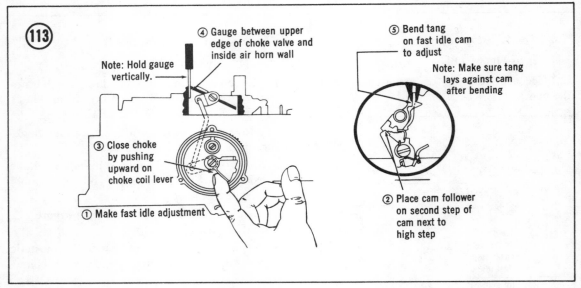

④ Gauge between upper edge of choke valve and inside air horn wall

⑤ Bend tang on fast idle cam to adjust

Note: Hold gauge vertically.

Note: Make sure tang lays against cam after bending

③ Close choke by pushing upward on choke coil lever

② Place cam follower on second step of cam next to high step

① Make fast idle adjustment

5. Bend tang on fast idle cam to adjust. Verify that tang lays against cam after bending.

6. Recheck fast idle speed, adjusting as required to match specifications on Emission Control decal.

Air Valve Dashpot Adjustment

Refer to **Figure 114**.

1. Use outside vacuum source to seat front vacuum break diphragm.

2. Completely close air valves.

3. Insert gauges between air valve dashpot rod and end of slot in the air valve lever. See Table 7 for specifications.

4. Bend rod at point shown if adjustment is required.

Front Vacuum Break Adjustment

Refer to **Figure 115**.

1. Loosen retaining screws and remove thermostatic cover and coil assembly from choke housing.

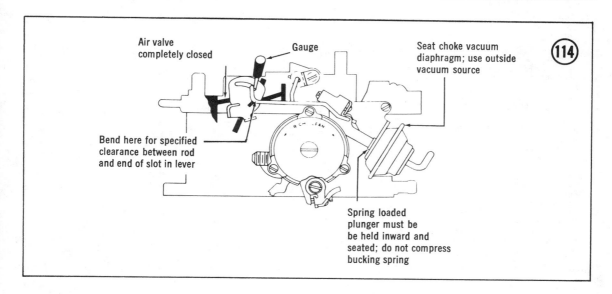

Air valve completely closed

Gauge

Seat choke vacuum diaphragm; use outside vacuum source

Bend here for specified clearance between rod and end of slot in lever

Spring loaded plunger must be be held inward and seated; do not compress bucking spring

(114)

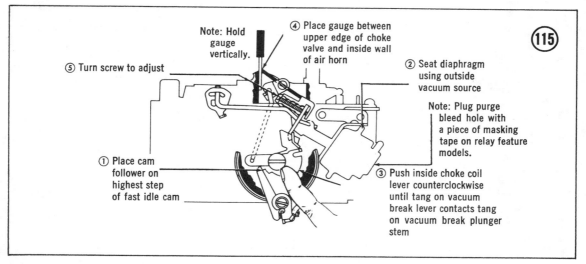

Note: Hold gauge vertically.

④ Place gauge between upper edge of choke valve and inside wall of air horn

⑤ Turn screw to adjust

② Seat diaphragm using outside vacuum source

Note: Plug purge bleed hole with a piece of masking tape on relay feature models.

① Place cam follower on highest step of fast idle cam

③ Push inside choke coil lever counterclockwise until tang on vacuum break lever contacts tang on vacuum break plunger stem

(115)

2. Place cam follower over on highest step of fast idle cam.

3. Use an outside vacuum source to seat front vacuum diaphragm.

4. Raise inside choke coil lever until tang on vacuum break lever contacts tang on vacuum break plunger.

5. Insert gauge (Table 7) between upper edge of choke valve and air horn inside wall.

6. If adjustment is required, turn adjustment screw on vacuum break plunger lever.

7. Replace thermostatic cover and coil assembly and tighten retaining screws. Adjust coil per procedure given below.

Rear Vacuum Break Adjustment

Refer to **Figure 116**.

1. Loosen retaining screws and remove thermostatic cover and coil assembly from choke housing.

2. Place cam follower lever on highest step of fast idle cam.

3. Using small piece of tape, cover bleed hole in end cover of vacuum break unit.

4. Use an outside vacuum source to seat rear vacuum brake diaphragm.

5. Raise choke coil lever inside choke housing toward closed choke position.

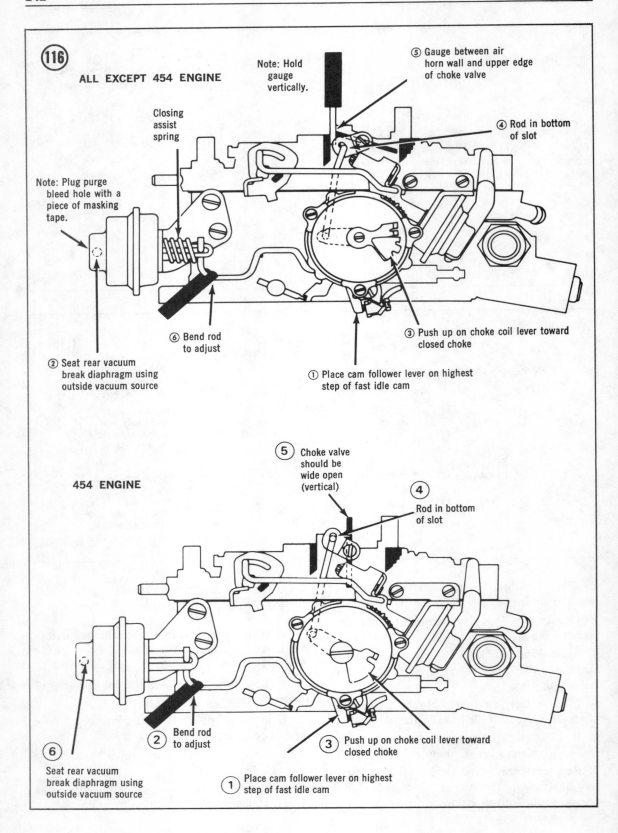

⑴⒃

ALL EXCEPT 454 ENGINE

Note: Hold gauge vertically.

⑤ Gauge between air horn wall and upper edge of choke valve

④ Rod in bottom of slot

Closing assist spring

Note: Plug purge bleed hole with a piece of masking tape.

⑥ Bend rod to adjust

② Seat rear vacuum break diaphragm using outside vacuum source

③ Push up on choke coil lever **toward** closed choke

① Place cam follower lever on highest step of fast idle cam

454 ENGINE

⑤ Choke valve should be wide open (vertical)

④ Rod in bottom of slot

② Bend rod to adjust

⑥ Seat rear vacuum break diaphragm using outside vacuum source

③ Push up on choke coil lever toward closed choke

① Place cam follower lever on highest step of fast idle cam

6. Verify that choke rod is in bottom of slot in choke lever and gauge between upper edge of choke valve and air horn inside wall. See Table 7 for correct gauge dimension.

7. If adjustment is necessary, bend vacuum break at point shown in Figure 116.

8. Replace coil assembly and thermostatic cover and tighten retaining screws. Adjust coil using procedure given below.

Automatic Choke Coil Adjustment

Refer to **Figure 117**.

1. Verify installation of thermostatic coil and cover assembly in choke housing. A gasket is required between cover and housing.

> NOTE: *Tang on thermostatic coil must be installed in slot on inside choke coil lever pickup arm.*

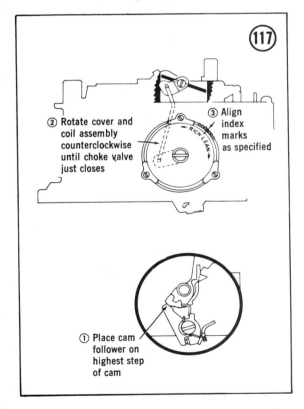

② Rotate cover and coil assembly counterclockwise until choke valve just closes

③ Align index marks as specified

① Place cam follower on highest step of cam

2. Place fast idle cam follower on highest step of fast idle cam.

3. Rotate thermostatic coil and cover assembly until choke valve barely closes.

4. Align index point on cover with proper index mark on choke housing.

5. Tighten retaining screws.

Unloader Adjustment

Refer to **Figure 118**.

1. Install and adjust thermostatic coil and cover assembly, using procedure given above.

2. With choke valve fully closed, hold throttle valves wide open.

> NOTE: *If engine is warm, close choke valve by pushing up on tang of intermediate choke lever that contacts fast idle cam. A rubber band may be used to hold choke in position.*

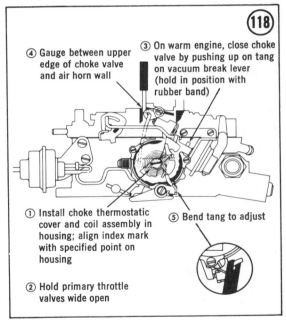

④ Gauge between upper edge of choke valve and air horn wall

③ On warm engine, close choke valve by pushing up on tang on vacuum break lever (hold in position with rubber band)

① Install choke thermostatic cover and coil assembly in housing; align index mark with specified point on housing

② Hold primary throttle valves wide open

⑤ Bend tang to adjust

3. Gauge between upper edge of choke valve and air horn inner wall.

4. Bend tang on fast idle lever as shown in Figure 118 to make any necessary adjustment.

CAUTION
After adjustment verify that fast idle lever tang is contacting center point of fast idle cam.

5. Remove rubber band, if it was used to hold choke closed.

Secondary Throttle Valve
Lockout Adjustment

Refer to **Figure 119**.

1. Hold choke valve and secondary throttle valves closed.

2. Measure clearances between lockout pin and lockout lever, as shown in Figure 119 (use 0.015 in. gauge).

3. If required, bend lockout pin at point shown to obtain proper clearance.

4. Hold choke valve wide open and secondary throttle valves slightly open.

5. Using 0.015 plug gauge, check clearance between end of lockout pin and toe of lockout lever, as shown in Figure 119.

6. If required, file off end of lockout lever to obtain proper clearance.

Secondary Closing Adjustment

Refer to **Figure 120**.

1. Set the idle speed screw to obtain the specified rpm.

2. With cam follower off steps of fast idle cam, hold choke wide open.

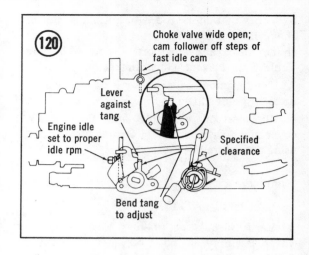

3. Gauge clearance between slot in secondary throttle valve pickup lever and secondary actuating rod. See Table 7 for specifications.

4. Bend secondary closing tang on primary throttle lever (Figure 120) to adjust.

Secondary Opening Adjustment

Refer to **Figure 121**.

1. Open primary throttle lever until link just contacts tang on secondary lever.

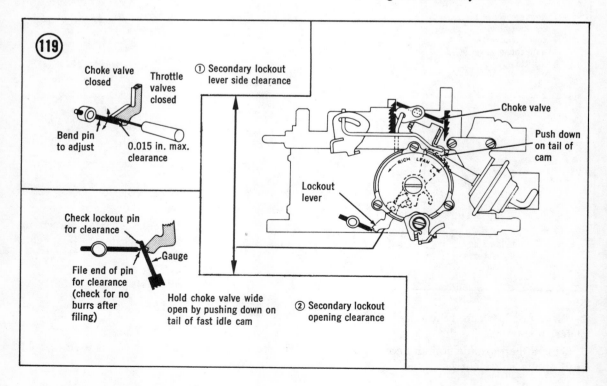

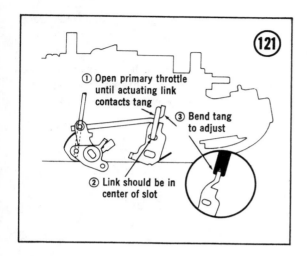

2. Hold link against tang. Link should be in center of slot in secondary lever.

3. If adjustment is required, bend tang on secondary lever (Figure 121).

Air Valve Spring Windup Adjustment

Refer to **Figure 122**.

1. Remove front vacuum break unit and air valve dashpot rod.

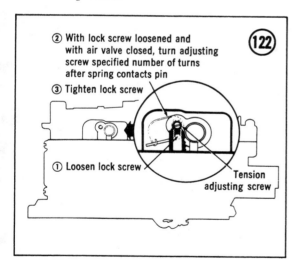

2. Using hex wrench, loosen lock screw (see Figure 122).

3. Turn the tension adjusting screw counter-clockwise until air valve starts to open.

4. Hold air valve closed and turn adjusting screw clockwise specified number of turns after spring contacts pin.

5. Tighten lock screw and replace parts removed in Step 1.

Deceleration Throttle Stop Adjustment

Refer to **Figure 123**.

1. Set idle speed to specification.

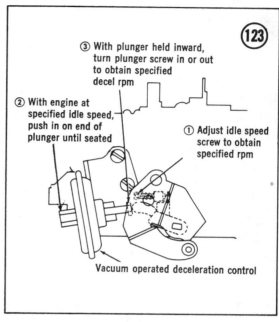

2. Push in on hex end of throttle stop plunger until plunger stem hits stop inside diaphragm unit.

3. Hold plunger against stop and turn plunger adjusting screw to obtain specified decel rpm.

FUEL PUMP

Two different diaphragm type fuel pumps are used on Corvette engines. The 1963-1966 327 cubic inch engines use a serviceable fuel pump which may be rebuilt or repaired. Larger engines through 1966 and *all* later engines use a non-serviceable fuel pump which cannot be repaired or rebuilt; the pump is replaced as a unit.

Removal/Installation

1. Disconnect fuel inlet and outlet pipes at fuel pump and fuel cover.

2. Remove 2 mounting bolts. Remove pump and gasket.

> NOTE: *Following 2 steps are not necessary unless operating pushrod requires service.*

3. Remove 2 adapter mounting bolts. Remove adapter and gasket from block.

4. Remove pushrod from block.

5. Installation is the reverse of these steps.

Disassembly

Refer to **Figure 124** for the following procedure.

1. Remove pulsator cover and diaphragm.

2. Mark edges of pump body and valve body so that parts will be assembled in same rotation.

3. Remove screws around valve body. Separate valve body from pump body. Use a light plastic hammer if necessary.

4. Lift fuel pump link with a screwdriver. See **Figure 125**. Unhook diaphragm from link by pressing down and away from rocker arm side.

5. Remove oil seal and retainer.

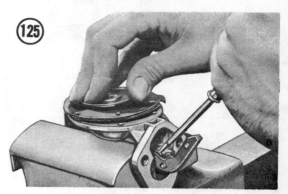

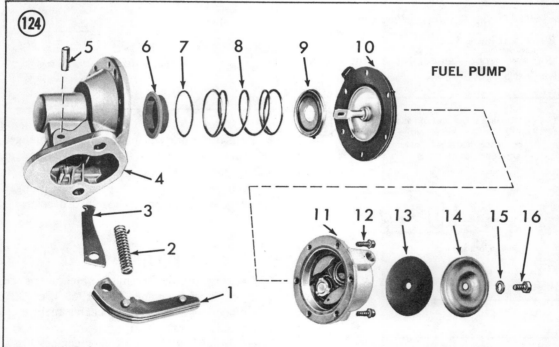

FUEL PUMP

1. Rocker arm
2. Rocker arm return spring
3. Actuating lever
4. Pump body
5. Arm and lever pivot pin
6. Oil seal
7. Oil seal retainer
8. Diaphragm and seal retainer spring
9. Diaphragm spring seat
10. Diaphragm assembly
11. Valve body and pump cover assembly
12. Valve body and fuel cover screws
13. Pulsator diaphragm
14. Pulsator cover
15. Pulsator cover lockwasher
16. Pulsator cover bolt

Cleaning and Inspection

1. Clean all metal parts in solvent.

2. Blow out all passages with compressed air.

3. Inspect pump body and valve body for cracks, breakage, and distorted gasket surfaces.

4. Check rocker arm and link for excessive wear and for a loose hinge pin.

5. Check condition of valves by pushing each off its seat with a pencil. If damaged or sticking, have your dealer replace the valve(s).

6. Discard diaphragm, rocker arm spring, diaphragm spring, and all gaskets.

Assembly

1. Install oil seal over pump body opening. Place oil seal retainer over lip of seal.

2. Install diaphragm spring.

3. Install spring seat and carefully insert diaphragm into pump body.

4. Lift pump lever with screwdriver (see Figure 125). Hook diaphragm pushrod over end of lever.

5. Install new pulsator diaphragm on valve body. Install cover with screw and fiber washer.

6. Install valve body on pump body. Align scribe marks and install screws with lockwashers. Do not tighten.

7. Tighten screws just enough to begin to compress lockwashers. Push locker arm fully to flex diaphragm, hold in this position then tighten screws.

FUEL TANK

Corvettes (1963-1973) have a standard 20 gallon steel tank, or optional 36 gallon fiberglass tank strapped in at the very rear of the vehicle. Corvettes manufactured in 1974-1975 have an 18 gallon steel tank, and 1976 Corvettes have a 17 gallon steel tank.

Too casual use of gasoline leads many to forget how dangerous and explosive it is. During the following procedures, ensure that the battery is disconnected and cannot accidently be reconnected. Prevent fuel spills and immediately wipe up any that do occur.

Removal (Standard)

1. Drain fuel tank.

> NOTE: *This is best done at a local service station which has the facilities to dispose of larger quantities of gasoline. Leave just enough in the tank to get home.*

2. Disconnect both battery cables.

3. Remove spare tire.

4. Remove spare tire carrier. See **Figure 126**.

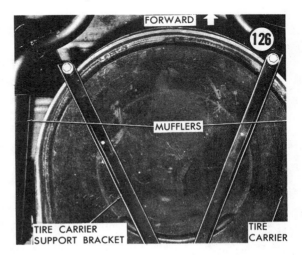

5. On 1967 and earlier models, remove U-bolts at both rear tailpipe shields. See **Figure 127**.

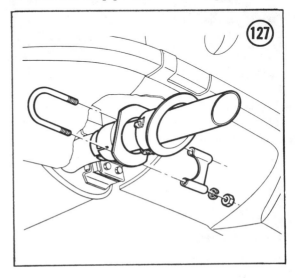

6. Separate exhaust system at the crossmember tube by loosening U-bolts. See **Figure 128**.

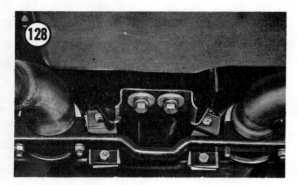

7. Remove both rear muffler brackets from frame and slide muffler system rearward.

8. Remove 2 fuel tank metal strap reinforcements and retaining bolts located at forward front side of tank.

9. Disconnect fuel gauge sender wires. See **Figure 129**.

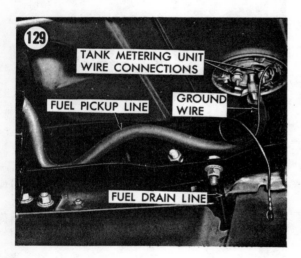

10. Disconnect fuel pickup line.

11. Remove gas cap and filler neck boot. On coupes, remove filler neck. Disconnect drain line.

12. Remove fuel tank support frame bolts and support.

13. Lower tank and rotate toward front of vehicle to remove.

Installation (Standard)

1. Push hoses and wires to one side of body.

2. Examine anti-squeak pads on crossmember support and tank. Cement new ones in place if necessary.

3. Hook reinforcement straps at rear frame crossmember. Crimp strap ends at rear frame attachment.

4. Rotate fuel tank into position.

5. Attach fuel tank support at frame side rails.

6. Attach reinforcement straps at front of tank to fuel tank support. Attach strap guide.

7. On coupes, install filler neck.

8. Connect filler neck boot to fuel tank drain hose. Install boot around filler neck.

9. Connect fuel pickup line and ground wire. Ensure that fuel drain line is flush to ½ in. inboard of rear bumper opening. See **Figure 130**.

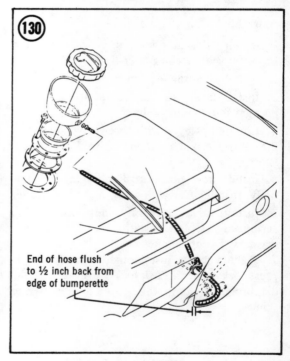

End of hose flush to ½ inch back from edge of bumperette

10. Connect fuel gauge sender wires.

11. Reconnect exhaust system by reversing Steps 5-7 of *Removal* procedure.

12. Install spare tire carrier and spare tire.

13. Fill fuel tank and install gas cap. Check for leaks while filling.

Removal/Installation (36 gallon)

1. Drain fuel tank.

> NOTE: *This is best done at a local service station which has the facilities*

to dispose of larger quantities of gaso-line. Leave just enough in the tank to get home.

2. Disconnect both battery cables.

3. Remove fuel tank cover. See **Figure 131**.

4. Disconnect hoses and remove 2 fittings at bottom of tank.

5. Disconnect fuel and vent lines at tank. See **Figure 132**.

6. Disconnect wires at tank.

7. Remove straps securing tank. Lift tank out.

8. Installation is the reverse of these steps.

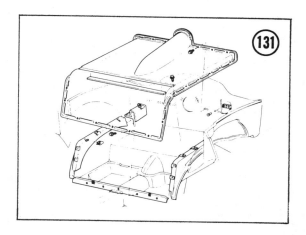

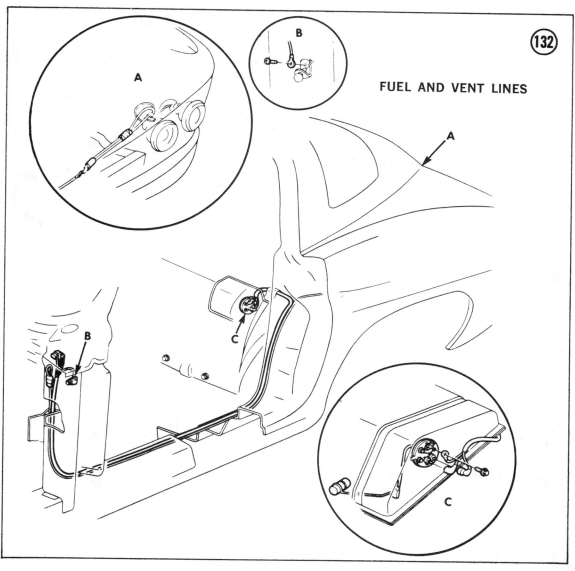

FUEL AND VENT LINES

CHAPTER SEVEN

ROCHESTER FUEL INJECTION

The Rochester fuel injection system consists of 3 basic components (**Figure 1**):

   a. Air meter

   b. Fuel meter

   c. Intake manifold with nozzles

The air meter controls intake of air to the engine and develops a vacuum control signal to the fuel meter in response to engine load. The fuel meter interprets the control signal and delivers the required fuel quantity through the injection nozzles. The intake manifold, housing the fuel distribution lines and nozzles, distributes rammed air flow to cylinders.

Figure 2 is a schematic of the 1965 system; earlier systems are similar. **Table 1** provides 1963-1965 specifications.

BASIC COMPONENTS

Air Meter

The air meter (**Figure 3**) consists of 4 main parts: throttle valve, cold enrichment valve, diffuser cone assembly, and the air meter body. The throttle valve, operated mechanically by the accelerator pedal, controls the flow of air into the system. The diffuser cone, suspended in the bore of the air meter inlet, provides a highly efficient annular venturi between the air meter

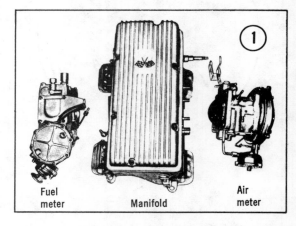

Fuel meter   Manifold   Air meter

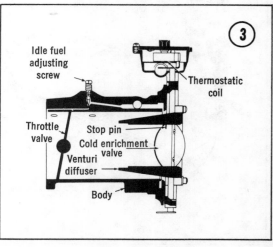

Idle fuel adjusting screw

Thermostatic coil

Throttle valve

Stop pin

Cold enrichment valve

Venturi diffuser

Body

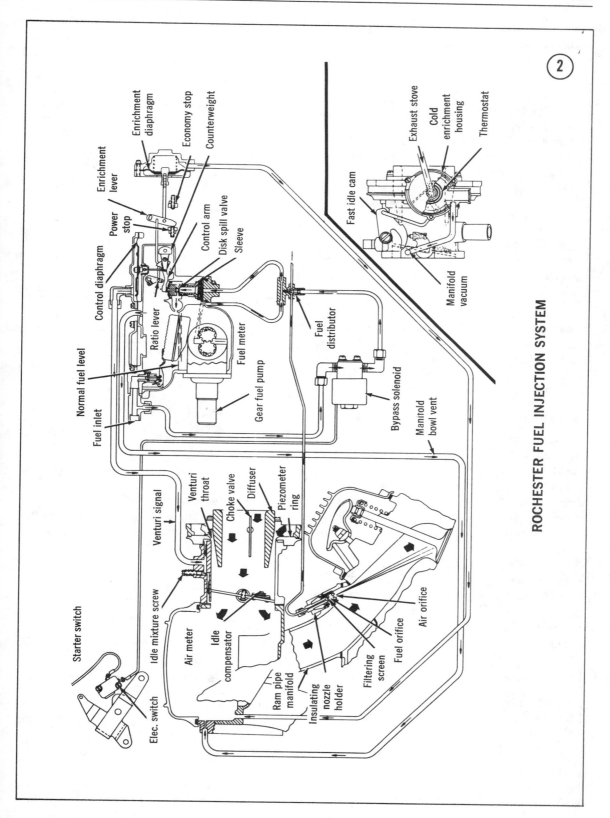

ROCHESTER FUEL INJECTION SYSTEM

Table 1   SPECIFICATIONS

	1963, 1964	1965
Fuel pressure		
Power stop @ 0.5" H₂O	1.2 (±0.1) Hg	1.9 (±0.1) Hg
Economy stop @ 0.5" H₂O	0.8 (±0.1) Hg	1.9 (±0.1) Hg
Fast idle speed (hot engine)	2,000 rpm	2,600 rpm
Enrichment diaphragm clearance (minimum)	0.040"	0.010"
Cold enrichment housing cover index	Index	Index
Cranking signal valve operating vacuum	1"	———
Enrichment diaphragm operating vacuum		
Economy stop	9"	6"
Power stop	3"	2"
Main signal diaphragm operating vacuum	1/2-30" H₂O	1/2" H₂O
Float level	2-9/32	2-9/32
Float drop	2-27/32	2-27/32

body and the cone. This type of venturi produces the minimum restriction to air flow, a vital factor in engine breathing capacity. The air meter body houses the foregoing components plus idle and main venturi signal systems.

Fuel Meter

The fuel meter contains a float-controlled fuel reservoir very similar to that used in conventional carburetion. An engine-mounted fuel pump, identical to that on carburetted models, delivers fuel through a 10 micron filter in the fuel meter. See **Figure 4**. A float-controlled inlet valve meters fuel into the fuel meter main reservoir.

The lower part of the fuel meter main reservoir contains a precision high-pressure wobble type pump. See **Figure 5**. The pump remains completely submerged. A flexible shaft driven by the distributor rotates the pump at ½ engine speed.

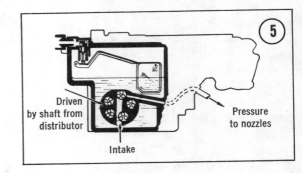

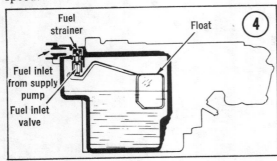

Nominal fuel pressures vary from near zero to 200 psi, depending on engine speed. Fuel not used by the engine spills back into the fuel meter by means of a fuel control system.

BASIC PRINCIPLES

Fuel Control System

A recirculating fuel flow system regulates fuel to the nozzles. The nozzles do not receive the full output of the wobble pump. Instead, a portion of the fuel delivered to the fuel distributor bypasses through the spill valve back into the main reservoir.

When the engine requires a high fuel flow, the spill valve or disc moves downward, closing off the spill ports to the fuel meter reservoir (**Figure 6**). This prevents fuel from bypassing the nozzles and thus increases fuel flow to the nozzles. Correspondingly, the spill valve or disc

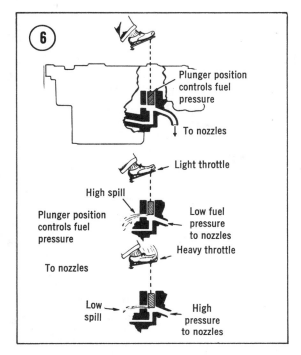

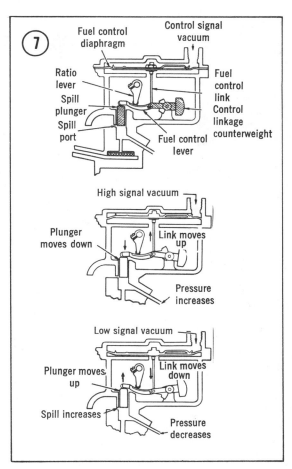

rises to allow the spill ports to be exposed when a low fuel flow is required. This causes the main output of the pump to bypass the nozzle circuits and re-enter the meter reservoir through the now-opened spill ports.

The accelerator pedal does not operate the plunger directly. The vacuum operated diaphragm, controlled by the air meter venturi vacuum, operates the plunger through a very precise counterbalanced linkage system. See **Figure 7**. Precision balancing makes the unit extremely sensitive to the slightest change in venturi vacuum and therefore to changes in the engine load.

One end of the fuel control lever rests directly on the spill plunger head and controls spill plunger or disc position. The other end of the control lever is connected by a link to the main control diaphragm. The control lever pivots on the ratio lever. When the diaphragm pulls the control lever upward, the roller end pushes the spill plunger or disc downward, closing off the spill ports and thus increasing fuel flow to the nozzles. When the diaphragm allows the control lever to fall, fuel pressure forces the spill plunger or disc upward and opens the spill ports to bypass fuel into the reservoir, reducing fuel flow to the nozzles.

The ratio of diaphragm vacuum to fuel pressure and thus fuel/air ratio is controlled by the location of the pivot point or ratio lever. Moving the ratio lever changes the mechanical advantage of the linkage system, thus providing fuel/air ratios for all driving conditions. For normal driving (engine manifold vacuum above 8 in. Hg), the ratio lever is held at the "economy" stop and fuel flow is a result of main control diaphragm vacuum. When a richer mixture is required, the ratio lever moves to the "power" stop. This increases the mechanical advantage during engine power demands, closes the spill ports and increases fuel flow to nozzles.

Starting System (1963-1964)

Cold engine starting conditions require extra fuel to compensate for poor fuel evaporation. See **Figure 8**. At starter cranking rpm, the signal generated at the idle needle and air meter ven-

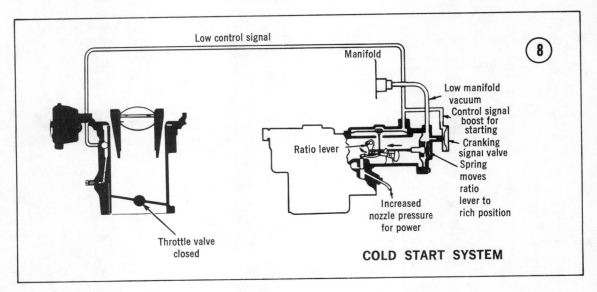

Low control signal

Manifold

⑧

Low manifold vacuum

Control signal boost for starting

Cranking signal valve

Spring moves ratio lever to rich position

Ratio lever

Increased nozzle pressure for power

Throttle valve closed

COLD START SYSTEM

turi is very low and must be boosted. Boost comes from a normally open cranking signal valve located at the enrichment diaphragm housing. The cranking signal valve allows direct manifold (cranking vacuum) to lift the main control diaphragm and close the spill valve. In addition, the enrichment diaphragm holds the ratio lever at the rich or "power" stop. Thus, maximum fuel flow at cranking speeds is directed to the nozzles. Immediately upon starting or when manifold vacuum reaches 1 in. Hg, the engine manifold vacuum overcomes the springs in the cranking signal valve and enrichment diaphragm, and the fuel injector system operates on the normal idle system.

Starting System (1965)

A bypass fuel circuit for cold starting replaces the cranking signal valve circuit on earlier injection systems. See Figure 2. Whenever the ignition switch is turned to START and the accelerator pedal is not depressed more than ⅓ of its travel, a bypass solenoid operates. This solenoid passes fuel directly from the *engine* fuel pump (not the wobble pump) through the fuel distributor to the nozzles. A ball check valve in the fuel distributor prevents the fuel from entering the fuel meter spill system.

Idle Air

Approximately 40% of the air requirement at idle enters the engine through the nozzle

blocks from an air connection on the air meter body. See **Figure 9**. The remaining air is controlled by adjusting throttle valve position with the positive idle stop screw on the air meter.

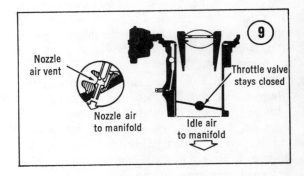

⑨

Nozzle air vent

Throttle valve stays closed

Nozzle air to manifold

Idle air to manifold

Fuel control during cold engine idling requires a maximum vacuum signal at the control diaphragm. This is accomplished by several components. The fast idle cam cracks the throttle valve open, increasing air velocity through the venturi, and increasing venturi vacuum signal to the main control diaphragm. The thermostatically controlled choke valve remains "closed" during initial cold engine operation, increasing air flow through the venturi. The enrichment diaphragm, connected directly to manifold vacuum, moves the ratio lever to the "economy" stop as soon as manifold vacuum overcomes the diaphragm spring. As the exhaust heated air relaxes the thermostat, allowing the choke valve to open, less air passes through the venturi and the boosted signal drops. The idle signal system then becomes the more important signal.

Fuel control during warm engine idle is performed by the main control signals action on the main control diaphragm. See **Figure 10**.

Hot Idle Compensator

During extreme heat conditions, fuel vapors can cause rich idling, resulting in engine roughness and stalling. A thermostatically operated valve located on the top side of the air meter throttle valve minimizes this problem. If idling temperature increases enough to affect the thermostatic spring, the valve opens, exposing a calibrated orifice through the throttle valve. A pre-determined amount of additional air bleeds into the manifold and restores the correct idle mixture ratio. Since the compensator is factory calibrated, no adjustment is necessary and the compensator should be replaced if defective.

Acceleration and Full Throttle Operation

At normal driving speeds, acceleration is instantaneous. As the throttle opens, 3 operations take place. See **Figure 11**. Increased air flow increases the venturi signal at the main diaphragm. Momentary reduction of manifold vacuum causes the ratio lever to move to the power stop. The calibrated restriction in the main control signal circuit retains any signal felt prior to the acceleration demands, thus increasing the total signal before bleeding through the restriction. Fuel/air ratios required for full throttle power are similar to acceleration requirement. See **Figure 12**.

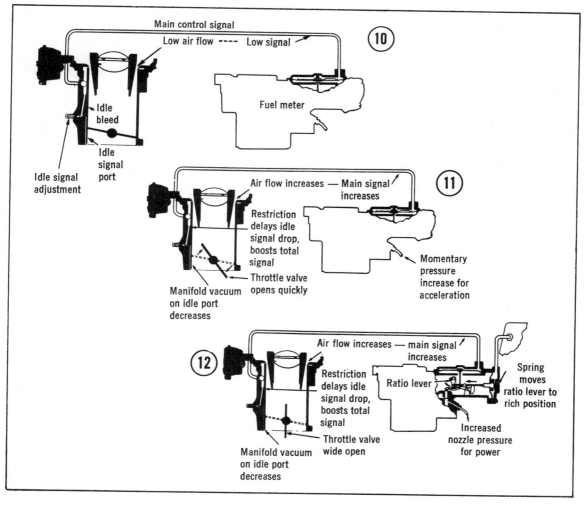

HOT STARTING AND UNLOADING

No separate circuits are included to perform these functions. For hot starting, the throttle valve must be held about ½ open. For unloading a flooded engine, hold the throttle wide open. In each case, the aim is to prevent additional fuel from being injected by the cold start circuits. On 1963-1964 models, holding the throttle wide open prevents high manifold vacuum which could operate the cranking signal valve. On 1965 models, a microswitch on the throttle linkage disables the cold start bypass solenoid when the throttle is opened.

INJECTION ASSEMBLY

Removal/Installation

Refer to **Figure 13** for the following procedure.

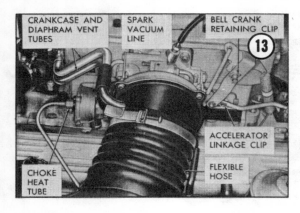

1. Disconnect washer vacuum line at manifold fitting.

2. Disconnect accelerator linkage at throttle bellcrank and bellcrank return spring.

3. Disconnect choke heat tubes.

4. Loosen clamps and disconnect all hoses to air meter and air cleaner cover. Remove air cleaner cover.

5. Disconnect fuel line at fuel meter.

6. Disconnect positive crankcase ventilation hoses at valve and oil filler tube.

7. Disconnect distributor spark advance hose at air meter.

8. Disconnect drive cable coupling at distributor. Slide cable into pump housing to disengage

it from distributor. Pull it clear and remove it from vehicle.

CAUTION
Do not lose fiber washer at distributor end of drive cable.

9. Remove 8 manifold-to-engine nuts.

10. Carefully remove injection assembly from engine.

11. Install a ⅜ x 2 in. bolt and nut in each outer mounting hole (**Figure 14**) to form feet. This prevents damage to nozzles during disassembly.

12. Installation is the reverse of these steps. Torque the mounting nuts to 15-20 ft.-lb.

13. Adjust speed and mixture as described in Chapter Three.

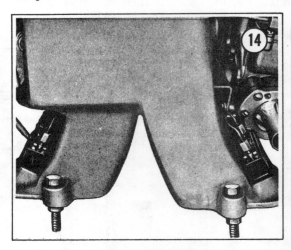

AIR METER

Removal/Installation

The air meter may be removed from engine without removing entire injection assembly. Refer to Figure 13 and **Figure 15**.

1. Disconnect throttle return spring and accelerator linkage at throttle bellcrank.

2. Remove bellcrank retaining clip. Slide bellcrank from pivot shaft; leave it attached to air meter.

3. Remove air cleaner flexible hose and cover.

4. Disconnect main control diaphragm vent tube and PCV tube at adapter.

5. Disconnect choke clean air tubes (one at choke housing, one at adapter).

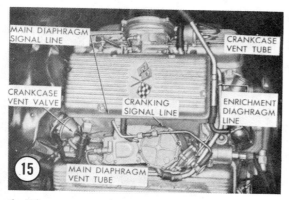

6. Disconnect main control signal tube at both ends. Lower it out of way.

7. Disconnect spark advance hose at air meter.

8. Remove 4 air meter-to-manifold nuts and lockwashers. Remove upper left nut last while moving air meter off studs. Disconnect rubber nozzle balance tube elbow. See **Figure 16**.

9. Installation is the reverse of these steps.

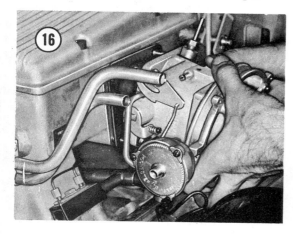

Disassembly/Assembly

Refer to **Figures 17 and 18**.

1. Remove 4 screws securing air cleaner adapter to air meter. Remove adapter.

2. Remove diffuser assembly.

3. Remove fast idle cam pivot screw, diffuser choke assembly and piezometer ring from air meter.

4. Remove idle speed and idle fuel adjusting screws. See **Figure 19**.

CAUTION

Do not put choke parts in solvent.

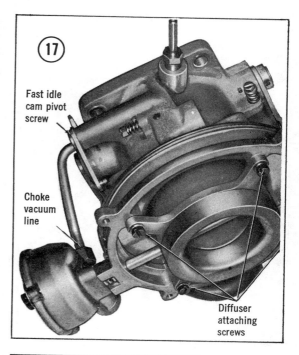

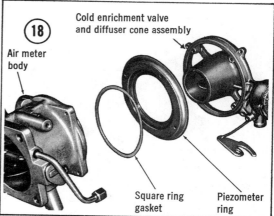

5. Remove 3 choke cover retaining screws. Disconnect heat tube and remove coil and cover.

6. Remove 2 choke housing screws and remove housing. See **Figure 20**.

7. Remove choke valve from shaft. Slide shaft from housing. Leave linkage on shaft.

CAUTION

Do not remove stop pin from diffuser cone.

NOTE: *Steps 8-10 are not necessary unless shaft binding exists. Try soaking assembly in carburetor cleaner first. If binding does not clear up, disassemble throttle valve.*

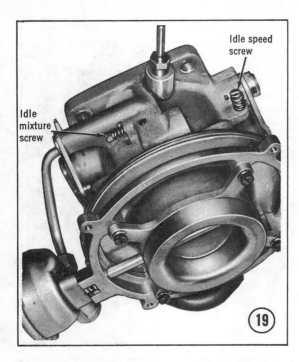

Idle speed screw

Idle mixture screw

19

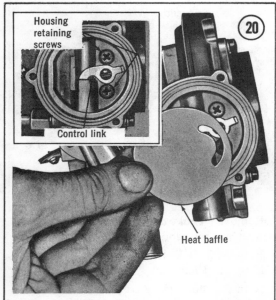

Housing retaining screws

Control link

Heat baffle

20

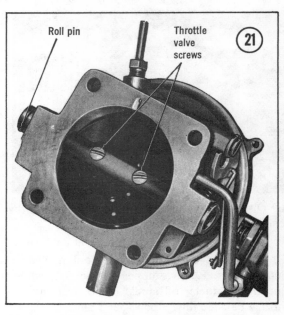

Roll pin

Throttle valve screws

21

12. Assembly is the reverse of these steps. Use Loctite on throttle valve screws, if removed. Preset idle speed and idle fuel screws 1½ turns out from bottom.

CAUTION
· *Do not screw these down tight or you may damage seats.*

FUEL METER

Entire injection assembly must be removed to remove fuel meter. See **Figure 22**.

1. Remove injection assembly as described earlier.

2. Remove main control signal tube from injection unit.

3. Disconnect main diaphragm vent tube and cranking signal line at fuel meter.

4. Disconnect enrichment diaphragm tube (both ends).

5. Invert injection assembly over a pan. Drain fuel bowl through cover vent.

6. Disconnect fuel pressure lines. See **Figures 23 and 24**.

CAUTION
Remove lines very carefully to avoid damage to nozzle tubes.

7. Remove screws at upper and lower brackets and remove fuel meter from injection assembly.

8. Remove roll pin securing throttle linkage to shaft linkage. See **Figure 21**.

9. Remove throttle valve screws.

10. Remove throttle valve from shaft. Remove shaft from air meter.

11. Clean and inspect parts as described in following procedure.

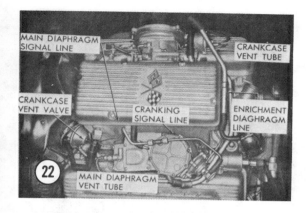

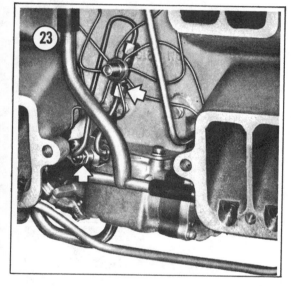

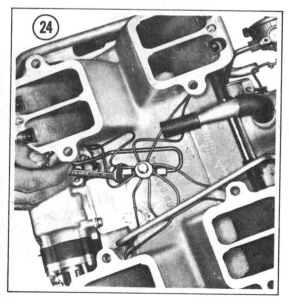

8. Installation is the reverse of these steps. Use new O-rings at fuel line connections (**Figure 25**).

CAUTION

O-rings must be absolutely clean and dry to prevent them from rolling over shoulder of nozzle distributor lines.

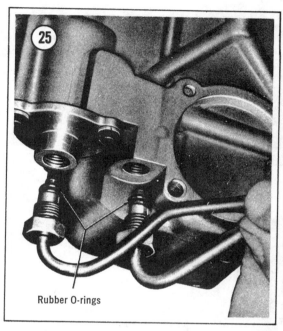

Rubber O-rings

Cranking Signal Valve
Removal/Installation (1963-1964)

This valve can be removed without removing fuel meter.

1. Disconnect vacuum line.
2. Unscrew valve. See **Figure 26**.
3. Screw new valve in. Connect vacuum line.

Enrichment Diaphragm
Removal/Installation

This valve can be replaced without removing fuel meter.

1. Remove ratio lever shield.

2. Remove vacuum lines from manifold and cranking signal valve.

3. Remove retaining clip and 2 screws shown in **Figure 27**. Remove enrichment assembly.

4. Disassemble enrichment diaphragm housing.

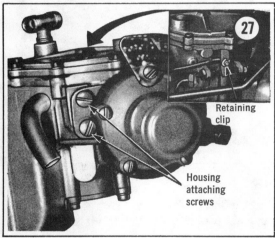

Retaining
clip

Housing
attaching
screws

3. Hold control link and remove retaining nut (**Figure 29**) and remove diaphragm.

4. Install new diaphragm and gasket. Tighten nut carefully while holding control link. Be sure that slots in diaphragm line up perfectly with screw holes in housing.

5. Install cover.

6. Reconnect vacuum lines.

5. Replace diaphragm. Center new diaphragm carefully.

6. Install enrichment assembly by reversing Steps 1-3.

7. Check clearance between housing and diaphragm with a 0.040 in. wire gauge. See **Figure 28**. Clearance must be 0.040 in. or greater to prevent interference during power stop operation. Correct diaphragm shaft length if necessary.

Main Control Diaphragm
Removal/Installation

1. Disconnect vacuum lines at diaphragm cover T-fitting.

2. Remove 8 cover screws. Separate cover from diaphragm carefully.

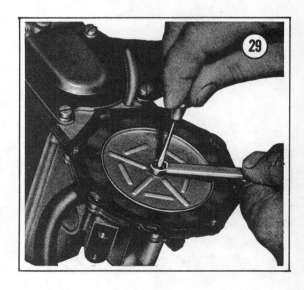

Spill Valve Removal/Installation

Injection assembly must be removed to service the spill valve.

1. Remove injection assembly from vehicle.

2. Disconnect fuel line at spill valve cover.

3. Remove 3 cover screws, cover, spring, and fuel filter screen. See **Figures 30 and 31**.

4. Carefully remove spill valve and sleeve assembly with a heavy hook shaped wire. See **Figure 32**.

5. Using fuel as a lubricant (do not oil), check valve for binding. Clean or replace valve if necessary.

6. Installation is the reverse of these steps.

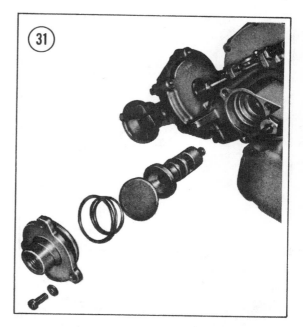

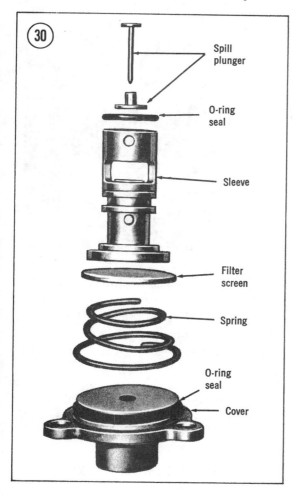

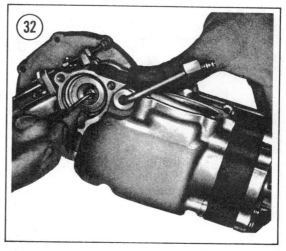

Control Arm and Counterweight Removal/Installation

Injection assembly must be removed from vehicle to perform this procedure.

1. Remove injection assembly from vehicle.

2. Remove main control diaphragm as described previously.

3. Remove nylon shield at diaphragm control link and 9 fuel bowl screws. See **Figure 33**.

CAUTION
Do not bend control link.

4. Carefully lift bowl cover, support bracket vent screen, and gasket from meter body.

5. Remove enrichment housing and cranking signal valve from fuel meter as described earlier.

6. Loosen ratio lever screw. See **Figure 34**. Slide ratio lever pivot shaft from meter body. Remove ratio lever. See **Figure 35**.

7. Rotate control arm and counterweights on

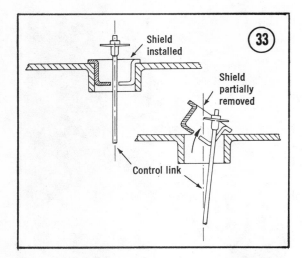

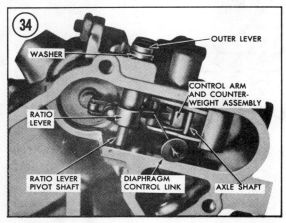

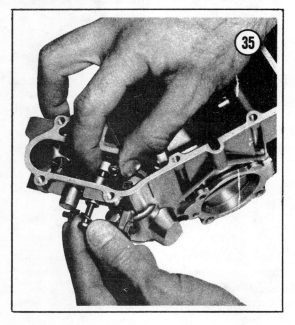

axle until axle shaft is exposed. Press axle from meter body with long nose pliers. See **Figure 36**.

NOTE: *Lead sealing ball will also come out.*

8. Position control arm and counterweight assembly in meter body. Install axle shaft and lead sealing plug.

9. Position ratio lever in meter. Install ratio lever shaft and tighten screw.

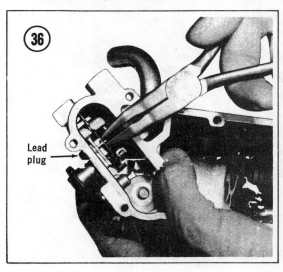

10. Check float level as shown in **Figure 37**. Bend float arm as necessary.

11. Check float drop as shown in **Figure 38**. Bend float tang if necessary.

12. Install fuel bowl gasket, cover, and upper support bracket on meter. See **Figure 39**.

13. Start control line into nylon shield slot and carefully work shield into position.

14. Install main control diaphragm and cover as described earlier.

HIGH PRESSURE PUMP

Removal/Installation

1. Remove injection assembly from engine as described earlier.

2. Remove fuel meter assembly from manifold as described earlier.

3. Remove 5 screws, pump, and gasket from fuel meter. See **Figure 40**.

4. Install pump on fuel meter with new gasket.

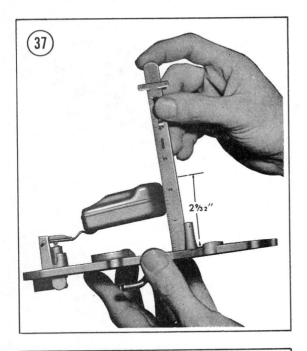

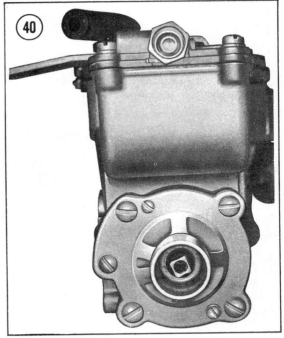

5. Install fuel meter on injection assembly.

6. Install injection assembly on engine.

Disassembly

A seal kit is available for service. However, if any other parts are damaged, the entire pump must be replaced. Disassemble pump in a large clean box as there are 48 parts, plus screws. Refer to **Figure 41**.

1. Remove 2 screws securing discharge housing and remove housing carefully.

2. Remove 5 discharge valves and springs.

3. Hold pump with inlet cover upward. Remove cover carefully.

4. Pull drive shaft out by holding wobble plate assembly.

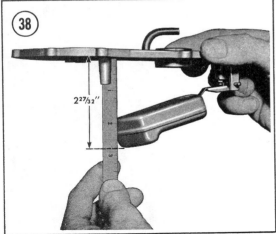

5. Remove pump pistons and inlet valve assemblies. See **Figure 42**.

6. Check all parts for dirt, warpage, nicks, burrs or other damage. Pistons must operate freely in their cylinders. Check wobble plate parts for wear or breakage.

7. Remove O-ring seals from housings.

8. If worn, measure location of drive shaft seal in discharge housing (not shown in Figure 41). Press it out with a suitable drift. See **Figure 43**.

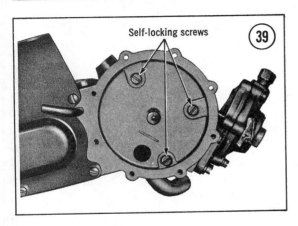

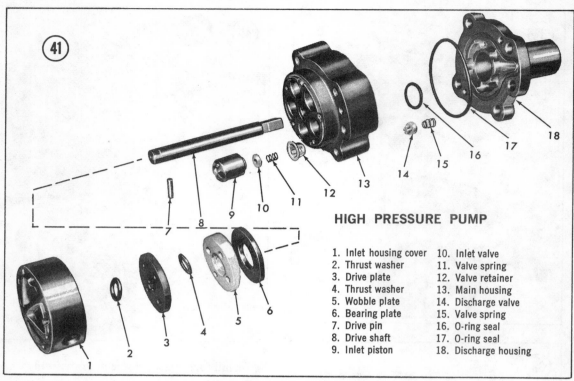

HIGH PRESSURE PUMP

1. Inlet housing cover
2. Thrust washer
3. Drive plate
4. Thrust washer
5. Wobble plate
6. Bearing plate
7. Drive pin
8. Drive shaft
9. Inlet piston
10. Inlet valve
11. Valve spring
12. Valve retainer
13. Main housing
14. Discharge valve
15. Valve spring
16. O-ring seal
17. O-ring seal
18. Discharge housing

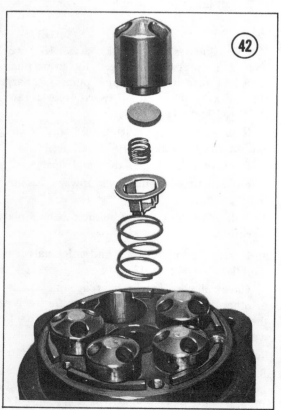

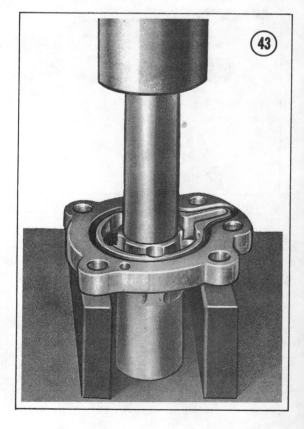

Assembly

1. If removed, coat outer diameter of drive shaft seal with good sealing compound. Press seal into housing to same location measured when old seal was removed.

2. Assemble inlet valve parts and pistons into housing. See Figure 42.

3. Assemble drive shaft and wobble plate as shown in **Figure 44**.

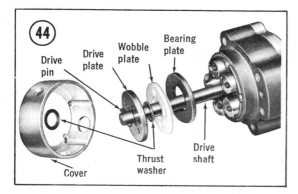

4. Carefully install drive shaft and wobble plate assembly over pistons and into pump housing.

5. Install thrust washer over end of drive shaft. Install cover.

> NOTE: *The 2 large inlet openings in cover go to the bottom of pump body.*

6. Depress cover, hold it in position and install cover screws.

7. Install new O-rings on pump body and seal groove of discharge housing. Lubricate small seal, but leave the other one dry.

8. Install 5 discharge valves and springs into discharge housing. See **Figure 45**.

9. Install pump body and drive shaft into discharge housing (Figure 45). Use a small wire to align valves during last 4 in. or so of assembly.

10. Install 2 pump body screws and lockwashers.

INTAKE MANIFOLD

Do not dismantle nozzle and fuel distribution system unless injection system requires complete overhaul.

To clean intake manifold:

1. Remove injection assembly.

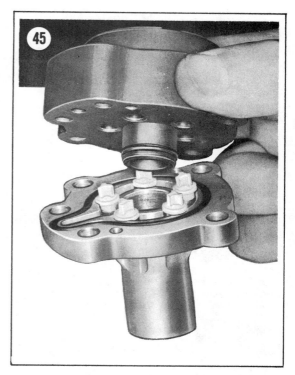

2. Remove air meter and fuel meter.

3. Remove fuel distribution lines.

4. Remove nozzles.

5. Separate cover from manifold. See **Figure 46**.

6. Wash in clean solvent and blow dry.

7. Reassemble by reversing procedure.

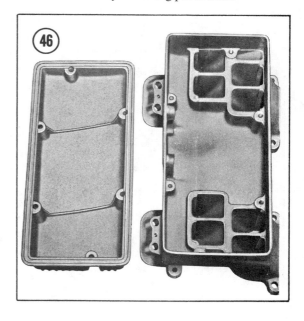

NOZZLES

Removal/Installation

1. Disconnect throttle bellcrank or fuel pump drive cable and move them out of way.

2. Disconnect and carefully move fuel lines out of way. See **Figures 47 and 48**.

3. Remove nozzle block and nozzles. See **Figure 49**.

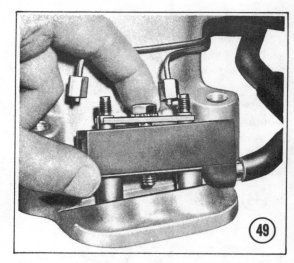

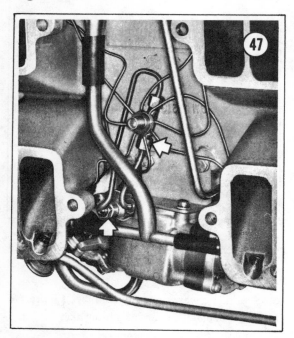

4. Remove individual nozzles from block. Remove old gaskets.

5. Install cleaned nozzles in nozzle block with new gaskets. Make certain gaskets remain in place and nozzles enter shield properly. See **Figure 50**.

6. Install nozzle blocks by reversing Steps 1-3.

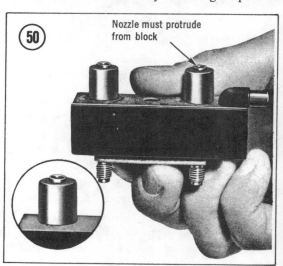

Nozzle must protrude from block

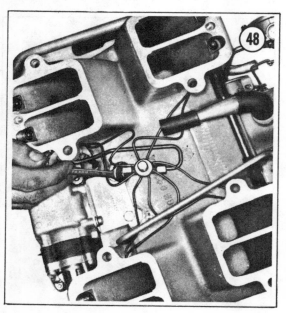

Disassembly, Cleaning, and Reassembly

1. Hold nozzle body and unscrew head with tool shown in **Figure 51**. Remove any burrs caused by disassembly.

CAUTION
Do not damage, lose, or mix up parts.
Nozzles are replaced as a unit.

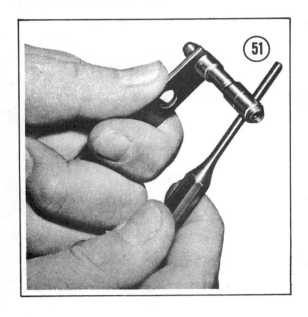

2. Clean nozzle parts in *clean* solvent.

CAUTION

Do not use wire to clean orifices. If plugged, replace nozzle as a unit.

3. Reassemble nozzle parts in order shown in **Figure 52**. Bright side of orifice disc faces nozzle head.

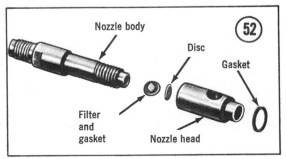

CHAPTER EIGHT

EMISSION CONTROL SYSTEMS

Harmful emissions from the Corvette are minimized by a number of systems depending on year:

a. Positive crankcase ventilation (PCV)
b. Controlled combustion system (CCS)
c. Air injection reaction (AIR)
d. Combination emission control system (CEC)
e. Fuel evaporation control system (ECS)
f. Exhaust gas recirculation system (EGR)
g. Catalytic converter (see Chapter Nine)

POSITIVE CRANKCASE VENTILATION

All Corvettes since 1963 have some form of positive crankcase ventilation. Early models have an "open" ventilation system. Fresh air is drawn through a vented oil filler cap. Later models and some early ones have a closed system. Clean air is drawn from the air cleaner; the oil filler cap is not vented.

In both open and closed systems, the fresh air scavenges emissions (e.g., piston blowby) from the crankcase and manifold vacuum draws the emissions into the carburetor. Eventually they can be reburned in the normal combustion process. **Figure 1** shows the closed system.

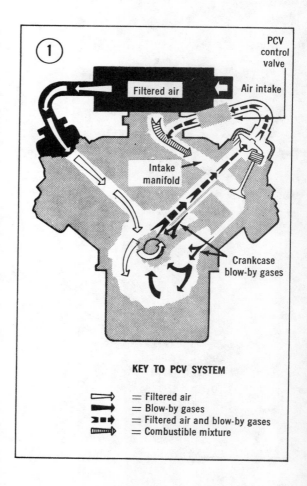

KEY TO PCV SYSTEM

⇨ = Filtered air
➡ = Blow-by gases
➤➤➡ = Filtered air and blow-by gases
▥▥▥⇨ = Combustible mixture

Either a PCV valve or fixed metered orifice mounted on the carburetor controls the volume of flow from crankcase to manifold. The valve or orifice tends to clog and must be removed and cleaned or replaced periodically. See Chapter Two.

A wide variety of systems have been used, but they differ mainly in minor ways. **Figure 2** shows typical systems.

CONTROLLED COMBUSTION SYSTEM

The controlled combustion system on 1970 and later Corvettes includes a special thermostatically controlled air cleaner, special calibrated carburetor and distributor, and a higher temperature thermostat. See **Figure 3**.

The thermostatically controlled air cleaner maintains air to the carburetor at 100°F or

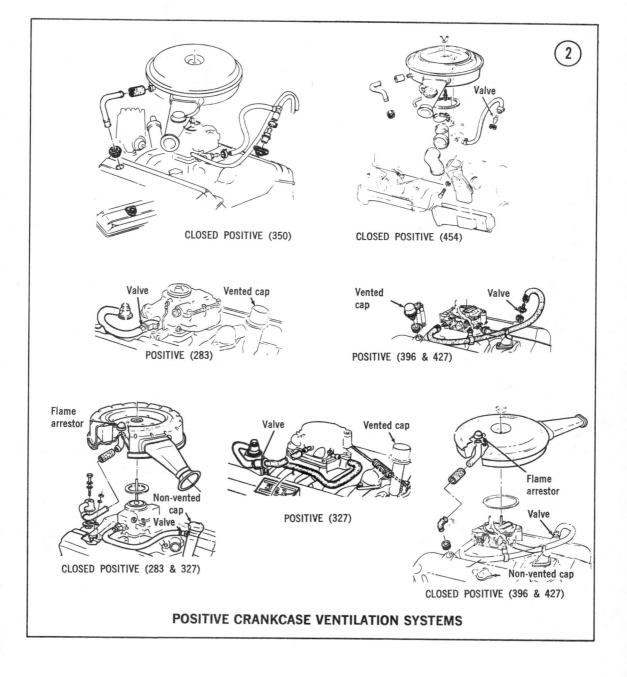

CLOSED POSITIVE (350)

CLOSED POSITIVE (454)

POSITIVE (283)

POSITIVE (396 & 427)

CLOSED POSITIVE (283 & 327)

POSITIVE (327)

CLOSED POSITIVE (396 & 427)

POSITIVE CRANKCASE VENTILATION SYSTEMS

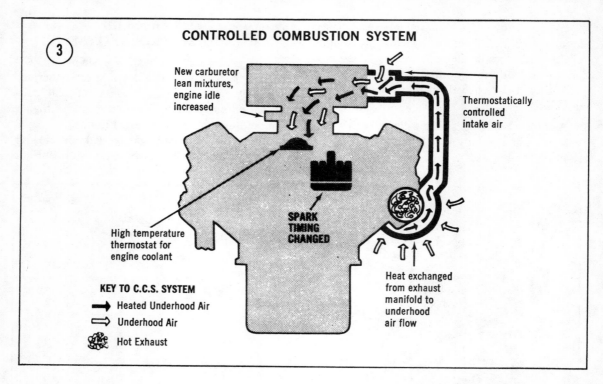

CONTROLLED COMBUSTION SYSTEM

New carburetor lean mixtures, engine idle increased

Thermostatically controlled intake air

SPARK TIMING CHANGED

High temperature thermostat for engine coolant

Heat exchanged from exhaust manifold to underhood air flow

KEY TO C.C.S. SYSTEM
➡ Heated Underhood Air
⇨ Underhood Air
🌀 Hot Exhaust

more. The air cleaner includes a temperature sensor, vacuum motor, and control damper assembly. See **Figure 4**.

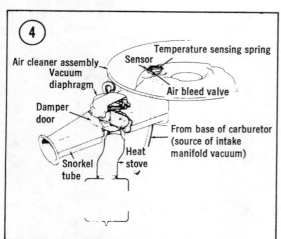

Air cleaner assembly
Vacuum diaphragm
Temperature sensing spring
Sensor
Air bleed valve
Damper door
From base of carburetor (source of intake manifold vacuum)
Snorkel tube
Heat stove

Operation of the air cleaner is shown in **Figure 5**. When the engine is off, absence of manifold vacuum permits the vacuum motor to close off the hot air pipe. When engine is running and underhood temperatures are below 85°F, the temperature sensor bleed valve is closed and manifold vacuum operates the vacuum motor.

The vacuum motor closes off the underhood air supply and the carburetor draws the much hotter air from the hot air pipe. Between 85°F and 128°F, the temperature sensor air bleed is partially open. The vacuum motor opens both the underhood air inlet and the hot air tube inlet. The resulting blend is maintained around 100°F or more. Finally, if the underhood temperature is above 128° F, the temperature sensor air bleed is fully open, the vacuum motor cannot operate and carburetor air is drawn from the underhood air inlet only.

Inspection

1. Check all heat pipe and hose connections.

2. Check for kinked or deteriorated hoses.

3. Remove air cleaner cover and install thermometer as close as possible to sensor. Install cover without wing nut. Lift cover after temperature stabilizes and read thermometer; temperature must be below 85°F before proceeding. Put cover back in place.

NOTE: *Use a relatively fast acting thermometer such as a photographic darkroom thermometer. See* **Figure 6**. *These are available for about $8.*

⑤

A—ENGINE OFF

Snorkel tube · Vacuum chamber · Diaphragm spring · Linkage · Diaphragm · Control damper assembly · Hot air pipe

B—UNDERHOOD TEMPERATURE BELOW 85°F.

Air bleed valve closed · Diaphragm spring · Vacuum chamber · Temperature sensing spring · Snorkel tube · Linkage · Diaphragm · Control damper assembly · Hot air pipe

C—UNDERHOOD TEMPERATURE ABOVE 128°F.

Air bleed valve open · Snorkel tube · Vacuum chamber · Diaphragm spring · Air inlet · Linkage · Diaphragm · Control damper assembly · Hot air pipe

D—UNDERHOOD TEMPERATURE BETWEEN 85°F. AND 128°F.

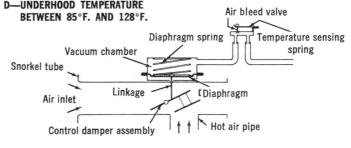

Air bleed valve · Diaphragm spring · Vacuum chamber · Temperature sensing spring · Snorkel tube · Linkage · Diaphragm · Air inlet · Control damper assembly · Hot air pipe

4. With engine off, observe damper door position through snorkel opening. Snorkel passage should be completely open (Figure 5, View A). If not, check for binds in linkage.

5. Start the engine. With the air temperature below 85°F, snorkel passage should close. When damper door begins to open passage, remove air cleaner cover and observe temperature, which should be between 85-115°F.

6. If damper door does not close completely or open at the right temperature, check the vacuum motor as described below.

Vacuum Motor Checking

1. Turn engine off. Disconnect vacuum hose between sensor and vacuum motor at sensor.

2. Suck on vacuum hose (or otherwise apply at least 9 in. Hg of vacuum). Damper door should completely close snorkel passage. If not, check for vacuum leak at other end of hose.

3. With vacuum applied, bend or tightly clamp hose to trap vacuum in motor. Damper door must remain in position. If not, the vacuum motor leaks and must be replaced.

4. If vacuum motor is good, yet system does not work properly, replace temperature sensor.

Vacuum Motor Replacement

Refer to **Figure 7** for the following procedure.

1. Remove air cleaner from engine.

2. Drill out spot welds fastening motor retaining strap to snorkel tube.

3. Unhook vacuum motor from damper door.

4. Drill 7/64 in. hole in snorkel tube at center of vacuum motor retaining strap.

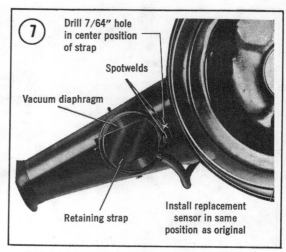

5. Connect vacuum motor to damper door.

6. Fasten retaining strap to air cleaner with sheet metal screw.

7. Install air cleaner and check operation of vacuum motor.

Temperature Sensor Replacement

1. Remove air cleaner from engine and disconnect vacuum hose at sensor.

2. Pry up sensor clip tabs. See **Figure 8**.

NOTE: *Observe position of sensor. New sensor must be installed in same position.*

3. Remove clip and sensor from air cleaner.

4. Install sensor and gasket in air cleaner in exactly the same position as the old one.

5. Press clip on sensor. Hold sensor by its sides only; do not touch control mechanism.

6. Install air cleaner and connect vacuum hoses.

AIR INJECTION REACTOR SYSTEM

The air injection reactor system reduces air pollution by oxidizing hydrocarbons and carbon monoxide as they leave the combustion chamber. See **Figures 9 and 10**.

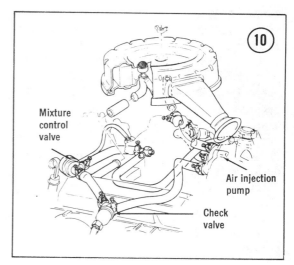

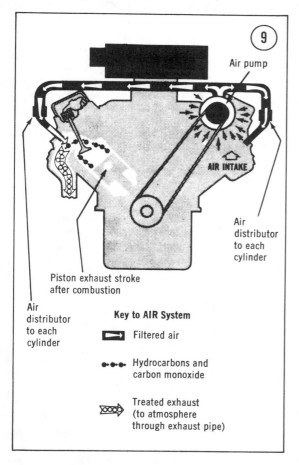

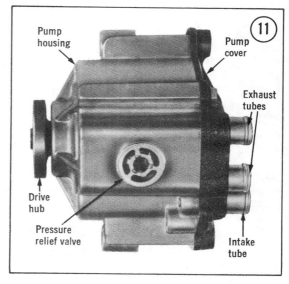

The air injection pump (**Figure 11**), driven by the engine, compresses filtered air and injects it at the exhaust port of each cylinder. The fresh air mixes with the unburned gases in the exhaust and promotes further burning.

On 1966 and 1967 systems, the mixture control valve (**Figure 12**) senses sharp increases in

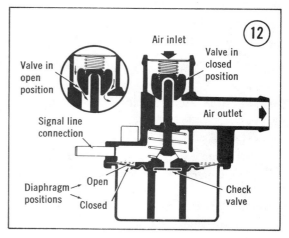

manifold vacuum, such as closed throttle deceleration. The increased vacuum opens the valve admitting fresh air into the intake manifold. This leans out the air/fuel mixture and prevents exhaust system backfire.

On 1968 and later systems, a diverter valve performs a function similar to the earlier mixture control valve. However, rather than admitting air from the pump into the intake manifold, backfire is prevented by cutting the fresh air to the exhaust system and diverting the pump output to the atmosphere. See **Figure 13**.

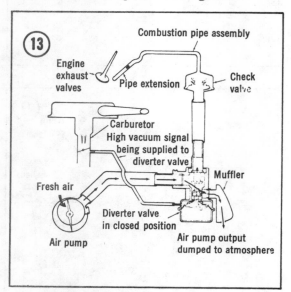

The check valves prevent exhaust gases from entering and damaging the air pump if the pump becomes inoperative, e.g., from a drive belt failure. Under normal conditions, the pump delivers sufficient air pressure to prevent exhaust gases from entering the pump.

The air injection reactor system also depends on a special calibrated carburetor, distributor, and other related components.

Air Injection Pump Removal/Installation

1. Disconnect hoses at pump.

2. Compress sides of pump belt tightly together to hold pump pulley. Loosen pump pulley bolts.

3. Loosen pump mounting bolt and pump adjustment bracket bolt. Swing pump until drive belt can be removed.

4. Remove pump pulley.

5. Remove pump mounting bolts and remove pump.

6. Installation is the reverse of these steps.

7. Adjust belt tension (Chapter Two).

> #### CAUTION
> *Air reactor system hoses are made from special materials to withstand high temperatures. Do not use substitutes.*

COMBINED EMISSION CONTROL SYSTEM

This system reduces exhaust emissions by permitting vacuum spark advance while in high gear only. It also prevents dieseling common to emission controlled engines.

The system consists of an electrically operated solenoid which shuts off the vacuum line between the carburetor and the distributor. See **Figure 14**. A switch on the transmission detects when the transmission is in a high gear; **Table 1** explains when vacuum is present and when it is shut off.

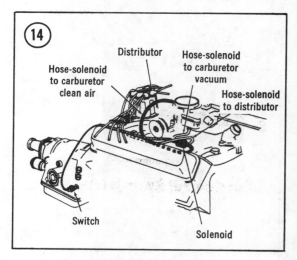

Figure 15 is a more detailed diagram of the 1970-1971 system. When the solenoid is not energized, vacuum to the distributor vacuum advance unit is shut off. The distributor is vented to atmosphere through a filter at the opposite end of the solenoid. When the solenoid is energized, the vacuum port uncovers and the plunger shuts off the clean air vent.

The solenoid performs another function besides that of a vacuum switch. When idling in a

Table 1   CEC SYSTEM OPERATION

Transmission	Gear						
	Park	Neutral	Reverse	1st	2nd	3rd	4th
3-speed	—	O	O	O	O	×	—
4-speed	—	O	O	O	O	×	×
Turbo-Hydramatic	O	O	×	O	O	×	—

X = Vacuum.   O = No vacuum.

low gear, e.g., during high gear deceleration with throttle closed, the solenoid is energized and the plunger is extended. This provides a higher idle rpm for reduced hydrocarbon emissions during high gear deceleration.

Two switches and 2 relays control the solenoid. When the transmission is in a low gear, the transmission switch contacts are closed and the reversing relay contacts are open and the solenoid is de-energized. When the transmission shifts to high gear, the transmission switch contacts open, the reversing relay de-energizes and the reversing relay contacts close. The solenoid energizes.

Two other circuits can energize the solenoid. The time delay relay holds its contacts closed for about 15 seconds after the ignition is turned on. The voltage developed across the resistor energizes the solenoid. Full vacuum during this time improves acceleration and eliminates stalling after a start. Finally, the water temperature switch provides an override when the temperature is below 82°F. The switch closes to ground below this temperature and energizes the solenoid.

The combined emission control system also provides methods to prevent dieseling which is a problem with emission controlled engines. One method is a by-product of the much lower "curb" idle rpm which occurs when the CEC solenoid is de-energized. The engine runs at such a low rpm it cannot diesel.

On air-conditioned vehicles with automatic transmission, the throttle is open more with the engine idling, and the engine tends to diesel if the air-conditioner compressor happens to be off. To prevent this, a solid state timer engages the air-conditioner clutch for 3 seconds after

the ignition is turned off. The additional compressor load stops the engine quicker, reducing its tendency to diesel. **Figure 16** shows location of components in the 1970-1971 system.

The system on 1972 350 cubic inch engines is similar to the earlier system with the following exceptions:

a. The transmission switch is open in low gears, eliminating the need for reversing relay.

b. A separate idle stop solenoid closes throttle completely when ignition is turned off to prevent dieseling.

c. The water temperature override operates below 82°F as before, but also operates above 232°F.

d. No time delay relay operates during startings.

e. A time delay prevents energizing vacuum advance solenoid for 23 seconds after shifting to high gear.

Figure 17 is a simplified schematic of the 350 cubic inch system. When the ignition is turned on, the idle stop solenoid cracks the throttle open to idle. If the engine cools and temperature is below 82°F, the solenoid operates. Vacuum advance when the engine is cold improves acceleration and helps minimize stalling. If the coolant is above 82°F, the solenoid does not energize.

When engine coolant rises above 82°F, the solenoid can energize only when transmission is in high gear and the 20 second time delay period has passed. In low gear, the transmission switch opens, de-energizing the solenoid. When the transmission is shifted to high gear, the

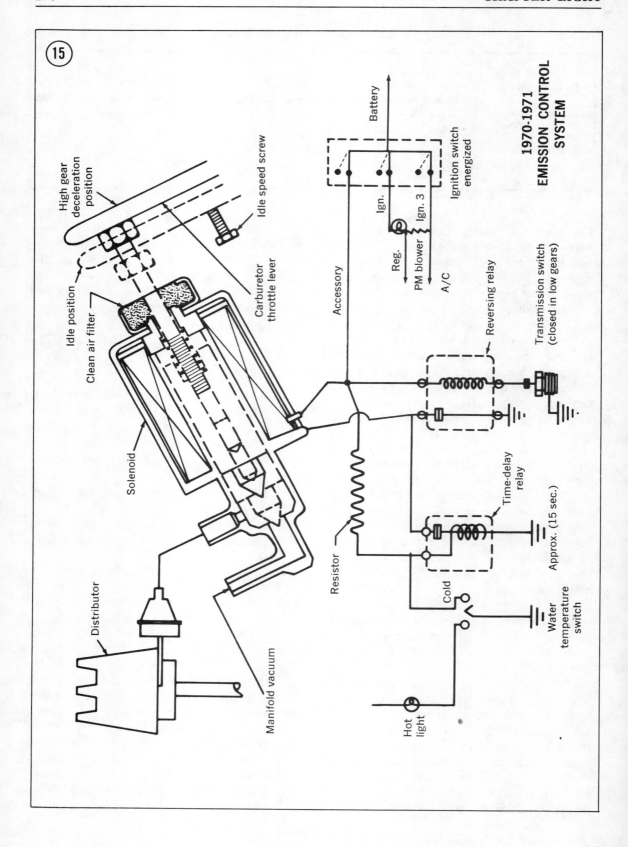

(15)

High gear deceleration position

Idle speed screw

Idle position

Clean air filter

Carburetor throttle lever

Solenoid

Distributor

Manifold vacuum

Resistor

Accessory

Battery

Ign.

Ign. 3

Ignition switch energized

Reg.

PM blower

A/C

Reversing relay

Transmission switch (closed in low gears)

Time-delay relay

Approx. (15 sec.)

Cold

Water temperature switch

Hot light

1970-1971 EMISSION CONTROL SYSTEM

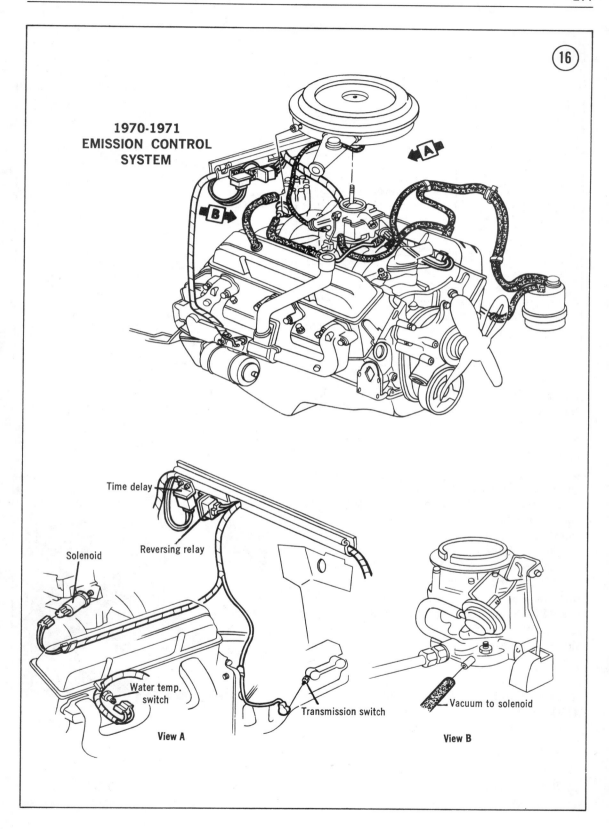

1970-1971 EMISSION CONTROL SYSTEM

Time delay

Reversing relay

Solenoid

Water temp. switch

Transmission switch

Vacuum to solenoid

View A

View B

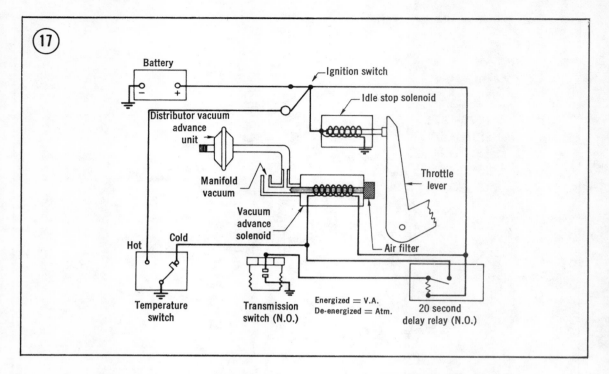

(17)

Battery — Ignition switch

Idle stop solenoid

Distributor vacuum advance unit

Manifold vacuum

Throttle lever

Vacuum advance solenoid

Air filter

Hot Cold

Temperature switch

Transmission switch (N.O.)

Energized = V.A.
De-energized = Atm.

20 second delay relay (N.O.)

transmission switch closes, but the time delay relay holds its contacts open for 20 seconds, preventing the solenoid from energizing. After 20 seconds, the solenoid energizes. If the transmission downshifts, even momentarily from high gear, the time delay relay will still prevent energizing the solenoid for 20 seconds.

If coolant temperature exceeds 232°F, regardless of gear, the temperature switch overrides the system and operates the solenoid to supply vacuum advance.

The system in the 454 cubic inch Corvette is identical to the 350 cubic inch model, except that there is no time delay circuit. See **Figure 18**. The solenoid energizes (and supplies full vacuum advance) as soon as the transmission switch closes.

Transmission Switch Replacement (1970-1971)

Refer to Figure 16.

1. Disconnect electrical wire.
2. Unscrew switch.
3. Screw in new switch and connect wire.
4. Test switch as described above.

Transmission Switch Replacement 1972-1973 Turbo Hydramatic 350

Figures 19 and 20 show location of the switch on the manual and Turbo Hydramatic 350 transmissions, respectively.

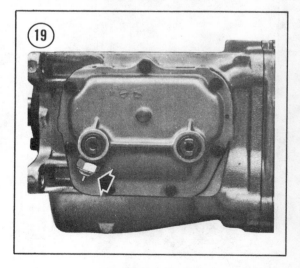

(19)

1. Disconnect electrical wire.
2. Unscrew switch.
3. Screw in new switch and connect wire.
4. Test switch as described above.

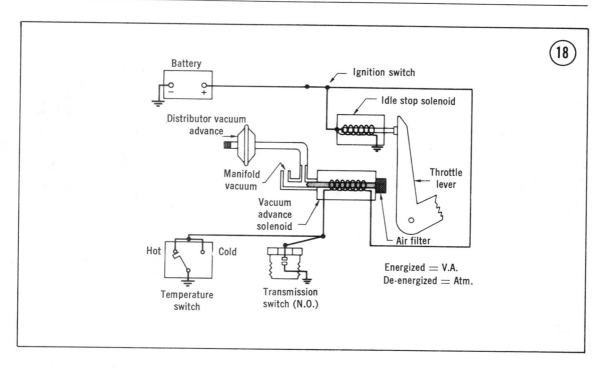

Transmission Switch Replacement
1972-1976 Turbo Hydramatic 400

The switch is located internally. See **Figure 21**. The transmission oil pan must be removed to reach the switch. Chapter Twelve explains pan removal.

A wire connects the switch to the externally mounted detent solenoid TCS connector. See **Figure 22**. Fortunately, the switch can be tested externally as described in Chapter Four.

CEC Solenoid Replacement (1970-1971)

See *Disassembly* procedure for your carburetor in Chapter Six.

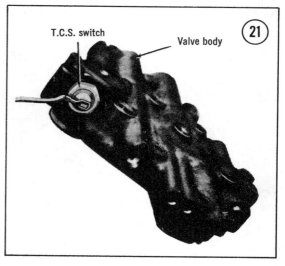

Vacuum Advance Solenoid Replacement (1972-1974)

On 350 engines, the solenoid is located on the right rear portion of the intake manifold. See **Figure 23**. On 454 engines, the solenoid is between the carburetor and the distributor. See **Figure 24**.

1. Disconnect vacuum hoses and electrical wires from solenoid.

2. Remove solenoid from bracket.

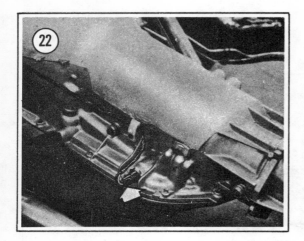

3. Install new solenoid. Connect vacuum hoses and wires.

Idle Stop Solenoid Replacement (1972-1976)

The idle stop solenoid is mounted on the carburetor. See **Figure 25**. Refer to *Disassembly* procedure in Chapter Six for your carburetor.

Relay Replacement (1970-1971)

Refer to Figure 16.

1. Disconnect cable from relay.

2. Unscrew relay bracket.

3. Install new relay and reconnect cable.

Time Delay Relay (1972-1974)

The time delay relay is located on the instrument panel reinforcement immediately behind the console instrument cluster assembly.

1. Disconnect cable from relay.

2. Unscrew relay bracket.

3. Install new relay and reconnect cable.

Water Temperature Switch Replacement (1970-1974)

The water temperature switch is located on the left cylinder head on 1970-1971 engines (Figure 16) and on the right cylinder head on 1972-1974 engines (**Figure 26**).

FUEL EVAPORATION CONTROL SYSTEM

All 1972 and later Corvettes (1970 and later in California) are equipped with a fuel evaporation control system which prevents release of fuel vapor into the atmosphere.

Refer to **Figure 27**. Fuel vapor from the fuel tank passes through the liquid/vapor separator to the carbon canister. The carbon absorbs and stores the vapor when the engine is stopped. When the engine runs, manifold vacuum draws the vapor from the canister. Instead of being released into the atmosphere, the fuel vapor takes part in the normal combustion process.

There is no preventive maintenance other than replacing the filter on the bottom of the carbon canister every 12,000 miles and checking tightness and conditions of all lines connecting the parts of the system. See Chapter Two.

Figures 28 and 29 show location of ECS components in the Corvette. **Figure 30** shows several ways in which hoses may be routed.

EXHAUST GAS RECIRCULATION (1973-1974)

The Exhaust Gas Recirculation (EGR) system is used to reduce the emission of nitrogen oxides (NOX). Relatively inert exhaust gases are introduced into the combustion process to slightly reduce peak temperatures. This reduction in temperatures reduces formation of NOX.

The exhaust gases are introduced into the intake manifold by way of an EGR valve (**Figure 31**). This shut off and metering valve operates on vacuum from the intake manifold via a signal port in the carburetor. On 1974 models a thermal vacuum switch cuts off vacuum to the EGR valve until water temperature reaches 100°F. At idle speed, recirculation is not required. Thus the carburetor signal port is located above the throttle valve and vacuum to the EGR valve diaphragm is cut off at idle speeds.

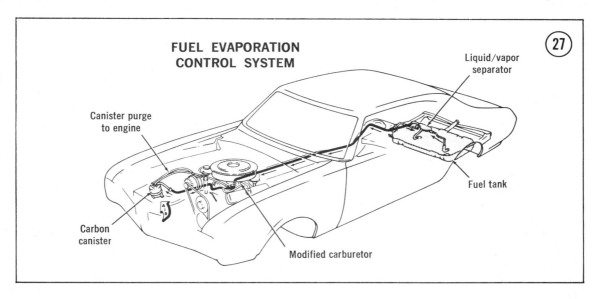

FUEL EVAPORATION CONTROL SYSTEM

Canister purge to engine

Liquid/vapor separator

Fuel tank

Carbon canister

Modified carburetor

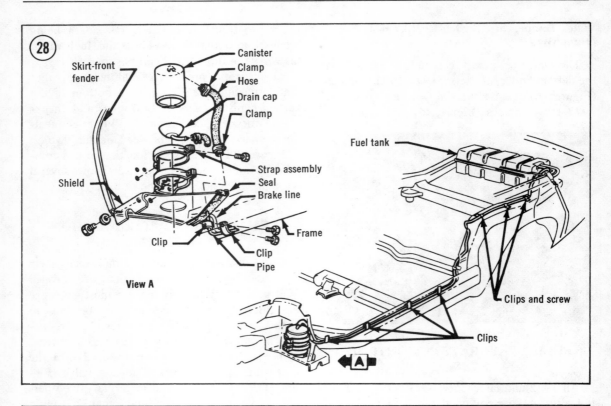

(28)

Skirt-front fender

Canister
Clamp
Hose
Drain cap
Clamp

Strap assembly
Seal
Brake line

Shield

Clip
Clip
Pipe

View A

Fuel tank

Frame

Clips and screw

Clips

A

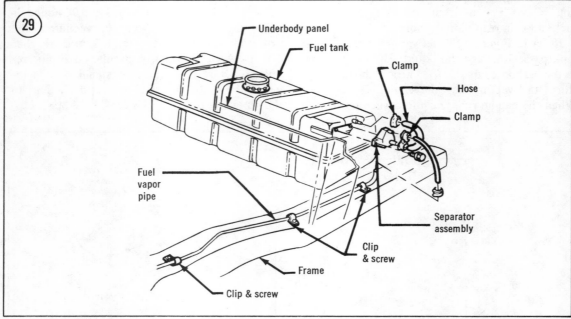

(29)

Underbody panel

Fuel tank

Clamp

Hose

Clamp

Fuel
vapor
pipe

Separator
assembly

Clip
& screw

Frame

Clip & screw

This causes the EGR valve to close, halting the introduction of exhaust gas to the intake manifold. As the throttle valve is opened, the signal port is again exposed to manifold vacuum. This actuates the EGR valve diaphragm, which opens the valve and allows exhaust gas to be metered (through an orifice) into the intake manifold (**Figure 32**).

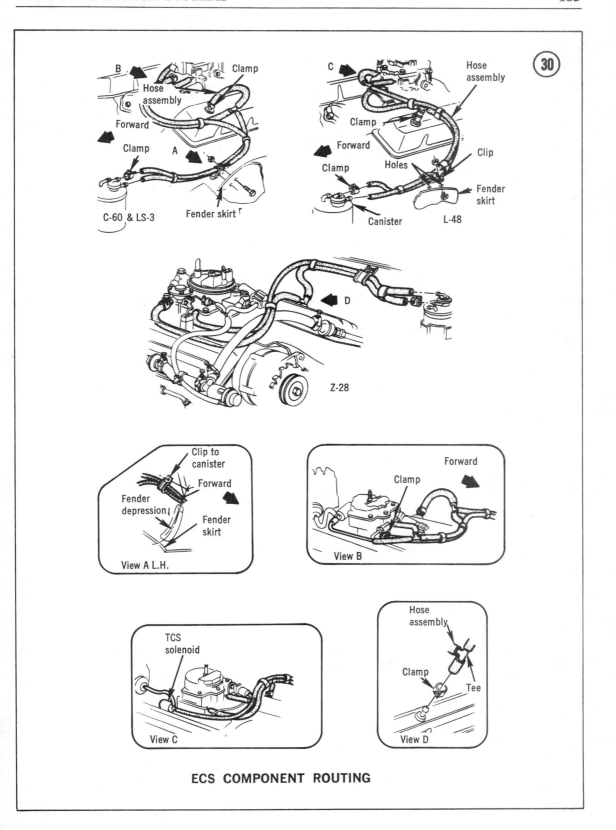

ECS COMPONENT ROUTING

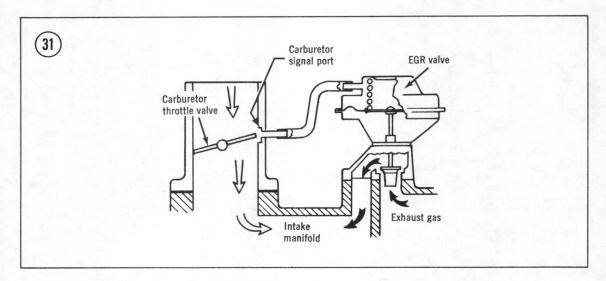

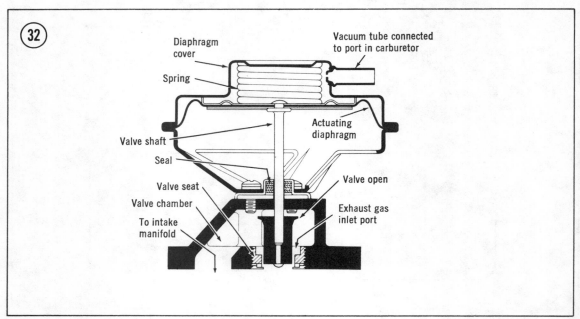

On Corvette engines, the valve is located externally on the right side of the intake manifold next to the rocker arm cover (**Figure 33**).

EGR Valve Replacement

1. Disconnect vacuum line at top of valve.

2. Remove bolt and clamp securing valve to manifold, then remove valve from manifold.

3. Reassemble valve to manifold, using new gasket, and torque bolt to 25 ft.-lb. Bend lock tab up over bolt head. Replace vacuum line.

EGR Valve Cleaning

CAUTION
Do not wash valve assembly in solvents or degreaser. Permanent damage could result.

1. Use wire brush or wire wheel to clean valve base and remove exhaust deposits from mounting surface.

2. A spark plug cleaner (sandblaster) can be used to clean valve seat and pintle. Insert valve and pintle into machine and blast for 30 seconds.

NOTE: *Many service stations have this type of spark plug cleaner and will clean the valve for a small fee.*

3. Compress diaphragm spring so valve is fully unseated and repeat sandblasting for 30 seconds.

4. Make sure all exhaust deposits have been removed. Repeat cleaning if required.

5. Use compressed air to remove all abrasive material from the valve.

Thermal Vacuum Switch Replacement (1974)

1. Disconnect vacuum lines and remove switch from thermostat housing.

2. Apply a sealer to switch threads and install switch in thermostat housing. Torque to 15 ft.-lb.

3. Rotate head of switch as required for proper hose routing and install vacuum hoses.

NOTE: *Thermal vacuum switch is nonrepairable. If defective, replace with new part.*

CHAPTER NINE

COOLING AND EXHAUST SYSTEMS

The cooling system is a pressurized type with thermostat control of circulation. The system consists of a pressurized radiator, pressure type radiator cap, centrifugal vane water pump, thermostat, and several water hoses. Pressurizing the system permits operating the coolant above its normal boiling point in order to raise the efficiency of the radiator.

All 1963-1974 Corvettes are equipped with dual exhaust systems. The system includes 2 front and rear exhaust pipe sections, mufflers, tailpipes and mounting hardware. See **Figure 1**. All 1975-1976 Corvettes have a catalytic converter mounted between the front exhaust pipes and the mufflers (**Figure 2**).

CLEANING AND FLUSHING

Cleaning

The cooling system should be cleaned with a good cleaning solution to loosen rust and scale before reverse flushing. Use GM Cooling System Cleaner or equivalent. Since procedure varies according to brand, follow manfacturer's directions exactly.

CAUTION
Some Corvettes have aluminum rather than conventional copper radiators. Do not use common "soda" or caustic base cleaners or any other cleaner generally used with copper radiators unless the container clearly recommends use for aluminum radiators.

Reverse Flushing

Reverse flushing is accomplished by forcing a water/air stream through the system in a direction opposite from the normal flow. The procedure requires special equipment and should be done by a professional radiator shop or your dealer.

If the system has not been seriously neglected, the following reverse flushing procedure (**Figure 3**) can be done by anyone with a garden hose. It is worth trying before paying for a more thorough, professional job.

> NOTE: *Always clean system as described above before flushing the system.*

1. Drain cooling system by removing the lower radiator hose. Do not open the engine block petcock. Once the radiator is drained, reconnect the lower radiator hose.

2. Remove radiator cap.

3. Remove thermostat.

4. Disconnect the heater hose from the thermostat housing. The open end of this hose will be a drain during flushing.

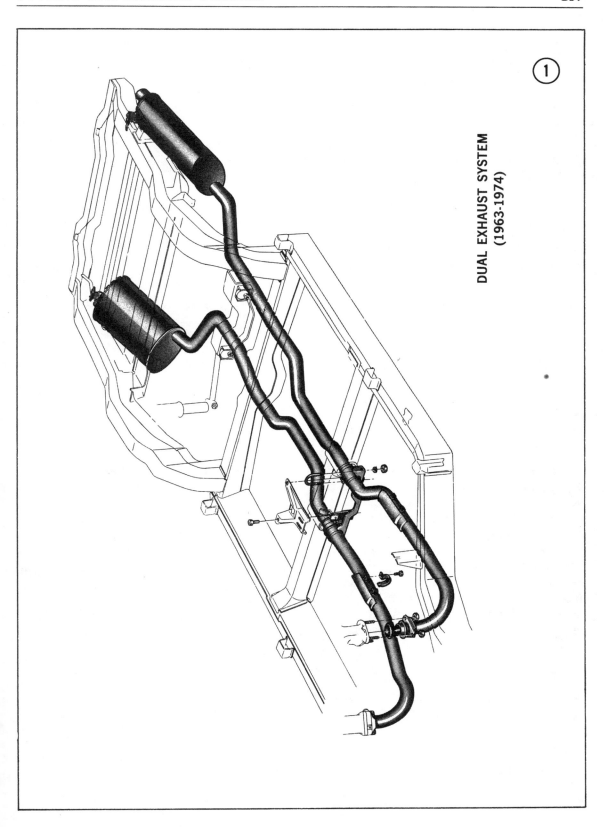

DUAL EXHAUST SYSTEM
(1963-1974)

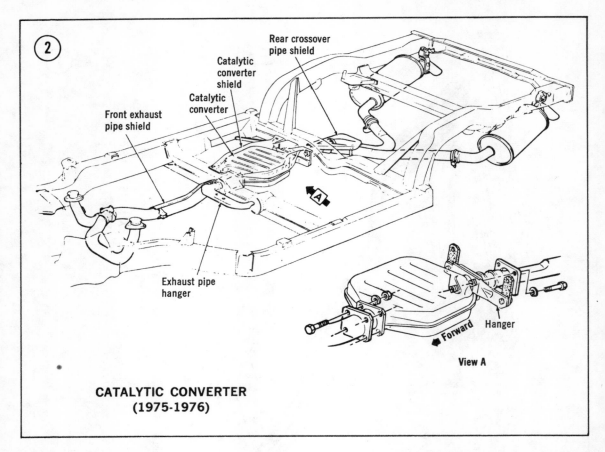

**CATALYTIC CONVERTER
(1975-1976)**

5. Connect a water supply, e.g., from a garden hose, to the rear engine block connection. This does not have to be a positive connection as long as most of the water enters the engine. If necessary, temporarily connect a length of heater hose to the rear block connection to make the garden hose connection more convenient.

6. Turn water on and flush for 3 to 5 minutes. It is not necessary to run engine. For the last minute of flushing, repeatedly squeeze upper radiator hose to expell any trapped coolant.

7. Turn water off. Reconnect heater hose to engine block on water pump.

8. Drain entire system by removing the lower radiator hose and opening the petcocks located at each side of the engine block.

Refilling

1. Be sure that all hoses are reconnected and all petcocks closed.

2. Set heater control to maximum.

3. Remove radiator cap and fill with an ethylene glycol/water mixture. The mixture must provide at least 0°F protection even if you live in a warmer climate; the anti-freeze makes a good rust inhibitor.

4. When system is full, install radiator cap.

5. Run engine at a fast idle and recheck coolant level. Top up if necessary. Also check system for leaks.

6. Recheck coolant level after driving several miles; it takes some time for all air to be removed from the system.

PRESSURE CHECK

If the coolant system requires frequent topping up, chances are there is a leak. Not only may coolant be lost, but without proper pressure, the coolant recovery system cannot function properly. To check the system, proceed as follows.

1. Remove radiator cap.

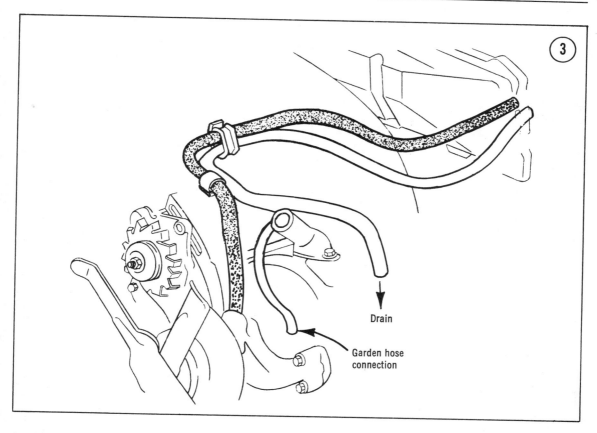

Drain

Garden hose connection

2. Dip the cap in water and attach to a cooling system pressure tester. See **Figure 4**.

3. Pump cap to pressure shown in **Table 1**. If the cap fails to hold pressure, replace it.

4. Pump cap pressure above Table 1 pressure. If cap fails to relieve pressure, replace it.

5. Attach pressure tester to filler hole on radiator. See **Figure 5**.

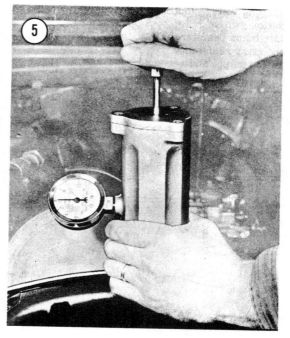

Table 1   COOLING SYSTEM SPECIFICATIONS

Radiator cap pressure	
1963-1965	13 psi
1966-1976	15 psi
Coolant capacity ①	
327 (1963-1964)	17 qt.
327 (1965-1968)	19 qt.
350 (1969-1974)	18 qt.
350 (1975-1976)	21 qt.
427	23 qt.
454	24 qt.
Thermostat	
1966-1969 without AIR system ②	180°
1966-1970 with AIR system ②	195°
1970-1974 (all engines)	180°
1975-1976 with optional 350 engine	180°
1975-1976 with standard 350 engine	195°

① Add 1 qt. for air-conditioned cars.
② AIR = Air Injection Reactor; See Chapter Eight.

6. Pump system to pressure in Table 1. There should be no noticeable pressure drop in 30 seconds. If pressure falls off, there is a leak which must be found and sealed.

WATER PUMP

Removal/Installation

1. Drain radiator.

2. Loosen fan drive bolts.

3. Loosen alternator bracket; rotate alternator and remove fan belt.

4. Loosen idler pulley bracket (or power steering pump bracket if so equipped) and remove drive belt.

5. Disconnect radiator hose and heater hose from water pump.

6. Remove 4 pump mounting bolts. Remove pump/fan assembly from vehicle.

7. Remove fan assembly from pump.

CAUTION
Thermostatic fan clutches must be kept vertical when removed to prevent leakage of silicone fluid.

8. Installation is the reverse of these steps.

9. Start engine and check for leaks.

RADIATOR

Removal/Installation

Refer to **Figure 6** for the following procedure.

1. Raise hood. On air-conditioned vehicles, remove hood (see Chapter Fifteen).

NOTE: *The following 2 steps apply to air-conditioned models only.*

2. Remove receiver dehydrator mounting bolts and let dehydrator rest in place.

3. Back out left front hinge-to-body bolt.

4. Drain radiator.

5. Remove radiator inlet and outlet hoses.

6. Remove supply tank hose at radiator.

7. Disconnect transmission cooler lines if so equipped.

8. Remove the shroud-to-radiator screws. Let shroud rest on fan.

9. Remove 4 upper support screws. Loosen 2 lower bolts. Carefully lift radiator from vehicle.

10. Installation is the reverse of these steps.

11. Start engine and check for leaks.

THERMOSTAT

Removal and Testing

1. Drain about 2 quarts of coolant from the radiator.

2. Unbolt cap screws holding the thermostat housing.

3. Lift out thermostat.

4. Heat a container of 33% glycol and water 25°F above the temperature stamped on the thermostat. Place thermostat in water and check that it is fully open. Replace if defective.

Installation

1. Test a brand new thermostat as in Step 4 above. Do not assume a new thermostat works properly. Replace if necessary.

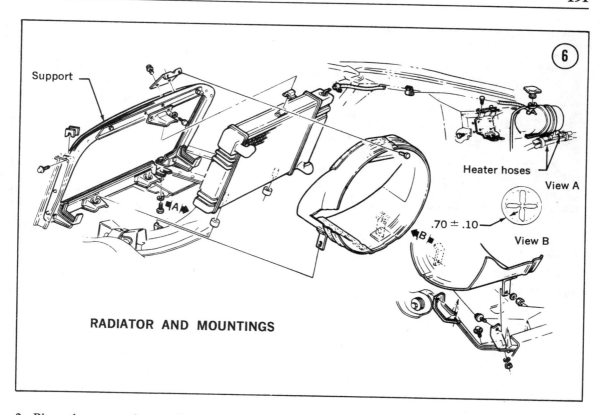

RADIATOR AND MOUNTINGS

2. Place thermostat in manifold. See **Figure 7**.

3. Install thermostat housing with new gasket.

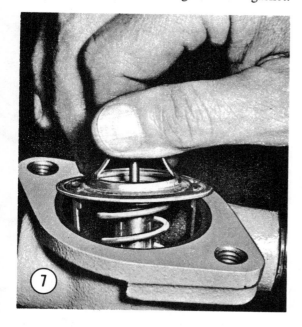

4. Fill cooling system.

5. Start engine and check for leaks.

EXHAUST SYSTEM

Muffler Replacement

1. Raise vehicle on hoist.

2. Remove U-bolts at both rear tailpipe shields. See **Figure 8**.

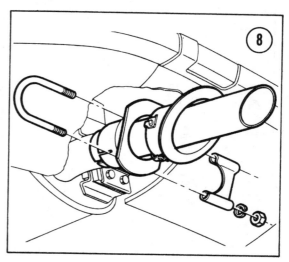

3. Separate exhaust system at crossmember tube by loosening U-bolts. See **Figure 9**.

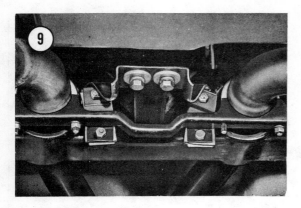

4. Remove both rear muffler brackets from frame and slide muffler system rearward.

5. Cut exhaust pipe near the muffler to allow sufficient pipe for muffler replacement.

CAUTION
Measure exhaust pipe end of new muffler and cut pipe to allow 1½ in. engagement of pipe into muffler.

6. Inspect rubber mounts. Replace if defective. See **Figures 10 and 11**.

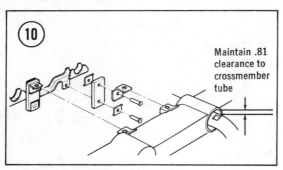

Maintain .81 clearance to crossmember tube

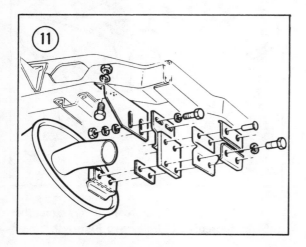

7. Install new muffler with new clamps.

> NOTE: *Clamps must be assembled with nuts toward rear of vehicle and 90° to sawcuts in muffler* (**Figure 12**).

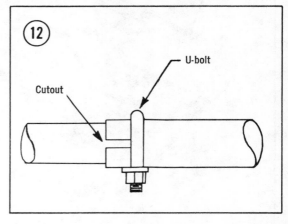

U-bolt

Cutout

8. Reverse Steps 1-4 of this procedure.

Rear Exhaust Pipe Replacement

1. Perform Steps 1-4, *Muffler Replacement*.

2. Cut rear exhaust pipe near muffler.

3. Remove rear exhaust pipe and install new one.

4. Perform Steps 6-8 of *Muffler Replacement* procedure.

Front Exhaust Pipe Replacement

1. Raise vehicle on hoist.

2. Disconnect exhaust pipe at manifold. See **Figure 13**.

3. Remove clamps at rear end of front exhaust pipe and remove pipe.

4. Connect new front pipe to rear pipe.

5. Attach front pipe to manifold with new packing and new nuts.

> NOTE: *Clean or replace manifold studs before installing nuts.*

6. Install new clamp at rear of front pipe.

7. Lower vehicle.

CATALYTIC CONVERTER

Exhaust systems on 1975-1976 models have a catalytic converter installed between the engine and the mufflers. This is an emission control

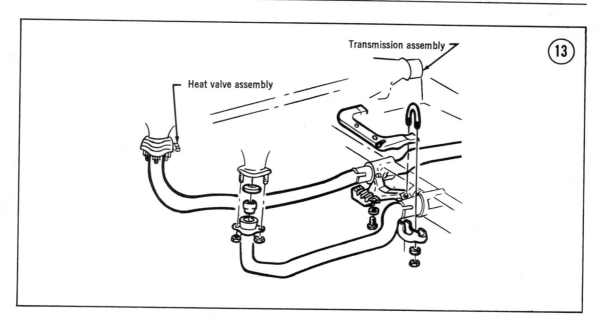

device that reduces hydrocarbon and carbon monoxide pollutants in the exhaust gases. The converter contains beads that are coated with a catalytic material containing platinum and palladium. The converter does not require periodic maintenance. However, it may become necessary to replace either the converter or the catalytic beads. Replacement of the catalytic beads requires expensive tools, making it more economical to have the job done by a dealer or qualified garage. A procedure for removing and replacing the converter is given below.

Removal/Installation

Refer to Figure 2.

1. Raise vehicle.
2: Disconnect converter at front and rear.
3. Remove converter.
4. Reverse procedure for installation.

CHAPTER TEN

ELECTRICAL SYSTEM

This chapter includes service procedures for the battery, starter, charging system, lighting system, fuses, instruments, windshield wipers, and ignition components. Specifications (**Tables 1 through 5**) are also included at end of chapter.

BATTERY

Care and Inspection

1. Remove battery hold-down clamps. Disconnect battery cables and remove battery.

2. Clean the top of the battery with baking soda solution. Scrub with a stiff bristle brush. Wipe clean with a cloth moistened in ammonia or baking soda solution.

> **CAUTION**
> *Keep cleaning solution out of battery cells or the electrolyte will be seriously weakened.*

3. Clean battery terminals with a stiff wire brush or one of the many tools made for this purpose.

4. Examine battery case for cracks.

5. Install battery and reconnect the battery cables. Observe polarity.

6. Coat battery connections with light mineral grease or Vaseline after tightening.

7. Check the electrolyte level and top up if necessary.

Testing

Hydrometer testing is the best way to check battery condition. Use a hydrometer with numbered graduations from 1.100 to 1.300 rather than one with color coded bands. To use the hydrometer, squeeze the rubber ball, insert the tip in the cell and release the ball (**Figure 1**). Draw in enough electrolyte to float the weighted float inside the hydrometer. Note the number in line with the surface of the electrolyte; this is the specific gravity for this cell. Be sure to return the electrolyte to the cell from which it came.

The specific gravity of the electrolyte in each battery cell is an excellent indication of that cell's condition. A fully charged cell will read 1.275 - 1.380, while a cell in good condition may read from 1.250 - 1.280. A cell in fair condition reads from 1.225 - 1.250 and anything below 1.225 is practically dead.

If the cells test in the poor range, the battery requires recharging. The hydrometer is useful for checking the progress of the charging operation. A reading from 1.200 to about 1.225 indicates a half charge; 1.275 - 1.380 indicates a full charge.

> **CAUTION**
> *Always disconnect both battery connections before connecting charging equipment. Make certain there are no*

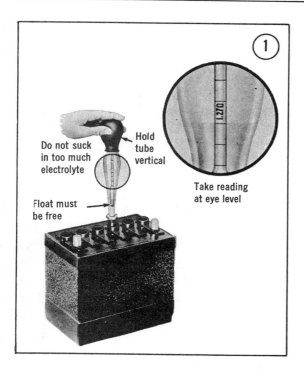

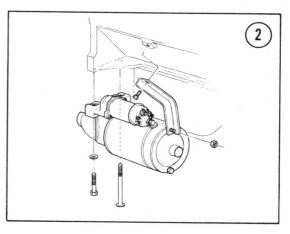

open flames, electrical sparks, or people smoking near a battery being charged. Highly explosive hydrogen gas is released during the process.

STARTER

Removal/Installation

1. Make a sketch of wire colors, or tag wires to aid installation.

2. Disconnect battery cables.

3. Disconnect lead wires from S and R terminals on solenoid.

4. Remove starter pad mounting bolts.

5. Remove stud nut at front of starter and rotate bracket out of the way. See **Figure 2**.

6. Pull the starter forward to clear housing and then remove.

7. Installation is the reverse of these steps. Tighten mounting bolts to 25-35 ft.-lb.

STARTER SOLENOID

Removal/Installation

1. Remove starter as described previously.

2. Remove outer screw and washer from starter connector strap terminal.

3. Remove the 2 screws securing solenoid to the starter frame.

4. Twist solenoid clockwise to remove flange keys from keyway slot in housing. Remove the solenoid.

Contact Replacement

Refer to **Figure 3**.

1. Remove solenoid from starter.

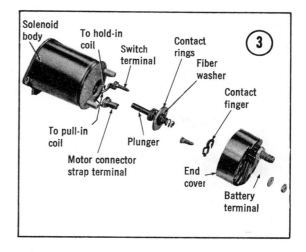

2. Remove end cover from solenoid.

3. Compress solenoid plunger contact ring slightly. Remove outer spring, retainer, fiber washer, and contact ring.

4. Remove battery terminal from end cover.

5. Remove the resistor bypass terminal and the contactor.

6. Remove motor connector strap terminal and solder new terminal in place.

7. Install new battery terminal in end cover.

8. Install bypass terminal and contactor.

9. Place new contact ring and fiber washer on plunger. Compress contact ring and install retainer and outer spring.

10. Install end cover.

11. Install on starter and bench test before installing starter to bell housing.

ALTERNATOR

The alternator generates alternating current (AC) which is converted to direct current (DC) by 6 internal silicon diodes.

Removal/Installation

1. Open engine hood and disconnect battery ground cable.

2. Disconnect wires from alternator.

3. Remove adjusting bolt. Push alternator toward engine and remove drive belt.

4. Remove mounting bolt.

5. Lift alternator out.

6. Installation is the reverse of these steps. Adjust belt tension as described in Chapter Two.

ALTERNATOR VOLTAGE REGULATOR

Adjusting the alternator voltage regulator requires special equipment not ordinarily available to a home mechanic. If trouble appears to be in the voltage regulator, take the job to your dealer or competent garage.

You might also consider replacing the regulator with a new one. The cost of adjusting an old regulator may be more than that of buying a new one. There is even a chance the old regulator cannot be adjusted; so you'll end up buying a replacement anyway.

Removal/Installation

1. Disconnect battery ground cable.

2. Disconnect wiring harness at regulator.

3. Remove screws securing regulator and remove regulator.

4. Installation is the reverse of these steps.

FUSES

Whenever a fuse blows, ascertain the reason for the failure before replacing the fuse. Usually the trouble is a short circuit in the wiring. This may be caused by worn through insulation or a wire which has worked its way loose and shorted to ground.

Always carry several spare fuses in the glove compartment.

> CAUTION
> *Never substitute tinfoil or wire for a fuse. An overload could result in fire and complete loss of the automobile.*

The fuse panel is located on the firewall just above the headlight dimmer switch. See **Figure 4**. **Tables 6 and 7** list the rating of each fuse. Fuse panel wiring is shown in a separate wiring diagram at the end of this chapter.

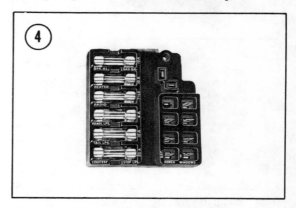

LIGHTING SYSTEM

The following procedures describe replacement of lamps, switches, and relays associated with the lighting system. Refer to **Tables 8 and 9** for the bulb used for each function.

Headlight Replacement (1963-1976)

Refer to **Figure 5**, page 200 (1963-1967) or **Figure 6** (1968-1976) for this procedure.

1. Open headlight panels.

2. Remove headlight bezel.

3. Disconnect spring from retainer ring and remove 2 retainer ring screws. Do not disturb adjusting screws.

4. Remove retainer ring.

5. Disconnect sealed beam lamp and remove it.

Table 6 FUSES AND CIRCUIT BREAKERS (1963-1967)

Circuit	Amperage rating	Type protection
Headlight	15	Circuit breaker
Headlight door	40	Circuit breaker
Power windows	40	Circuit breaker
Parking brake alarm and gas gauge	10	Fuse
Heater		
except 1967	10	Fuse
1967	25	Fuse
Radio (AM/FM)		
except 1967	2.5	Fuse
1967	10	Fuse
Instruments, radio (AM) clock lights	4	Fuse
Tail/back-up lights (except 1967)	10	Fuse
Stop/license lights (except 1967)	20	Fuse
Stop/taillights (1967)	20	Fuse
Air conditioning	30	Fuse
High speed blower	30	Fuse

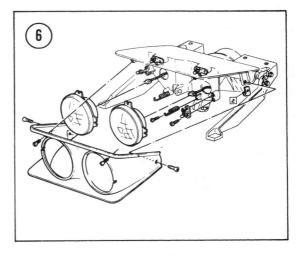

6. Install new sealed beam lamp with molded numbers on lens at the top.

NOTE: *Outboard headlights are 3-prong, while inboard headlights are 2-prong.*

7. Reverse Steps 1-4 to complete installation.

Table 7   FUSES AND CIRCUIT BREAKERS (1968-1976)

Circuit	Amperage Rating			Type Protection
	1968-1973	**1974**	**1975-1976**	
Headlights	30	15	15	Circuit breaker
Power windows	30	30	30	Circuit breaker
Stoplights/hazard flasher	20	20	20	Fuse
Heater and air conditioning	25	25	25	Fuse
Radio, rear defogger	10	20	20	Fuse
Wiper/washer	25	25	25	Fuse
Directional signals/ back-up lights	20	20	25	Fuse
Instrument lights	5	5	5	Fuse
Gauges and warning lights	10	10	10	Fuse
Clock, cigarette lighter	25	20	20	Fuse
Tail, license, marker, luggage, and parking lights	20	20	20	Fuse

Table 8   LAMPS (1963-1967)

Bulb circuit	Bulb Type		
	1963-1964	1965-1966	1967
Headlamps			
Outer	4002	4002L	4002
Inner	4001	4001L	4001
Front parking lamp/turn signal	1034	1157	1157
Tail/stop/turn signal	1034	1157	1157
Turn signal indicator	1816	1816	1816
High beam indicator	53	1445	1445
Cigarette lighter lamp	53	1445	1445
Ignition lock lamp	53	1445	1445
Instrument lamps	1816	1816	1816
Courtesy lamp	90	90	90
License plate lamp	67	67	67
Radio dial lamp	1816	1816	1816
Clock lamp	1816	1816	1816
Brake alarm	257	257	1816
Headlamp door warning lamp	257	257	257
Back-up lamp	——	1156	1156
Glove box lamp	——	1893	1893
Heater control panel	——	1893	1893
Air conditioning control panel	——	1893	1893

Headlight Motor Replacement (1963-1967)

1. Raise hood.

2. Disconnect battery ground cable.

3. Disconnect motor lead wires.

4. Turn knurled knob at inboard end of motor until gear turns freely. Turn knob in one direction until definite drag is felt on gear, then rotate knob 6 complete turns in the opposite direction.

5. Remove retainer from groove in motor locating stud. Remove motor-to-support screw. Lift motor assembly out.

6. Rotate new motor and/or headlight panel as required to align slot in motor with headlight panel pivot shaft. Install motor on shaft so that bracket aligns with locating stud.

7. Slide the motor onto the shaft until it seats against shoulder.

8. Install retainer in groove on locating stud.

9. Install retaining screw with ground wire between screw head and bracket.

10. Connect motor lead wires.

11. Connect battery ground cable.

12. Close hood and check operation of motor.

Headlight Actuator Removal/Installation (1968-1976)

Refer to **Figure 7** (a typical illustration) for this procedure.

1. Remove the radiator grille.

2. Partially open headlight panels.

3. Remove long spring on either side of pivot link pin.

4. Disconnect vacuum hoses from actuator.

5. Remove cotter pin and slide pivot pin out.

6. Remove 4 nuts from actuator studs. Slide actuator down and out of grille opening.

7. Installation is the reverse of these steps.

Table 9   LAMPS (1968-1976)

Bulb Circuit	Bulb Type				
	1968	1969	1970-1972	1973	1974-1976
Headlamps					
Outer	4002	4002	4002	4002	4000
Inner	4001	4001	4001	4001	5001
Front parking lamp/turn signal	1157NA	1157NA	1157NA	1157NA	1157NA
Tail/stop/turn signal	1157	1157	1157	1157	1157
Turn signal indicator	1895	1895	1895	1895	1895
High beam indicator	1895	1895	1895	1895	1895
Cigarette lighter lamp	1445	1445	1445	1445	1445
Ignition lock lamp	1895	—	—	—	—
Instrument lamps	1895	1895	1895	1895	1895
Courtesy lamp	631	90	90	90	212
License plate lamp	67	97	97	97	168
Radio dial lamp	1893	1893	1893	1893	1893
Clock lamp	1895	1895	1895	1895	1895
Brake alarm	1895	1895	1895	1895	1895
Headlamp door warning lamp	—	1895	1895	1895	1895
Back-up lamp	1156	1156	1156	1156	1156
Glove box lamp	1895	1895	1895	1895	1895
Heater control panel	1895	1895	1816	1816	1816
Air conditioning control panel	1895	1895	1816	1816	1816
Side marker					
Front	194A	194	168	168	168
Rear	194	194	168	168	168
Door ajar warning	—	1895	1895	1895	1895
Seat belt warning	—	1895	194	1895	1895
Windshield fluid level	—	—	168	1445	1445
Stereo indicator	—	—	2182	2182	2182

Headlight Vacuum Tank Replacement

Refer to **Figure 8** for this procedure.

1. Remove power brake booster and master cylinder. See Chapter Twelve.

2. Disconnect vacuum lines from tank. Sketch connectors showing color stripe on lines to aid installation. Tape ends of lines to keep out contaminants.

3. Remove tank retaining screws from underside of left fender skirt.

4. Lift tank out through engine compartment.

5. Installation is the reverse of these steps.

Headlight Vacuum Line Replacement

Replace leaking or deteriorated lines. **Figure 9** shows typical routing. Do not pinch hoses during installation.

CAUTION
Actuator to relay valve lines are cut to a specific length.

Lighting Switch Replacement (1965-1967)

Refer to **Figure 10** for this procedure.

1. Disconnect battery ground cable.

2. Pull switch to full ON position.

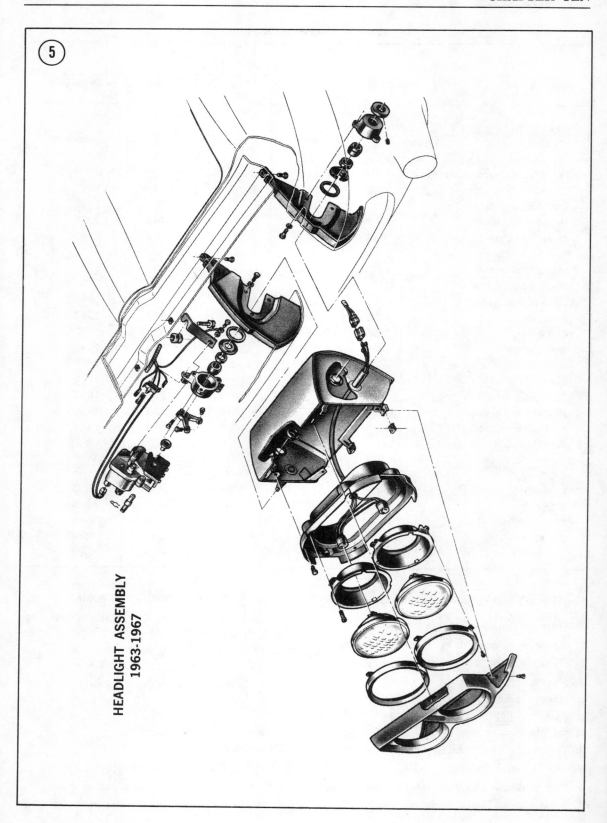

⑤

HEADLIGHT ASSEMBLY
1963-1967

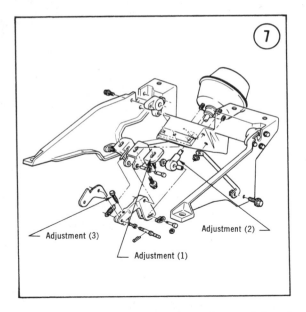

⑦

Adjustment (3)

Adjustment (2)

Adjustment (1)

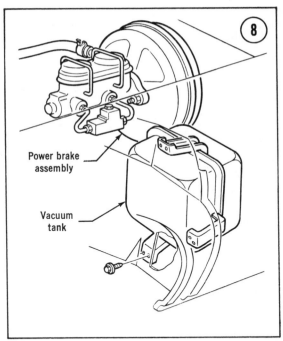

⑧

Power brake
assembly

Vacuum
tank

3. Depress switch shaft retainer (detent pin) and remove knob/shaft assembly.

4. Remove retaining nut with tool J-7673 or wide blade screwdriver.

5. Remove the bezel and switch from instrument panel.

6. Disconnect electrical connector from switch.

7. Installation is the reverse of these steps.

Lighting Switch Replacement (1968-1973)

1. Disconnect battery ground cable.

2. Remove mast jacket trim covers. Lower steering columns. See Chapter Thirteen.

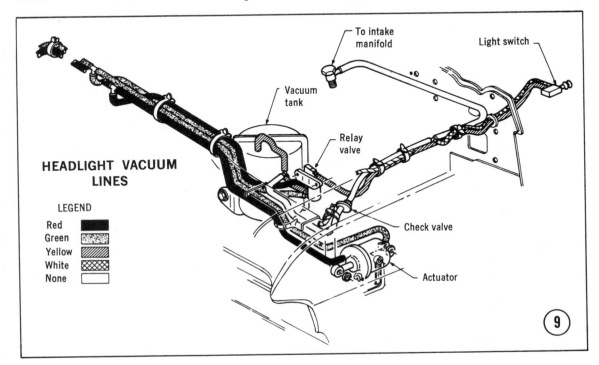

To intake
manifold

Light switch

Vacuum
tank

Relay
valve

**HEADLIGHT VACUUM
LINES**

LEGEND

Red	
Green	
Yellow	
White	
None	

Check valve

Actuator

⑨

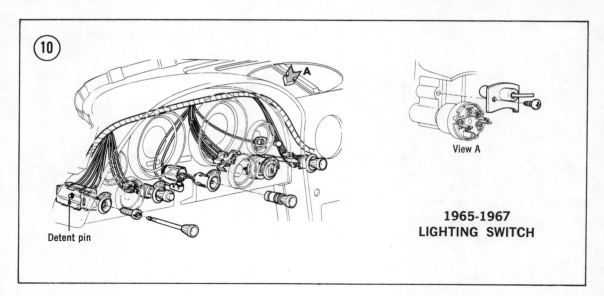

10

Detent pin

View A

**1965-1967
LIGHTING SWITCH**

3. Remove screws around left instrument panel. See **Figure 11**.

4. Unclip floor console forward trim panels.

5. Pull cluster assembly forward slightly.

6. Pull switch to full ON position.

7. Depress switch shaft retainer and remove knob/shaft assembly.

8. Remove bezel and switch from panel.

9. Disconnect and mark vacuum lines at switch.

10. Pry electrical connector from switch.

11. Installation is the reverse of these steps.

**Lighting Switch Replacement
(1974-1976)**

1. Disconnect ground cable from battery.

2. Remove mast jacket trim cover screws to allow access to steering column and instrument panel mounting bracket. Unclip and remove left side console forward trim panel.

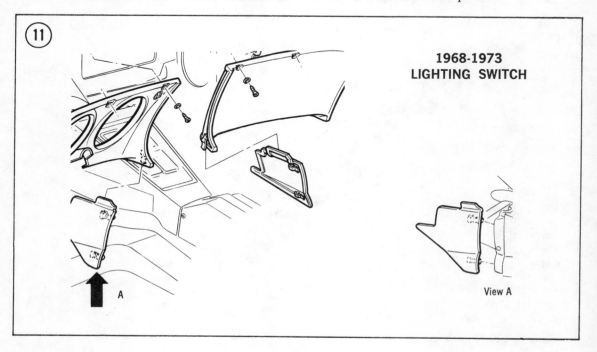

11

**1968-1973
LIGHTING SWITCH**

A

View A

3. Lower steering column.

4. Remove left instrument panel attaching screws at door opening, to left of dash, and left side of center instrument panel.

5. Pull cluster assembly down. Tip the assembly forward for access to lighting switch.

6. Refer to **Figure 12**. Depress switch/shaft retainer and remove knob and shaft assembly. Remove bezel.

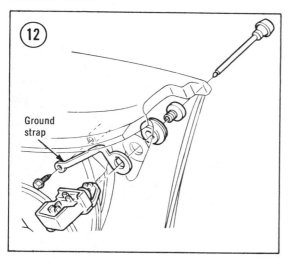

7. Tag vacuum hoses for reassembly and remove them from switch. Remove electrical connector, then remove switch.

8. To replace, reverse the above procedure.

Headlight Dimmer Switch Replacement

1. Disconnect battery ground cable.

2. Fold back upper left corner of floor mat.

3. Remove 2 screws securing switch to floor pan. See **Figure 13**.

4. Remove connector from switch.

5. Installation is the reverse of these steps.

Parking Brake Alarm Switch Replacement

Refer to **Figure 14** for this procedure.

1. Disconnect battery ground cable.

2. Remove 2 wires from switch.

3. Remove screw securing switch and remove it from brake lever housing.

4. Pull parking brake fully on. If necessary, adjust parking brake (Chapter Twelve).

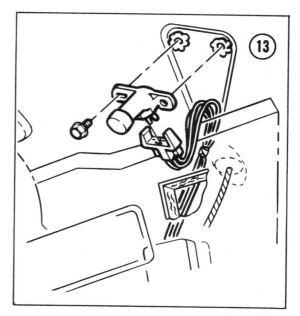

5. Locate switch on lever housing so that spring tab on switch engages its slot in brake lever housing.

6. Position clamp to switch, install retaining screw and connect wires to switch.

7. Connect battery ground cable.

Brake Light Switch Replacement

Refer to **Figure 15** for this procedure.

1. Disconnect battery ground cable.

2. Disconnect the 2 electrical connectors or wiring harness from the brake light switch.

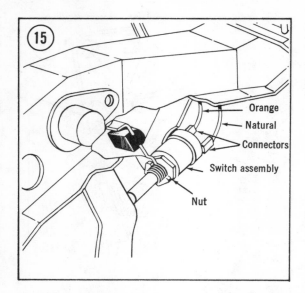

3. Remove locknut from plunger end of switch. Remove switch.

4. Installation is the reverse of these steps.

5. Adjust switch position so that brake lights come on when pedal is depressed ⅝ in.

License Plate Light

Remove screws securing lens and remove lens. See **Figure 16**. Replace bulb, then install lens. Do not overtighten the screws or the lens may crack.

Taillight Replacement

Refer to **Figure 17**. Remove screws securing lens and remove lens. Replace bulb, then install lens. Do not overtighten the screws or the lens may crack.

Front Parking Light Replacement (1963-1973)

Refer to **Figure 18**. Remove screws securing lens and remove lens. Replace bulb, then install

lens. Do not overtighten the screws or the lens may crack.

Front Parking Light Replacement (1974-1976)

1. Reach through valance air slot and remove nuts holding grille to valance panel. Refer to **Figure 19**.

2. Remove twist lock socket from rear of parking light housing.

3. Replace bulb, then reinstall twist lock socket in parking light housing.

4. Replace grille with attaching nuts.

Side Marker Lights (1968-1973)

Refer to **Figure 20**. Remove screws securing radiator grille and swing grille to one side. Reach through grille opening and turn plug connector ¼ turn counterclockwise. Remove lamp holder. Replace lamp and reinstall holder and grille.

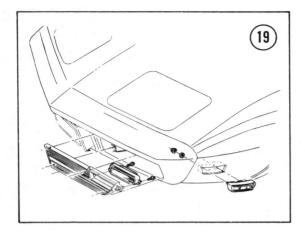

Back-up Lights

Refer to Figure 17. Remove screws securing lens and remove lens. Replace bulbs, then install lens. Do not overtighten the screws or the lens may crack.

Instrument Panel Lamp Replacement

1. Reach behind instrument cluster and pull defective lamp holder from cluster.

2. Replace the lamp and push the holder back into cluster.

INSTRUMENTS

Instrument Cluster Removal/Installation (1963-1967)

1. Remove mast jacket and steering shaft assembly as described in Chapter Thirteen.

2. Disconnect the tachometer drive cable at distributor.

3. Remove headlight switch.

4. Disconnect cowl vent cable brackets and headlight panel switch from cluster.

5. Disconnect parking brake lever support bracket at cowl crossmember.

6. Disconnect the oil pressure line at oil pressure gauge.

7. Disconnect and mark wires from ammeter, wiper switch, and cigarette lighter. See **Figure 21**.

8. Disconnect the trip odometer at the mast jacket support.

9. Remove screws securing cluster. Pull cluster forward slightly. Reach behind cluster and disconnect speedometer cable, tachometer cable, cluster ground wire, fuel gauge wires, and remaining indicator and illumination lights.

10. Installation is the reverse of these steps.

Instrument Removal/Installation (1963-1967)

1. Remove the instrument cluster as described in the preceding sequence.

2. Remove 5 screws securing cluster back panel to the cluster assembly. Carefully lift the back panel off.

3. Remove screws securing desired instrument to back panel.

4. Installation is the reverse of these steps.

Speedometer/Tachometer Cable Replacement

1. Disconnect cable from instrument.

2. Pull the cable out of the conduit from the instrument end.

> NOTE: *If cable is broken, disconnect cable at lower end also and pull remaining piece of cable out.*

3. Lubricate lower ¾ of new cable with AC speedometer cable lubricant or equivalent.

4. Push cable into conduit from instrument end.

5. Connect upper end to instrument.

6. Road test car to check for proper operation.

Instrument Cluster Removal/Installation (1968-1976)

Left-hand Cluster

1. Disconnect battery ground cable.

2. Lower steering column. See Chapter Thirteen.

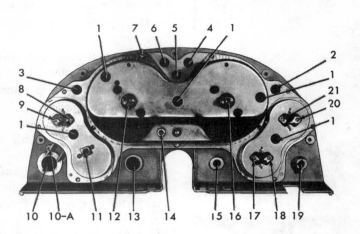

INSTRUMENT CLUSTER — 1963-1967

1. Cluster illuminating bulbs — gray leads
2. Direction signal indicator bulb left hand — light blue lead
3. Direction signal indicator bulb right hand — dark blue lead
4. Headlamp actuating motor indicator — light blue and gray and blue stripe leads
5. Headlamp hi beam indicator — light green lead
6. Parking brake alarm indicator — black lead
7. Ground lead attaching point — black and white stripe lead
8. Temperature indicator "I" terminal — light green lead
9. Temperature indicator "S" terminal — dark green lead
10. Ignition switch receptacle
10A. Ignition switch illuminating bulb attaching point — gray lead
11. Oil pressure indicator
12. Tachometer
13. Lighter receptacle
14. Trip odometer
15. Wiper switch receptacle
16. Speedometer
17. Ammeter "gen." terminal — red lead
18. Ammeter "battery" terminal — black lead
19. Lighting switch receptacle
20. Fuel gauge "I" terminal — light green lead
21. Fuel gauge "S" terminal — brown lead

3. Remove screws around left instrument panel. See **Figure 22** (1968-1973) **or** 23 (1974-1976).

4. Unclip floor console forward trim panel.

5. Pull cluster assembly forward slightly to obtain clearance.

6. Disconnect speedometer cable, tachometer cables, headlight, and ignition switch connector and instrument panel lights.

7. Installation is the reverse of these steps.

Center Instrument Cluster

1. Disconnect battery ground cable.

2. Remove right side dash pad.

3. Unclip center console trim pads.

4. Remove radio knobs and nuts on front bezel.

5. Disconnect antenna, speaker, and electrical connections from back of radio.

6. Remove rear support from radio and slide radio out right side.

7. Remove upper center console trim plate screws. Tip plate forward enough to remove windshield wiper switch connector. Lift trim plate out.

8. Remove screws at left side of center console.

9. Remove nuts at underside of console. See **Figure 24**.

10. Tilt center console forward. Remove oil line, electrical connectors, and lamps from the rear console.

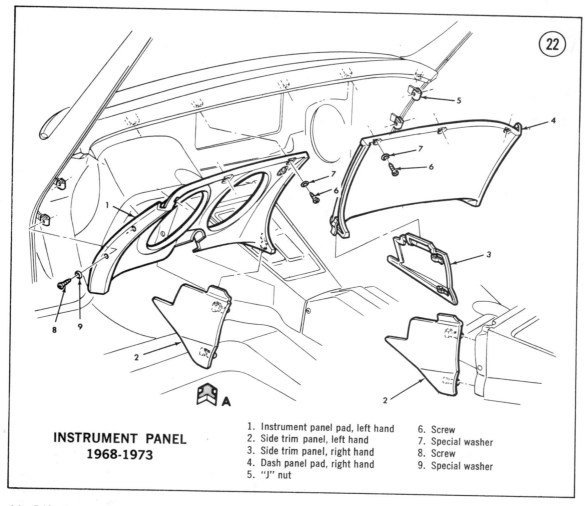

**INSTRUMENT PANEL
1968-1973**

1. Instrument panel pad, left hand
2. Side trim panel, left hand
3. Side trim panel, right hand
4. Dash panel pad, right hand
5. "J" nut

6. Screw
7. Special washer
8. Screw
9. Special washer

11. Lift the center console up and forward to remove it.

12. Installation is the reverse of these steps.

Instrument Removal/Installation (1968-1976)

1. Remove left or center instrument cluster.

2. Remove screws securing instrument to cluster. Remove instrument.

3. Installation is the reverse of these steps.

DIRECTIONAL SIGNAL LAMPS

Front directional signal lamps are part of parking lamps. See *Front Parking Light Replacement* procedure.

Rear directional signal lamps are part of brake lamps. See *Taillight* procedure.

HORNS

Horn Adjustment

1. Connect a 0-20 ampere ammeter in series with horn terminal.

2. Operate horn and check current draw. Each horn should draw 7.0-11.0 amperes at 12 volts.

3. Turn adjusting screw a fraction of a turn at a time if necessary to bring current within specifications. See **Figure 25**. If current cannot be adjusted, replace horn.

Horn Replacement

1. Raise hood.

2. Disconnect wire from hood.

3. Remove retaining screw and horn.

4. Installation is the reverse of these steps.

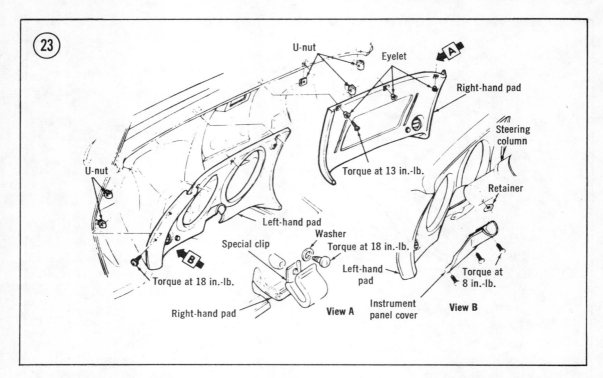

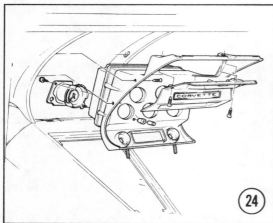

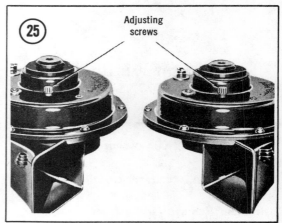

Horn Relay Replacement

1. Open hood.

2. Disconnect wires from horn relay.

3. Remove retaining screws and relay.

4. Installation is the reverse of these steps.

WINDSHIELD WIPER SYSTEM

Wiper Motor Removal/Installation

1. Raise the hood and disconnect the battery ground cable.

2. Remove distributor shielding and vertical shield for left spark plug wires.

3. Disconnect loom for left spark plug wires.

4. Disconnect ignition ballast resistor at firewall.

5. Disconnect washer pump inlet and outlet hoses at pump valve assembly.

6. Remove distributor cap (leave wires connected) and push to one side.

7. Disconnect wires at wiper motor.

8. Remove glove box door and compartment.

9. Disconnect wiper linkage from motor crank arm. See **Figure 26**.

10. Remove 4 wiper motor-to-dash bolts and remove motor.

11. Mount motor to dash wall. Motor must be in parked position.

12. Install left linkage over motor crank arm, then install spacer and right linkage. Secure with retaining clip. See Figure 26.

13. Remainder of installation is the reverse of Steps 1-8.

Wiper Arm and Linkage Removal

1. Remove wiper block and arm assembly from linkage. See Figure 26.

2. Remove glove box door and compartment.

3. Remove 3 wiper block retaining bolts.

4. Disconnect the wiper linkage from motor crank arm. Remove the linkage through the glove box opening.

5. Installation is the reverse of these steps.

Wiper Switch Replacement

1. Disconnect battery ground cable.

2. On 1968-1976 models, remove "Corvette" cover plate from upper portion of center console.

3. Remove wiring connector from switch.

4. Remove switch and plate.

5. Hold the switch arm with pliers. Gently pry knob off switch, then remove the screws securing switch.

6. Installation is the reverse of these steps.

IGNITION SYSTEM

The ignition system consists of the battery, ignition switch, ignition coil, capacitor-discharge system (some models), high energy system (1975-1976), distributor, spark plugs, and associated wiring. The following describes replacement procedures.

Ignition Coil Replacement (1963-1974)

A defective ignition coil must be replaced. Disconnect primary and secondary wires from coil and remove coil from its bracket. Install new coil; connect wire.

Ignition Switch Replacement

> NOTE: *On 1974-1976 models, ignition switch is located on steering column. Replacement procedure is given in Chapter Thirteen,* Front Suspension and Steering.

1. On 1968-1973 models, remove "Corvette" cover plate at top center of cluster assembly.

2. Disconnect battery ground cable.

3. With key, turn switch to LOCK or ACC.

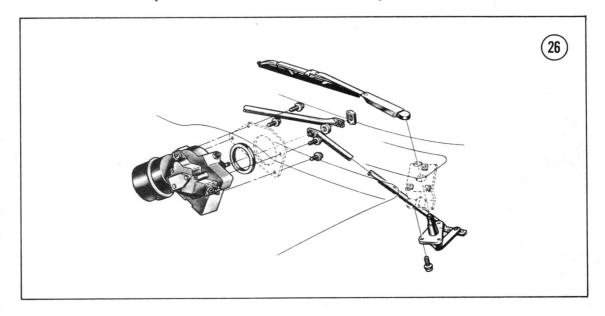

4. Insert stiff wire in small hole in the cylinder face. Push wire into the depress plunger. Turn key counterclockwise until the lock cylinder can be removed.

5. Remove bright metal ignition switch nut from passenger side of dash. See **Figure 27**.

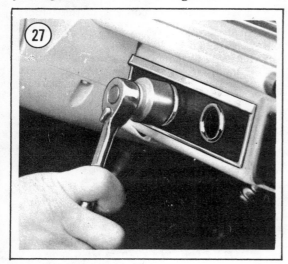

6. Pull ignition switch out from under dash. Remove wiring connector, lamp socket, and bulb. See **Figures 28 and 29**.

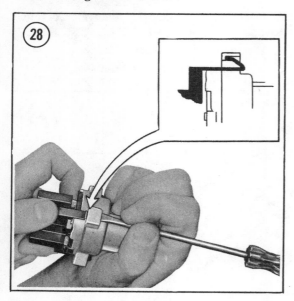

7. Snap connector and lamp socket onto the new switch.

8. Place switch into position from behind dash. Secure with ignition switch hub.

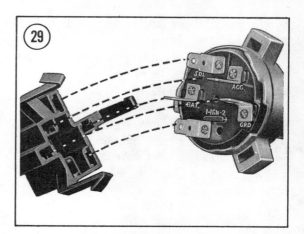

9. Insert lock cylinder.

10. Install battery ground cable.

Distributor Removal/Installation

1. Remove distributor shield.

2. Disconnect tachometer and fuel injection pump drive cables if so equipped.

3. Disconnect pickup coil leads at connector on breakerless distributor.

4. Remove distributor cap.

5. Crank engine so rotor is in position to fire cylinder No. 1 and timing mark on harmonic balancer is indexed with pointer.

6. Mark position of rotor arm on distributor housing on breaker-type distributors. On breakerless distributors the rotor will rotate as distributor is pulled out. Mark position of rotor on housing *after* distributor is removed.

7. Remove the distributor clamp and pull the distributor out.

> NOTE: *Do not rotate engine while distributor is removed.*

8. Installation is the reverse of these steps.

9. Adjust ignition timing (see Chapter Three).

Table 1   BATTERY SPECIFICATIONS

Voltage	12 volts
Size	
66 plates (1963-1967)	61 Ah
78 plates (1968-1972)	62 Ah
72 plates (1973 350 engine)	76 Ah
90 plates (1973 454 engine)	76 Ah

Table 2   ALTERNATOR SPECIFICATIONS

	Model						
	1100693 1100628	1100694	1100857 1100859 1100833 1100696	1100697	1100825 1100750	1100544	1102353 1100950 1100543
Voltage	14	14	14	14	14	14	14
Output current (hot)	37	55	42	60	61	61	42
Field current	1.9-2.3	2.2-2.6	2.2-2.6	2.8-3.2	2.2-2.6	4.0-4.5	4.0-4.5

Table 3   STARTER SPECIFICATIONS

	Model				
	1108430 1108418 1108400 1108429	1108351	1108338	1107365 1107352	1107320 1107388 1107242
Free speed					
Voltage	9	9	9	10.6	10.6
Current	65-95	65-95	55-80	70-99	65-100
rpm	7,500-10,500	5,300-10,500	3,500-6,000	7,800-12,000	3,600-5,100

Table 4   IGNITION COIL TYPES

	Model Number				
	1115091	1115207	1115202	1967-1974 (Non-transistor)	1967-1973 (Transistor)
Primary resistance	1.02-1.13	0.38-0.51	1.24-1.46	1.77-2.05	0.41-0.51
Secondary resistance	8,000-10,500	8,200-12,400	6,500-9,500	3,000-20,000	3,000-20,000
Ballast resistance	1.4-1.62	0.43-0.68	1.8	1.35	0.43-0.68

Table 5   DISTRIBUTOR SPECIFICATIONS

Model	1111022 1111024	1111076	1111070 1111069	1111087	1111060 1111064
Dwell angle	28-32°	28-32°	28-32°	28-32°	——
Centrifugal advance	0° @ 700	0° @ 750	0° @ 800	0° @ 750	0° @ 800
(crankshaft degrees	11° @ 1,600	15° @ 1,500	24° @ 2,350	15° @ 1,500	26° @ 2,500
@ engine rpm)	24° @ 4,600	26° @ 4,100		30° @ 5,100	
Vacuum advance	0° @ 8″	0° @ 4″	0° @ 4″	0° @ 4″	0° @ 4″
(crankshaft degrees @ ″Hg vacuum)	15° @ 15.5″	16.5° @ 8.2″	16.5° @ 8.2″	16.5° @ 8.2″	16.5° @ 8.2″

Model	1111153	1111141 1111142	1111157	1111294 1111293 1111247 1111926	1111196
Dwell angle	28-32°	28-32°	——	28-32°	28-32°
Centrifugal advance	0° @ 900	0° @ 900	0° @ 900	0° @ 900	0° @ 900
(crankshaft degrees	15° @ 1,500	14° @ 1,200	17° @ 1,600	8.5° @ 1,250	9° @ 1,200
@ engine rpm)	26° @ 4,100	19° @ 1,600	28° @ 4,600	17° @ 2,000	15° @ 1,500
		30° @ 5,000		32° @ 5,000	30° @ 5,100
Vacuum advance	0° @ 6″	0° @ 6″	0° @ 4″	0° @ 7″	0° @ 6″
(crankshaft degrees @ ″Hg vacuum)	15° @ 12″	15° @ 12″	16° @ 7″	12° @ 12″	16° @ 7″

Model	1111194	1111438	1111296	1111295	1111441
Dwell angle	28-32°	28-32°	28-32°	28-32°	28-32°
Centrifugal advance	0° @ 900	0° @ 950	0° @ 900	0° @ 1,200	0° @ 900
(crankshaft degrees	9° @ 1,200	14° @ 1,400	30° @ 3,800	18° @ 1,900	16.5 @ 1,400
@ engine rpm)	15° @ 1,500	20° @ 1,800		30° @ 5,000	30° @ 4,400
	30° @ 5,100	30° @ 4,700			
Vacuum advance	0° @ 6″	0° @ 8″	0° @ 8″	——	0° @ 8″
(crankshaft degrees @ ″Hg vacuum)	15° @ 12″	15° @ 15.5″	15° @ 15.5″	——	15° @ 15.5″

Model	1111490	1111493 1111491	1111928	1111927	1111496
Dwell angle	28-32°	28-32°	——	——	29-31°
Centrifugal advance	0° @ 900	0° @ 1,000	0° @ 900	0° @ 1,200	0° @ 1,200
(crankshaft degrees	9° @ 1,200	10° @ 1,700	2° @ 1,100	16° @ 1,900	12° @ 2,000
@ engine rpm)	15° @ 1,500	26° @ 5,000	30° @ 3,800	29° @ 5,000	20° @ 4,600
	30° @ 1,500				
Vacuum advance	0° @ 8″	0° @ 7″	0° @ 7″	——	0° @ 7″
(crankshaft degrees @ ″Hg vacuum)	10° @ 17″	15° @ 12″	15° @ 15.5″	——	12° @ 12″

Table 5   DISTRIBUTOR SPECIFICATIONS (continued)

Model	1111971	1111954	1112050	1112038	1112051
Dwell angle	——	——	29-31°	——	29-31°
Centrifugal advance	0° @ 950	0° @ 900	0° @ 865	0° @ 1,060	0° @ 857
(crankshaft degrees	2° @ 1,200	8° @ 1,200	2° @ 1,335	2° @ 1,340	2° @ 1,143
@ engine rpm)	12° @ 2,000	17° @ 2,000	11° @ 2,400	17° @ 2,400	14° @ 2,000
	20° @ 4,600	26° @ 3,700	18° @ 4,200	24° @ 4,800	22° @ 3,900
Vacuum advance	0° @ 7″	0° @ 7″	0° @ 8″	0° @ 8″	0° @ 8″
(crankshaft degrees @ ″Hg vacuum)	12° @ 12″	12° @ 12″	15° @ 15.5″	15° @ 15.5″	20° @ 17″

Model	1112076	1112053	1112101	1112114	1112098
Dwell angle	——	——	29-31°	29-31°	29-31°
Centrifugal advance	0° @ 1,100	0° @ 1,090	0° @ 1,090	0° @ 65	0° @ 1,100
(crankshaft degrees	3° @ 1,300	2° @ 1,310	2° @ 1,310	2° @ 1,335	2° @ 1,550
@ engine rpm)	10.8° @ 1,590	22° @ 2,400	21° @ 2,350	11° @ 2,400	6° @ 2,410
	25° @ 2,350	28° @ 5,450	28° @ 5,000	18° @ 4,200	12° @ 3,300
	32° @ 5,000				14° @ 4,200
Vacuum advance	0° @ 7″	0° @ 7″	0° @ 8″	0° @ 6″	0° @ 6″
(crankshaft degrees @ ″Hg vacuum)	12° @ 12″	12° @ 12″	15° @ 15.5″	20° @ 15″	15° @ 14″

Model	1112850	1112851	1112247	1112853	1112880
Dwell angle	29-31°	29-31°	29-31°	29-31°	——
Centrifugal advance	0° @ 1,000	0° @ 1,100	0° @ 1,100	0' @ 1,000	0° @ 1,200
(crankshaft degrees	10° @ 1,800	11° @ 2,400	11° @ 2,400	12° @ 2,200	12° @ 2,000
@ engine rpm)	15° @ 2,400	18° @ 4,200	18° @ 4,200	20° @ 5,000	22° @ 4,200
	22° @ 4,200				
Vacuum advance	0° @ 2-4″	0° @ 2-4″	0° @ 5-7″	0° @ 2-4″	0° @ 4″
(crankshaft degrees @ ″Hg vacuum)	14° @ 7.5-8.5″	14° @ 7.5-8.5″	15° @ 13-14″	14° @ 7.5-8.5″	18° @ 12″

Model	1112888	1112883
Dwell angle	——	——
Centrifugal advance	0° @ 1,100	0° @ 1,100
	12° @ 1,600	12° @ 1,600
	16° @ 4,200	16° @ 2,400
		22° @ 4,600
Vacuum advance	0° @ 4″	0° @ 4″
(crankshaft degrees @ ″Hg vacuum)	18° @ 12″	15° @ 10″

CHAPTER ELEVEN

CLUTCH AND TRANSMISSION

This chapter provides replacement and repair procedures for all 3- and 4-speed transmissions and clutches used from 1963-1976. In addition, removal and installation procedures are provided for automatic transmissions.

Repairs requiring disassembly are not recommended for home mechanics nor garage mechanics without special skills and a large assortment of special tools. The price of necessary tools far exceeds the price of a professionally rebuilt transmission.

Considerable money can be saved by removing the old transmission and installing a new or rebuilt one yourself. This chapter includes removal and installation procedures, plus other simple repairs. See Chapter Two for lubrication and preventive maintenance.

Tables 1 through 5 (end of chapter) give clutch specifications, transmission gear ratios, and transmission tightening torques.

CLUTCH

All 1963-1976 Corvettes use a bent-finger centrifugal diaphragm clutch. See **Figure 1**. The integral release fingers are bent back to gain a centrifugal boost and insure quick re-engagement at high engine speeds.

With this type clutch, pressure plate load increases as the drive plate wears. In addition, pedal effort is lower without requiring over-center booster springs on the clutch linkage.

Clutch Pedal Free Play Adjustment

To check free play, depress clutch pedal by hand. Free play should be ¾-1 in. on 1963-1964 models, 1¼-1¾ in. on 1965-1973 models, and 1-1½ in. on 1974-1976 models. Refer to **Figure 2**.

1. Remove clutch pedal return spring.

2. Loosen nut (A) and back off from swivel about ½ in.

3. Hold clutch pedal pushrod so pedal is against bumper stop.

4. Hold cross shaft lever in the opposite direction so the throwout bearing is against the clutch fingers.

5. Adjust nut (B) to obtain about ⅛-3/16 in. clearance between nut (B) and upper edge of swivel.

6. Release pushrod and cross shaft lever. Tighten nut (A) to lock swivel against nut (B).

7. Check free pedal play.

Clutch Pedal Travel Adjustment

Total pedal travel should be 6½ in. when linkage is set normally and 5 in. when linkage is

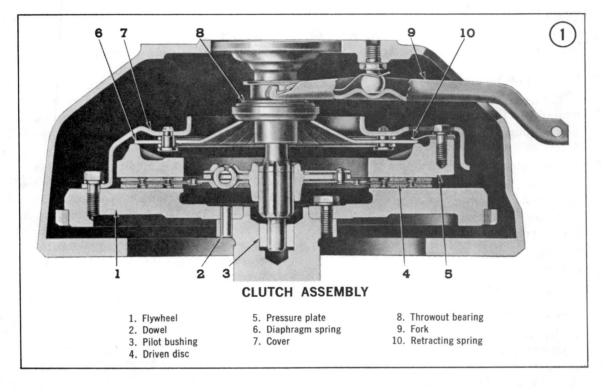

CLUTCH ASSEMBLY

1. Flywheel
2. Dowel
3. Pilot bushing
4. Driven disc

5. Pressure plate
6. Diaphragm spring
7. Cover

8. Throwout bearing
9. Fork
10. Retracting spring

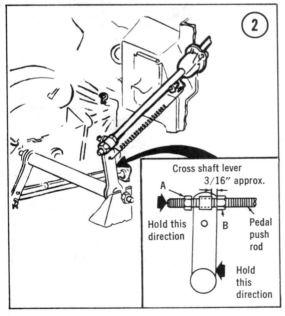

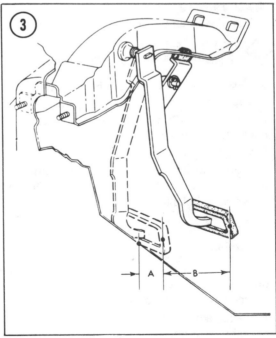

set to fast release position. Refer to **Figure 3** for this procedure.

1. Hold clutch against floor stop. Measure distance (A). This dimension may be as little as ⅛ in.

2. Release pedal and measure distance (B).

3. Subtract distance (A) from (B). The result is pedal travel.

4. To increase pedal travel, turn the rubber bumper as necessary. To decrease pedal travel, adjust pedal free-play as necessary.

Clutch Pedal Linkage Adjustment

The clutch linkage is normally set for 6½ in. total travel. To provide faster release for quick gear shifting, the linkage can be readjusted to 5 in. total travel.

1. Disconnect clutch return spring.

2. Loosen pedal bracket lower bolt. Remove upper bolt.

3. Rotate bracket to align alternate upper bolt hole in bracket and install upper bolt.

4. Disconnect pedal pushrod at cross shaft. Rotate 180° and reconnect.

5. Tighten bracket bolts.

Clutch Mechanism Removal

1. Support engine and remove transmission as described later.

2. Disconnect clutch fork pushrod and spring.

3. Remove flywheel housing.

4. On 1965-1973 models, slide clutch fork from ball stud and remove fork from dust boot.

> NOTE: *Ball stud is threaded into clutch housing and is easily replaced.*

5. Install tool J-5824 or equivalent clutch pilot to support clutch.

6. Look for "X" mark on flywheel and clutch cover. If not visible, make small punch marks on these parts to aid reassembly.

7. Loosen clutch-to-flywheel bolts evenly, one turn at a time, until spring pressure is released.

8. Remove bolts and clutch assembly.

Inspection

Never replace clutch parts without giving thought to the reason for failure. To do so only invites repeated troubles.

1. Clean the flywheel face and pressure plate assembly in a non-petroleum base cleaner such as tricloroethylene.

2. Check the friction surface of the flywheel for cracks and grooves. Attach a dial indicator and check runout. Compare with specifications for

your engine. If necessary, have the flywheel reground; replace it in cases of severe damage.

3. Check the pressure plate for cracked or broken springs, evidence of heat, cracked or scored friction surface and looseness. Check release lever ends for wear. On diaphragm spring clutches, check the spring fingers for wear. If there is any damage, replace with a professionally rebuilt pressure plate assembly.

4. Check the clutch disc (drive plate) lining for wear, cracks, oil, and burns. The assembled thickness of the disc should be at least 0.36 in. (**Figure 4**). Check for loose rivets and cracks in the spring leaves or carrier plate. Ensure that the disc slides freely on the transmission spline without excessive radial play. If the disc is defective, replace it with a new one.

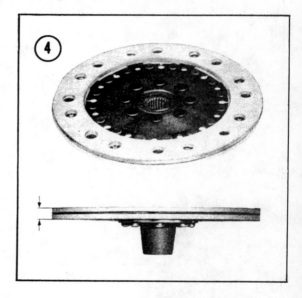

5. Check the release bearing for wear to determine if it caused the original trouble. Never reuse a release bearing unless necessary. When other clutch parts are worn, the bearing is probably worn. If it is necessary to reinstall the old bearing, do not wash it in solvent; wipe it with a clean cloth.

Installation

1. Wash your hands *clean* before proceeding.

2. Sand the friction surface of the flywheel and pressure plate with a medium-fine emery cloth. Sand lightly across the surfaces (not around)

until they are covered with fine scratches. This breaks the glaze and aids seating a new clutch disc.

3. Clean the flywheel and pressure plate with tricloroethylene or equivalent.

4. Position clutch disc and pressure plate on engine and support with tool J-5824 or equivalent pilot tool. Clutch disc damper springs face the pressure plate.

> NOTE: *An excellent pilot tool can be made by cutting off about 1 foot from the forward end of an old transmission main shaft. Other tools made from wooden dowelling are available from most auto parts suppliers.*

5. Align "X" marks or punch marks on clutch cover and flywheel. Install bolts finger-tight.

6. Tighten diagonally opposite bolts a few turns at a time until are tight. Torque to 11 ft.-lb.

7. Remove pilot tool.

8. Unhook clutch fork. Lubricate ball socket with high melting point grease, e.g., graphite, and reinstall fork on ball stud.

9. Lubricate recess on inside of throwout bearing with molybdenum grease. See **Figure 5**.

10. On 1965-1973 models, install clutch fork and dust boot into clutch housing.

11. Install throwout bearing to fork.

12. Install flywheel housing.

13. Install transmission.

14. Connect fork pushrod and spring.

15. Adjust clutch pedal travel and free play.

Clutch Pilot Bearing Removal/Installation

The clutch pilot bearing should be removed for inspection whenever the clutch is removed.

1. Pull bearing from crankshaft with tool J-1448 or equivalent puller. See **Figures 6 and 7**.

2. Clean bearing with a clean cloth dipped in solvent.

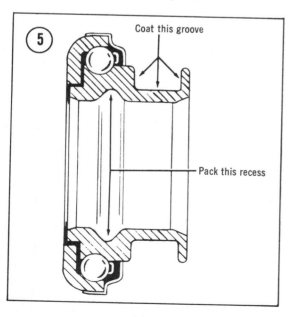
Coat this groove

Pack this recess

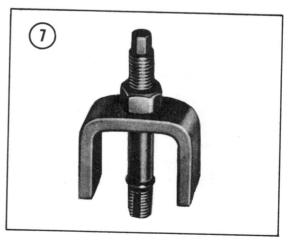

3. Check bearing for excessive wear or other damage. Replace if necessary.

4. Drive bearing into the crankshaft with tool J-1522 or equivalent driver. See **Figure 8**.

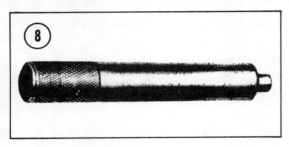

3-SPEED TRANSMISSION (1963-1965)

This 3-speed synchromesh transmission is standard equipment on 1963-1965 Corvettes. See **Figures 9 and 10**.

Removal/Installation

1. Raise vehicle on jackstands or hoist.

2. Disconnect speedometer cable.

3. Disconnect rods (D and E) from levers (B and C). See **Figure 11**.

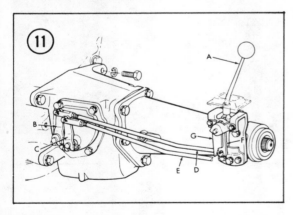

4. Disconnect control lever and bracket assembly. Tie out of way.

5. Remove propeller shaft. See Chapter Fourteen.

6. Support engine at oil pan rail with a jack.

7. Remove bracket connecting transmission extension mount to center crossmember.

8. Remove 2 top clutch housing bolts. Insert 2 guide pins in these holes. Then remove the 2 lower retaining bolts.

NOTE: *The guide pins support the transmission during removal and prevent clutch disc damage. The guide pins can be made by cutting the heads off 2 appropriately sized bolts.*

9. Slide the transmission straight back on the guide pins until the input shaft is free of the splines in the clutch disc.

10. Tilt forward end of transmission downward and withdraw transmission from vehicle.

11. Installation is the reverse of these steps. Torque transmission mounting bolts to 40-50 ft.-lb.

12. Fill transmission to proper level with correct lubricant. See Chapter Two.

13. Lower vehicle and check shift pattern. Adjust linkage as described below.

Shift Linkage Adjustment

1. Set levers (A, B, and C) shown in Figure 11 in neutral detent position.

2. Install rod (D) on lever (F) and install clip.

3. Adjust clevis until clevis pin fits easily in the clevis holes in lever (B). Install clevis pin and cotter pin.

4. Move shift lever (A) to the left to engage the first and reverse lever (G), but keep the shift lever in the neutral position.

5. Install rod (E) on lever (G) and insert clip.

6. Adjust clevis on rod (E) until clevis pin fits easily through clevis holes and lever (C). Install clevis pin and cotter pin.

7. Tighten locknuts at clevis on rods (D and E).

8. Check shift pattern for proper operation.

3-SPEED TRANSMISSION (1966-1968)

This transmission is standard on 1966-1968 Corvettes. See **Figure 12** for cutaway view.

Removal/Installation

1. Disconnect battery ground cable.

2. Unscrew ball from shift lever. Lift out T-handle spring and T-handle and remove the anti-rattle bushing.

3. Place front and rear of vehicle on jackstands or hoist.

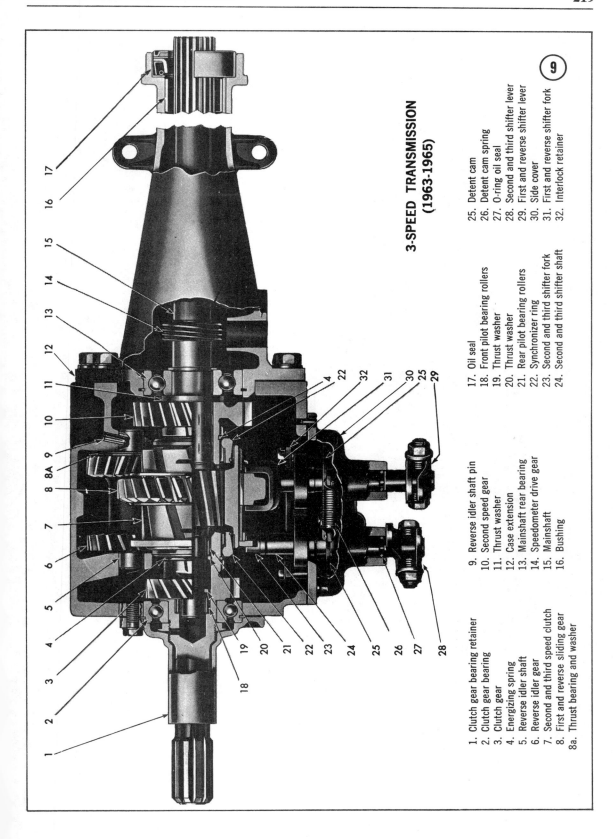

3-SPEED TRANSMISSION (1963-1965)

1. Clutch gear bearing retainer
2. Clutch gear bearing
3. Clutch gear
4. Energizing spring
5. Reverse idler shaft
6. Reverse idler gear
7. Second and third speed clutch
8. First and reverse sliding gear
8a. Thrust bearing and washer

9. Reverse idler shaft pin
10. Second speed gear
11. Thrust washer
12. Case extension
13. Mainshaft rear bearing
14. Speedometer drive gear
15. Mainshaft
16. Bushing

17. Oil seal
18. Front pilot bearing rollers
19. Thrust washer
20. Thrust washer
21. Rear pilot bearing rollers
22. Synchronizer ring
23. Second and third shifter fork
24. Second and third shifter shaft

25. Detent cam
26. Detent cam spring
27. O-ring oil seal
28. Second and third shifter lever
29. First and reverse shifter lever
30. Side cover
31. First and reverse shifter fork
32. Interlock retainer

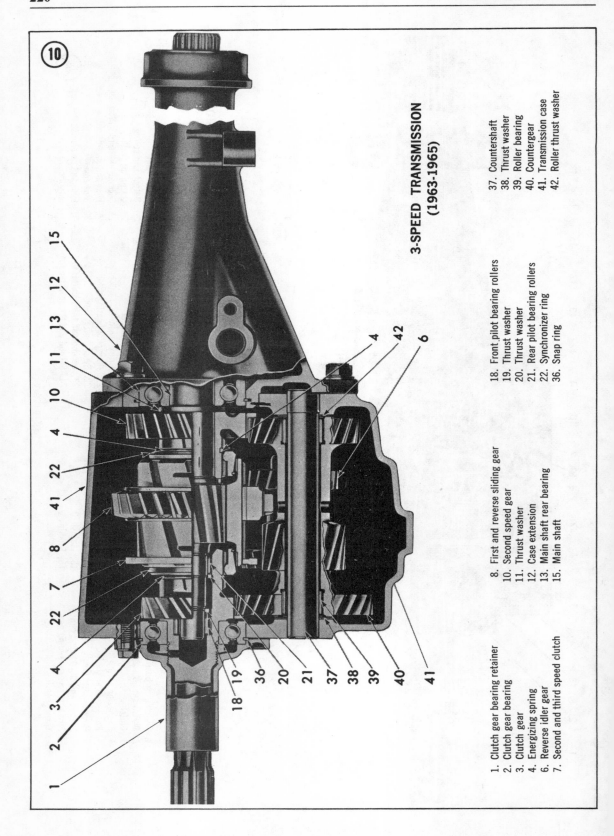

⑩

**3-SPEED TRANSMISSION
(1963-1965)**

1. Clutch gear bearing retainer
2. Clutch gear bearing
3. Clutch gear
4. Energizing spring
6. Reverse idler gear
7. Second and third speed clutch

8. First and reverse sliding gear
10. Second speed gear
11. Thrust washer
12. Case extension
13. Main shaft rear bearing
15. Main shaft

18. Front pilot bearing rollers
19. Thrust washer
20. Thrust washer
21. Rear pilot bearing rollers
22. Synchronizer ring
36. Snap ring

37. Countershaft
38. Thrust washer
39. Roller bearing
40. Countergear
41. Transmission case
42. Roller thrust washer

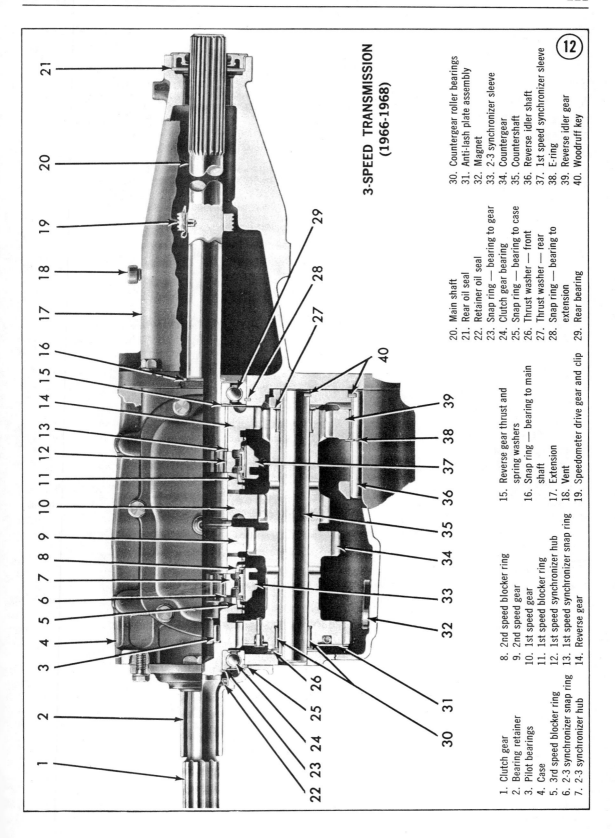

3-SPEED TRANSMISSION (1966-1968)

1. Clutch gear
2. Bearing retainer
3. Pilot bearings
4. Case
5. 3rd speed blocker ring
6. 2-3 synchronizer snap ring
7. 2-3 synchronizer hub
8. 2nd speed blocker ring
9. 2nd speed gear
10. 1st speed gear
11. 1st speed blocker ring
12. 1st speed synchronizer hub
13. 1st speed synchronizer snap ring
14. Reverse gear
15. Reverse gear thrust and spring washers
16. Snap ring — bearing to main shaft
17. Extension
18. Vent
19. Speedometer drive gear and clip
20. Main shaft
21. Rear oil seal
22. Retainer oil seal
23. Snap ring — bearing to gear
24. Clutch gear bearing
25. Snap ring — bearing to case
26. Thrust washer — front
27. Thrust washer — rear
28. Snap ring — bearing to extension
29. Rear bearing
30. Countergear roller bearings
31. Anti-lash plate assembly
32. Magnet
33. 2-3 synchronizer sleeve
34. Countergear
35. Countershaft
36. Reverse idler shaft
37. 1st speed synchronizer sleeve
38. E-ring
39. Reverse idler gear
40. Woodruff key

4. Remove the propeller shaft as described in Chapter Fourteen.

5. Remove heat deflectors from right and left exhaust pipes.

6. Remove left and right exhaust pipes and heat riser as described in Chapter Nine.

7. Remove 2 bolts attaching rear transmission mount cushion to rear mount bracket.

8. Support engine at oil pan rail with a jack. Raise the engine just enough to remove the load from the rear mount cushion.

9. Remove transmission mount bracket.

10. Remove 2 bolts from mount pad on transmission case. Remove rubber mount cushion and exhaust pipe yoke.

11. Disconnect transmission linkage by removing shift levers at transmission side cover.

12. Disconnect speedometer cable at transmission extension.

13. Remove the slip yoke and transmission output shaft.

14. Disconnect gear control lever and bracket assembly from adapter plate on side of transmission. Lower the assembly from the vehicle, letting the gear shift lever slide down and out through the dust boot.

15. Remove transmission mounting bolts from bell housing.

16. Slide transmission rearward until it is clear of the clutch. Rotate transmission to gain access to the 3 flat head machine screws on the control lever bracket adapter plate. Remove the adapter plate and rotate the transmission back to the upright position.

17. Lower the rear of the engine slowly until the tachometer drive cable at the distributor just clears the horizontal ledge across the front of the dash. This allows sufficient room to remove the transmission.

18. Slide transmission rearward until it is clear of the clutch, then lower it out of vehicle.

19. Installation is the reverse of these steps.

20. Adjust shift linkage as described in the following procedure.

Shift Linkage Adjustment

Refer to **Figure 13** for this procedure.

1. Set levers (K and L) in neutral detent position.

2. Move shift lever (A) to NEUTRAL position and insert locating pin (D) into notch of lever and bracket assembly.

3. Install nut (N) and clevis (M) on rod (J) loosely, then attach rod to lever (B); secure with retainer.

4. With lever (B) against locating pin, adjust clevis at lever (L) until clevis pin fits easily through the holes. Then secure the clevis pin with a washer and cotter pin. Tighten nut (N).

5. With lever (C) against locating pin, attach swivel (F) to lever and secure with the retainer. Run nut (G) against the swivel and tighten nut (E) against swivel.

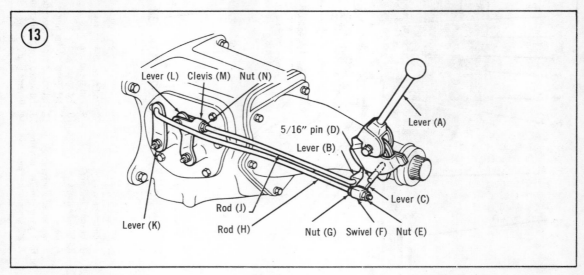

Figure 13: Lever (L) Clevis (M) Nut (N), Lever (A), 5/16" pin (D), Lever (B), Lever (C), Lever (K), Rod (J), Rod (H), Nut (G) Swivel (F) Nut (E)

6. Remove locating pin and check shifting for proper operation. Readjust clevis and swivel if necessary.

4-SPEED TRANSMISSION

The 4-speed synchromesh transmission is optional on 1963-1968 Corvettes and standard on 1969-1976 Corvettes. A cutaway view of the 1963-1973 transmission is shown in **Figure 14**. The 1975-1976 transmissions are shown in **Figures 15 and 16**.

Removal/Installation (1963-1964)

1. Raise vehicle on jackstands or hoist.

2. Disconnect speedometer cable.

3. Disconnect shift levers at transmission. See **Figure 17**.

4. Disconnect control lever and bracket assembly. Tie out of way.

5. Remove propeller shaft (Chapter Fourteen).

6. Support engine at oil pan rail with a jack.

7. Remove bracket connecting transmission extension mount to center crossmember.

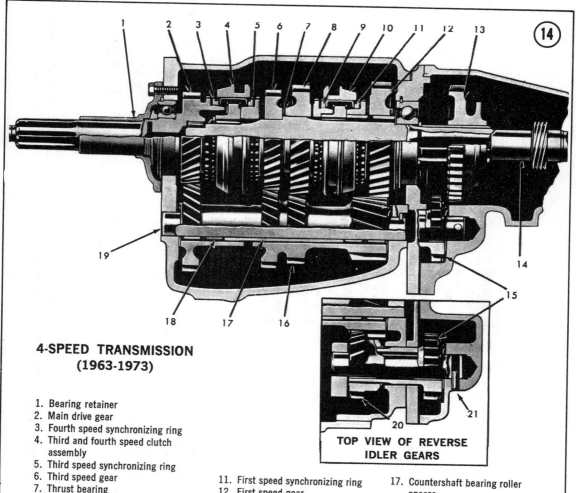

4-SPEED TRANSMISSION (1963-1973)

1. Bearing retainer
2. Main drive gear
3. Fourth speed synchronizing ring
4. Third and fourth speed clutch assembly
5. Third speed synchronizing ring
6. Third speed gear
7. Thrust bearing
8. Second speed gear
9. Second speed synchronizing ring
10. First and second speed clutch assembly
11. First speed synchronizing ring
12. First speed gear
13. Reverse gear
14. Main shaft
15. Reverse idler gear (rear)
16. Countershaft gear
17. Countershaft bearing roller spacer
18. Countershaft bearing roller
19. Countershaft
20. Reverse idler gear (front)
21. Reverse idler shift lock pin

TOP VIEW OF REVERSE IDLER GEARS

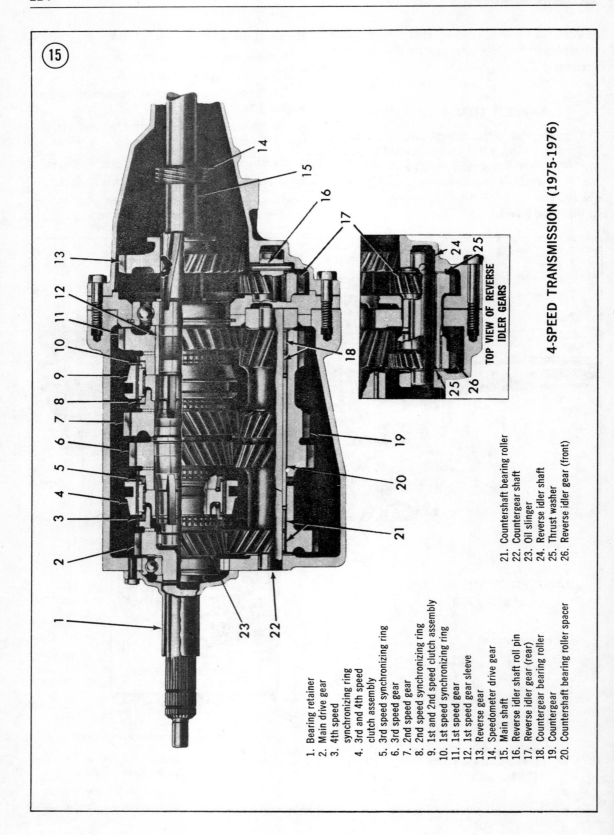

⑮

4-SPEED TRANSMISSION (1975-1976)

TOP VIEW OF REVERSE IDLER GEARS

1. Bearing retainer
2. Main drive gear
3. 4th speed synchronizing ring
4. 3rd and 4th speed clutch assembly
5. 3rd speed synchronizing ring
6. 3rd speed gear
7. 2nd speed gear
8. 2nd speed synchronizing ring
9. 1st and 2nd speed clutch assembly
10. 1st speed synchronizing ring
11. 1st speed gear
12. 1st speed gear sleeve
13. Reverse gear
14. Speedometer drive gear
15. Main shaft
16. Reverse idler shaft roll pin
17. Reverse idler gear (rear)
18. Countergear bearing roller
19. Countergear
20. Countershaft bearing roller spacer
21. Countershaft bearing roller
22. Countergear shaft
23. Oil slinger
24. Reverse idler shaft
25. Thrust washer
26. Reverse idler gear (front)

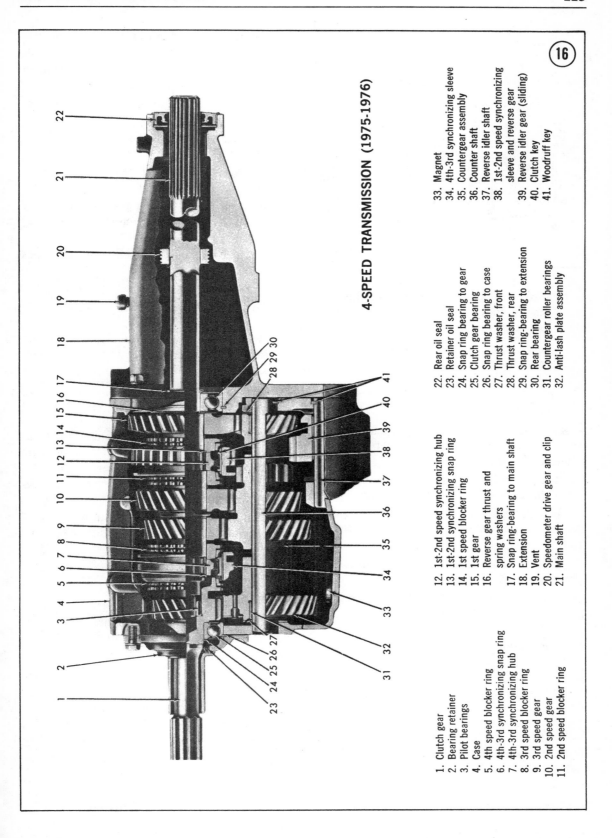

4-SPEED TRANSMISSION (1975-1976)

1. Clutch gear
2. Bearing retainer
3. Pilot bearings
4. Case
5. 4th speed blocker ring
6. 4th-3rd synchronizing snap ring
7. 4th-3rd synchronizing hub
8. 3rd speed blocker ring
9. 3rd speed gear
10. 2nd speed gear
11. 2nd speed blocker ring
12. 1st-2nd speed synchronizing hub
13. 1st-2nd synchronizing snap ring
14. 1st speed blocker ring
15. 1st gear
16. Reverse gear thrust and spring washers
17. Snap ring-bearing to main shaft
18. Extension
19. Vent
20. Speedometer drive gear and clip
21. Main shaft
22. Rear oil seal
23. Retainer oil seal
24. Snap ring bearing to gear
25. Clutch gear bearing
26. Snap ring bearing to case
27. Thrust washer, front
28. Thrust washer, rear
29. Snap ring-bearing to extension
30. Rear bearing
31. Countergear roller bearings
32. Anti-lash plate assembly
33. Magnet
34. 4th-3rd synchronizing sleeve
35. Countergear assembly
36. Counter shaft
37. Reverse idler shaft
38. 1st-2nd speed synchronizing sleeve and reverse gear
39. Reverse idler gear (sliding)
40. Clutch key
41. Woodruff key

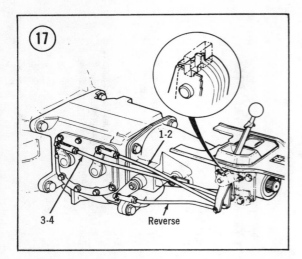

8. Remove 2 top clutch housing bolts. Insert 2 guide pins in these holes. Then remove the 2 lower retaining bolts.

> NOTE: *The guide pins support the transmission during removal and prevent clutch disc damage. The guide pins can be made by cutting the heads off 2 appropriately sized bolts.*

9. Slide the transmission straight back on the guide pins until the input shaft is free of the splines in the clutch disc.

10. Tilt forward end of transmission downward and withdraw transmission from vehicle.

11. Installation is the reverse of these steps. Torque transmission mounting bolts to 40-50 ft.-lb.

12. Fill transmission to proper level with correct lubricant. See Chapter Two.

13. Lower vehicle and check shift pattern. Adjust linkage as described below.

Removal/Installation (1975-1976)

> NOTE: *On 1975-1976 models it may be necessary to remove the catalytic converter to provide necessary clearance.*

1. Disconnect battery ground cable.

2. From inside the vehicle, remove the shifter ball and T-handle.

3. Remove console trim plate.

4. Raise vehicle on hoist.

5. Remove right and left exhaust pipes as described in Chapter Nine.

6. Remove the propeller shaft as described in Chapter Fourteen.

7. Remove bolts attaching rear mount to rear mount bracket.

8. Raise rear of engine with jack to lift transmission off mounting bracket.

9. Remove bolts retaining transmission linkage mounting bracket to frame.

10. Remove bolts securing gear shift assembly to mounting bracket and remove the mounting bracket.

11. Remove the shifter mechanism with the rods attached.

12. Disconnect shift levers at transmission.

13. Disconnect speedometer cable and TCS switch wiring.

14. Remove bolts securing transmission mount bracket to crossmember and remove mount bracket. Remove bolts securing rear mount cushion and exhaust pipe yoke.

15. Remove bolts securing transmission to bell housing and remove lower left extension bolt.

16. Lower the rear of the engine until the tachometer drive cable at the distributor just clears the horizontal ledge across the front of the dash. This will provide additional clearance for removing the transmission.

17. Pull the transmission rearward until it is clear of the bell housing. Rotate clockwise while pulling to the rear.

18. Installation is the reverse of these steps.

Shift Linkage Adjustment

A simple gauge shown in **Figure 18** is necessary for this procedure. Make the gauge from a block of wood.

1. Remove transmission gear shift lever seal from floor pan.

2. Place transmission in NEUTRAL and install the gauge block as shown in the inset in Figure 15.

3. Remove the cotter pin, anti-rattle washer, and clevis pin at each shift lever. Adjust the threaded clevis on each shift rod until the clevis pin fits easily in the shift lever hole.

4. Reconnect the clevises to the shift levers.

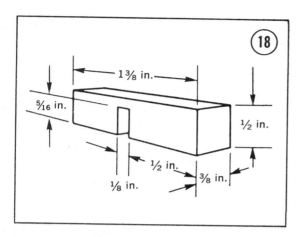

5. Remove the gauge block and check the transmission shifting. Readjust if necessary.

POWERGLIDE TRANSMISSION

This transmission is optional equipment on 1963-1967 Corvettes.

Removal/Installation

1. Disconnect battery ground cable.

2. Remove ball from transmission shift control lever. See **Figure 19**.

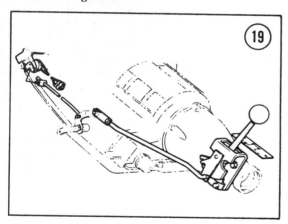

3. Raise entire car on jackstands or hoist.

4. Remove the propeller shaft as described in Chapter Fourteen.

5. Remove left and right exhaust pipes.

6. Remove 2 bolts securing rear mount cushion to rear mount bracket.

7. Support engine under oil pan and raise engine to remove load from rear mount cushion.

CAUTION
Use a wide base, heavy wood platform between the jack pad and the oil pan to prevent damage to the pan.

8. Remove 3 transmission mount bracket-to-crossmember bolts, then remove the mount bracket.

9. Remove 2 bolts from mount pad to transmission case and remove rubber mount cushion and exhaust pipe yoke.

10. Disconnect oil cooler lines at transmission and swing the lines clear.

11. Remove converter underpan.

12. Remove converter-to-flywheel which connects the bolts.

13. Disconnect vacuum modulator line and speedometer from transmission.

14. Disconnect transmission shift linkage from transmission gear shift control lever. See Figure 19. Remove shift lever.

15. Remove throttle valve linkage and disconnect neutral safety switch linkage at transmission. Also remove gear shift control linkage.

16. Remove neutral safety switch from transmission.

17. Remove transmission output shaft, slip yoke and insert a plastic plug in the end of the extension to prevent spillage of transmission fluid.

18. Remove bright metal ignition shielding from distributor area.

19. Remove the transmission dipstick and tube assembly.

20. Disconnect vacuum modulator line at distributor advance line T-fitting.

21. Position transmission hoist or floor jack under transmission.

22. Remove transmission-to-engine mounting bolts and slide the transmission rearward.

NOTE: *Make certain that converter moves with the transmission. If not, pry it free of the flywheel before proceeding.*

23. Install converter retaining strap. **Figure 20**.

24. Lower and remove the transmission from the vehicle.

25. Installation is the reverse of these steps.

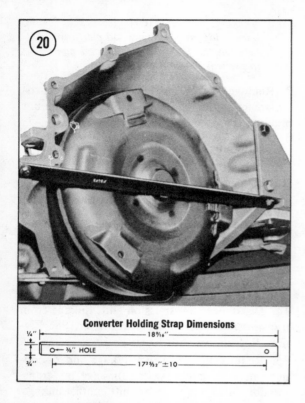

Converter Holding Strap Dimensions

POWERGLIDE ADJUSTMENTS

Shift Linkage Adjustment

Refer to **Figure 21** for this procedure.

1. Set transmission bellcrank (E) in PARK position.

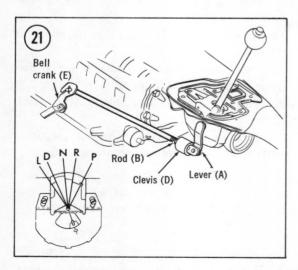

2. Set shift lever in PARK position.

3. Install clevis (D) on rod (B) loosely.

4. Connect rod to bellcrank and secure with retainer.

5. Adjust clevis until clevis pin fits easily through holes and secure with washer and cotter pin.

6. Check shifts to insure proper operation. Readjust clevis as necessary.

Low Band Adjustment

1. Tighten the low servo adjusting screw to 40 in.-lb. See **Figure 22**.

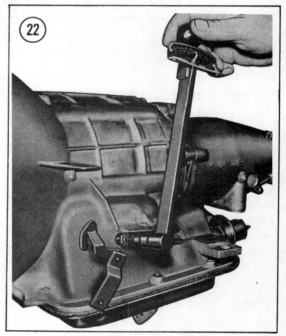

2. Back off 4 complete turns for a band which has been in use for 1,000 miles or more, or 3 turns for a new band.

3. Tighten the locknut to 15 ft.-lb.

TURBO HYDRAMATIC TRANSMISSION

This transmission is optional equipment on 1968-1976 Corvettes.

Removal/Installation

1. Disconnect battery ground cable.

2. Raise front and rear of car on jackstands or a hoist.

3. Remove the propeller shaft as described in Chapter Fourteen.

4. Disconnect speedometer cable, electrical lead to case connector, vacuum line modulator, and oil cooler lines.

5. Disconnect shift control linkage.

6. Support transmission with suitable floor jack.

7. Disconnect the rear mount from the frame crossmember.

8. Remove 2 bolts at each end of the frame crossmember and through bolt at inside of the frame and parking brake pulley and remove the crossmember.

9. Remove converter underpan.

10. Remove converter-to-flywheel bolts.

11. Lower transmission until jack is barely supporting its weight.

12. Remove transmission-to-engine mounting bolts, and remove oil filler tube at transmission.

13. Raise transmission to its normal position, support engine with jack, and slide transmission rearward from engine. Lower transmission from the vehicle.

CAUTION
*Secure the torque converter with tool J-5384 or equivalent (**Figure 23**) when lowering the transmission, or keep the rear of the transmission lower than the front so as not to lose the converter.*

14. Installation is the reverse of these steps.

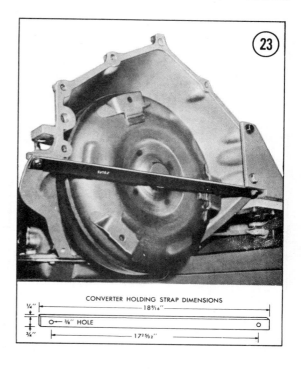

CONVERTER HOLDING STRAP DIMENSIONS

TURBO HYDRAMATIC ADJUSTMENTS

Shift Linkage Adjustment

Refer to **Figure 24** for this procedure.

1. Disconnect shift cable at both ends.

2. Place transmission control lever in DRIVE.

3. Place selector lever in DRIVE position.

4. Install cable as shown in Figure 22.

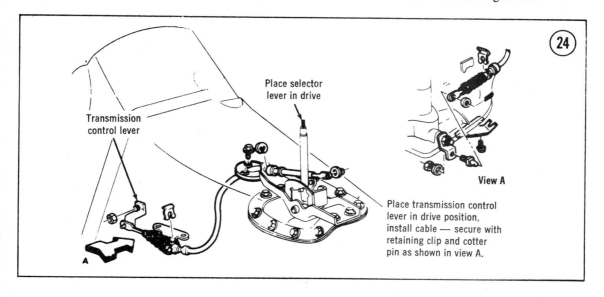

Transmission control lever

Place selector lever in drive

View A

Place transmission control lever in drive position, install cable — secure with retaining clip and cotter pin as shown in view A.

Table 1   CLUTCH SPECIFICATIONS

Type	Centrifugal diaphragm
Frictional area	
10 in. disc	90.7 in.²
10.7 in. disc	103.5 in.²
Disc facing thickness (each disc)	0.135 in.

Table 2   MANUAL TRANSMISSION GEAR RATIOS

3-Speed	1963-1964	1965	1966-1973
1st gear	2.47	2.58	2.54
2nd gear	1.53	1.48	1.50
3rd gear	1.00	1.00	1.00
Reverse	2.80	2.58	2.63

4-Speed	1963-1964 (Standard)	1963-1964 (Close Ratio)	1965 (Standard)	1965-1974 (Close Ratio)
1st gear	2.54	2.20	2.56	2.20
2nd gear	1.89	1.64	1.91	1.64
3rd gear	1.51	1.31	1.48	1.28
4th gear	1.00	1.00	1.00	1.00
Reverse	2.61	2.26	2.64	2.26

4-Speed	1966-1974 (Standard)	1975-1976 (Close Ratio)	1975-1976 (Standard)
1st gear	2.52	2.43	2.64
2nd gear	1.88	1.76	1.75
3rd gear	1.46	1.47	1.33
4th gear	1.00	1.00	1.00
Reverse	2.59	2.35	2.55

Table 3   AUTOMATIC TRANSMISSION GEAR RATIOS

Powerglide (1963-1967)		Turbo Hydramatic (1968-1976)	
Torque multiplication	2.10	1st	2.5:1
Low	1.76	2nd	1.5:1
Drive	1.00	3rd	1.0:1
Reverse	1.76	Reverse	3.70:2

Table 4   MANUAL TRANSMISSION TIGHTENING TORQUES

Transmission	Ft.-lb.	Transmission	Ft.-lb.
3-speed Muncie		Power take off cover bolts	18
Clutch gear retainer to case bolts	15	Parking brake	22
Side cover to case bolts	15	Countergear front cover screws	25
Extension to case bolts	45	Transmission to clutch housing bolts	75
Shift lever to shifter shaft bolts	25	Crossmember to mount	40
Lubrication filler plugs	18	Mount to transmission	50
Transmission case to clutch housing bolts	75		
Crossmember to frame nuts	25		
Crossmember to mount bolts	40		
Transmission drain plug	30		
2-3 crossover shaft bracket retaining nut	18	**4-speed Saginaw**	
1-revolution swivel attaching bolt	20	Clutch gear retainer to case bolts	15
Mount to transmission bolt	50	Side cover to case bolts	15
		Extension to case bolts	45
		Shift lever to shifter shaft bolts	25
		Lubrication filler plug	13
3-speed Saginaw		Transmission case to clutch housing bolts	75
Clutch gear retainer to case bolts	15	Crossmember to frame nuts	25
Side cover to case bolts	15	Crossmember to mount and mount to	40
Extension to case bolts	45	extension bolts	
Shift lever to shifter shaft bolts	25	Mount to transmission bolts	32
Lubrication filler plug	18		
Transmission case to clutch housing bolts	75		
Crossmember to frame nuts	25		
Crossmember to mount bolts	40	**4-speed Warner**	
2-3 crossover shaft bracket retaining nut	18	Clutch gear retainer to case bolts	18
1-revolution swivel attaching bolt	20	Side cover to case bolts	18
Mount to transmission bolt	50	Extension to case bolts	40
		Shift lever to shifter shaft bolts	20
		Lubrication filler plug	15
		Transmission case to clutch housing bolts	52
4-speed Muncie		Crossmember to mount and mount to	25
Rear bearing retainer	18	extension bolts	
Cover bolts	25	Rear bearing retainer to case bolts	25
Filler plug	35	Extension to rear bearing retainer	25
Drain plug	35	bolt (short)	
Clutch gear bearing retainer bolts	18	Retainer to case bolts	35
Universal joint front flange nut	95	Transmission drain plug	20

Table 5   AUTOMATIC TRANSMISSION TIGHTENING TORQUES

Transmission	Ft.-lb.	Transmission	Ft.-lb.
Powerglide		**Turbo Hydramatic**	
Transmission case to engine	35	Transmission to engine bolts	35
Oil pan bolts	8	Rear mount to transmission bolts	40
Low band adjustment locknut	15	Rear mount to crossmember bolt	40
Converter to engine bolts	35	Crossmember mounting bolts	25
Oil pan drain plug	20	Strainer retainer bolt	10
		Converter to flywheel bolts	35

CHAPTER TWELVE

BRAKES

Corvettes use conventional hydraulically operated brakes on all 4 wheels. Models from 1963-1964 use drum brakes. The manual brakes and the standard power brakes use a single circuit braking system which operates both front and rear brakes. When the heavy duty brake system with metallic linings is installed, a dual circuit hydraulic system is used; one circuit operates front brakes, the other circuit operates the rear brakes. All Corvettes from 1965-1976 have 4-wheel disc brakes. All 1965-1966 manual brakes use a single hydraulic circuit; while 1965-1966 power brakes and all 1967-1976 systems use a dual hydraulic circuit.

Dual system brakes provide a safety margin not found in single circuit systems. If one circuit should fail, the other remains intact permitting a safe stop with 2 wheels. A warning circuit in 1968-1976 models indicates that pressure in one circuit is defective. Increased pedal travel and decreased braking also indicate trouble.

Cable operated mechanical hand brakes act on the rear wheels. When the hand lever is drawn back, the rear brake shoes expand to provide emergency or parking brakes. On 1963-1964 drum brake systems, the existing brake drums are used for this purpose. On 1965-1976 disc brake systems, special brake shoes are used. The rear brake disc acts as a parking brake drum.

This chapter describes repair procedures for all parts of the brake system. **Tables 1, 2, and 3** at the end of this chapter list specifications and tightening torques. A variety of brake components are used, depending on year. Where differences exist, they are pointed out. Because of these differences, always order brake parts by year and compare new parts to old parts before installation.

SINGLE MASTER CYLINDERS

Removal/Installation

Refer to **Figure 1** for this procedure.

1. Disconnect the hydraulic lines from the main cylinder.

2. Cap line fittings to prevent entry of dirt and moisture.

3. Remove the clip and clevis pin from the brake pedal arm.

4. Remove master cylinder retaining nuts and lockwasher securing master cylinder to the front dash panel. Remove master cylinder.

5. Installation is the reverse of these steps. Refill master cylinder and bleed all brake lines as described later.

6. Adjust pushrod clearance as described later.

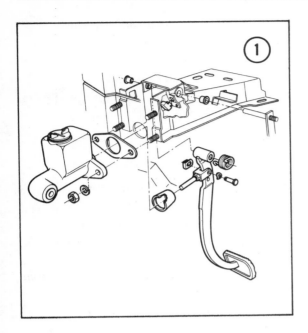

Pushrod Clearance

1. Loosen locknut on clevis.

2. Turn pushrod in direction necessary until the pushrod just contacts the master cylinder piston.

3. Turn pushrod in the opposite direction until pedal moves ⅛-⅜ in. before pushrod contacts master cylinder piston.

4. Tighten locknut on clevis.

Disassembly

Refer to **Figure 2** for this procedure.

1. Remove 2 hydraulic line nuts from the master cylinders. See **Figure 3**. Remove check valves and springs.

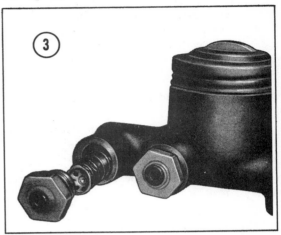

2. Remove pushrod assembly.

3. Remove boot.

4. Remove end plug. Insert wire in end plug hole and push out primary cup, spring, valve assembly, and valve seat.

5. Remove reservoir cover components from master cylinder.

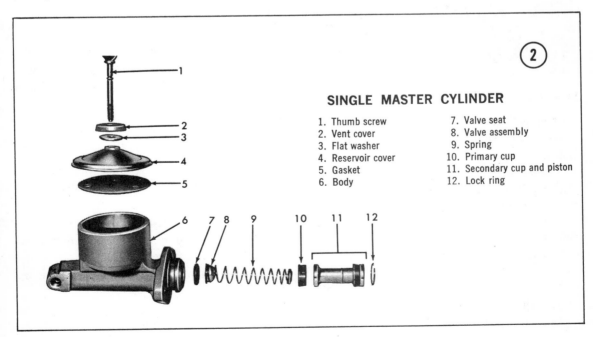

SINGLE MASTER CYLINDER

1. Thumb screw
2. Vent cover
3. Flat washer
4. Reservoir cover
5. Gasket
6. Body
7. Valve seat
8. Valve assembly
9. Spring
10. Primary cup
11. Secondary cup and piston
12. Lock ring

Cleaning and Inspection

1. Clean all parts in denatured alcohol or clean brake fluid.

CAUTION
Never use gasoline, kerosene, or any solvent other than alcohol for rubber brake parts. You may wash metal brake parts in other solvents if you blow them dry, rinse several times in clean alcohol and blow dry again before installing.

2. Inspect the cylinder bore for scoring, pitting, or heavy corrosion. Very light scratches and corrosion may be removed with crocus cloth. Discard the master cylinder if damage is more severe.

3. Inspect the piston for scoring, pitting, or heavy corrosion.

4. Check piston clearance in cylinder bore as shown in **Figure 4**. Clearance between piston and wall of the cylinder should be 0.001-0.005 in.

Assembly

Refer to Figure 2 for this procedure.

1. Lubricate cylinder walls with brake fluid.

2. Install valve seat, valve assembly, and spring into master cylinder.

3. Dip primary cup into clean brake fluid and install into master cylinder with the flat side toward the pushrod end. Make certain it seats over end of spring.

4. Dip secondary cup in clean brake fluid and install on piston.

5. Assemble secondary cup and piston in the body so that the bleeder hole end of the piston is toward the end plug.

6. Install the piston stop and snap ring.

7. Install the boot.

8. Install the end plug.

9. Install pushrod, locknut, and clevis.

10. Install check valves and springs. Secure with 2 hydraulic nuts. See Figure 3.

DUAL MASTER CYLINDERS
Removal/Installation (Manual 1967-1976)

1. Wipe away dirt around hydraulic lines and disconnect hydraulic lines from master cylinder. Cover ends to prevent entry of dirt and moisture.

2. Disconnect pushrod from brake pedal.

3. Unbolt and remove master cylinder from firewall.

4. Remove master cylinder mounting gasket and boot.

5. Remove master cylinder cover and dump out fluid. Pump remaining fluid from cylinder by depressing the pushrod.

6. Install is the reverse of these steps. Fill the reservoirs with brake fluid and bleed the system as described later.

7. Adjust pushrod clearance as described below if necessary.

Pushrod Clearance

1. Loosen locknut on clevis.

2. Turn pushrod in direction necessary until the pushrod just contacts the master cylinder piston.

3. Turn pushrod in the opposite direction until pedal moves 1/8-3/8 in. before pushrod contacts master cylinder piston.

4. Tighten locknut on clevis.

Disassembly

Refer to **Figure 5** for this procedure.

1. Clamp master cylinder in a vise.

2. Remove pushrod retainer.

3. Remove secondary piston stop bolt from bottom of front fluid reservoir.

4. Remove snap ring retainer and primary piston assembly.

5. Remove secondary piston, piston spring and retainer by blowing compressed air through the

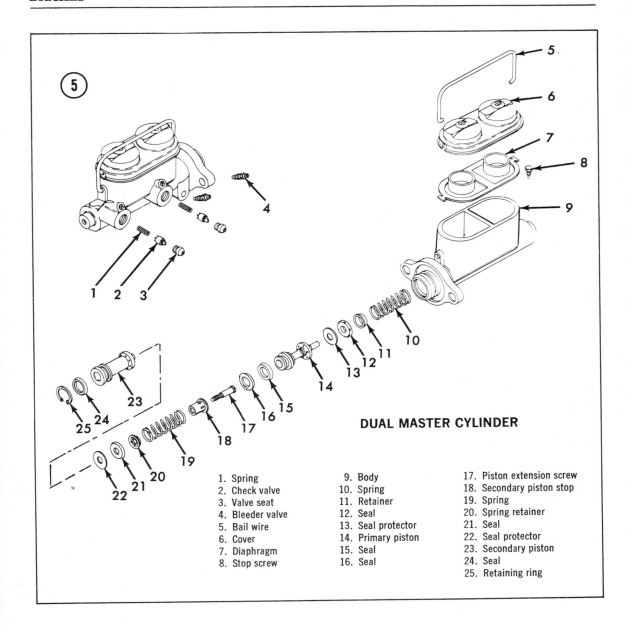

DUAL MASTER CYLINDER

1. Spring
2. Check valve
3. Valve seat
4. Bleeder valve
5. Bail wire
6. Cover
7. Diaphragm
8. Stop screw
9. Body
10. Spring
11. Retainer
12. Seal
13. Seal protector
14. Primary piston
15. Seal
16. Seal
17. Piston extension screw
18. Secondary piston stop
19. Spring
20. Spring retainer
21. Seal
22. Seal protector
23. Secondary piston
24. Seal
25. Retaining ring

stop bolt hole. If air is not available, use a piece of stiff wire with approximately ¼ in. of one end bent over at a right angle. Hook the secondary piston and pull it out.

6. Reposition master cylinder in vise with outlet holes facing up.

7. Drill a 13/64 in. hole through both check valve seats.

8. Tap out both seats using a ¼ in.-20 tap.

9. Install a spare brake line tube nut in the outlet hole. Place a flat washer on a one in. long

¼ in.-20 screw. Thread the screw into the threaded hole in the tube seat. Hold the screw to keep it from turning and back out the tube nut. This will pull the tube seat out of the master cylinder.

10. Repeat Step 9 on second tube seat.

11. Remove the primary seal, primary seal protector, and secondary seals from the secondary piston.

12. Remove the piston extension screw securing the primary spring to the primary piston.

13. Remove the spring retainer, primary seal, primary seal protector, and secondary seal from the primary piston.

Cleaning and Inspection

1. Clean all parts in denatured alcohol or clean brake fluid.

CAUTION
Never use gasoline, kerosene, or any solvent other than alcohol for rubber brake parts. You may wash metal parts in other solvents if you blow them dry, rinse several times in clean alcohol, and blow dry again.

2. Inspect the cylinder bore for scoring, pitting, or heavy corrosion. Very light scratches and corrosion may be removed with crocus cloth. Discard the master cylinder if damage is more severe.

3. Inspect the pistons for scoring, pitting, and heavy corrosion.

Assembly

Refer to Figure 5 for this procedure.

1. Hold master cylinder in a vise with the outlet holes facing up.

2. Install new brass tube seats in the outlet holes. Be sure seats are not cocked as this would turn up burrs as the tube seats are pressed in. Thread a spare brake line tube nut into the outlet hole and turn the nut down until the tube seat bottoms. Do this for both outlets.

3. Place new secondary seal in the 2 grooves in the flat end of the secondary piston assembly. The seal nearest the flat end has its lips facing toward the flat end. On Delco units, the seal in the second groove has its lips facing toward the small compensating holes. On Bendix units, the seal in the second groove is an O-ring.

4. Assemble new primary seal and primary protector over the end of the secondary piston opposite the secondary seals.

5. Lubricate the cylinder walls and all internal parts with brake fluid.

6. Insert the secondary piston spring retainer into the secondary piston spring. Place the retainer and spring down over the end of the secondary piston so that the retainer locates inside the lips of the primary seal.

7. Hold the master cylinder with the open end of the bore up. Push the secondary piston into the bore so that the spring seats against the closed end of the bore.

8. Push the primary piston into the bore of the master cylinder. Hold the piston down and snap the lock ring into place in the bore.

9. While still holding the primary piston down, install the stop screw in the master cylinder and tighten to 33 in.-lb.

10. Install the reservoir diaphragm in the reservoir cover and install the cover on the master cylinder.

11. Bench bleed the master cylinder as described in the following procedure.

Bench Bleeding

1. Install plugs in both outlet ports.

NOTE: *Plastic plugs which come with a replacement cylinder are recommended for this operation.*

2. Clamp the master cylinder in a vise with the front end tilted slightly down.

CAUTION
Do not tighten vise too tight as damage to the master cylinder could result.

3. Fill both reservoirs with clean brake fluid.

4. Insert a rod with a smooth, round end into the primary piston and press in to compress the piston return spring.

5. Release pressure on rod. Watch for air bubbles in the reservoir fluid.

6. Repeat Step 5 until bubbles no longer appear.

7. Reposition master cylinder in vise so front end tilts slightly up.

8. Repeat Steps 4-6.

9. Install diaphragm and cover on reservoir.

POWER CYLINDER
Moraine Removal/Installation (1963-1967)

1. Disconnect clevis at brake pedal assembly.

2. Remove vacuum hose from vacuum check valve.

3. Disconnect hydraulic line at master cylinder.

4. Remove 2 nuts and lockwashers on the inside of firewall.

5. Remove 2 bolts from the top engine side of the firewall and remove power cylinder.

> NOTE: *Remove unit carefully so that the rubber pushrod boot is not torn.*

6. Installation is the reverse of these steps. Adjust clevis on pushrod to obtain a pedal height of 4⅝ in. from floor to top of pedal. Check stoplight operation after adjusting pedal height.

7. Refill master cylinder and bleed brakes as described later.

Bendix Removal/Installation (1968-1976)

1. Disconnect pushrod at brake pedal arm.

> NOTE: *It may be necessary to remove the clevis from the pushrod. Note the approximate location of clevis on the rod.*

2. Remove vacuum hose from check valve.

3. Disconnect hydraulic lines at master cylinder.

4. Remove master cylinder attaching nuts, lockwashers, rubber seal, and metal retainer.

5. Remove 4 nuts and lockwashers securing power cylinder to firewall. Remove power cylinder from engine compartment.

6. Installation is the reverse of these steps.

7. Refill master cylinder and bleed brake system as described later.

BRAKE DRUMS (1963-1964)

Removal/Installation

1. Raise vehicle on jackstands or hoist.

2. Remove wheels.

3. Pull brake drum off. See **Figure 6**.

> NOTE: *If the brake drums are severely worn, it may be necessary to retract the adjusting screw. The lanced area in the web of the brake drum must be knocked out with a chisel or similar tool to gain access to the adjusting screw star wheel. Be sure to clean*

away all metal from the brake area. Install a new cover when the drum is reinstalled.

4. Installation is the reverse of these steps.

Inspection

1. Blow brake dust and dirt from the brake drum. Remove grease and oil with cleaning solvent. Blow dry.

2. Clean the drum braking surface with alcohol.

3. Inspect brake drums for scoring, cracking, taper, out-of-roundness, heat evidence, etc. Drums which are scored or worn should be turned and brake shoes replaced by oversize shoes. Cracked drums cannot be turned; replace them.

4. Remove glaze on serviceable drums with fine emery cloth.

BRAKE SHOES (1963-1964)

Brake shoes require relining or replacement when linings are soaked with oil, grease, or brake fluid. In addition, replace linings worn to less than 1/16 in.; check by removing brake drums. If brake drums have been turned, use oversize linings. Always replace linings on all 4 wheels to ensure uniform braking.

NOTE: *Corvette brake shoes normally have a glazed appearance; this is a normal condition with the hard lining used. Do not use a wire brush or abrasive on the lining to destroy the glazed surface.*

Removal

1. Raise the vehicle on jackstands.

2. Loosen locknuts at forward end of parking brake cable (A and B, **Figure 7**) sufficiently to remove all tension from brake cable.

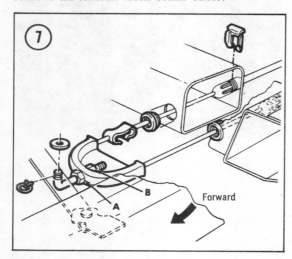

3. Remove wheels and drums as described earlier.

4. Unhook brake shoe return springs from anchor pin and link end. See **Figure 8**.

5. Remove the actuator return spring.

6. Disengage the link end from the anchor pin and other end from the secondary shoe.

7. Remove hold-down pins and springs with a pair of needlenose pliers. See **Figure 9**.

8. Remove the actuator assembly.

NOTE: *The actuator pivot and override spring are an assembly. Do not disassemble them unless they are broken; it is much easier to assemble and disassemble the brakes, leaving them intact.*

9. Separate the brake shoes by removing adjusting screw and spring. See **Figure 10**.

10. On rear brakes only, remove parking brake lever from secondary brake shoe.

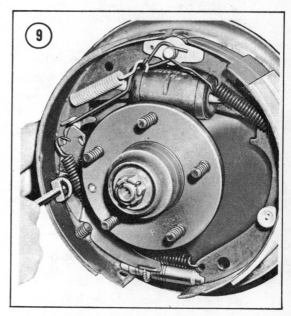

Inspection

1. Clean and inspect brake drums as described earlier.

2. Inspect wheel bearings and oil seal and replace if necessary.

3. Carefully pull lower edges of wheel cylinder boots away from cylinders and note whether interior is wet with brake fluid. A slight amount

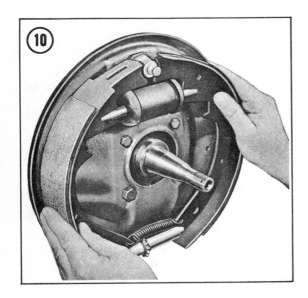

of fluid is normal. Excessive fluid at this point indicates leakage past the piston cups, requiring wheel cylinder overhaul.

4. On rear wheels, inspect backing plate for oil leakage past axle shaft oil seals. Install new seals if necessary.

5. Make sure all backing plate bolts are tight. Clean all rust and dirt from shoe contact faces on backing plate, using fine emery cloth. See **Figure 11**.

Installation

1. Lubricate parking brake cable.

2. Lubricate fulcrum end of parking brake lever

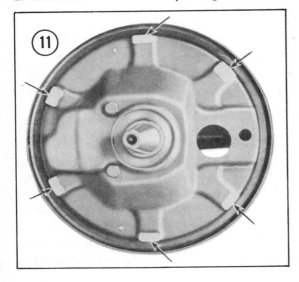

and the bolt with brake lube. Attach lever to secondary shoe with bolt, spring washer, lockwasher, and nut. Make sure that the lever moves freely.

3. Make certain the adjusting screw is clean and properly lubricated.

4. Connect brake shoes together with adjusting screw spring. Place adjusting screw, socket, and nut in position.

CAUTION
The starwheel must be installed nearest the secondary shoe and the adjusting screw spring installed to prevent interference with the starwheel.

5a. On standard brakes, secure the primary brake shoe (short lining) with the hold-down pin and spring. The primary brake shoe faces forward. Be sure that the brake shoes fit in the wheel cylinder connecting links.

5b. On metallic brakes, secure the secondary brake shoe (long lining) with the hold-down pin and spring. The secondary shoe faces rearward. Be sure that the brake shoes fit in the wheel cylinder connecting links.

6a. On standard brakes, secure the actuator assembly, override spring, and return spring on the secondary shoe.

6b. On metallic brakes, secure the actuator assembly, override spring, and return spring on the primary shoe.

7a. On standard brakes, secure actuator assembly and secondary brake shoe with the hold-down pin and spring.

7b. On metallic brakes, secure actuator assembly and primary brake shoe with the hold-down pin and spring.

8. Install guide plate over anchor pin.

9. Install the wire link.

10. On rear brakes, connect cable to parking brake lever and install strap between lever and primary shoe.

11. Install return spring as shown in **Figure 12**. If old springs are nicked, distorted, or strength is doubtful, use new springs.

12. Pry shoes away from backing plate and lubricate shoe contact surfaces with a thin coat of brake fluid.

CAUTION
Do not get lubricant on linings.

13. Make certain that actuator lever works easily by hand. See **Figure 13**.

14. Disengage actuator from starwheel and rotate starwheel until brake drums just fit over linings. Back the starwheel off 1¼ turns to retract the shoes.

15. Install brake drums and wheels as described earlier.

16. Make several forward and reverse stops with the vehicle to allow the self-adjusters to adjust the brakes.

> NOTE: *These steps apply to metallic linings only. They seat the linings.*

17. Make 6-8 stops from 30 mph with moderate pedal pressure.

18. Make 6-8 complete stops from 65 mph at approximately one mile intervals.

WHEEL CYLINDERS (1963-1964)

Removal

1. Raise vehicle on jackstands.

2. Remove wheels and drum as described earlier.

3. Disconnect brake lines.

4. Disconnect brake shoe retracting spring from brake shoes.

5. Remove 2 bolts which hold rear wheel cylinder to brake flange plate, and remove rear wheel cylinder.

6. Remove anchor pin which holds front wheel cylinder to flange plate and remove front wheel cylinder.

Rebuilding

Refer to **Figure 14** for this procedure.

1. Remove both rubber boots.

2. Remove pistons, cups, cup expanders, and spring.

3. Remove bleeder valve.

4. Clean all parts in alcohol or brake fluid.

5. Examine the cylinder bore for scoring, pitting, or heavy corrosion. Very light scratches may be removed with crocus cloth. Flush out with alcohol and blow dry. Replace wheel cylinders which show more extensive damage.

6. Check piston clearance in bore as shown in **Figure 15**. Clearance should be 0.003-0.006 in.

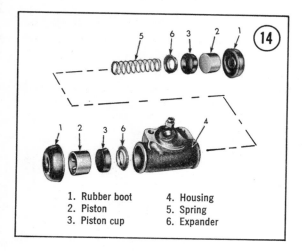

1. Rubber boot
2. Piston
3. Piston cup
4. Housing
5. Spring
6. Expander

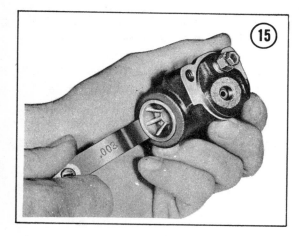

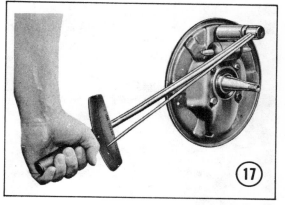

If clearance exceeds 0.006 in., replace piston and cup, if bore is not damaged. Replace cylinder assembly if bore is scored or damaged.

7. Lubricate all parts with brake fluid.

8. Install new cups, cup expanders, and springs provided in the repair kit. Do not use old parts.

9. Install pistons and new rubber boots.

10. Install bleeder valve.

Installation

1. Mount front wheel cylinders to the brake flange plate with the threaded anchor pin. See **Figure 16**. Tighten to 65 ft.-lb. See **Figure 17**.

CAUTION
Peen over the flat washer on the anchor pin to prevent the anchor pin from loosening.

2. Mount the rear wheel cylinder to the brake flange plate and install 2 bolts. Tighten securely and install the 2 connecting links.

3. On both front and rear, replace the brake shoe retracting springs.

4. Connect the brake line to the wheel cylinder.

5. Install the rear brake drums, and install the wheels.

6. Install front drum and adjust wheel bearings as described in Chapter Thirteen.

7. Bleed all brake lines.

8. Adjust brakes as described later.

BRAKE PAD REPLACEMENT

Brake pads on all 4 wheels should be inspected every 6,000 miles as described in Chapter Two. Replace brake when the groove in the center of the shoe is gone. This leaves approximately 1/16 in. of lining.

It is rarely necessary to bleed the brake system after a simple brake pad replacement.

1. Siphon all brake fluid from master cylinder reservoirs.

2. Raise car on jackstands and remove the wheels.

3. Remove retainer pin clip on brake caliper and remove pin.

4. Pull brake pads out. See **Figure 18**.

CAUTION
If brake pads are to be reinstalled, mark them so they can be replaced in the same position.

5. Clean out the cavity which holds the brake pads. Inspect the rubber dust covers; if they are damaged, replace them. If dirt has penetrated the cylinders due to damaged cover, recondition the brake caliper as described later.

6. Push both pistons back into the caliper housing and place piston retaining clips (tool J-21938), or equivalent, down over the caliper to hold the pistons in retracted position.

NOTE: *Open the bleed valve(s) to make this easier.*

7. Install new brake pads and remove the piston retaining clips.

8. Install brake pad retaining pin and secure both ends with clips.

9. Refill master cylinder and if necessary bleed brakes as described later. Install wheels and lower vehicle.

10. Depress brake pedal several times before driving the car so that the pads can assume correct alignment with respect to the brake disc.

BRAKE CALIPERS

Removal/Installation

1. Raise vehicle on jackstands.

2. Remove wheel(s).

3a. On front caliper, disconnect brake hose at brake line support bracket.

3b. On rear caliper, disconnect brake tubing from the inboard caliper and tape the hole to prevent entry of dirt and moisture.

4. Remove brake pads as described previously.

5. Unbolt caliper from mounting bracket.

6. Installation is the reverse of these steps. Torque mounting bolts to 60-90 ft.-lb.

Reconditioning

Refer to **Figure 19** for this procedure.

1. Clean outside of caliper thoroughly with Declene or clean alcohol.

2. Remove brake hose from front caliper.

3. Remove 2 large bolts from caliper and disassemble caliper housing halves. Remove small O-rings (2 on front calipers, one on rear calipers) from the cavities around the transfer holes.

4. Push each piston down into the caliper so the end is below the level of the steel ring on the boot. Insert a small screwdriver blade under inner edge of the steel ring and pry the boot from its seat.

CAUTION
Do not damage the insulators or puncture the seal.

5. Remove the piston assembly and piston spring from the caliper half.

6. Remove the screw which holds the insulator and boot on each piston. Remove the seal from the piston groove.

7. Clean all parts in Declene, alcohol, or clean brake fluid.

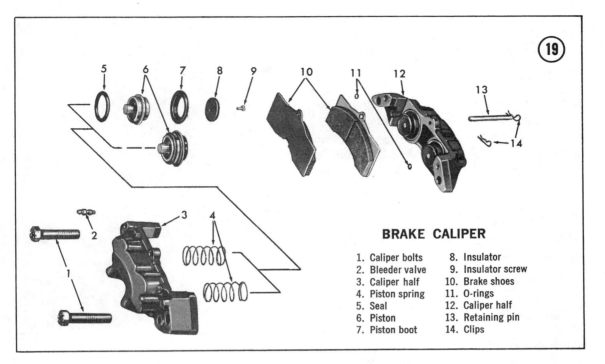

BRAKE CALIPER

1. Caliper bolts
2. Bleeder valve
3. Caliper half
4. Piston spring
5. Seal
6. Piston
7. Piston boot
8. Insulator
9. Insulator screw
10. Brake shoes
11. O-rings
12. Caliper half
13. Retaining pin
14. Clips

8. Inspect cylinder bore for scoring or other damage.

9. Check piston clearance in bore with a feeler gauge. See **Table 4** for proper clearance. If the bore is undamaged and the clearance exceeds upper limit, replace the piston.

Table 4   CALIPER/PISTON CLEARANCES

Bore	Clearance
1⅞″ (front)	0.0045 - 0.010″
1⅜″ (rear)	0.0035 - 0.009″

10. Place boots on end of pistons so that the inside diameter fits on the steps in the end of the pistons. Fold the boot in toward the piston groove.

11. Install new seals on the pistons with the lips of the seals facing away from the boot ends of the pistons.

12. Install the insulator on the end of the piston with the screw. Make sure that the inside diameter of the boot remains in the groove between the insulator and the piston. Torque the screws to 11-14 in.-lb.

13. Place the piston spring in the bottom of the cylinder bores.

14. Lubricate the piston seal with clean brake fluid. Install pistons in bores with the boot end up.

15. Press the steel retaining ring in evenly until it is flush or slightly below the machined surface of the caliper. See **Figure 20**.

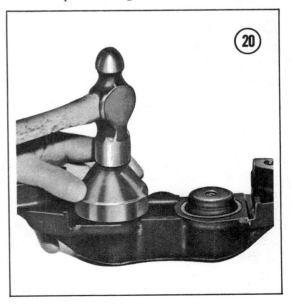

CAUTION
*Any distortion or uneven seating of
the steel retaining ring could allow
contaminating and corrosive elements
to enter the bore.*

16. Install new O-rings in the small cavities around the brake fluid transfer holes.

17. Lubricate the 2 housing bolts with clean brake fluid. Torque to a 120-140 ft.-lb. on the front calipers, and 55-65 ft.-lb. on the rear calipers.

CAUTION
These torque values are very critical.

18. On front calipers only, connect brake hose to calipers with a new washer.

BRAKE DISC

The brake disc is riveted to the wheel hub or spindle on production models. When the brake disc is removed for any reason, the rivets must be drilled out. However, it is not necessary to install new rivets when the disc is installed since the wheel lugs will hold the disc in place.

Removal/Installation

1. Raise the vehicle on jackstands and remove wheels.

2. Remove caliper as described previously.

3. Drill out the 5 rivets attaching the disc to the hub or spindle.

4. Remove brake disc from vehicle.

5. Remove remnants of the 5 rivets from the hub or spindle.

6. Installation is the reverse of these steps.

NOTE: *On the rear wheels, be sure the emergency brake adjusting holes of the spindle and disc are in line with each other.*

Inspection

Check the brake disc for deep scratches, excessive runout, and uneven thickness. Small marks on the disc are not important, but deep radial scratches reduce braking effectiveness and increase pad wear.

To check disc runout, mount the dial indicator as shown in **Figure 21**. On front wheels, tighten

the wheel bearing adjustment nut until all bearing play has been removed. The nut should be just loose enough to allow the wheel to turn. When the brake disc is turned, the dial indicator reading should not exceed 0.002 in. when measured one in. from the outer edge. If runout exceeds this amount, the hum and disc assembly should be replaced. Because of the close tolerances involved, do not machine the front discs or replace discs separately from the hub. After checking runout, readjust the wheel bearings as described in Chapter Thirteen.

Rear wheel brake discs are checked in a similar manner. Move the wheel in and out to measure rear wheel bearing end play. When the brake disc is turned, lateral runout should not exceed bearing end play by more than 0.040 in.; if it does, replace the disc.

BRAKE LINE DISTRIBUTOR

The brake line distributor is mounted just below the master cylinder.

Removal/Installation

1. Disconnect the battery ground cable.

2. Disconnect the electrical lead from the switch assembly.

3. Place dry rags below switch to absorb any brake fluid spilled during removal of switch.

CAUTION
Spilled brake fluid can damage paint.

4. Disconnect 4 hydraulic lines from connections at switch. Cover open ends of lines with clean, lint-free material to prevent entry of dirt and moisture.

5. Remove mounting screw and remove combination valve from vehicle.

6. Make sure new switch is clean and free of dust and lint. If any doubt exists, wash switch in Declene or clean alcohol and dry with air.

7. Mount combination valve with screw.

8. Connect hydraulic lines to switch.

9. Connect electrical lead to switch.

10. Connect battery ground cable.

11. Bleed the brake system as described later.

PRESSURE REGULATOR VALVE

Some Corvettes with a heavy duty brake option include a pressure regulator valve mounted in the rear brake line just below the master cylinder. See **Figure 22**. This valve balances pressure between the front and rear hydraulic systems and prevents premature wheel lockup when the brakes are applied hard.

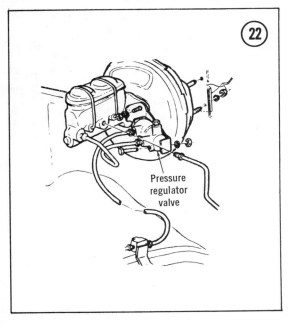

Pressure
regulator
valve

Removal/Installation

1. Disconnect hydraulic line between master cylinder and pressure regulator valve.

2. Disconnect hydraulic line between pressure regulator valve and brake line distributor.

3. Remove bolt securing the pressure regulator valve to bracket.

4. Installation is the reverse of these steps.

5. Bleed the brake system as described later.

PARKING BRAKES (1963-1964)

Lever Handle Replacement

Refer to **Figure 23** for this procedure.

1. Remove pin securing handle to lever assembly with a small screwdriver.

2. Steady lever assembly and remove handle.

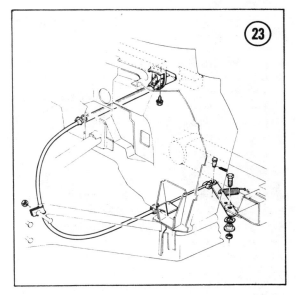

3. Replace handle.

4. Align handle with lever assembly and position vertically.

5. Insert pin with a small punch.

Front Cable Replacement

Refer to Figure 23 for this procedure.

1. Remove clip retainer on the firewall in the engine compartment.

2. Remove lever handle as described in previous procedure.

3. Remove bolts, lockwashers, and nuts securing front cable.

4. Disconnect front cable ball at idler lever.

5. Remove front cable.

6. Installation is the reverse of these steps. Lubricate cables and all moving parts with Lubriplate.

Rear Cable Replacement

Refer to Figure 23 for this procedure.

1. Remove cable clip retainers from each of the rear brake cable assemblies.

2. Disconnect cable at rear wheel backing plate.

3. Disconnect rear end of cable from brake lever assembly clevis.

4. Disconnect clips and retainers along the frame rail and at the differential support carrier bracket.

5. Disconnect cable at equalizer and remove cables. See **Figure 24**.

6. Installation is the reverse of these steps. Lubricate cable and all moving parts with Lubriplate.

PARKING BRAKES (1965-1976)

Lever Removal

Refer to **Figure 25** for this procedure.

1. Release handbrake.

2. Under vehicle, unhook and remove return spring.

3. Remove rear nut from cable stud at equalizer. Allow front cable to hang down.

4. Remove 6 screws securing cover to underbody. See **Figure 26**. Remove the retainer and lift the cover upward and to the rear to allow seal to slide out of cover slot. Remove cover.

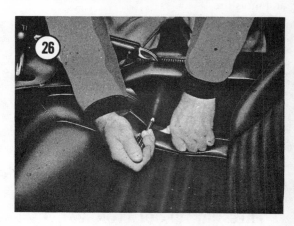

5. Remove trim seal from lever. See **Figure 27**.

6. Remove screw and washer securing parking brake alarm switch to side of lever.

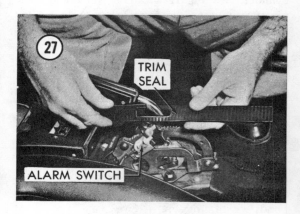

7. Remove 4 bolts securing lever assembly to underbody. Lift lever assembly upward. Remove forward mounting bracket for lever.

8. Remove front cable from lever assembly using long nose pliers as shown in **Figure 28**.

Lever Installation

1. Install front cable in lever assembly as shown in Figure 28.

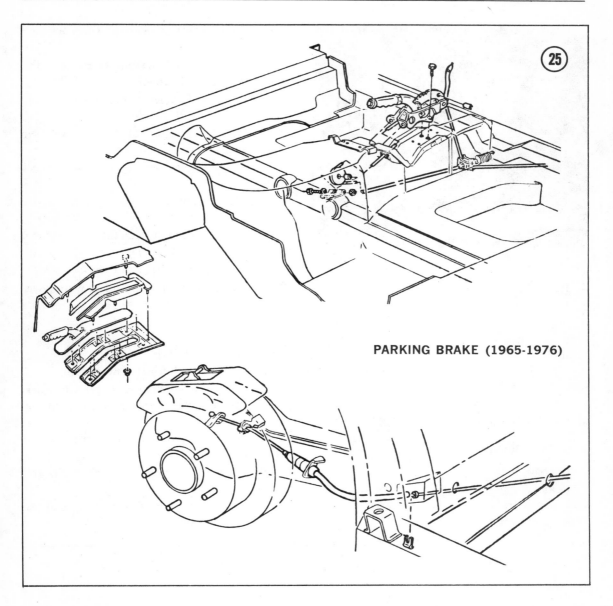

PARKING BRAKE (1965-1976)

2. Place forward mounting bracket in position and secure plate and lever assembly to underbody with 4 mounting screws.

3. Secure parking alarm switch to side of lever assembly with washer and screw.

4. Install trim seal on lever.

5. Insert end of trim seal into slot in the cover. Slide the cover forward and down into position.

6. Place retainer in position. Secure retainer and cover with 6 screws.

7. Insert front cable stud through equalizer assembly and secure with nut. See Figure 24.

8. Install return spring.

9. Adjust parking brake as described later.

Front Cable Replacement

Refer to Figure 25 for this procedure.

1. Remove parking brake lever as described previously.

2. From under vehicle, remove nut, washer, and bolt securing pulley to pulley bracket.

3. Remove the seal grommet from the underbody cable hole.

4. Pull cable out of vehicle.

5. Install seal grommet around front cable.

6. Slide front cable into position through cable hole and work seal grommet into installed position.

7. From under vehicle, loop front cable around pulley wheel and secure pulley wheel to bracket with bolt, washer, and nut.

8. Install parking brake lever.

Rear Cable Replacement

Refer to Figure 25 for this procedure.

1. Remove the cable clip retainers on the back side of the frame rail from each of the rear brake cable ends.

2. Disconnect cable at the rear wheel backing plate.

3. Remove the cable ball from the recess in the brake lever assembly clevis.

4. Disconnect the cables at the equalizer connector and remove the cables.

5. Connect the rear cable ball to the brake lever assembly clevis.

6. Connect the cable assembly to the rear wheel backing plate.

7. Connect the cable assembly along the frame rail area.

8. Insert the cable end through the equalizer and attach it to the equalizer connector.

9. Adjust the parking brake as described later.

10. Lubricate the cables and all moving parts with Lubriplate.

Brake Shoe Replacement

Refer to **Figure 29** for this procedure.

1. Remove rear brake discs as described earlier.

2. Remove retractor spring at the top of the shoes.

3. Remove hold-down springs on primary and secondary shoes.

4. Pull shoes away from the anchor pin and remove them.

5. Remove the adjusting screw spring and the adjusting screw from the shoes.

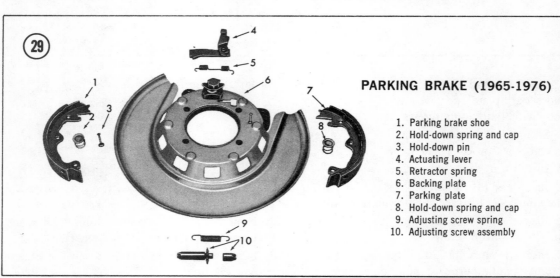

PARKING BRAKE (1965-1976)

1. Parking brake shoe
2. Hold-down spring and cap
3. Hold-down pin
4. Actuating lever
5. Retractor spring
6. Backing plate
7. Parking plate
8. Hold-down spring and cap
9. Adjusting screw spring
10. Adjusting screw assembly

6. Clean all dirt from brake backing plate.

7. Lubricate contact surfaces on backing plate and the threads of the adjusting screw with Lubriplate.

8. Connect adjusting screw spring to the bottom hole in each shoe.

9. Insert the starwheel between the shoes. On the left-hand brake, the starwheel goes next to the rear shoe. On the right-hand brake, the starwheel goes next to the forward shoe.

10. Install the shoes on the backing plate by spreading them and placing them around the anchor pin.

11. Install hold-down springs on the hold-down nails.

12. Install retractor spring on one shoe and stretch to other shoe.

CAUTION
Make sure that the lever assembly which spreads the shoes is located so that the notches on the lever fit against the shoes.

13. Install brake disc and brake calipers as described previously.

14. Adjust parking brake.

BRAKE BLEEDING

Brakes require bleeding whenever air enters the system, lowering the effective braking pressure. Air can enter when the master cylinder or wheel cylinders are serviced, or if the fluid in the reservoir runs dry. Air can also enter through a leaky brake line or hose. Find the leaky line and replace it before bleeding.

Whenever handling brake fluid, do not get any on the brake shoes or body paint. Brake shoes will be permanently damaged, requiring replacement. Body paint can be damaged also unless you wipe the area with a clean cloth, then wash it with a soapy solution immediately.

1. Ensure that the brake fluid reservoir is full and that the vent in the cap is open.

2. Connect a plastic or rubber tube to the bleeder valve on the left rear wheel. Suspend the other end of the tube in a jar or bottle filled with a few inches of clean brake fluid. See **Figure 30**. During the remaining steps, keep this

end submerged at all times and never let the level in the brake fluid reservoir drop below about ½ full.

3. Open the bleeder valve on the left rear wheel about one turn. Have an assistant depress the brake pedal slowly to the floor. As soon as the pedal is all the way down, close the bleeder valve and let the pedal up. Repeat this step as many times as necessary, i.e., until fluid with no air bubbles issues from the tube.

4. Bleed the remaining valves in the same manner described in the above steps. Follow the sequence shown in **Figure 31**. Keep checking the brake fluid reservoir to be sure it doesn't run out of fluid.

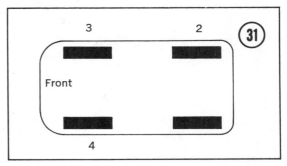

BRAKE ADJUSTMENT

Foot Brakes

Both drum brakes and disc brakes are self-adjusting. Therefore, no foot brake adjustment is necessary.

Handbrake (1963-1964)

1. Raise rear of car on jackstands. Release handbrake.

2. Loosen locknut (A) shown in **Figure 32**.

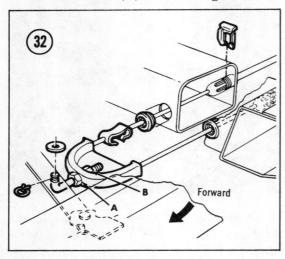

3. Turn rear nut (B) until rear wheels turn by hand with only slight drag. Loosen the nut until the drag disappears.

4. Pull handbrake lever up 2 notches. Turn the wheels by hand and ensure that the same effort is required for each wheel.

5. Pull the handbrake lever up an additional 2 notches. It should not be possible to turn either wheel by hand.

6. Tighten nut (A) against the equalizer.

7. Road test the car to ensure that the brakes hold properly.

Handbrake (1965-1976)

1. Raise rear of car on jackstands.

2. Remove rear wheels.

3. Release the handbrake.

4. Loosen brake cables at the equalizer until the cables are slack. See **Figure 33**.

5. Turn the brake discs until the adjusting screw can be seen through the hole in the discs.

6. Tighten the adjusting screw until the disc will not move (**Figure 34**). Back off the screw 6-8 notches.

7. Apply the parking brake 2 notches.

8. Tighten the brake cables at the equalizer until there is slight drag with the wheels mounted.

9. Fully release the parking brake and rotate the rear wheels. No drag should be evident.

10. Lower the vehicle.

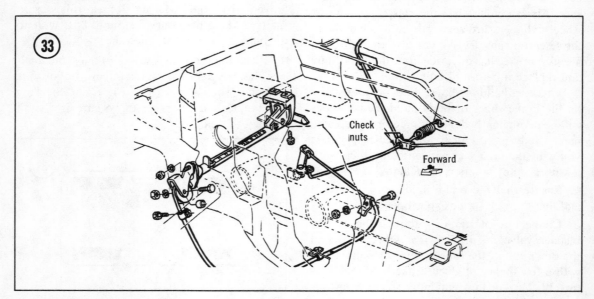

Table 2   BRAKE SPECIFICATIONS (1965-1976)

Foot brake	
Master cylinder bore	1.0"
Brake caliper piston bore	
Front	1.875"
Rear	1.375"
Disc diameter	11.75"
Brake pad	
Width	2.21"
Thickness	0.41"
Length	5.96"
Hand brake	
Drum diameter	6.5"
Lining	
Width	1.25"
Thickness	0.175"

Table 1   BRAKE SPECIFICATIONS (1963-1964)

Brake drum diameter	11"
Brake lining width	
Front	2.75"
Rear	2.00"
Brake lining thickness (min.)	0.168"
Total effective lining area	185.2 in.^{2}
Master cylinder	
Diameter	1.0"
Piston travel	1.329"
Wheel cylinder bore	
Front	1.1875"
Rear	1.00"

Table 3   TORQUE SPECIFICATIONS

Component	Torque
Master cylinder to dash	24 ft.-lb.
Master cylinder to booster	24 ft.-lb.
Vacuum booster to dash	24 ft.-lb.
Pushrod to clevis	14 ft.-lb.
Brake line nuts (to master cylinder & valves)	150 in.-lb.
Brake line nuts (to front brake hose)	150 in.-lb.
Brake line nut (to rear brake hose)	115 in.-lb.
Brake line clip to frame	100 in.-lb.
Brake bleeder valves	65 in.-lb.
Caliper mounting bolt	70 ft.-lb.
Caliper housing bolt	130 ft.-lb.
Flex hose to caliper bolt	22 ft.-lb.
Distribution switch mounting	100 in.-lb.
Parking brake equalizer	70 in.-lb.
Parking brake assembly (to dash or floor)	100 in.-lb.
Rear cable bracket	100 in.-lb.

CHAPTER THIRTEEN

FRONT SUSPENSION AND STEERING

The Corvette independent front suspension is conventional. It uses unequal upper and lower control arms and coil springs. The shock absorbers mount inside the coil springs. A stabilizer bar attaches to the lower control arms and the frame. **Figure 1** shows the complete front suspension.

Figure 2 shows the steering system. Pitman arm motion is transmitted to a center relay rod supported at one side by an idler arm. Center relay rod movement in turn moves the steering knuckles through two adjustable outer tie rods. Overall steering ratio may be changed from a standard road ratio to a faster ratio by moving each tie rod from one steering mounting hole to the other. See **Table 1**, end of chapter, for actual ratios possible. A steering damper incorporated in the steering linkage dampens road shock.

The power steering system uses the same recirculating ball steering gear, and linkage, with an added hydraulic power assist. An engine driven vane-type pump delivers hydraulic pressure to a control valve. The control valve senses the requirement for power assistance and supplies the power cylinder which operates the linkage.

WHEEL ALIGNMENT

Several front suspension dimensions affect running and steering of the front wheels. These variables must be properly aligned to maintain directional stability, ease of steering, and proper tire wear.

The dimensions involved define:
- a. Caster
- b. Camber
- c. Toe-in
- d. Steering axis inclination
- e. Front axle height

All except steering axis inclination are adjustable. Since these adjustments are critical, they must be done by a competent front end alignment shop or your dealer.

Pre-alignment Check

Several factors influence the suspension angles, or steering. Before any adjustments are attempted, perform the 10 following checks.

1. Check tire pressure and wear.
2. Check play in front wheel bearings. Adjust if necessary.
3. Check play in ball-joints.
4. Check for broken springs.
5. Remove any excessive load.
6. Check shock absorbers.
7. Check steering gear adjustments.
8. Check play in pitman arm and tie rod parts.

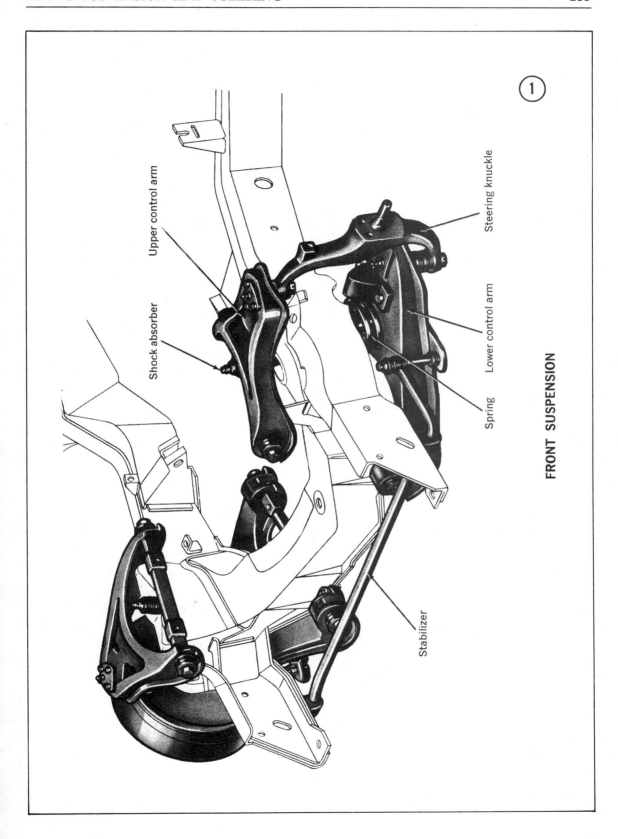

FRONT SUSPENSION

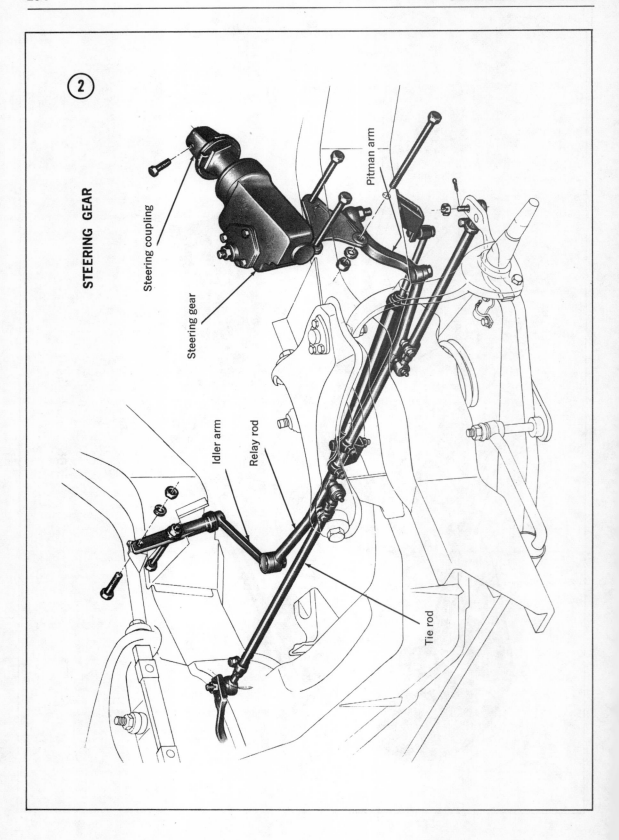

② STEERING GEAR

Steering coupling
Steering gear
Pitman arm
Idler arm
Relay rod
Tie rod

9. Check wheel balance.

10. Check *rear* suspension for looseness.

A proper inspection of front tire wear can point to several alignment problems. Tires worn primarily on one side show problems with toe-in. If toe-in is incorrect on one wheel, the car probably pulls to one side or the other. If toe-in is incorrect on both wheels, the car probably is hard to steer in either direction.

Incorrect camber may also cause tire wear on one side. Tire cupping (scalloped wear pattern) can result from worn shock absorbers, one wheel out of alignment, a bent spindle, or a combination of all. Tires worn in the middle, but not the edges, or worn nearly even on both edges, but not in the middle are probably over inflated or under inflated, respectively. These conditions are not caused by suspension misalignment.

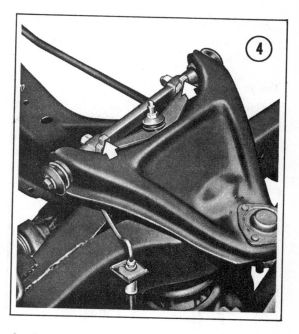

Camber

Camber is the inclination of the wheel from vertical as shown in **Figure 3**. Note that camber angle is positive camber, i.e., the top of the tire inclines outward more than the bottom.

Camber is adjusted by adding or removing shims at both front and rear bolts of upper control arm shaft. See **Figure 4**.

Caster

Caster is the fore and aft inclination of the steering knuckle centerline from vertical. See Figure 3. The Corvette has positive caster, i.e.,

the bottom of the wheel is shifted forward. Caster causes the wheel to return to a position straight ahead after a turn. It also prevents the car from wandering due to wind, potholes, or uneven road surfaces.

Caster is adjusted by adding or subtracting shims to the front bolt *or* the rear bolt of the upper control arm shaft. See Figure 4.

Steering Axis Inclination

Steering axis inclination, shown in Figure 3, is the inward inclination of the steering knuckle

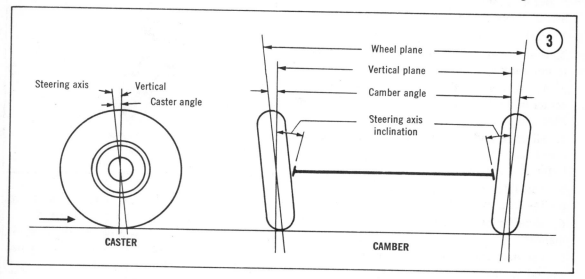

centerline from vertical. This angle is not adjustable, but can be checked with proper front end racks to find bent suspension parts.

Toe-in

Camber and rolling resistance tend to force the front wheels outward at their forward edge. To compensate for this tendency, the front edges are turned slightly inward when the car is at rest. This is toe-in. See **Figure 5**.

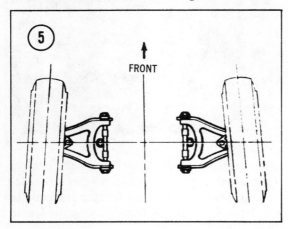

Toe-in is adjusted by lengthening or shortening the tie rods. Each tie rod is threaded so that the center section can be rotated to make the adjustment.

Ride Height

Before making any other suspension adjustments, check ride height as follows.

1. Park car on smooth, level floor.

2. Bounce car several times to permit it to settle to normal height.

3. Measure and record distance from floor to center of the front inner pivot of lower arm. See **Figure 6**.

4. Measure and record distance from floor to lower face of lower steering knuckle boss. See Figure 6.

5. The difference in the 2 measurements should be $3\frac{5}{8} \pm \frac{1}{2}$ in.

6. Measure other side of vehicle in the same manner.

7. The differences recorded in Step 5 must not exceed $\frac{1}{2}$ in.

SHOCK ABSORBERS

Replacement

Refer to **Figure 7**.

1. Raise front of vehicle on hoist or jackstands.

2. Hold upper stem of shock absorber with a $\frac{1}{4}$ in. wrench. Remove upper nut, retainer and grommet.

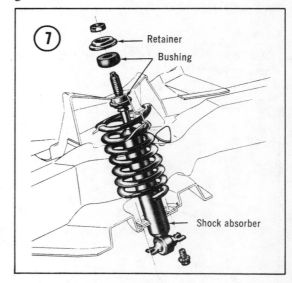

3. Disconnect lower shock mount from control arm. Pull shock out of arm. See **Figure 8**.

4. Installation is the reverse of these steps. Tighten upper nut to 15-25 foot-pounds. Tighten lower bolts to 8-11 foot-pounds.

and thread into tool J-6874. Tighten snugly. See **Figure 10**.

FRONT SPRINGS

WARNING
Due to the danger of working with a compressed spring, special tools must be used. Do not improvise.

Removal (1963-1967)

1. Raise car on jackstands.

2. Remove wheel and tire.

3. Remove stabilizer bar and shock absorber.

4. Loosen the lower ball-joint to steering knuckle nut.

5. Loosen lower control arm cross shaft bushing bolts.

6. Place tool J-6874-1 (**Figure 9**, next page) across top of 6th coil. Loosely secure tool J-6874-2 to the upper shoe. The V-notch in the upper shoe of the tool and the raised bank on the lower shoe should contact the spring.

7. Insert tool J-6874 up through center of spring and attach to upper and lower shoe assembly.

8. Position spacers under shock absorber mounting hole and against bottom of lower control arm. Install special bearing washer and tool J-6874-5. Locate bearing against spacer and large washer against bearing. Feed screw up through large washer, bearing and spacer

9. Center the shoe assembly on spring and tighten screw to compress spring slightly.

10. Tighten 2 capscrews securing upper and lower shoes to lock shoes on spring.

11. Compress spring with tool until spring clears spring tower.

> NOTE: *You may have to pry spring out of tower with a pry bar. See* **Figure 11.**

12. Remove the lower ball-joint to steering knuckle nut.

13. Disconnect lower ball-joint from spring knuckle and lower control arm with spring.

WARNING
Spring is under considerable tension and could cause serious injury if it is accidently released. Wrap spring and control arm as securely as possible with an old blanket to minimize danger in case of accident. Also, release spring compression as soon as spring is removed.

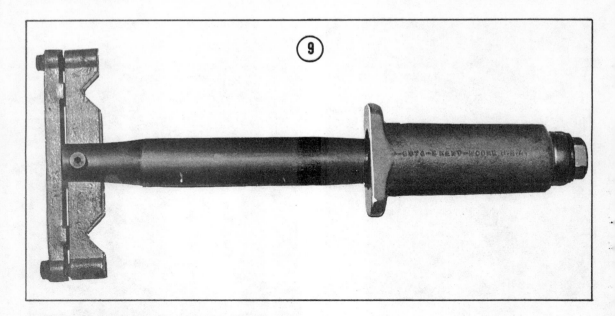

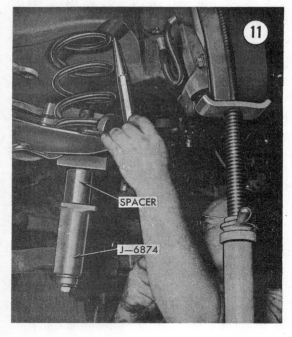

6. Position the spacers under the shock absorber mounting hole.

7. Install the bearing, large washer and tool J-6874-5. Locate bearing against spacer and large washer against bearing. Feed screw up through large washer, bearing, and spacer. Thread into yoke rod. Tighten slightly but do not compress spring.

8. Center shoe assembly on spring and tighten lug screw to compress spring slightly. Tighten capscrews on shoe assembly.

9. Turn lug screw until spring is compressed enough to clear spring tower.

10. Install lower ball-joint into steering knuckle and secure in place with nut.

11. Release spring slowly. Use a drift if necessary to seat spring properly. The end of the coil must be ⅜ in. from coil stops in seat.

12. Tighten lower ball-joint to steering knuckle nut. Lock with cotter key.

13. Install shock absorber and stabilizer bar.

14. Install wheel.

15. Lower car.

16. Tighten the lower control arm bushing bolts to 45-55 ft.-lb.

Removal (1968-1976)

1. Raise car on hoist so that the control arms hang free.

Installation (1963-1967)

1. Position spring with small end up.

2. Place tool J-6874-1 across top of 6th coil.

3. Loosely attach tool J-6874-2.

4. Insert tool J-6874 up through center of spring. Attach to upper and lower shoe assembly with bolt and nut.

5. Set spring in its seat on the lower control arm.

2. Remove shock absorber and disconnect stabilizer link.

3. Bolt tool J-23028 to floor jack and hoist it into position, cradling the inner bushings. See **Figure 12**.

4. Raise jack to remove tension on lower control arm.

5. Wrap heavy chain around spring and control arm to prevent it from flying out if the jack or tool should slip. See **Figure 13**.

6. First remove rear bolt from control arm, then all remaining nuts and bolts.

7. Lower control arm slowly with the jack until spring can be removed.

Installation (1968-1976)

1. Fit spring in control arm. Align as shown in **Figure 14**.

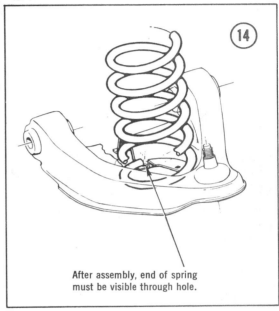

After assembly, end of spring must be visible through hole.

2. Lift control arm into position with tool J-23028 fitted to floor jack.

3. Install pivot bolts (front bolt first) and nuts.

CAUTION
In order to maintain adequate steering linkage clearance, install bolts in directions shown in **Figure 15.**

4. Lower jack.

5. Connect stabilizer link and shock absorber.

6. Lower car.

BALL-JOINTS

Replacement

1. Raise vehicle on jackstands and remove wheels.

2. Remove cotter pin, loosen ball-joint stud nut about one turn.

3. Place jack under lower control arm. Jack the arm up just enough to support control arm.

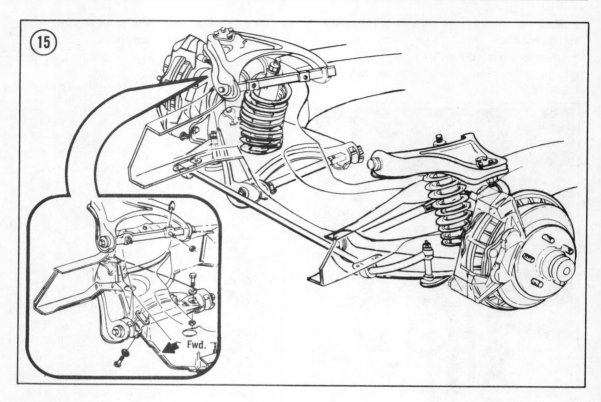

4. Install tool J-23742-1 or equivalent between ball studs as shown in **Figure 16**. Turn threaded end of tool until stud is free of steering knuckle.

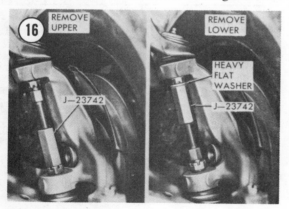

5. Remove ball-joint stud nut and disconnect steering knuckle from ball-joint.

6. Grind or chisel rivets off ball-joint assembly and remove ball-joint.

7. Check ball-joint mounting area on control arm for cracks or metal fatigue.

8. Drill rivet holes in control arm to diameter specified in ball-joint service kit.

9. Install new ball-joint with special bolts supplied in service kit. Insert bolts from bottom with nut on top. Torque bolts to 15-25 foot-pounds.

10. Turn ball stud cotter pin hole so it faces fore and aft.

11. Raise control arm and insert upper ball stud into steering knuckle. Install ball stud nut and torque to 50 foot-pounds. Secure with new cotter pin. If cotter pin hole does not line up, *tighten* nut additionally; do not *loosen* nut.

12. Connect stabilizer link to control arm bracket. Torque to 9-12 foot-pounds.

STABILIZER BAR

Refer to **Figure 17** for these procedures.

Removal

1. Raise car on jackstands.

2. Disconnect both stabilizer links from control arms. Remove link bolt bushings and retainers.

3. Remove bolts securing stabilizer supports

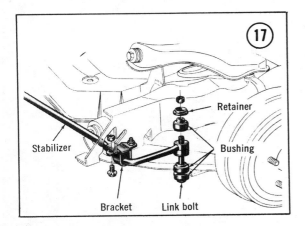

Stabilizer

Retainer

Bushing

Bracket   Link bolt

to frame. Bolt heads are accessible through holes in frames.

4. Remove stabilizer bar.

Installation

1. Secure stabilizer bar with brackets.

2. Assemble link bolts, bushings and retainers. See Figure 17. Secure to control arms.

3. Lower car. Bounce front several times to settle rubber bushings.

4. Retighten all bolts.

STEERING KNUCKLE

Removal

1. Raise vehicle on jackstands. Support lower control arms with jacks so that spring stays compressed as if car were on floor.

2. Remove front wheels.

3a. On 1963-1964 models with front drum brakes, remove brake drum, wheel hub and brake shoes. Disconnect backing plate and steering knuckle. See Chapter Twelve.

3b. On 1965-1976 models with disc brakes, remove brake caliper and disc. See Chapter Twelve.

4. Remove upper and lower ball-joint nuts.

5. Loosen steering knuckle from ball-joints by tapping knuckle bosses with hammer.

6. Installation is the reverse of these steps. Tighten ball-joint nuts to 60-94 foot-pounds. Use new cotter pins.

7. Adjust wheel bearings as described earlier.

8. Check wheel alignment.

FRONT WHEEL HUB (DRUM BRAKES)

Removal/Installation

1. Perform Steps 1 and 2 of *Wheel Bearing Replacement* procedure to remove hub.

2. Remove, clean and repack bearings as described in Steps 3-5, 11 and 12, *Wheel Bearing Replacement*.

3. Reinstall wheel hub by following Steps 13-18, *Wheel Bearing Replacement*.

WHEEL BEARINGS

Adjustment

1. Raise front of vehicle until tires clear the ground.

2. Remove hub cap and dust cap. Remove cotter pin from spindle.

3. Tighten spindle nut to 15 foot-pounds while rotating wheel.

4. Back off nut one flat (1/6 turn) and insert cotter pin. If slot and hole do not line up, back off an additional ½ flat or less, as necessary.

5. Spin wheel to be sure it turns freely.

6. Install dust cap and hub cap.

7. Lower vehicle.

Replacement

1a. On 1963-1964 models, remove brake drums as described in Chapter Twelve. Remove hub dust cap, cotter pin, spindle nut and washer. Pull hub off.

1b. On 1965-1976 models, remove brake caliper and disc.

2. Remove outer bearing from hub on the brake disc.

3. Pry out inner grease seal from hub on brake disc and remove inner bearing.

4. Clean wheel bearings in hub or brake disc in solvent. Blow dry. Check bearing rollers for scores, wear and evidence of overheating (bluish tint). Check bearing races in hub or brake disc. Do not mix bearings up if they are good; they must be replaced on the same wheel assembly.

CAUTION
If a bearing race is damaged, the bearing and *race must be replaced.*

5. If bearings and races are good, reinstall by following Steps 11-17. Otherwise, proceed to Step 6.

6. Make 2 bearing race removers out of 7/16 in. square steel stock as shown in **Figure 18**.

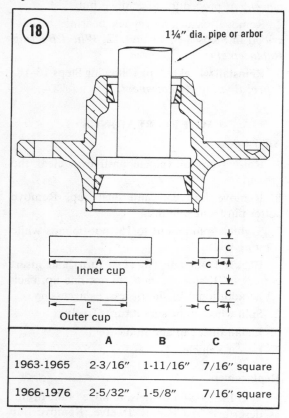

	A	B	C
1963-1965	2-3/16"	1-11/16"	7/16" square
1966-1976	2-5/32"	1-5/8"	7/16" square

7. Lay remover across race in hub (see Figure 18). Ends fit in slots in hub shoulder.

8. Press race from hub with a pipe or rod which bears on the remover.

9. Press new races into hub using tool J-8849 (outer race), tool J-8850 (inner race) or equivalents. See **Figure 19**. Be sure that the races seat fully against hub shoulder and do not cock in seats.

10. Pack inner and outer bearings with high temperature wheel bearing grease. Do not pack cavity in hub with grease.

11. Fit inner bearing in hub or brake disc. Install new grease seal with flange facing bearing race.

12a. On 1963-1964 models, install wheel hub over steering spindle.

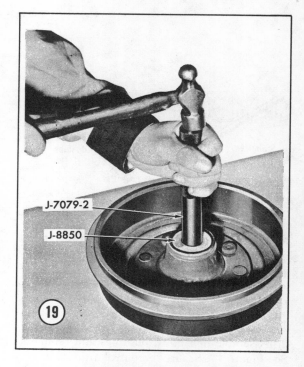

12b. On 1965-1976 models, install brake disc.

13. Install outer bearing. Press it in firmly by hand.

14. Install spindle washer and adjusting nut.

15. Adjust wheel bearings as described earlier.

16a. On 1963-1964 models, install brake drum and wheel.

16b. On 1965-1976 models, install brake caliper and wheel.

17. Lower vehicle.

STEERING ADJUSTMENTS

Before attempting to correct steering deficiencies with these adjustment, carefully check:

   a. Front end alignment

   b. Shock absorber condition

   c. Wheel balance

   d. Tire pressure

Steering Gear Adjustment

1. Remove pitman arm nut. Mark relation of pitman arm on sector shaft.

2. Remove pitman arm as shown in **Figure 20**. Use tool J-6632 or suitable puller.

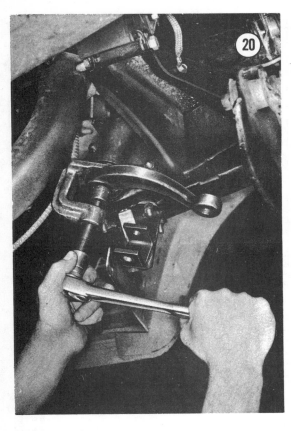

3. Loosen lash adjuster locknut (see **Figure 21**) and turn adjuster a few turns counterclockwise.

4. Turn steering wheel very gently and slowly in one direction until stopped by gear. Back away about one turn.

CAUTION
Do not turn wheel hard against stops when relay rod is disconnected or ball guides in steering gear will be damaged.

5. Using a spring scale, measure pull required to keep wheel in motion. See **Figure 22**. Scale centerline must remain at right angles to wheel spoke. From ⅜ to ¾ pound force should be required; adjust worm bearings if force is higher or lower.

6. To adjust worm bearings, loosen worm adjuster locknut. See Figure 21. Turn adjuster until there is no appreciable end play in worm. Tighten locknut.

7. Repeat Steps 5 and 6 as necessary.

8. If gear feels rough after adjustment, bearings are probably damaged.

9. Count number of turns required to turn steering wheel from one stop to the other. Turn

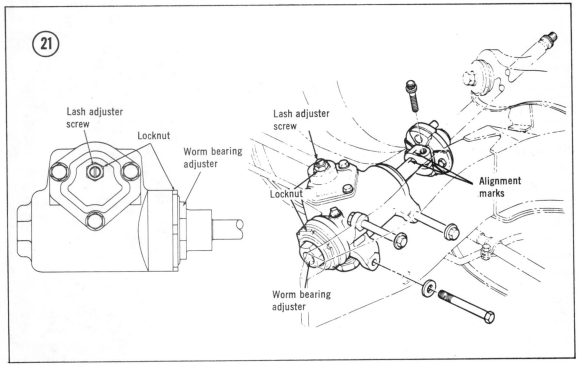

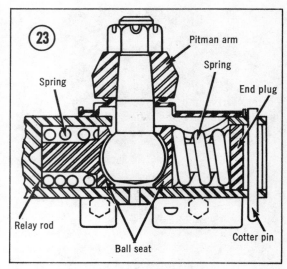

3. Connect tie rod ends to forward holes for fast ratio or rear holes for standard ratio. See **Figure 24**. Table 1 lists actual steering ratios possible for each year.

CAUTION
Do not use rearward (slow) steering arm holes on models with power steering or interference will result.

wheel back from stop exactly ½ the number of turns. Mark on top of wormshaft just below clamp should be at top of shaft and in line with the sawcut at the lower coupling clamp.

10. Turn lash adjuster screw clockwise to take out all lash in gear teeth. Tighten locknut.

11. Check force required to pull wheel through center position with spring scale. From ⅞ to 1½ pounds should be required. Repeat Steps 9-11 as necessary to obtain correct force.

12. Reassemble pitman arm to sector shaft. Line up marks made during disassembly. Torque nut to 100-150 foot-pounds.

Pitman Arm to Relay Rod Ball-joint Adjustment

1. Remove cotter pin from end of relay rod.

2. Tighten end plug until springs are compressed and plug bottoms. See **Figure 23**.

3. Back off end plug ¾ turn (slightly more if necessary) to align cotter pin holes. Install new cotter pin.

Steering Ratio Adjustment

1. Raise car on jackstands or hoist.

2. Disconnect tie rod ends from steering arms. See *Tie Rod Replacement*.

Steering Wheel Alignment

1. Drive the car onto any level smooth surface such as a driveway or parking lot. The front wheels must point straight ahead. One method to ensure this is to take advantage of wheel caster. Drive the car straight forward without touching the steering wheel. Stop the car with the handbrake. The wheels should stop straight ahead.

2. Mark on top of wormshaft just below clamp should be at top of shaft and in line with sawcut on lower coupling clamp.

3. If mark on wormshaft is not at top of shaft when wheels are straight ahead, loosen both clamps on left and right tie rods. See **Figure 25**. Turn each tie rod sleeve an equal amount in the *same direction* to bring mark to the top. Tighten clamps.

> NOTE: *If tie rod sleeves are turned unequally, toe-in will be changed.*

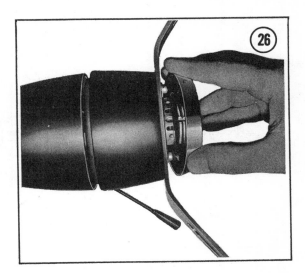

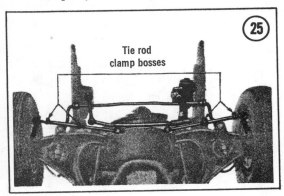

4. If the steering wheel is not centered, remove it and reinstall so that it is centered.

STEERING WHEEL

Removal/Installation (1963-1965)

1. Disconnect battery ground cable.

2. Carefully pry horn cap off. See **Figure 26**.

3. Remove steering wheel nut and washer from steering shaft.

4. Remove steering wheel from shaft. Use suitable puller if necessary. See **Figure 27**.

5. Install steering wheel over splines on shaft. Align mark on steering wheel hub with mark on shaft.

6. Install washer and nut. Torque nut to 35-40 foot-pounds.

7. Snap horn cap over hub.

Removal/Installation (1966-1976)

Refer to **Figure 28** for this procedure.

1. Disconnect column harness at wiring connector.

2. Disconnect battery ground cable.

3. Pry off horn button cap.

4. Remove 3 screws securing horn contact to spacer and hub.

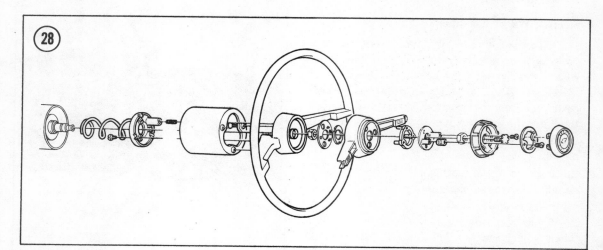

5. Remove 2 screws securing lock screw to lock knob and remove lock screw, lock knob and spacer.

6. Remove 6 screws securing steering wheel to hub and remove wheel.

7. Installation is the reverse of these steps.

Steering Coupling Removal/Installation

Refer to **Figure 29** for this procedure.

1. Remove steering coupling upper and lower clamp bolts.

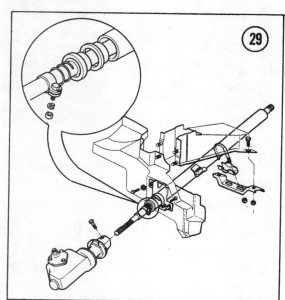

2. Remove mast jacket escutcheon screws (see **Figure 30**) and loosen mast jacket U-bolt clamp nuts (see **Figure 31**) under instrument panel.

3. Disconnect instrument panel harness from mast jacket lower switch.

4. Loosen mast jacket lower clamp at firewall. See **Figure 32**.

5. Pull mast jacket and steering shaft assembly up and out of steering coupling. When sufficient clearance is obtained, pull coupling off steering gear.

6. Scribe alignment marks on coupling so that upper and lower halves may be reassembled in the same relative position.

7. Separate upper and lower halves by removing attaching nuts and bolts.

8. Inspect flexible coupling for damage and replace if necessary.

9. Reassemble upper and lower flanges, align scribe marks and assemble with attaching nuts. Torque nuts 15-20 foot-pounds.

10. Install coupling over steering shaft splines, lining up mark on shaft with coupling clamp sawcut.

11. Insert steering gear wormshaft into lower coupling clamp, lining up mark on shaft with coupling clamp sawcut.

12. Install the coupling clamp bolts and torque to 25 foot-pounds.

Mast Jacket Removal/Installation (1963-1964)

1. Pull instrument panel harness from mast jacket lower switch. Disconnect switch from mast jacket.

2. Remove steering wheel as described in previous procedure.

3. Remove mast jacket escutcheon screws. See Figure 30. Remove mast jacket support U-bolt and nuts. See Figure 31.

4. Loosen mast jacket lower clamp at firewall. See Figure 32.

5. Loosen lower spring stop clamp. Slide stop and spring down on steering shaft.

6. Paint mark on steering shaft and coupling. Remove coupling upper clamp bolt.

7. Remove mast jacket and steering shaft assembly from steering coupling. Carefully withdraw through dash panel while sliding lower spring stop, spring, bearing, and seat off steering shaft.

8. Carefully insert mast jacket assembly into instrument panel down through firewall. At the same time, slide lower mast jacket seat, bearing, spring, and stop assembly over steering shaft over lower splines. Feed shaft into steering coupling, lining up mark on shaft with coupling clamp. Install upper clamp bolt, but do not tighten.

9. Assemble mast jacket escutcheon to instrument panel, making sure insulator is seated in escutcheon groove.

10. Loosely assemble mast jacket support U-bolt under instrument panel.

11. Adjust mast jacket so that dimple in lower support indexes in depression in mast jacket.

12. Install lower switch to mast jacket and connect wiring harness to switch. Connect horn wire and install wire and cable clips to mast jacket.

13. Install steering wheel and horn cap as described elsewhere in this chapter.

Mast Jacket Adjustments (1963-1964)

1. Adjust directional signal housing set screw until there is an 0.070-0.090 in. gap between housing and steering wheel hub. See **Figure 33**.

2. Compress lower spring with an 0.010-0.020 in. shim inserted between two coils. Tighten spring stop clamp in this position and remove shims. See **Figure 34**.

3. Grasp steering wheel, and by moving mast jacket in or out of dash panel, adjust to desired fore and aft steering position. Tighten lower clamp bolt and support U-bolts.

> NOTE: *Lower end of steering shaft is splined to allow a variation in steering wheel positions.*

Telescoping Mast Jacket Removal (1965-1976)

1. Disconnect battery ground cable.
2. Disconnect directional signal wiring at multiple connector.

3. Remove 2 screws securing jacket escutcheon to dash panel.
4. Remove mast jacket-to-dash bracket bolts.
5. Remove odometer reset control.
6. Remove clutch return spring.
7. Remove mast jacket-to-firewall clamp and bolt.
8. Remove 2 bolts retaining mast jacket cover plate and seal to firewall.

> NOTE: *Lower bolt has clutch spring retaining clip.*

9. Remove steering coupling-to-steering shaft clamp bolt.

> NOTE: *Mark steering coupling to steering shaft alignment.*

10. Lock column in full down position and carefully pull steering and mast jacket assembly from opening in firewall.

Telescoping Mast Jacket Installation (1965-1976)

1. Lock column in full down position, then install mast jacket and wheel assembly through firewall.
2. Install seal, plate, and loosely install bolts. Be sure clutch return spring clip is in place on lower bolt.
3. Install clamp over steering shaft.
4. With the help of an assistant, position steering shaft on coupling using previous made alignment marks.
5. Position shaft so the notch lines up with bolt hole and install coupling clamp bolt. Don't tighten at this time.
6. Install upper mast jacket bracket bolts. Leave support bolts finger-tight until mast jacket is correctly positioned.
7. Position escutcheon and install attaching screws.
8. Position steering column so that a minimum gap of 0.060 in. remains between the lower edge of the directional housing and the dash escutcheon with the column in the full down position. Then tighten all column bolts.
9. Install trip odometer cable to bracket and install retaining nut.

10. Connect directional signal harness to instrument panel harness assembly.

11. Tighten steering shaft coupling bolt. Torque to 30 ft.-lb.

12. Tighten firewall bracket bolts.

13. Tighten band-type clamp bolt.

14. Install clutch return spring.

Ignition Switch Removal/Installation (1974-1976)

1. Disconnect ground cable from battery.

2. Remove steering wheel as described under *Steering Wheel Removal/Installation (1966-1976)* elsewhere in this chapter.

3. Lower steering column as described in *Telescoping Mast Jacket Removal (1965-1976)* elsewhere in this chapter.

> NOTE: *It is not necessary to remove the steering column from the vehicle unless desired. However, make sure the column is properly supported before proceeding.*

4. Make sure switch is in LOCK position. If cylinder has been removed from lock, pull up on actuating rod until there is a definite stop, then move rod down one detent to the LOCK position.

5. Remove 2 attaching screws and remove ignition switch.

6. Make sure replacement switch is in LOCK position (**Figure 35**). Use a screwdriver in slot to position switch in LOCK, if necessary.

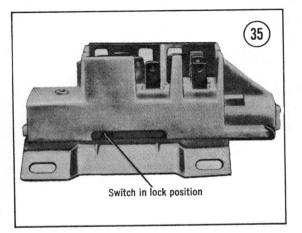

Switch in lock position

7. Install actuating rod in switch and attach switch to column with screws.

CAUTION
Use only original or identical attaching screws, as over-length screws will cause interference.

8. Reinstall steering column and steering wheel, as described in *Telescoping Mast Jacket Installation (1965-1976)* and *Steering Wheel Removal/Installation (1966-1976)* elsewhere in this chapter.

STEERING GEAR

Removal/Installation

1. Remove lower clamp bolts on steering coupling to wormshaft.

2. Raise vehicle on hoist or jackstands.

3. Remove pitman arm with suitable puller. See **Figure 36**.

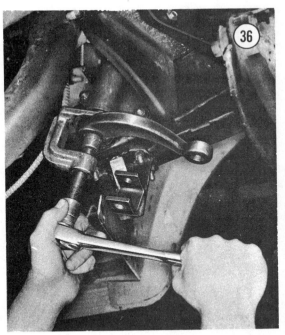

4. Remove steering gear mounting bolts and remove steering gear.

5. Installation is the reverse of these steps. Be sure that wheels are straight ahead, steering wheel is straight, and steering gear is set to the middle of its travel.

Disassembly

Refer to **Figure 37** for this procedure.

1. Clean exterior thoroughly in solvent to remove road dirt and grease.

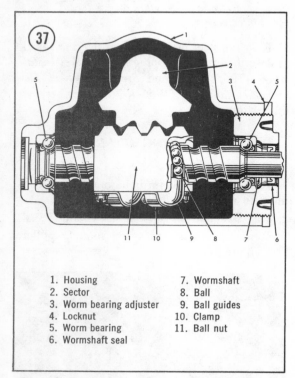

1. Housing
2. Sector
3. Worm bearing adjuster
4. Locknut
5. Worm bearing
6. Wormshaft seal
7. Wormshaft
8. Ball
9. Ball guides
10. Clamp
11. Ball nut

2. Cover *clean* work surface with clean paper or rags.

3. Hold gear in vise by lower mounting ear.

4. Loosen lash adjuster locknut and turn lash adjuster several turns counterclockwise.

5. Remove 3 cap screws holding side cover. Pull side cover/sector shaft assembly out. See **Figure 38**.

> NOTE: *Turn wormshaft if necessary until sector clears opening.*

6. Remove worm bearing adjuster, locknut and upper ball bearing from housing.

7. Remove wormshaft and ball nut assembly from housing. See **Figure 39**. Remove lower ball bearing.

8. Remove locknut from lash adjuster and unscrew adjuster clockwise from side cover. Slide adjuster and shim out of slot in end of sector shaft.

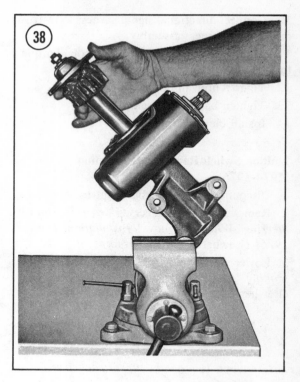

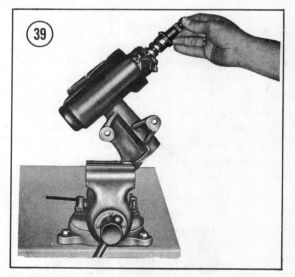

9. Remove sector shaft seal.

10. Remove wormshaft seal.

> NOTE: *Further disassembly is usually not necessary unless ball nut binds or is rough when rotated on worm. Don't allow ball nut to be rotated far enough to bottom on either end of the worm. This could damage the ball guides.*

11. Remove clamp retaining ball guides in nut. Draw guides out of nut.

12. Turn nut upside down and rotate worm-shaft back and forth until all the balls have dropped out into a clean pan.

13. Pull nut off worm.

Inspection

1. Wash all parts in solvent. Dry them with clean rags.

2. Check ball bearings, races, worm and nut grooves for signs of wear and scoring.

3. Inspect sector shaft and bushings for wear and check the fit of the shaft in the housing bushings.

4. Check ball guides for damaged ends. Replace if necessary.

5. Check wormshaft assembly for damage.

Rebuilding and Assembly

NOTE: *Bushings require replacement only if worn or damaged. Consider dealer replacement with proper tools.*

1. Press both sector shaft bushings out of housing. See **Figure 40**.

2. Coat new bushings with steering gear lube.

3. Press new sector shaft bushings into each end of bore so that bushing is flush with, or slightly lower than, end of bore.

NOTE: *Wormshaft seal and sector shaft seal must be replaced anytime steering gear is assembled.*

4. Remove old seals using a suitable slide hammer.

5. Coat new seals with steering gear lube inside and out.

6. Position new wormshaft seal over center hole in worm bearing adjuster and press in using socket of suitable outside diameter. Seal edge should be flush with inner edge of small bore adjuster.

7. Position new sector shaft seal over sector shaft bore. Press in with same method used for wormshaft seal.

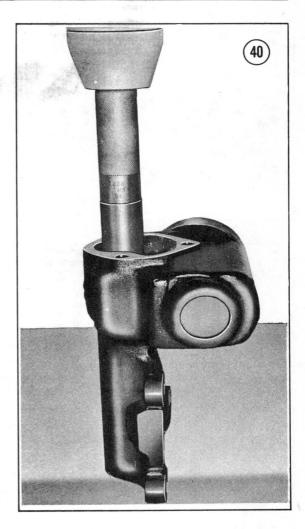

NOTE: *Wormshaft bearing races require replacement only if worm is damaged. Consider dealer replacement with proper tools.*

8. Place steering gear housing or worm adjuster in vise with bore horizontal.

9. Pull race out with suitable slide hammer and accessories. See **Figure 41**.

10. Press new bearing races in with tool J-5755. See **Figure 42**.

NOTE: *Steps 11-20 assemble ball nut on wormshaft.*

11. Lay wormshaft flat on bench. Slip ball nut over worm with ball guide holes up and the shallow end of the rack teeth to the left as viewed from the steering wheel position. See **Figure 43**.

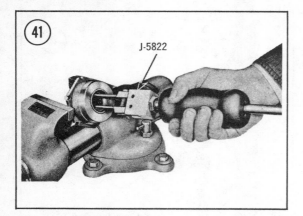

J-5822

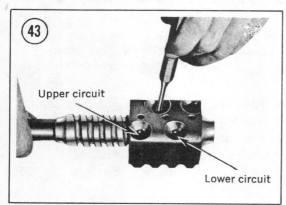

Upper circuit

Lower circuit

12. Count 27 balls into a clean shallow container like a pie tin. Each circuit requires 27 steel balls.

13. Align grooves in the worm and nut by sighting through the ball guide holes.

14. Insert balls for one circuit into one of the guide holes one at a time while gradually turning the worm away from that hole. Continue until ball circuit is full from bottom of one guide hole to bottom of other.

> NOTE: *If you reach end of worm before circuit is full, hold the balls in the nut down with a blunt, clean rod or punch. See Figure 43. Now rotate worm in opposite direction a few turns, then continue inserting balls as in Step 14. It may be necessary to work worm back and forth several times while holding the balls down with the punch in one guide hole, then the other, to close up spaces between balls and pack the circuit as solidly as possible.*

15. Place remaining balls (from original 27) in ball guide. See **Figure 44**. Close the 2 halves together and plug each end with petroleum jelly so that balls will not fall out.

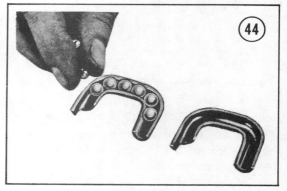

16. Push guide into guide holes in nut. See **Figure 45**. Tap guide down lightly with small piece of hardwood if necessary to seat it. Don't tap it hard or with a hammer.

17. Fill second circuit by repeating Steps 12 through 16.

18. Mount ball guide clamp on nut. Use lockwasher under clamp screw.

19. Rotate nut on worm to be sure it rotates freely. Do not bottom nut on either end of worm. If nut binds slightly, ball guide ends are probably damaged and require replacement.

20. Hold steering gear housing in vise with the wormshaft bore vertical and the side cover opening up.

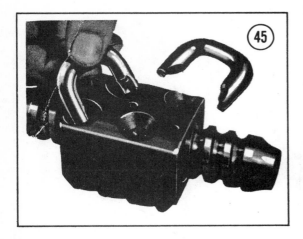

21. Install wormshaft bearing.

22. Slide adjuster assembly with bearing over end of wormshaft and lower wormshaft into housing. Index end of shaft in bearing.

CAUTION
Tape ball nut in center of worm to prevent it from bottoming on end of worm.

23. Thread worm bearing adjuster into housing until nearly all slack is out of wormshaft bearings. Remove tape from ball nut.

24. Assemble lash adjuster with shim in slot in end of sector shaft.

25. Check end clearance as shown in **Figure 46**. End clearance should not exceed 0.002 in. Change shim installed in Step 24 if necessary. Shims are available 0.063-0.069 in. thick, but only in 0.002 in. increments.

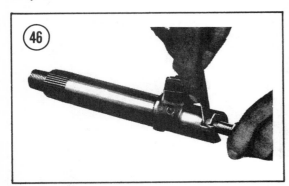

26. Install gasket on side cover and insert sector shaft into housing. Do not damage seal. Be sure to index center tooth of sector in center space of ball nut rack.

27. Align holes in side cover with holes in housing. Install upper cap screw.

28. Hold steering gear housing in vise in its approximate position when installed in car.

29. Inject steering gear lubricant into lowest side cover cap screw opening until lubricant appears in another opening. Install 2 remaining cap screws and lockwashers.

Preliminary Adjustment

Worm bearing and lash adjustments may be made before gear is installed in car.

1. Hold steering gear in vise in its approximate position when installed in car.

2. Temporarily install steering wheel on wormshaft.

3. Perform Steps 5-7, *Steering Gear Adjustment* procedure described earlier.

STEERING LINKAGE

Tie Rod Replacement

Refer to **Figure 47** on the following page for this procedure.

1. Raise car on jackstands and remove front wheels.

2. Remove cotter pins and nuts from ball studs.

3. Hold heavy hammer as backing. Tap steering arm with another hammer to loosen ball stud. See **Figure 48**.

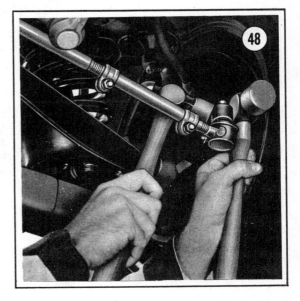

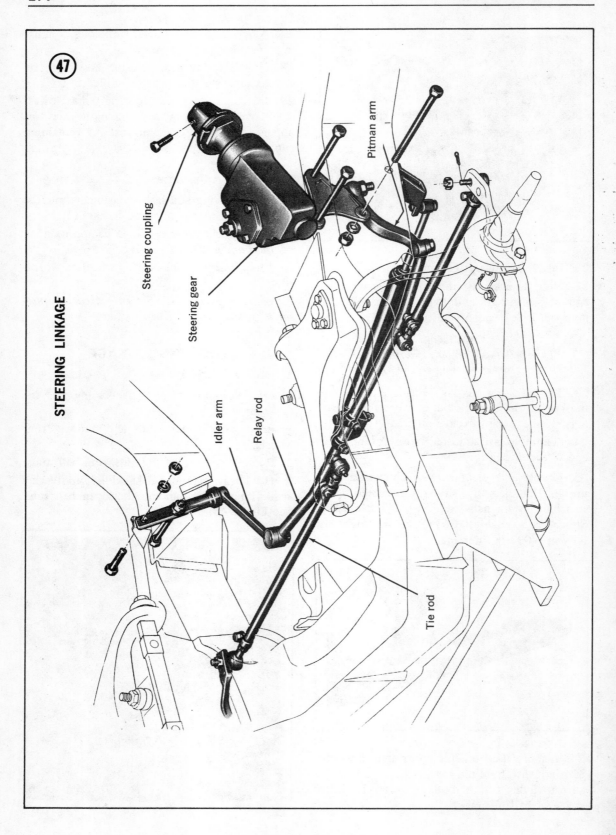

STEERING LINKAGE

Steering coupling

Steering gear

Pitman arm

Idler arm

Relay rod

Tie rod

4. Remove inner ball stud in a similar manner.

5. Loosen clamp bolts and unscrew tie rod ends.

6. Install tie rod ends on tie rod. Make sure both ends are threaded on an equal amount.

7. Make sure that ball stud threads and nut threads are perfectly clean and smooth.

8. Install neoprene seals on ball studs.

9. Install ball studs in the steering arms and the relay rod.

10. Install ball stud nuts. Torque to 45 ft.-lb. Tighten additionally if necessary to align cotter pin holes; do not loosen nut.

11. Install new cotter pin.

12. Lubricate tie rod ends. See Chapter Two.

13. Adjust toe-in.

CAUTION
Before locking clamp bolts, make sure that tie rod ends are aligned with their ball studs. Otherwise, binding will result.

Steering Damper Replacement

1. Raise car on jackstands and remove front wheels.

2. Remove bolt securing damper pivot bracket at relay rod.

3. Remove nut from damper pivot at frame bracket.

4. Remove damper.

5. Installation is the reverse of these steps.

Relay Rod Replacement

See Figure 47 and **Figure 49** for this procedure.

1. Raise car on jackstands.

2. Remove steering damper.

3. Remove anchor bracket from relay rod.

4. Disconnect inner ends of tie rods from relay rod. See Steps 3 and 4, *Tie Rod Replacement.*

5. Remove cotter pin and nut on ball stud at pitman arm.

6. Tap ball stud out of pitman arm and lower relay rod.

7. Remove cotter pin and nut from idler arm.

8. Disconnect relay rod from idler arm.

9. Remove washer and seal from idler arm.

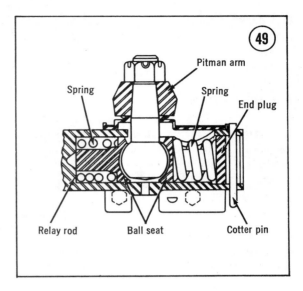

10. Clean relay rod assembly with solvent.

11. Place relay rod on idler arm stud. Make sure that stud seal and washer are in place. Install nut and tighten to 45 ft.-lb. Tighten nut additionally if necessary to align cotter pin holes.

12. Install new seal and clamp over ball at end of pitman arm.

13. Install inner spring seat and spring to the relay rod.

14. Install end of rod on pitman arm.

15. Install spring seat, spring, and end plug.

16. Tighten end plug until springs are compressed and the plug bottoms out. Back off ¾ turn (slightly more if necessary) to align cotter pin holes. Install cotter pin.

17. Connect tie rod ends to relay rod.

18. Lubricate tie rod ends and pitman arm ball-joint. See Chapter Two.

19. Install steering damper.

20. Adjust toe-in.

Idler Arm Removal/Installation

Refer to Figure 47.

1. Raise car on jackstands.

2. Remove cotter pin and nut from idler arm.

3. Disconnect relay rod from idler arm.

4. Remove idler arm from frame.

5. Remove stud seals and clean idler arm in solvent.

6. Check for damage and wear. Make sure studs turn smoothly. A grating noise indicates dirt within unit.

7. Hold idler arm in a vise and check torque required to rotate idler shaft. Torque should be from 30-55 in.-lb.

8. Attach nut to ball stud and check torque required to rotate the ball stud. The torque should be 10-35 in.-lb. Replace idler arm if torque values are not within specifications.

9. Mount idler arm on frame. Torque the bolts to 25-35 ft.-lb.

10. Connect relay rod to idler arm. Use new seal and tighten nut to 45 ft.-lb.

11. Install cotter pin. Tighten nut additionally if necessary to align cotter pin holes.

POWER STEERING PUMP

Belt Tension Adjustment

1. Loosen power steering bracket-to-power steering pump attaching bolts.

2. Move pump, with belt in place, until belt tension is correct. This occurs when a 15 pound force applied at the midpoint between the power steering pump pulley and the drive pulley causes ½-¾ in. belt deflection.

3. Tighten pump mounting bolts.

Removal/Installation

Refer to **Figure 50** for this procedure.

1. Disconnect hoses at pump. Secure ends to prevent drainage of oil. Cap or tape the ends of the hose to prevent entry of dirt.

2. Install 2 caps at pump fittings to prevent drainage of oil from pump.

3. Loosen bracket-to-pump mounting nuts.

4. Remove pump belt.

5. Remove bracket-to-pump bolts and remove pump from vehicle.

6. Remove drive pulley attaching nut.

7. Slide pulley from shaft.

CAUTION
Do not hammer pulley off shafts as this will damage the pump.

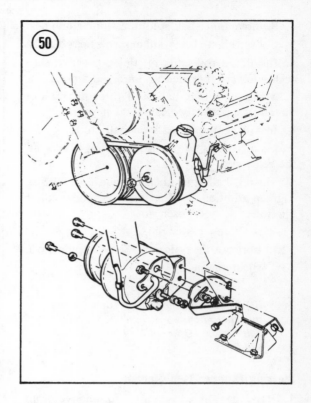

Disassembly

Refer to **Figure 51** for this procedure.

1. Clean outside of pump in solvent before disassembly.

2. Clamp front hub of housing in a vise with soft jaws.

CAUTION
Do not exert excessive force on front hub or you may distort the bushings.

3. Remove union and seal.

4. Remove pump reservoir retaining studs.

5. Remove reservoir from housing.

6. Remove mounting bolt and union O-rings.

7. Remove filter and filter cage. Discard filter element.

8. Remove end plate retaining ring. Compress end plate retaining ring by inserting small punch into the hole in the pump housing (**Figure 52**). Once the ring is compressed, remove the ring with a screwdriver as shown in the figure.

9. Remove end plate. If end plate sticks, slightly rock the end plate or tap it lightly with a hammer to free it.

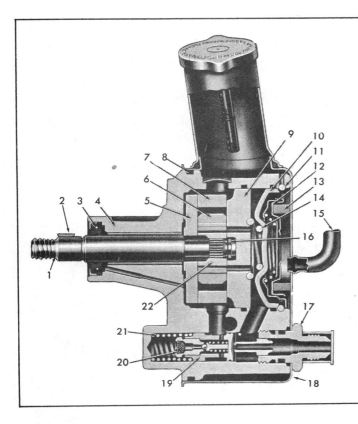

POWER STEERING PUMP (51)

1. Shaft
2. Woodruff key
3. Shaft seal
4. Pump housing
5. Thrust plate
6. Vanes
7. Pump ring
8. Reservoir O-ring seal
9. Pressure plate
10. End plate retaining ring
11. End plate
12. Filter cage assembly
13. Filter element
14. Pressure plate spring
15. Pump inlet tube
16. Rotor-to-drive shaft retaining ring
17. Pump outlet union
18. Reservoir
19. Flow control valve
20. Flow control valve cap screw
21. Flow control valve spring
22. Rotor

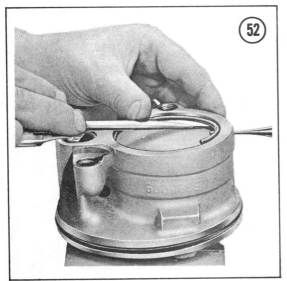

(52)

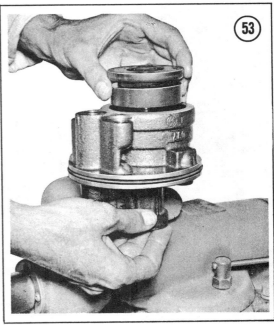

(53)

10. Remove Woodruff key from shaft.

11. Tap end of shaft gently with a soft hammer until pressure plate, pump ring, rotor assembly, and thrust plate may be removed as a unit. See **Figure 53**.

12. Remove end plate O-ring.

13. Separate parts removed in Step 11.

Inspection

1. Clean all parts in solvent.

2. Ensure that flow control valve slides freely in housing bore. If it sticks, check for dirt and burrs.

3. Check cap screw in the end of the flow control valve for looseness. If necessary, tighten it, being careful not to damage machined surfaces.

4. Be sure that pressure plate and pump plate surfaces are flat and parallel with pump ring. Check all these parts for cracks and scoring.

> NOTE: *A high polish is always present on rotor pressure plate and thrust plate as a result of normal wear. Do not confuse this with scoring.*

5. Make certain that the vanes are installed with radiused edge towards pump ring to see that they move freely in rotor slots.

6. Check drive shaft for worn splines, brakes, bushing material pickup, etc.

7. Check reservoir, studs, castings, and other parts for burrs and other faults which impair proper operation.

Assembly

1. Install shaft seal, using tool J-8818 as shown in **Figure 54**.

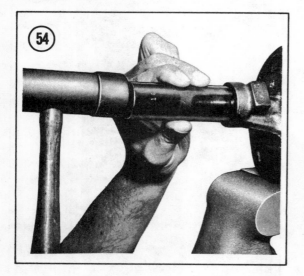

2. Insert shaft into housing as in **Figure 55**.

3. Install thrust plate on dowel pins with ported face to rear of pump housing. See **Figure 56**.

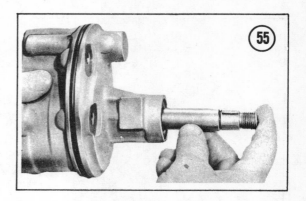

4. Install rotor on pump shaft over splined end. Rotor must be free on splines.

> NOTE: *Countersunk side of rotor is toward the shaft.*

5. Install shaft retaining ring. See **Figure 57**.

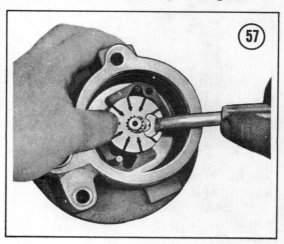

6. Install pump ring on dowel pins. The arrow indicating direction of rotation should face toward the rear of the pump housing (**Figure 58**).

> NOTE: *The pump rotates counterclockwise as viewed from the pulley.*

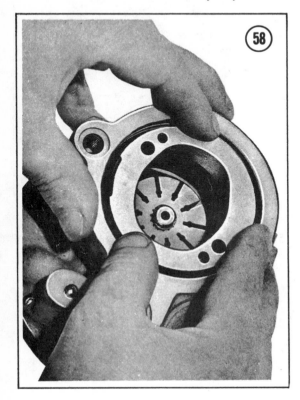

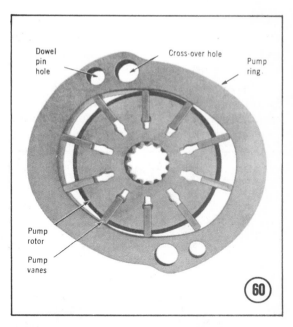

7. Install vanes in rotor slots with radiused edge towards outside as shown in **Figures 59 and 60**.

8. Lubricate outside diameter and chamfer of pressure plate with petroleum jelly.

9. Install pressure plate on dowel pins with ported face towards the pump ring. Seat pressure plate by placing large socket on top of plate and pushing down by hand.

10. Install pressure plate spring in center groove of pressure plate. See **Figure 61**.

11. Install end plate O-ring.

12. Lubricate outside diameter and chamfer of end plate with petroleum jelly. Install in housing, using an arbor press.

13. Install end plate retaining ring while pump is still in press. Be sure that it is completely seated in the groove of the housing and that the ring gap is in position shown in **Figure 62**.

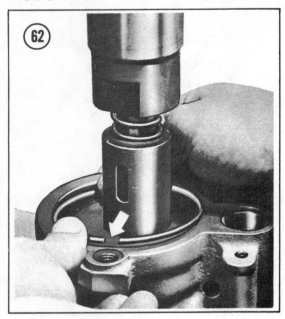

14 Install flow control spring and flow control plunger. Be sure that hex head screw goes into bore first. See **Figure 63**. Install filter cage, new filter stud seals, and union seal.

15. Place reservoir in position and press down until reservoir seats in housing. Check position of stud seals and union seal.

16. Install studs, union, and drive shaft Woodruff key. Support the shaft on the opposite side of key when tapping key into place.

Installation

1. Slide pulley on shaft.

CAUTION
Do not hammer pulley on shaft.

2. Install pulley nut and torque to 35-45 ft.-lb. Use a new pulley nut.

3. Position pump assembly on vehicle and install nuts loosely.

4. Connect and tighten hose fittings.

5. Fill reservoir. Bleed pump by turning pulley backward (counterclockwise as viewed from front) until air bubbles cease to appear.

6. Install pump belt over pulley.

7. Adjust belt tension as described earlier.

8. Bleed hydraulic system as described later.

POWER STEERING CONTROL VALVE

Removal

Refer to **Figure 64** for this procedure.

1. Raise the front of the vehicle on jackstands or hoist.

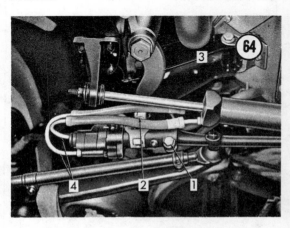

1. Clamp bolt	3. Pitman arm
2. Ball stud nut	4. Valve-to-power piston lines

2. Remove clamp bolt between relay rod and control valve.

3. Disconnect the 2 pump-to-control valve hose connections. Allow fluid to drain into a container.

4. Disconnect the 2 remaining valve-to-power cylinder hoses.

5. Remove the retaining nut from the ball stud to the pitman arm connection and disconnect the control valve from the pitman arm.

6. Turn the pitman arm to the right, clear of the control valve and unscrew the control valve from the relay rod.

7. Remove the control valve from the vehicle.

Disassembly

1. Place valve in a vise as shown and remove the dust cover. See **Figure 65**.

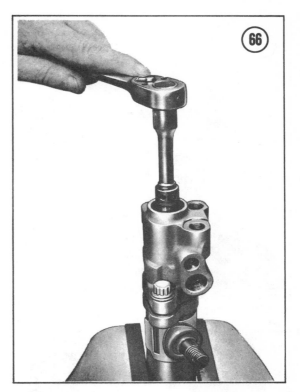

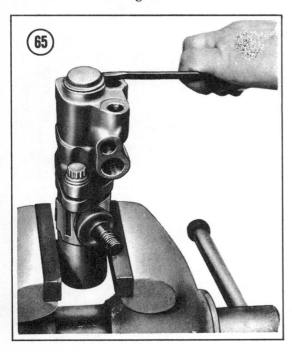

2. Remove adjusting nut. See **Figure 66**.

3. Remove valve-to-adapter bolts and remove valve housing and spool from adapter.

4. Remove spool from housing. See **Figure 67**.

5. Remove spring, reaction spool, washer, reaction spring, spring retainer, and seal. See **Figure 68**. Remove O-ring from the reaction spool.

6. Remove the annulus spacer, valve shaft washer, and plug-to-sleeve key. See Figure 68 and **Figure 69**.

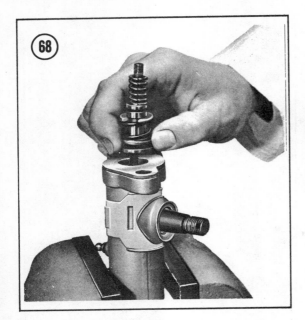

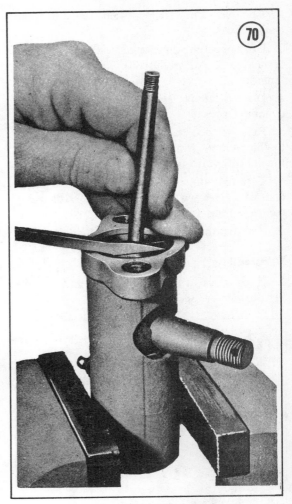

2. Inspect all parts for scratches, burrs, distortion, evidence of wear, and replace all worn or damaged parts.

3. Discard all seals and gaskets. New ones will be installed during assembly.

Assembly

Refer to **Figure 71** for the following procedure.

1. Install the sleeve and one ball seat in the adapter. Install the ball stud and the other ball seat. Install the small spring with the small coil facing out.

2. Clamp the adapter in a vise. Put the valve shaft through the seat in the ball adjuster plug and screw the adjuster plug in the sleeve. See **Figure 72**.

7. Carefully turn adjuster plug out of sleeve. See **Figure 70**. Do not nick the top surface.

8. Remove the housing from the vise and invert it. Shake out the spring and 2 ball seats.

9. Remove the ball stud and the other ball seat. The sleeve bearing will fall free.

Inspection

1. Wash all metal parts in solvent and blow dry with compressed air.

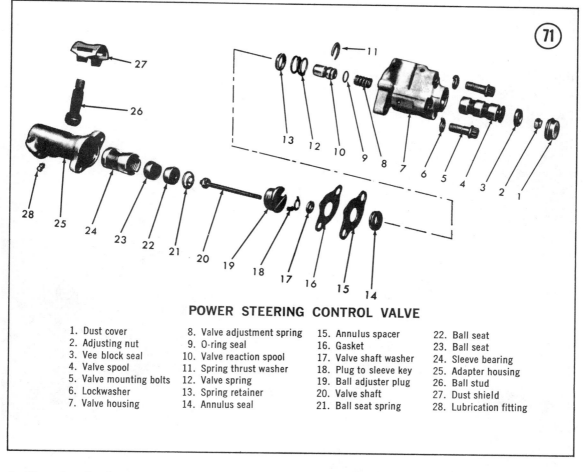

POWER STEERING CONTROL VALVE

1. Dust cover
2. Adjusting nut
3. Vee block seal
4. Valve spool
5. Valve mounting bolts
6. Lockwasher
7. Valve housing
8. Valve adjustment spring
9. O-ring seal
10. Valve reaction spool
11. Spring thrust washer
12. Valve spring
13. Spring retainer
14. Annulus seal
15. Annulus spacer
16. Gasket
17. Valve shaft washer
18. Plug to sleeve key
19. Ball adjuster plug
20. Valve shaft
21. Ball seat spring
22. Ball seat
23. Ball seat
24. Sleeve bearing
25. Adapter housing
26. Ball stud
27. Dust shield
28. Lubrication fitting

3. Turn the plug in until it is tight, then back it off until the slot lines up with the slots in the sleeve.

4. Insert the key, making sure that the small tangs on the ends of the key fit into the notches in the sleeve. See **Figure 73**.

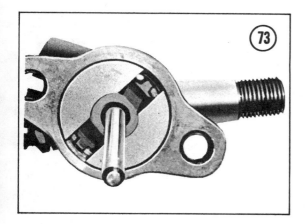

5. Install O-ring seal on reaction spool.

6. Install the valve shaft washer, annulus spacer, and the reaction seal with the lip up.

7. Install the spring retainer, reaction spring and spool, washer and adjustment spring. Install washer with the chamfer up.

8. Install the seal on the valve spool with the lip down. Install the spool in the housing, being careful not to jam the spool.

9. Install housing and spool onto adapter. The side ports should be on the same side as the ball stud. Bolt housing to the adapter.

10. Depress valve spool and turn the locknut onto the shaft about 4 turns with a clean wrench or socket.

NOTE: *Always use a new nut. Do not install the dust cap until the control valve has been installed and balanced. See procedures below.*

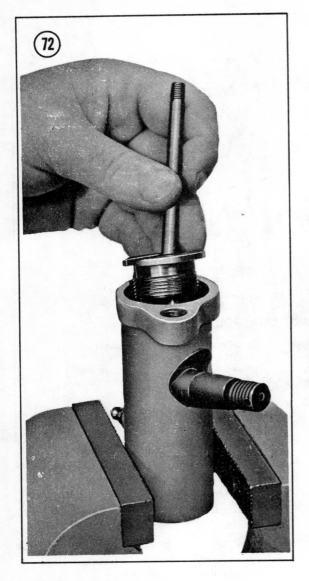

Installation

1. Install the control valve on the relay rod so the control valve bottoms. Back off the control valve if necessary to install clamp bolt. Do not exceed 2 full turns of the valve.

2. Tighten the control valve clamping bolt. Assemble the ball stud to the pitman arm.

3. Reconnect the 4 hydraulic hoses to the control valve.

4. Fill the system with Type A automatic transmission fluid. Bleed the system as described later and grease the valve.

5. Balance the control valve as described below.

Control Valve Balancing

1. Raise the vehicle on a hoist with an assistant inside.

2. Disconnect the power cylinder piston rod from the frame bracket.

3. Have the assistant start the engine.

4. If the piston rod remains retracted, turn the adjusting nut on the control valve (**Figure 74**) clockwise until the rod just begins to move out. Turn the nut counterclockwise until the rod just begins to move back in. Note the amount of rotation required. Now turn the nut clockwise exactly ½ the rotation required to change the direction of the piston rod.

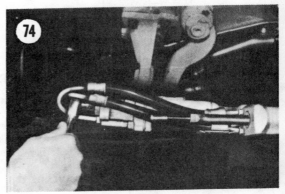

5. The piston rod extends when the engine is started. Move the adjusting nut on the control valve counterclockwise until the rod begins to retract. Then turn the adjusting nut clockwise until the rod just begins to move out again. Now turn the rod counterclockwise exactly ½ the rotation required to change direction of the piston rod.

CAUTION
Do not turn the nut back and forth more than is absolutely necessary to balance the valve.

6. With the valve balanced, it should be possible to move the rod in and out manually.

7. Turn off the engine and connect the piston rod to the frame bracket.

8. Restart the engine. If the front wheels do not turn in either direction from center, the valve is properly balanced. If the wheels move, repeat the procedure as often as necessary to balance the valve.

9. Once the valve is balanced, grease the end of the valve and install the dust cap.

Ball Stud Seal Replacement (1965-1976)

This seal can be replaced without removing the control valve.

1. Disconnect control valve ball stud from pitman arm.

2. Remove seal retaining clamp. Pull seal off end of stud.

3. Install new seal and clamp over stud so lip on seal mates with clamp. See **Figure 75**.

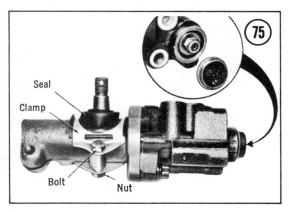

4. Connect ball stud to pitman arm and secure with retaining nut.

POWER CYLINDER

Removal / Installation

1. Disconnect the 2 hydraulic lines connected to the power cylinder and drain fluid into a container. Do not reuse.

2. Remove retaining nut, washer, and rubber grommet at the bracket attached to the frame.

3. Remove the cotter pin, retaining nut, and pull stud out of relay rod.

4. Remove the power cylinder from the vehicle.

5. Installation is the reverse of these steps.

6. Fill the system with Type A automatic transmission fluid and bleed as described later. Grease the ball-joint.

Disassembly / Assembly

Refer to **Figure 76** for the following procedures.

1. Remove the snap ring, then pull out the rod. Remove the back-up washer, piston rod scraper, and piston rod seal from rod.

2. Depress the end plug and remove the snap ring. Push on the end of the ball stud and the end plug, spring, spring seat, ball stud and seal may be removed.

3. Press the ball seal out as shown in **Figure 77**.

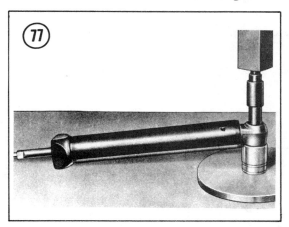

4. Installation is the reverse of these steps. Apply a thin coating of Lubriplate on the inner surfaces of the seal and scraper element before assembly.

BLEEDING
HYDRAULIC SYSTEM

1. Fill fluid reservoir to proper level and let fluid remain undisturbed for at least 2 minutes.

2. Start engine and run for several seconds.

3. Add fluid if necessary.

4. Repeat above 3 steps until fluid level remains constant after running engine.

5. Raise front of vehicle so that wheels are off the ground.

6. Start engine and run at about 1,500 rpm.

7. Turn the front wheels right and left lightly from stop to stop.

8. Add fluid if necessary.

9. Lower the car and turn wheels right and left on the ground.

10. Again check the fluid level and refill if necessary.

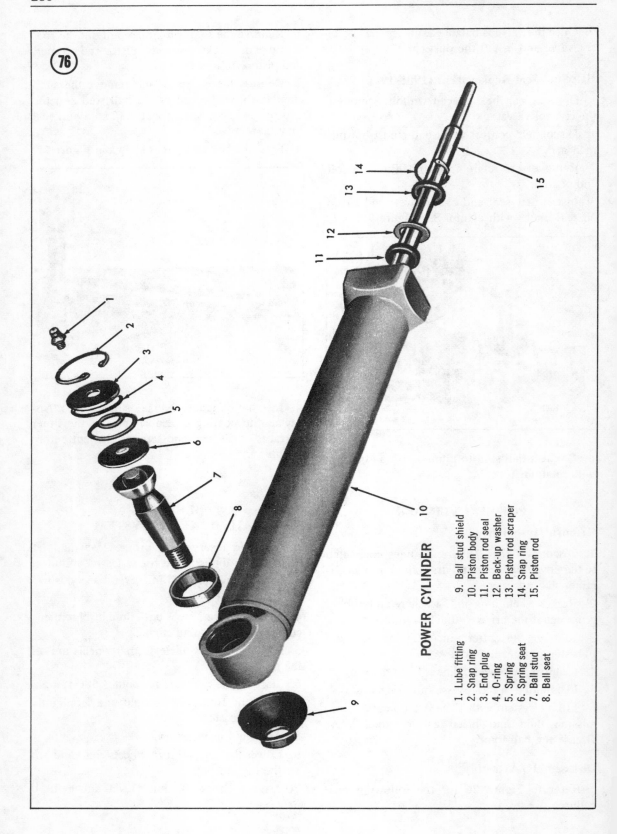

76

POWER CYLINDER

1. Lube fitting
2. Snap ring
3. End plug
4. O-ring
5. Spring
6. Spring seat
7. Ball stud
8. Ball seat
9. Ball stud shield
10. Piston body
11. Piston rod seal
12. Back-up washer
13. Piston rod scraper
14. Snap ring
15. Piston rod

11. If fluid is extremely foamy, allow vehicle to stand a few minutes with engine off and repeat above procedure.

Table 1   STEERING SPECIFICATIONS 1968-1976

	1963-1967	1968-1976
Wheel alignment		
Caster	$+1° 45' \pm 30'$	$+1° \pm 30'$ [1]
Camber	$0° 45' \pm 30'$	$+0° 45' \pm 30'$
Toe-in	⅛″ - ⅜″	¼″ $\pm$ 1/16″
Springing	Coil springs	Coil springs
Steering gear ratio	16.0 : 1	16.0 : 1
Overall steering ratio		
Normal	20.2 : 1	20.2 : 1
Fast adjustment	17.6 : 1	17.6 : 1
Power steering	17.6 : 1	17.6 : 1

1. For power steering models, caster is $+2° 15' \pm 30'$

Table 2   TIGHTENING TORQUES

	Foot-pounds	
	1963-73	1974-76
Shock absorber		
Upper	15-25	7-8
Lower	9-11	12-13
Stabilizer link bolt	9-12	18-20
Control arm		
Upper	65-75	50-55
Lower nut	120-150	60-65
Lower bolt	65-75	60-65
Ball stud		
Upper	42-47	50-55
Lower	60-94	80-85
Control arm cross shaft	30-40	35-40
Wheel stud nuts	75	70-75

CHAPTER FOURTEEN

PROPELLER SHAFT AND REAR SUSPENSION

All 1963-1976 Corvettes have an independent rear suspension with semi-trailing (control) arms. See **Figure 1**. Control arms are sprung by transverse left springs and located by adjustable strut rods.

Double-articulated drive shafts with universal joints drive the rear wheels. The differential is fixed-mounted to the frame at 3 points.

The propeller shaft is a single tubular piece with a universal joint at each end. Because the differential is fixed, drive line angles do not change with suspension height variations.

This chapter contains repair and replacement procedures for the propeller shaft, rear axles, differential carrier, and rear suspension components. **Table 1**, which lists specifications, is at the end of the chapter.

WHEEL ALIGNMENT

Wheel alignment on an independent rear suspension is as important to handling and tire wear as front suspension wheel alignment. Wheel camber angle and toe-in are adjustable and should be checked periodically on an alignment ramp.

It is not possible to adjust camber or toe-in without an alignment ramp. If you have disassembled any part of the rear suspension, take the car to your dealer or other front end specialist immediately after reassembling.

CAUTION
Drive slowly and carefully as handling is affected. Don't drive too far as tires can wear extremely quickly when scrubbed sideways by a misalinged suspension.

Camber

Camber is the inclination of the wheel from vertical. Corvette rear wheels have negative camber, i.e., the top of the wheel inclines inward.

Rear wheel camber is adjusted by rotating an eccentric cam at the inner end of each strut rod. See **Figure 2**. This moves the strut rod in or out to achieve $-0°\ 20' \pm 30'$ camber.

Toe-in

Camber and rolling resistance tend to force the front wheels outward at their forward edge. To compensate for this tendency, the front edges are turned slightly inward when the car is at rest; this is toe-in.

Toe-in is adjusted by inserting shims inside the frame member on both sides of the control arm pivot bushing. See **Figure 3**.

REAR SUSPENSION

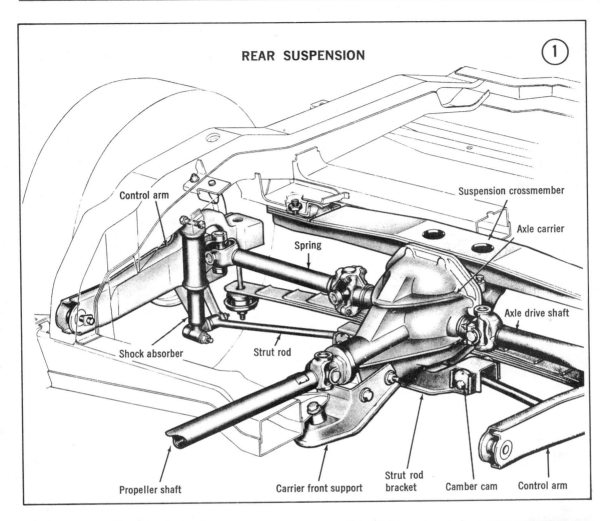

Control arm

Suspension crossmember

Axle carrier

Spring

Axle drive shaft

Shock absorber

Strut rod

Propeller shaft

Carrier front support

Strut rod bracket

Camber cam

Control arm

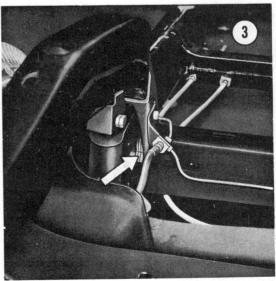

AXLE DRIVE SHAFTS

Removal/Installation

1. Disconnect inboard end of drive shaft by removing U-bolts at joint. See **Figure 4**.

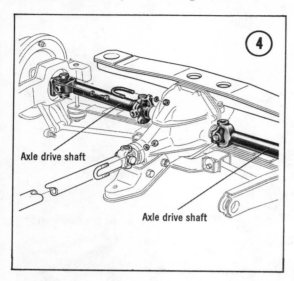

Axle drive shaft

Axle drive shaft

2. Remove 4 bolt securing shaft flange to spindle flange.

3. Pry drive shaft out of outboard flange pilot and remove by withdrawing outboard end first. See **Figure 5**.

4. Installation is the reverse of these step. Tighten outboard flange bolts to 70-90 foot-pounds. Tighten inboard U-bolt nuts to 14-18 foot-pounds.

U-joint Disassembly/Assembly

1. Remove bearing lock ring from trunnion yoke. See **Figure 6**.

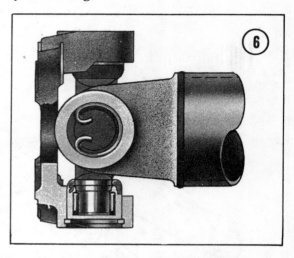

2. Support trunnion yoke on a piece of 1-¼ in. pipe.

3. Press trunnion down far enough to drive opposite bearing cup from yoke. Use a metal punch and a bench vise or hydraulic press, as shown in **Figures 7 and 8**.

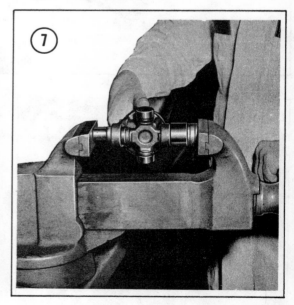

4. Disassemble trunnion and yoke at other end in a similar manner.

5. Clean and inspect the bearing rollers and the trunnion.

6. Relubricate with high temperature wheel bearing grease.

7. Partially install 1 bearing cup into yoke.

8. Place trunnion in yoke and into bearing cup.

9. Install other bearing cup and press both bearing cups into yoke. Keep trunnion aligned with cups.

> NOTE: *A large vise is an excellent tool for pressing both cups in evenly. See* **Figure 9.**

10. Press bearing cups in far enough to install lock rings.

PROPELLER SHAFT

Removal/Installation

1. Raise rear of vehicle on jackstands.

2. Place ½ in. thick blade of wood between upper surface of differential carrier behind the companion flange.

> NOTE: *This prevents carrier assembly from twisting upward when front support bracket is removed.*

3. Remove nut securing front carrier bracket to frame crossmember.

4. Remove front bolt and loosen rear bolt securing front carrier bracket to carrier. Swing bracket down. See **Figure 10**.

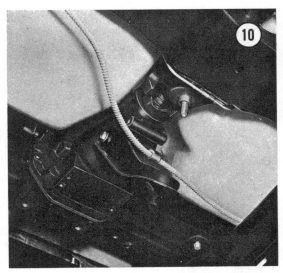

5. Remove trunnion U-bolts at carrier companion flange and at transmission yoke.

6. Slide transmission yoke forward to provide clearance and lower propeller shaft to rear. See **Figure 11**.

7. Installation is the reverse of these steps. Torque U-bolts to 14-18 foot-pounds. Torque front support bracket nut to 20-30 foot-pounds and bolts to 45-55 foot-pounds.

U-joint Disassembly/Assembly

1. Remove bearing lock ring from trunnion yoke. See Figure 6.

2. Support trunnion yoke on a piece of 1-¼ in. pipe.

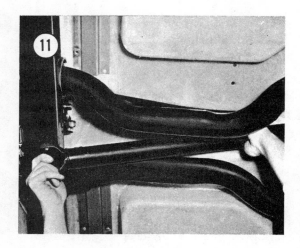

3. Press trunnion down far enough to drive opposite bearing cup from yoke. Use a metal punch and a bench vise or hydraulic press, as shown in Figures 7 and 8.

4. Remove trunnion and press other bearing cup from yoke. Do not drop cup or lose bearing rollers.

5. Disassemble trunnion and yoke at other end in a similar manner.

6. Clean and inspect the bearing rollers and the trunnion.

7. Relubricate with high temperature wheel bearing grease.

8. Partially install bearing cup into yoke.

9. Place trunnion in yoke and into bearing cup.

10. Install other bearing cup and press both bearing cups into yoke. Keep trunnion aligned with cups.

> NOTE: *A large vise is an excellent tool for pressing both cups in evenly. See Figure 9.*

11. Press bearing cups in far enough to install lock rings.

DIFFERENTIAL CARRIER

Removal

1. Raise vehicle on hoist.

2. Disconnect spring end link bolts as described in Steps 1-6, *Spring Removal*.

3. Disconnect axle drive shafts at carrier. See *Axle Shaft Removal*.

4. Remove carrier front support bracket.

5. Remove propeller shaft.

6. Mark relative alignment of camber cam and bolt on strut rod bracket and loosen cam bolts. See **Figure 12**.

7. Remove 4 bolts securing strut rod bracket to carrier. See **Figure 13**. Lower bracket.

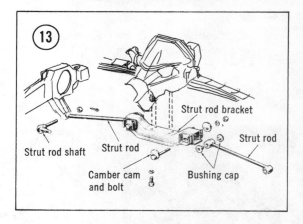

8. Remove camber cam bolts and swing strut rods out of the way.

9. Loosen 8 carrier cover bolts enough to allow gear oil to drain out. Remove carrier cover bolts.

10. Pull carrier partially out of cover which remains in vehicle. Drop front of carrier to clear crossmember and gradually work carrier down and out.

11. Clean inside of carrier cover and liberally grease gasket surface. Place new gasket on cover.

12. Cut heads off two ¼ in. - 13 x 1¼ in. bolts. Slot the cutoff end to accept screwdriver. Install these aligning studs into any 2 below-center cover bolt holes, one on each side.

13. Raise carrier into position, aligning studs into cover. See **Figures 14 and 15**.

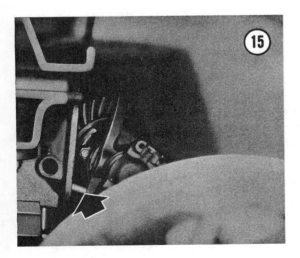

14. Install 6 carrier cover bolts, remove aligning studs, and install remaining 2 bolts. Tighten bolts to 45-55 foot-pounds.

15. Install propeller shaft.

16. Install front support bracket with the rear bolt only. Place rubber cushion on bracket, swing it into place, and secure with front bolt and nut. Tighten nut to 20-30 foot-pounds. Tighten bolts to 45-55 foot-pounds.

17. Install axle drive shafts.

18. Assemble strut rods to bracket and raise bracket into position under carrier. Install 4 bolts and torque to 15-22 foot-pounds.

19. Move camber cams to original marked position and tighten cam nuts to 55-70 foot-pounds.

20. Connect spring end link bolts as described in Steps 4-8, *Spring Installation.*

21. Remove filler plug located on right side of cover. Fill with hypoid lubricant (see Table 4, Chapter Two) to level of filler hole.

22. Lower vehicle and road test for leaks, noise, and general performance.

Carrier Cover Removal/Installation

The carrier cover normally need not be removed unless it is damaged. See *Suspension Crossmember Removal/Installation.*

Pinion Oil Seal Replacement

1. Raise rear of vehicle on jackstands.

2. Place ½ in. thick block of wood between upper surface of differential carrier behind the companion flange.

> NOTE: *This prevents carrier assembly from twisting upward when front support bracket is removed.*

3. Remove nut securing front carrier bracket to frame crossmember.

4. Remove front bolt and loosen rear bolt securing front carrier bracket to carrier. Swing bracket down. See **Figure 16**.

5. Remove propeller shaft as described elsewhere.

6. Mark companion flange nut and threaded pinion so that nut can be tightened to exact same spot.

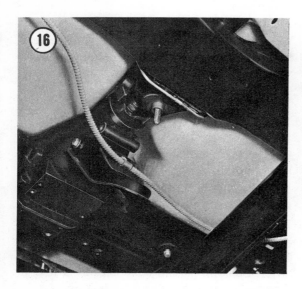

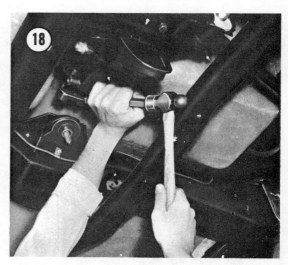

7. Hold flange and remove flange nut and washer. See **Figure 17**.

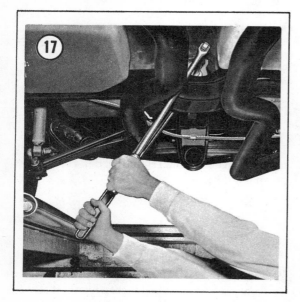

possible leaks. Tap seal into position until there is a ⅛ in. gap between seal flange and carrier. See **Figures 19 and 20**.

12. Lubricate flange splines and tap into place.

13. Install flange washer and nut. Tighten nut so that marks made in Step 6 line up.

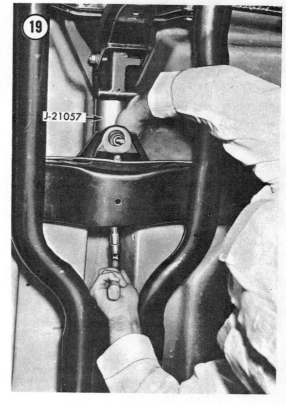

8. Drive flange off with *brass* drift and hammer. See **Figure 18**.

9. Pry old oil seal out with screwdriver.

CAUTION
Do not nick sealing surfaces of carrier.

10. Coat outside diameter of new seal with sealing compound.

11. Install new seal in bore. Seal must be started squarely to prevent seal distortion and

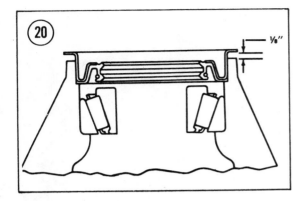

14. Install propeller shaft.

15. Install front bracket. Tighten to 45-55 foot-pounds.

16. Install crossmember nut and torque it to 20-30 foot-pounds.

Disassembly

Rear axle disassembly and repair requires many special tools and professional experience. The cost of the tools alone would exceed the cost of professional repair by your dealer.

Considerable expense can be saved by removing the rear axle yourself and making a preliminary examination.

1. Remove differential carrier.

2. Clean gear teeth and examine contact pattern (see **Figure 21**). The shiny, smooth pattern should be right in the middle of the tooth face. If the pattern is too high, too low, or off to one side of the tooth, the rear axle needs adjustment or repair. Also look for egg-shaped patterns or tilted patterns; these also require attention.

3. If the rear axle needs service, install the inspection cover and take the assembly to your dealer. Do not dismantle any farther than indicated.

REAR SUSPENSION

Rear Shock Absorber Replacement

1. Raise rear of vehicle on jackstands.

2. Disconnect upper mounting nut from shock absorber.

3. Remove lower mounting nut and lockwasher.

4. Slide upper end out of frame bracket and pull lower end and rubber grommets off strut rod shaft. See **Figure 22**.

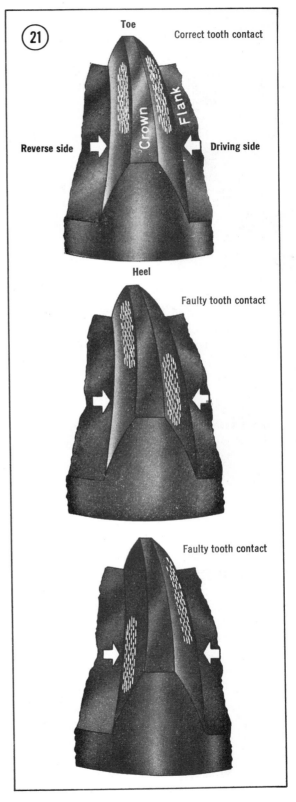

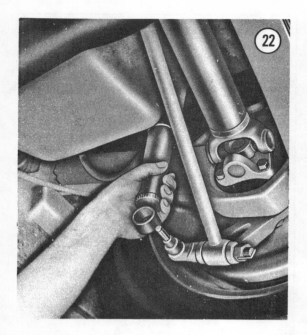

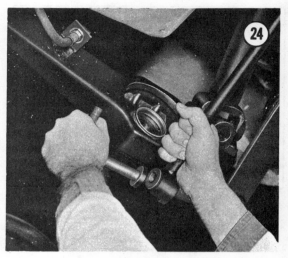

5. Installation is the reverse of these steps. Tighten upper nut to 40-60 foot-pounds. Tighten lower nut to 50-60 foot-pounds.

Strut Rod Removal

Refer to **Figure 23** for this procedure.
1. Raise rear of vehicle on jackstands.

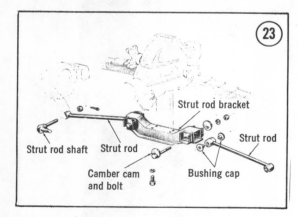

Strut rod bracket

Strut rod shaft   Strut rod   Strut rod

Camber cam   Bushing cap
and bolt

2. Disconnect lower end of shock absorber.

3. Remove cotter pin and nut from strut shaft. Pull shaft toward front of vehicle to remove it. See **Figure 24**.

4. Mark relative alignment of camber cam and bolt on strut rod bracket and loosen cam bolts. See **Figure 25**.

5. Remove 4 bolts securing strut rod bracket to carrier. See Figure 23. Lower bracket.

6. Remove camber cam bolts and pull strut rods out. Remove bushing caps from rod.

7. Inspect strut rod bushings and make sure rod is straight. If necessary, replace bushing or rod. Bushing should be replaced by Chevrolet dealer with special tools. Refer to **Table 2** for tightening torques.

8. Installation is the reverse of these steps.

Spring Removal

Refer to **Figure 26** for this procedure.
1. Raise vehicle on hoist or jackstands. Jackstands should be placed under frame slightly forward of torque control arm pivot points.

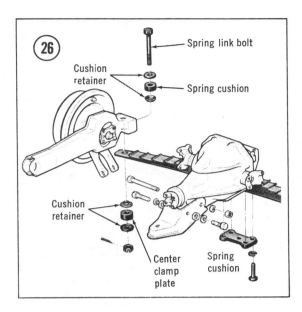

2. Remove wheels.

3. Place floor jack under spring at link bolt and raise spring until nearly flat.

4. Wrap ¼ in. or 5/16 in. chain with grab hook around suspension crossmember and spring. Secure chain to spring with large C-clamp to prevent slipping. See **Figure 27**.

WARNING

This procedure can be dangerous if not done exactly. Use only 1/4 in. or 5/16 in. chain with a safe grab hook. Do not use rope, wire, cable or any other method of retaining spring.

5. Lower jack when chain is secure.

6. Remove link bolt and rubber cushions.

7. Raise end of spring again with floor jack. Remove chain and carefully lower jack to release spring tension.

8. Repeat Steps 3-7 for other side of spring.

9. Remove 4 bolts securing center clamp plate. See **Figure 28**.

10. Remove spring. See **Figure 29**.

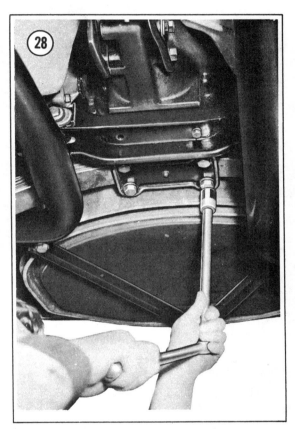

Spring Installation

1. Place spring on mounting surface. Index center bolthead with hole in carrier cover.

2. Install center clamp plate. Torque bolts to 55-75 foot-pounds.

3. Raise one end of spring with floor jack until end is nearly flat. Secure with chain as described in Step 4, *Spring Removal*. Lower jack.

4. Align torque control arm with spring end. Insert link bolt, rubber cushions and retainers. See Figure 26. Install castellated nut on link

bolt. Tighten nut until cotter pin hole is visible, then install *new* cotter pin and bend ends over.

5. Raise end of spring with jack under link bolt. Remove chain.

6. Carefully lower jack. Make certain that rubber cushions remain in place in retainers.

7. Repeat Steps 3-6 for other side of spring.

8. Install wheels and lower vehicle.

Spring Disassembly/Assembly

1. Clamp center of spring in vise (see **Figure 30**) and remove center bolt.

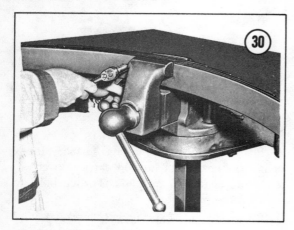

2. Release vise. Remove spring and separate leaves.

3. Replace worn or damaged liners and any broken leaves.

4. Replace damaged spring cushion retainers on main leaf by chiseling over flared portion until retainer can be knocked out. Place new retainer in position and flare over with a ball peen hammer.

5. Reassemble leaves and liners. Insert a drift into center bolt holes in leaves to align them.

6. Compress leaves and secure with center bolt. See **Figure 31**.

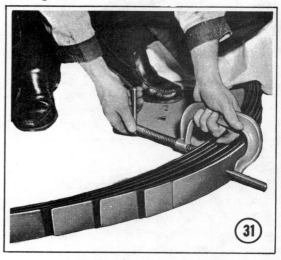

Control Arm Removal

Refer to **Figure 32** for this procedure.

1. Remove wheel spindle as described earlier.

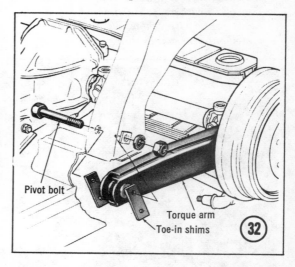

Pivot bolt

Torque arm

Toe-in shims

2. Disconnect spring on side. Control arm is to be removed. Follow Steps 1-7, *Spring Removal*, precisely.

3. Disconnect lower end of shock absorber.

4. Disconnect strut rod from strut shaft. See Figures 23 and 24. Swing strut down.

5. Remove 4 flange bolts from outboard end of axle drive shaft.

6. Disconnect brake hose and parking brake cable from control arm.

7. Loosen control arm pivot bolt and remove toe-in shims. Tape shims together and mark for correct reinstallation.

8. Remove pivot bolt. Pull control arm out of frame.

Control Arm Bushing Replacement

Refer to **Figure 33** for this procedure.

1. Drill out flared end of bushing retainer with an 11/16 in. drill. See **Figure 34**.

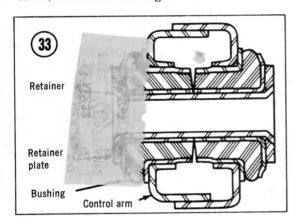

2. Remove special retainer plate and tap retainer out of bushing.

3. Spread bushings apart with chisel. (see **Figure 35**) and tap them out of control arm.

> NOTE: *If bushings are severely rusted, clamp arm end in a C-clamp to prevent the arm from spreading with the bushings.*

4. Take arm to Chevrolet dealer for installation of new bushings. Special tools not easily improvised are required.

Wheel Spindle Removal/Installation

Refer to **Figure 36** for this procedure.

1. Raise rear of vehicle on jackstands and apply parking brake.

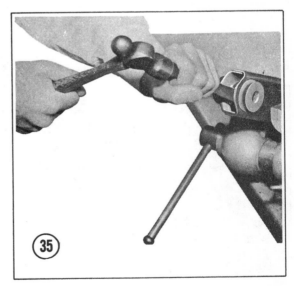

2. Remove the wheel and the brake caliper on 1965-1973 models.

3. Remove spindle cotter pin, nut, and washer from inner end of spindle.

4. Pull spindle drive flange off inner end of spindle.

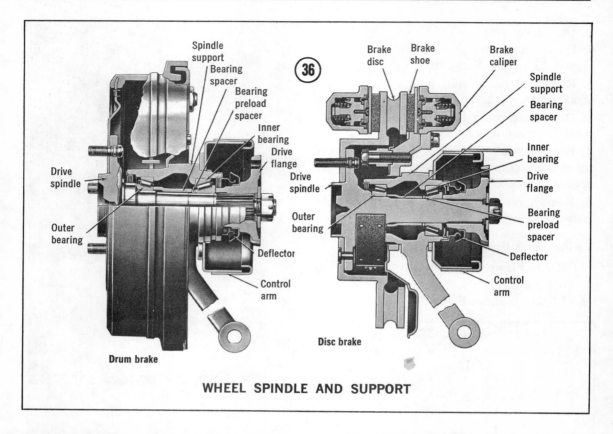

Drum brake

Disc brake

WHEEL SPINDLE AND SUPPORT

5a. On 1963-1964 models, remove brake drums (see Chapter Twelve) and pull spindle out. See **Figure 37**.

5b. On 1965-1976 models, install spindle nut until flush with end of spindle. Drive spindle out with a removal tool. See **Figure 38**.

6. On 1965-1976 models, remove dust deflector from spindle support.

7. Pry inner and outer seals out.

8. Remove inner and outer bearing race and roller assemblies.

9. Remove shim and bearing spacer.

10. Installation is the reverse of these steps if original wheel bearings are reinstalled. Otherwise, install by performing *Wheel Bearing Adjustment*. Pack bearings with high temperature wheel bearing grease.

Wheel Bearing Replacement

1. Remove the wheel bearings as described in Steps 1-8, *Wheel Spindle Removal/Installation*.

2. Lay a piece of ⅜ in. square steel bar stock across bearing races from inside (see **Figure 39**) and press races out.

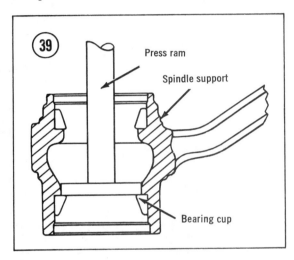

3. Press new bearing races into place.

4. Pack bearings and reassemble parts by reversing Steps 1-8, *Wheel Spindle Removal/ Installation*. Use a new 0.145 in. shim.

5. Check wheel bearing adjustment. Change shim if necessary.

Wheel Bearing Adjustment

1. Raise rear of vehicle on jackstands with wheels clear of ground.

2. Disconnect outboard end of axle drive shafts at flange.

3. Mark camber cam and bolt in relation to bracket. See **Figure 40**.

4. Loosen and turn camber bolt until strut rods are forced outward. This will move control arm

outward and provide enough clearance to drop axle drive shaft.

5. Mount dial indicator on inboard surface of control arm with pointer resting on spindle end. See **Figure 41**.

6. Move spindle in and out and measure total play on dial indicator. If it is 0.001-0.008 in., it is within specifications. If over 0.008 in., perform following steps to adjust end play.

7. Remove wheel spindle components following Steps 1-8, *Wheel Spindle Removal/Installation*.

8. Measure thickness of original shim. If dial indicator reading in Step 6 was over 0.007 in., select a shim thinner by the amount needed to bring play into specifications. Shims are available from 0.097 to 0.148 in., in 0.008 in. increments.

NOTE: *For example, if play is 0.011 in., it is 0.003 in. over limit. Select a shim 0.006 in. thinner than the original. If original is 0.145 in. thick, use one 0.139 in. thick.*

9. Pack bearing and install spindle parts by reversing Steps 1-8, *Wheel Bearing Removal/Installation.*

10. Remeasure wheel bearing end play and repeat Steps 1-3 if necessary.

Suspension Crossmember Removal

1. Remove spring as described previously.
2. Remove differential carrier.
3. Remove bolts securing crossmember isolation mounts to frame and lower crossmember. See **Figure 42**.

4. Remove bolts securing carrier cover to crossmember.
5. Inspect rubber isolation mounts for deterioration. Replace if necessary.

6. Installation is the reverse of these steps. Torque carrier cover-to-crossmember bolts to 25-35 ft.-lb. Torque crossmember mounting bolts to 20-30 ft.-lb.

Table 2   TIGHTENING TORQUES

	Foot-pounds
Lower control arm	50
Rear shock absorber	
Upper	50
Lower	35
Leaf spring retainer	70
U-joint flange	15
Wheel stud nut	75
Axle drive shaft to spindle	75
Axle drive shaft to yoke	15
Carrier cover	50
Filler plug (differential)	20
Stabilizer shaft	
Bracket to frame	10
Bracket to torque arm	10
Link bushing bolts	25
Rebound bumper to frame	20
Crossmember to carrier	60
Carrier front support	
To crossmember	65
Front bolt	50
Rear bolt	50
Drive spindle nut	100
Drive spindle support to torque arm	30
Strut rod	
To spindle support	75
Bracket to carrier	35
Camber cam	65
Torque arm pivot	50

Table 1   SPECIFICATIONS

	1963-1967	1968-1973	1974	1975	1976
Type	①	①	①	①	①
Springing	②	②	②	②	②
Wheel alignent					
Camber	−0°20′ ± 30′	+0°52′ ± 15′	−0°52′ ± 15′	−0°30′ ±30′	−0°52′ ± 15′
Toe-in	1/32-3/32 in.	1/16 ± 1/32 in.	1/16 ± 1/32 in.	3/32 ± 1/32 in.	1/16 ± 1/32 in.
Rear track	57.6 in.	59.4 in.	59.5 in.	59.5 in.	59.5 in.

① Independent double-jointed half axles   ② Transverse leaf springs

INDEX